critical thinking
A Guide to Logical Problem Solving

DeVry Institute of Technology
Phoenix, Arizona

contributors

Marie Hallinan
Dean of General Education

Lou Ascione
Assistant Professor

Steven H. Brown
Senior Professor

Robert Diehl
Senior Professor

Joe Friona
Assistant Professor

Jennifer M. Townsley
Assistant Professor

PEARSON PUBLISHING SOLUTIONS

Cover image: "Belvedere," by M. C. Escher. Copyright © Cordon Art, b.v. Baarn, The Netherlands, All rights reserved.

Excerpts taken from:
Strategies for Creative Problem Solving, by H. Scott Fogler and Steven E. LeBlanc: "Problem Definition," pp. 29–59; "Generating Solutions," pp. 61–85; "Deciding the Course of Action," pp. 87–117; and "Implementing the Solution," pp. 119–132.
Copyright © 1995 by Prentice-Hall, Inc.
Pearson Publishing Solutions/A Pearson Education Company
Upper Saddle River, New Jersey 07458

Becoming A Critical Thinker: A User-Friendly Manual, by Sherry Diestler: "Foundations of Arguments," pp. 1–22; "Values and Ethics," pp. 23–68; and "Reality Assumptions," pp. 69–82.
Copyright © 1998 by Prentice-Hall, Inc.

Keys to Effective Learning, by Carol Carter, J. Bishop, and S.L. Kravits: "Reading and Studying: Your Keys to Knowledge," pp. 173–212; "Note Taking and Research: Learning From Others," pp. 261–294; and "Test Taking: Showing What You Know," pp. 339–369.
Copyright © 1998 by Prentice-Hall, Inc.

Copyright © 1999 by Pearson Publishing Solutions.
All rights reserved.

This copyright covers material written expressly for this volume by the editor/s as well as the compilation itself. It does not cover the individual selections herein that first appeared elsewhere. Permission to reprint these has been obtained by Pearson Publishing Solutions for this edition only. Further reproduction by any means, electronic or mechanical, including photocopying and recording, or by any information storage or retrieval system, must be arranged with the individual copyright holders noted.

Printed in the United States of America

10 9 8 7 6 5 4 3 2 1

Please visit our website at www.sscp.com

ISBN 0-536-02116-3

BA 98755

PEARSON PUBLISHING SOLUTIONS
160 Gould Street/Needham Heights, MA 02494
A Pearson Education Company

Copyright Acknowledgments

Grateful acknowledgment is made to the following sources for permission to reprint material copyrighted or controlled by them:

"Learning to Work Together," by Peter R. Scholtes, reprinted from *The Team Handbook*, 1998, Joiner Associates, Inc.

"Participating in Work Groups" and "Leadership in Groups," by Rudolph F. Verderber, from *Communicate! 8th Edition*, 1996, edited by K. Hartlove. Reprinted by permission of Wadsworth Publishing Company.

"Conflict in Interpersonal Relationships," by Joseph A. DeVito, from *The Interpersonal Communication Book, 7th Edition*, 1995. Copyright © 1995 by Joseph A. DeVito. Reprinted by permission of Addison-Wesley Publishers, Inc.

"Quality and Process," by R. Dozar and J. McNeil, reprinted from *Introduction to Engineering Design: The Workbook*, 1998, McGraw-Hill.

Contents

Preface vii

Critical Thinking at DeVry ix

Section I—Teambuilding Tools 1
    Chapter 1: Learning to Work Together 5
    Chapter 2: Participating in Work Groups 33
    Chapter 3: Leadership in Groups 53
    Chapter 4: Conflict in Interpersonal Relationships 71

Section II—Problem Solving Tools 89
    Chapter 5: Problem Definition 93
    Chapter 6: Generating Solutions 121
    Chapter 7: Deciding the Course of Action 147
    Chapter 8: Implementing the Solution 179

Section III—Logical Reasoning Tools 191
    Chapter 9: Foundations of Arguments 195
    Chapter 10: Values and Ethics 209
    Chapter 11: Reality Assumptions 243
    Chapter 12: Logic: The Practical Science of Inference 253

Appendix A—Quality 301

Appendix B—Reading and Studying:
Your Keys to Knowledge 319

Appendix C—Note Taking and Research:
Learning from Others 363

Appendix D—Test Taking:
Showing What You Know 399

Preface

DeVry Institute of Technology has systematically positioned itself to accomplish two critical objectives: to provide the high-quality, career-oriented, hands-on education that is being demanded in the marketplace; and to facilitate the success of its students within that provision.

Few institutions have adapted themselves to the kind of high-energy and high-contact guidance that is demanded by today's post-secondary educational experience. Freshman at DeVry, even in their first few weeks of school, are guided through significant problem solving experiences in a team environment that would be impossible without the strategic collaboration of their instructors and the careful integration of curricula. The interdependence of each lesson taught and singleness of purpose developed by the team of freshman instructors facilitate a learning experience that is simply the best available.

In the same spirit of excellence, this text is being offered to the freshman of DeVry. It is designed to support the learning experience in Critical Thinking (COLL115) and contains what we believe to be the most important elements of an excellent educational foundation. Critical Thinking in turn is designed as the support, or hub, of the freshman experience. The concepts taught in Critical Thinking—effective communication, team member skills, persuasive logic, and problem solving techniques—will be used across all freshman courses and beyond. In short, this book had been uniquely designed to support the educational experience at DeVry, just as the educational experience at DeVry has been uniquely designed for its students.

Critical Thinking at DeVry

Critical thinking is both an activity and an academic field of study. As a field of study, the subject matter of critical thinking is logical reasoning, and includes specific concepts, skills and attitudes that are necessary for effectively evaluating truth claims. As an activity, however, critical thinking functions as a means for intelligent problem solving and decision making. The relationship between these two sides of critical thinking is one of theory versus practice, so that the purpose of studying critical thinking is to maximize the efficiency and effectiveness of critical thinking as an activity. In other words, we study critical thinking to become better critical thinkers, but the value of critical thinking lies in its instrumental capacity to guide the achievement of practical goals intelligently.

Most critical thinking courses focus on the academic study of critical thinking and therefore on logical reasoning. On the other hand, some courses in critical thinking focus solely on the practical application of critical thinking to a specific area of inquiry such as any of the physical or social sciences. The critical thinking program at DeVry, however, is distinctive in that it combines both aspects of critical thinking: theory and practice. The theoretical side of critical thinking is the standard study of logical reasoning, while the practical side involves learning problem solving and decision making skills in class and practicing them in lab. Because a large percentage of applied critical thinking outside of academia involves not individuals but groups of individuals, almost all problem solving and decision making labs are conducted using teams, so that teamwork and teambuilding have become integral parts of our critical thinking course.

This textbook is an anthology which has been compiled by the critical thinking instructors as well as the Dean of General Education at the Phoenix campus of DeVry as a resource to help achieve specific course objectives for which the critical thinking course was designed. The text is divided into three sections, namely, team-building, problem solving and logical reasoning, with each section responsible for a particular set of course objectives. The following is a list of general course objectives followed by the specific course objectives for the teambuilding, problem solving and logical reasoning sections:

General

1. Given a course capstone project, operate in a team to select a problem. Define that problem by collecting and analyzing information, brainstorm possible solutions, select the most viable solution, present a plan for implementation to the appropriate persons, and receive and respond to feedback.
2. Given the general problem solving process, be able to apply it to personal, academic, and work related problems.

Teambuilding

3. Given a problem, in which team members are assigned roles with conflicting interests, work through the problem-solving process to arrive at a solution amenable to all interests, applying appropriate teamwork and negotiation skills.
4. Given a teambuilding/group activity use interpersonal skills to solve a problem effectively.
5. Given the characteristics of effective problem-solvers, assess personal and team behaviors and make appropriate plans for capitalizing on strengths and correcting weaknesses through conflict management strategies, group dynamics, and interpersonal skills.

Problem Solving

6. Given a set of symptoms or an ill-defined task, apply appropriate strategies to define a problem.
7. Given a clearly defined problem, define in concrete, measurable terms the characteristics of an acceptable solution.
8. Given clearly defined criteria, apply appropriate strategies to generate possible solutions.
9. Given a set of potential solutions, select the most appropriate action to be taken.
10. Given a solution that requires complex implementation planning, use various project management strategies to plan for implementation of that solution.
11. Given problems that vary in complexity, selectively apply strategies necessary for solving the problems and provide well-supported rationales for the decisions.

Logical Reasoning

12. Given any issue, precisely state the arguments, locating both the premise and the conclusion, and frame the argument in standard form.
13. Given an argument in standard form, evaluate its validity, truth and soundness.
14. Given invalid arguments, evaluate them in terms of fallacies or be able to explain the reasons why the arguments are invalid.

While the course objective list represents the order of the sections as they appear in the text, the presentation of this material is determined at the discretion of the instructor. Furthermore, this text is designed to function as support for all DeVry programs. To this end, each instructor may focus more or less on a specific section depending on the overall needs of the students in his or her program. Finally, the purpose of the critical thinking course is to improve the critical thinking abilities of students in their personal, academic and career experiences. It is the aim of this book to provide a full range of resources with which to meet the varied needs of our students in these experiences.

SECTION I

Teambuilding Tools

INTRODUCTION

Each day presents you with several different opportunities to interact and communicate with others. Most of us have had feelings of intrigue, frustration, concern and interest when interacting with others in various team situations. Whether we have been assigned to a committee at work or school, are involved in a family discussion or are a member of a recreational sports team, we require team specific skills and strategies to be successful in accomplishing our goals.

Teamwork, or group based learning and problem solving, has rapidly become an important component of industry today. Organizations, corporations and institutions are not only requiring their employees to participate in teams but are also requiring these employees to use the appropriate skill sets and strategies necessary for team success. This section, therefore, will offer a discussion and review of teambuilding skills and strategies.

The following chapters have been identified to assist you in building your skills as an effective team member. *Learning to Work Together* offers an understanding of the team formation process as well as 14 quality improvement strategies for developing effective and successful teams. *Participating in Work Groups* provides an in-depth discussion of the key roles and characteristics of effective team communication, while *Leadership in Groups* discusses the characteristics of effective leadership and identifies key leadership functions. Finally, *Conflict in Interpersonal Relationships* provides a practical model for conflict resolution and offers several conflict management strategies.

The above combination of teambuilding strategies, team member characteristics and group communication skills has been designed to assist you in transferring your knowledge base into actual hands-on practice and performance. This team performance, or group synergy, is a primary goal of groups working in problem based learning environments. With this goal in mind, we encourage you to actively develop and enhance your team communication skills, group member characteristics and overall teaming success strategies.

CHAPTER 1

Learning to Work Together

The ordinary project team is a complicated creature. Members must work out personal differences, find strengths on which to build, balance commitments to the project against the demands of their everyday jobs, and learn how to improve quality.

Dealing with internal group needs that arise from these pressures is as important as the group's external task of making improvements. Yet even teams that grasp the importance of improving quality often underestimate the need for developing themselves as teams. When a team runs smoothly, members can concentrate on their primary goal of improving a process. In contrast, a team that fails to build relationships among its members will waste time on struggles for control and endless discussions that lead nowhere.

The more you know about what to expect as your group progresses, the better equipped you will be to handle difficulties. You will be able to recognize and avoid many disruptions, and together work through those that cannot be avoided. To build the group skills needed to achieve these goals, you must start by understanding what lies behind most troubles.

I. Undercurrents in Team Dynamics

To outside observers, the only obvious team efforts are associated with the *task* of improving a process: having meetings, gathering data, planning improvements, making changes, writing reports, and so forth. If, indeed, these were the team's only concerns, progress would be very fast. But when people form into groups, something always seems to get in the way of efficient progress.

The problem is that there are hidden concerns that, like undercurrents, pull team members away from their obvious tasks. When they walk through the door into a meeting, team members are beset by conflicting emotions: excitement and anxiety about being on the team, loyalty to their divisions or departments, nervous anticipation about the project's success.

If left unattended these undercurrents can inhibit a group's chance of becoming an effective team. Every group must therefore spend time on activities not directly related to a task, activities that build understanding and support in the group. You need to resolve issues that fall into what one author, William Schutz, calls the "interpersonal underworld."

These are issues not often spoken about, but common to us all, and they fall into three categories:

1. **Personal identity in the team**

   It is natural for team members to wonder how they will fit into the team. The most common worries are those associated with:

   - *Membership, Inclusion:* "Do I feel like an insider or outsider? Do I belong? Do I want to belong? What can I do to fit in?"
   - *Influence, Control, Mutual Trust:* "Who's calling the shots here? Who will have the most influence? Will I have influence? Will I be listened to? Will I be able to contribute? Will I be allowed to contribute?"
   - *Getting Along, Mutual Loyalty:* "How will I get along with other team members? Will we be able to develop any cooperative spirit?"

2. **Relationships between team members**

   With few exceptions, team members want the team to succeed, to make improvements, and to work cooperatively with each other. They extend personal concerns to the team: "What kind of relationships will characterize this team? How will members of different ranks interact? Will we be open or guarded in what we say? Will we be able to work together, or will we argue and disagree all the time? Will people like or dislike me? Will I like or dislike them?"

3. **Identity with the organization**

   Team members usually identify strongly with their departments or divisions, and they will need to know how membership in the team will affect those roles and responsibilities: "Will my loyalty to the team conflict with loyalty to my co-workers? Will my responsibilities as a team member conflict with my everyday duties?" Usually it is the project that suffers if the two compete.

   Just as team members must reach outside the group to maintain ties with their departments, so must the team as a whole build relationships throughout the organization. Political astuteness is crucial. Finding influential people to champion the team and its project can make a big difference in the support your team receives from the organization. The more people you convince that quality improvement projects are worthwhile, the better off your team and the entire organization will be. A team's relationship with its guidance team is one avenue for creating such support within the organization.

II. Stages of Team Growth

As the team matures, members gradually learn to cope with the emotional and group pressures they face. As a result, the team goes through fairly predictable stages:

Stage 1: Forming

When a team is forming, members cautiously explore the boundaries of acceptable group behavior. Like hesitant swimmers, they stand by the pool, dabbling their toes in the water. This is a stage of transition from individual to member status, and of testing the leader's guidance both formally and informally.

Forming includes these feelings . . .

- Excitement, anticipation, and optimism
- Pride in being chosen for the project
- Initial, tentative attachment to the team
- Suspicion, fear, and anxiety about the job ahead

. . . and these behaviors.

- Attempts to define the task and decide how it will be accomplished
- Attempts to determine acceptable group behavior and how to deal with group problems
- Decisions on what information needs to be gathered
- Lofty, abstract discussions of concepts and issues; or, for some members, impatience with these discussions
- Discussion of symptoms or problems not relevant to the task; difficulty in identifying relevant problems
- Complaints about the organization and barriers to the task

Because there is so much going on to distract members' attention in the beginning, the team accomplishes little, if anything, that concerns its project goals. This is perfectly normal.

Stage 2: Storming

Storming is probably the most difficult stage for the team. It is as if team members jump in the water, and, thinking they are about to drown, start thrashing about. They begin to realize the task is different and more difficult than they imagined, becoming testy, blameful, or overzealous.

Impatient about the lack of progress, but still too inexperienced to know much about decision making or the scientific approach, members argue about just what actions the team should take. They try to rely solely on their personal and professional experience, resisting any need for collaborating with other team members.

Storming includes these feelings . . .

- Resistance to the task and to quality improvement approaches different from what each individual member is comfortable using
- Sharp fluctuations in attitude about the team and the project's chance of success

. . . and these behaviors.

- Arguing among members even when they agree on the real issue
- Defensiveness and competition; factions and "choosing sides"
- Questioning the wisdom of those who selected this project and appointed the other members of the team
- Establishing unrealistic goals; concern about excessive work
- A perceived "pecking order"; disunity, increased tension, and jealousy

Again, this many pressures mean team members have little energy to spend on progressing towards the team's goal. But they are beginning to understand one another.

Stage 3: Norming

During this stage, members reconcile competing loyalties and responsibilities. They accept the team, team ground rules (or "norms"), their roles in the team, and the individuality of fellow members. Emotional conflict is reduced as previously competitive relationships become more cooperative. In other words, as team members realize they are not going to drown, they stop thrashing about and start helping each other stay afloat.

Norming includes these feelings . . .

- A new ability to express criticism constructively
- Acceptance of membership in the team
- Relief that it seems everything is going to work out

. . . and these behaviors.

- An attempt to achieve harmony by avoiding conflict
- More friendliness, confiding in each other, and sharing of personal problems; discussing the team's dynamics
- A sense of team cohesion, a common spirit and goals
- Establishing and maintaining team ground rules and boundaries (the "norms")

As team members begin to work out their differences, they now have more time and energy to spend on the project. Thus they are able to at last start making significant progress.

Stage 4: Performing

By this stage, the team has settled its relationships and expectations. They can begin performing—diagnosing and solving problems, and choosing and implementing changes. At last team members have discovered and accepted each other's strengths and weaknesses, and learned what their roles are. Now they can swim in concert.

Performing includes these feelings . . .

- Members having insights into personal and group processes, and better understanding of each other's strengths and weaknesses
- Satisfaction at the team's progress

. . . and these behaviors.

- Constructive self-change
- Ability to prevent or work through group problems
- Close attachment to the team

The team is now an effective, cohesive unit. You can tell when your team has reached this stage because you start getting a lot of work done.

The duration and intensity of these stages vary from team to team. Sometimes Stage 4, performing, is achieved in a meeting or two; other times it may take months. Use the descriptions here to compare your team with the normal pattern for maturing groups. Understanding these stages of growth will keep you from overreacting to normal problems and setting unrealistic expectations that only add to frustration. Don't panic. With patience and effort this assembly of independent individuals *will* grow into a team.

III. Roller Coaster of Highs and Lows

Knowing about the typical stages a team passes through—forming, storming, norming, and performing—should relieve much of the fear team members have about the project's success. It is also helpful to be aware of the roller coaster of highs and lows every team experiences.

A team's mood usually reflects its fortune: With every step forward, the future looks bright and team members are optimistic. But no matter how well a team works together, progress is never smooth. As progress swings from forward to stalled, and then from stalled to backward, the team mood will swing, too. These swings are only partly linked to the stages of growth, and usually the changes are unpredictable.

As shown (above), the team begins with hopefulness and optimism. These positive feelings may last a while, but usually change to boredom and impatience as the project gets underway and members feel overwhelmed when they realize just how much they have to learn about quality improvement. Somewhere in here the storming starts.

When they finally begin collecting data, team members again feel encouraged—at last they are making progress! Rarely does this elation last: since few people are experts in scientific methods the first time out, team members almost always uncover mistakes in data collection procedures, and realize they must go back and do it again. The mood swings down. Recovery comes as the team learns from experience, makes another attempt, and gathers good, reliable data.

The pattern is different for each team. Team members' attitudes depend on both the speed of progress and the resistance or encouragement they receive from the guidance team and their departments.

The best way to deal with this cycle is to understand and accept it with a "this too shall pass" attitude. Changes in attitude, just like growth stages, are normal. The team must cultivate patience, and pass it on to its guidance team. Eventually, everyone will better understand how projects unfold, and will be able to set a realistic pace for the project.

Teams can also take a more active approach to dealing with the stages and cycles they experience by learning when and how to avoid or work through group problems. The rest of this chapter describes approaches for improving the group's ability to solve and prevent problems.

IV. Recipe for a Successful Team

No team exists without problems. But some teams—particularly those who have learned to counter the negative team dynamics—seem to be especially good at preventing many typical group problems. How close a team comes to this ideal depends on the following ten essential ingredients.

1. *Clarity in Team Goals*

A team works best when everyone understands its purpose and goals. If there is confusion or disagreement, they work to resolve the issues.

Ideally, the team . . .

- agrees on its mission, or works together to resolve disagreement;
- sees the mission as workable or, if necessary, narrows the mission to a workable size;
- has a clear vision and can progress steadily towards its goals;
- is clear about the larger project goals and about the purpose of individual steps, meetings, discussion, and decisions.

Indicators of potential trouble

- Frequent switches in directions
- Frequent arguments about what the team should do next
- Feelings that the project is too big or inappropriate
- Frustration at lack of progress
- Excessive questioning of each decision or action taken
- Floundering

Recommendations

If team members feel they don't understand the mission, emphasize the right of each team member to ask questions about a decision or event until satisfied with the answers. If you find a mission is too broad, work with the guidance team to find something workable.

2. An Improvement Plan

Improvement plans help the team determine what advice, assistance, training, materials, and other resources it may need. They guide the team in determining schedules and identifying mileposts.

Ideally, the team...

- has created an improvement plan, revising it as needed during the project;
- has a flowchart or similar document describing the steps of the project;
- refers to these documents when discussing what directions to take next;
- knows what resources and training are needed throughout the project, and plans accordingly.

Indicators of Potential Trouble

- Uncertainty about the team's direction (the team muddles through each step without a clear idea of how to get the information it needs)
- Being "lost in the woods" (when one step is completed there is little or no idea of what to do next)
- "Fishing expeditions" (the team plunges ahead, hoping to stumble across improvement ideas)
- "Filling the sky with lead" (launching many improvement activities without thinking about what each is supposed to do, hoping at least one will hit the target)

Ten Ingredients For a Successful Team

1. Clarity in Team Goals
2. An Improvement Plan
3. Clearly Defined Roles
4. Clear Communication
5. Beneficial Team Behaviors
6. Well-defined Decision Procedures
7. Balanced Participation
8. Established Ground Rules
9. Awareness of the Group Process
10. Use of the Scientific Approach

Recommendations

Seek assistance from a competent technical advisor. Ask yourselves what you need in order to fulfill your mission. Ask your guidance team to review or, if necessary, help formulate your plan.

3. Clearly Defined Roles

Teams operate most efficiently if they tap everyone's talents, and all members understand their duties and know who is responsible for what issues and tasks.

Ideally, the team . . .

- has formally designated roles (all members know what is expected of everyone, especially the leader, facilitator, technical expert, and quality advisor);
- understands which roles belong to one person and which are shared, and how the shared roles are switched (for instance, using an agreed-upon procedure to rotate the job of meeting facilitator);
- uses each member's talents, and involves everyone in team activities so no one feels left out or taken advantage of (for example, not always having women take the notes).

Indicators of potential trouble

- Roles and duty assignments that result from a pecking order
- Confusion over who is responsible for what
- People getting stuck with the same tedious chores

Recommendations

The team must decide on how roles will be assigned and changed. Have the team leader and quality advisor discuss their responsibilities and those of any other designated roles. The team leader might facilitate discussions on what duties must be assigned, how they will be assigned, and how they can be changed. Reach consensus about roles within the team.

4. Clear Communication

Good discussions depend on how well information is passed between team members.

Ideally, team members should . . .

- speak with clarity and directness (for example, avoid using questions to disguise statements);
- be succinct, avoiding long anecdotes and examples;
- listen actively, explore rather than debate each speaker's ideas;
- avoid interrupting and talking when others are speaking;

- share information on many levels, for example:
  * *sensing statements* ("I don't hear any disagreements with John's point. Do we all agree?")
  * *thinking statements* ("There seems to be a correlation between the number of errors and the volume of work.")
  * *feeling statements* ("I'm disappointed that no one has taken care of this yet.")
  * *statements of intentions* ("My question was not a criticism. I simply wanted more information.")
  * *statements of actions* ("Let's run a test on the machine using materials of different thickness.")

Indicators of potential trouble

- Poor speaking skills (mumbling, rambling, speaking too softly, little eye contact)
- Members are unable to say what they really feel; cautiousness; lots of tentative, conditional statements ("Do you think, maybe, that sometimes it might be that . . .")
- Everyone senses there is more going on than meets the eye; people's words do not match their tone of voice or mannerisms
- Opinions expressed as facts or phrased as questions
- Plops: statements that receive no acknowledgement or response
- Bullying statements ("What you don't understand is. . .")
- Discounts ("That's not important. What's worse is. . .")

Recommendations

Develop communication skills, and learn to recognize problems that result from poor communication. Use the meeting evaluation to discuss how well team members communicate. Have observers (team members or outsiders) watch the group and give honest feedback on communication dynamics. Videotape a discussion; review and critique it.

5. Beneficial Team Behaviors

Teams should encourage all members to use the skills and practices that make discussions and meetings more effective.

Ideally, team members should . . .

- initiate discussions;
- seek information and opinions;
- suggest procedures for reaching a goal;
- clarify or elaborate on ideas;
- summarize;

- test for consensus;
- act as gate-keepers: direct conversational traffic, avoid simultaneous conversations, throttle dominant talkers, make room for reserved talkers;
- keep the discussion from digressing;
- compromise and be creative in resolving differences;
- try to ease tension in the group and work through difficult matters;
- express the group's feeling and ask others to check that impression;
- get the group to agree on standards ("Do we all agree to discuss this for 15 minutes and no more?");
- refer to documentation and data;
- praise and correct others with equal fairness; accept both praise and complaints.

Indicators of potential trouble

- Failure to use discussion skills
- Reliance on one person (the leader) to manage the discussion; no shared responsibility
- People repeating points, unsure whether anyone heard them the first time
- Discussions that are stuck; wheel-spinning; inability to let go of one topic and move onto the next
- Discussions in the hallway after the meeting are more free and more candid than those during the meeting

Recommendations

Refer to our three-part discussion on "Working Through Group Problems" that appears later in this chapter (Constructive Feedback, General Guidelines, Ten Common Problems and What to do About Them). The team leader can also create an exercise out of effective discussion skills. For example, team members could pick two or three skills for the whole team to practice at a meeting, reviewing their performance during the meeting evaluation.

6. *Well-defined Decision Procedures*

You can tell a lot about how well a team is run by watching its decision-making process. A team should always be aware of the different ways it reaches decisions.

Ideally, the team should . . .

- discuss how decisions will be made, such as when to take a poll, when to decide by consensus (are there times when a decision by only a few people is acceptable?);
- explore important issues by polling (each member is asked to vote or state an opinion verbally or in writing);
- decide important issues by consensus;

- test for consensus ("This seems to be our agreement. Is there anyone who feels unsure about the choice?");
- use data as the basis of decisions.

Indicators of potential trouble

- Conceding to opinions that are presented as facts with no supporting data
- Decisions by one or two people in the group, without team members agreeing to defer to their expertise
- Decision by a minority
- Too-frequent recourse to "majority rules" or other easy approaches that bypass strong disagreement
- Decision by default; people do not respond to a statement (the "plop"); silence interpreted as consent

Recommendations

Have the team leader (or, if necessary, the quality advisor) lead a discussion on decision-making in the team. Occasionally designate a member or outsider to watch and give feedback on how decisions are made so the group can talk about necessary changes in the group.

7. Balanced Participation

Since every team member has a stake in the group's achievements, everyone should participate in discussions and decisions, share commitment to the project's success, and contribute their talents.

Ideally, the team should . . .

- have reasonably balanced participation, with all members contributing to most discussions;
- build on members' natural styles of participation.

Indicators of potential trouble

- Some team members have too much influence, others, too little
- Participation depends on the subject being discussed (for example, only those who know the most about a subject are actively involved; others do not even ask questions)
- Members too often contribute only at certain times in a conversation or meeting
- Some members speak only about a certain topic ("hot buttons"—participation only when the subject touches, for example, money or training)

Recommendations

Use brainstorming and nominal group technique to elicit input from all team members during discussions.

8. Established Ground Rules

Groups invariably establish ground rules (or "norms") for what will and will not be tolerated in the group.

Ideally, the team should ...

- have open discussions regarding ground rules, where the group discusses what behaviors are acceptable and unacceptable;
- openly state or acknowledge norms ("We all agreed to decide the issue this way").

Indicators of potential trouble

- Certain important topics are avoided; too many subjects are taboo; conversations recur that are irrelevant to the task and harmful to the group
- No one acknowledges the norms; everyone acts as they *think* the group wants them to act; no one is able to say exactly what ground rules the team follows (for example, no one cracks jokes even though it was never stated that jokes would be out of place)
- Recurring differences about what is or is not acceptable behavior
- Behavior that signifies irritation; for example, repeated disregard for starting and ending times
- Conflict over assumed norms or conflicting expectation.

Recommendations

Groups must take time at the beginning of the group to discuss and agree on obvious ground rules. From time to time, review the ground rules, adding, deleting, or revising them as needed. Particularly pay attention to current and possible ground rules during times of conflict and antagonism.

9. Awareness of the Group Process

Ideally, all team members should be aware of the group process—how the team works together—along with paying attention to the content of the meeting.

Ideally, team members should ...

- be sensitive to nonverbal communication, for example, be aware that silence may indicate disagreement, or knowing that physical signs of agitation might indicate someone is uncomfortable with a discussion;
- see, hear, and feel the group dynamics;
- comment and intervene to correct a group process problem;
- contribute equally to group process and meeting content;
- choose to work on group process issues and occasionally designate a team member or outsider to officially observe and report on group interactions at a meeting.

Indicators of potential trouble

- Lack of reference to undercurrent issues, particularly when the group is having difficulty
- Pushing ahead on the task when there are nonverbal signs of resistance, confusion, or disappointment
- Inattention to obvious nonverbal clues and shifts in the group mood
- Members attributing motives to nonverbal behavior ("You've been quiet during the last 30 minutes. You must not be interested in what's being said.")
- Remarks that discount someone's behavior or contribution, or group process issues ("Let's get on with the task and stop talking about that stuff.")

Recommendations

Use the quality advisor as an observer to evaluate how well the group handles problems, confusion, discussions, and so forth. Encourage the team to have several "process checks," times when members can say how they think the meeting is going, or express thoughts for which there were no appropriate times in the meeting. Routinely include group process issues in meeting evaluations.

10. *Use of the Scientific Approach*

Teams that use a scientific approach, the reliance on good data for problem solving and decision making, have a much easier time arriving at permanent solutions to problems. Failure to use a scientific approach seriously compromises a basic principle of quality improvement and can ruin the team's chance for success. The scientific approach helps avoid many group problems and disagreements. Many arguments are between individuals with strong opinions. The scientific approach insists that opinions be supported by, or at least defer to, data.

Ideally, the team should . . .

- demand to see data before making decisions and question anyone who tries to act on hunches alone;
- use basic statistical tools to investigate problems and to gather and analyze data;
- dig for root causes of problems;
- seek permanent solutions rather than rely on quick fixes.

Indicators of potential trouble

- Team members insist they don't need data because their intelligence and experience are enough to tell them what the problems and solutions are
- Wild stabs at supposed solutions jumping to conclusions, too many inferences and assumptions, shooting from the hip
- Hasty action, a "ready, *fire*, aim!" approach

Recommendations

Make sure the team has access to an expert for training and guidance (usually this is the quality advisor). Every team should talk about the importance of enforcing a scientific approach, especially when decisions or actions are needed.

V. Working Through Group Problems, Part 1: *Constructive Feedback*

No matter what pressures a team encounters, a fundamental message of this handbook is that it can work hard at its task *and* support member's needs. The single most important skill to have in working through any problem is the ability to give constructive feedback.

Why? Because most often problems are expressed as criticism of someone's action. When you are criticized by someone, it is difficult to know what to do. A common reaction is to feel critical of them: "What right do they have to criticize *me*?" Suppose it is you reacting negatively to behavior that truly disrupts the group's progress. Do you sit on your negative feelings for the sake of group harmony? Is there a way to express dissatisfaction without provoking a confrontation that might disrupt the group even more?

There are proven methods for giving and receiving criticism, methods that work equally well for giving and receiving praise. The goals are to give constructive feedback, whether positive or negative, and to make sure that any feedback you receive is constructive. While there is no guarantee, following the guidelines below will minimize the possibility of provoking a bad scene. Use them to help you decide when to give feedback, how to tell a person or group what you think, and how to listen to their feedback.

> Five authors have made significant contributions to the formulation of these rules: Norman Berkowitz, a professor of psychology at Boston College with insight into what happens when a simple disagreement turns into hostility; Chris Argyris, a well-known author in the field of organizational change; Eric Berne, the founder of Transactional Analysis; Virginia Satir, an eminent family therapist; and Dr. Thomas Gordon, psychologist and author of *Leader Effectiveness Training*.

Guidelines for Constructive Feedback

Useful feedback comes in several forms. *Statistical data* provide feedback from a process, measurements that tell you how well a process is running, whether changes you tried were effective, and so forth. *Market research* provides feedback from customers, telling you how well your organization is doing and whether your product or service meets customers' needs. The most common form of feedback (and our focus here) is simply *one person talking to another*.

Many people know that to get good data or useful market information you must plan carefully and follow established rules and guidelines. Few people know that the same ideas apply to person-to-person feedback. Thinking ahead of time about what you are going to say and how you increase the value of what you say to another person.

To make personal feedback constructive, you must:

- **Acknowledge the need for feedback**

    The first thing to recognize is the value of giving feedback, both positive and negative. Feedback is vital to any organization committed to improving itself, for it is the only way to know what needs to be improved. Giving and receiving feedback should be more than just a part of a team member's behavior; it should be part of the whole organization's culture.

    You will need good feedback skills to improve your team meetings, and, more generally, interactions between team members.

    These skills will also help you communicate more effectively with customers and suppliers (both internal and external). In fact, you will find many opportunities to apply these skills in your work. First, however, your team should agree that giving and receiving feedback is an acceptable part of how you will improve the way you work together. This agreement is necessary so that no one is surprised when he or she receives feedback.

- **Give both positive and negative feedback**

    Many people take good work for granted and give feedback only when there are problems. This is a bad policy: people will more likely pay attention to your complaints if they have also received your compliments. It is important to remember to tell people when they have done something well.

Guidelines for Constructive Feedback

- **Acknowledge the need for feedback**
- **Give both positive and negative feedback**
- **Understand the context**
- **Know when to give feedback**
- **Know how to give feedback**
    * Be descriptive.
    * Don't use labels.
    * Don't exaggerate.
    * Don't be judgmental.
    * Speak for yourself.
    * Talk first about yourself, not about the other person.
    * Phrase the issue as a statement, not a question.
    * Restrict your feedback to things you know for certain.
    * Help people hear and accept your compliments when giving positive feedback.
- **Know how to receive feedback**
    * Breathe.
    * Listen carefully.
    * Ask questions for clarity.
    * Acknowledge the feedback.
    * Acknowledge valid points.
    * Take time to sort out what you heard.

- **Understand the context**

  The most important characteristic of feedback is that it always has a context where it happened, why it happened, what led up to the event. You never simply walk up to a person, deliver a feedback statement, and then leave. Before you give feedback, review the actions and decisions that led up to the moment.

- **Know when to give feedback**

  Before giving feedback, determine whether the moment is right. You must consider more than your own need to give feedback. Constructive feedback can happen only within a context of listening to and caring about the person.

  Do not give feedback when:

  * You don't know much about the circumstances of the behavior.
  * You don't care about the person or will not be around long enough to follow up on the aftermath of your feedback. Hit and run feedback is not fair.
  * The feedback, positive or negative, is about something the person has no power to change.
  * The other person seems low in self-esteem.
  * You are low in self-esteem.
  * Your purpose is not really improvement, but to put someone on the spot ("gotcha!"), or demonstrate how smart or how much more responsible you are.
  * The time, place, or circumstances are inappropriate (for example, in the presence of outsiders).

- **Know how to give feedback**

  If the circumstances are appropriate for giving feedback, use the following guidelines for compliments as well as complaints. Use the "Easy-to-Remember Guide for Giving Constructive Feedback" (facing page) the first few times—though it may feel awkward, you will soon get more comfortable and be able to give constructive feedback without having to refer to the guide.

  * *Be descriptive.*

    Relate, as objectively as possible, what you saw the other person do or what you heard the other person say. Give specific examples, the more recent, the better. Examples from the distant past are more likely to lead to disagreement over "facts."

  * *Don't use labels.*

    Be clear, specific and unambiguous. Words like "immature," "unprofessional," "irresponsible," and "prejudiced" are labels we attach to sets of behaviors. Describe the behavior and drop the labels. For example, say, "You missed the deadline we had all agreed to meet" rather than "You're being irresponsible and I want to know what you're going to do about it!"

* *Don't exaggerate.*

   Be exact. To say "You're always late for deadlines" is probably untrue and, therefore, unfair. It invites the feedback receiver to argue with the exaggeration rather than respond to the real issue.

* *Don't be judgmental.*

   Or at least don't use the rhetoric of judgment. Words like "good," "better," "bad," "worst," and "should" place you in the role of a controlling parent. This invites the person receiving your comments to respond as a child. When that happens, and it will most of the time, the possibility of constructive feedback is lost.

An Easy-to-Remember Guide for Constructive Feedback

Sequence	Explanation
1. "When you . . ."	Start with a "When you . . ." statement that describes the behavior without judgment, exaggeration, labeling, attribution, or motives. Just state the facts as specifically as possible.
2. "I feel . . ."	Tell how their behavior affects you. If you need more than a word or two to describe the feeling, it's probably just some variation of joy, sorrow, anger, or fear.
3. "Because I . . ."	Now say why you are affected that way. Describe the connection between the facts you observed and the feelings they provoke in you.
(4. Pause for discussion)	Let the other person respond.
5. "I would like . . ."	Describe the change you want the other person to consider . . .
6. "Because . . ."	. . . and why you think the change will alleviate the problem.
7. "What do you think?"	Listen to the other person's response. Be prepared to discuss options and compromise on a solution.

How the feedback will work:

When you [do this], I feel [this way], because [of such and such]. What I would like you to consider is [doing X], because I think it will accomplish [Y]. What do you think?

Example:

"When you are late for meetings, I get angry because I think it is wasting the time of all the other team members and we are never able to get through our agenda items. I would like you to consider finding some way of planning your schedule that lets you get to these meetings on time. That way we can be more productive at the meetings and we can all keep to our tight schedules."

* *Speak for yourself.*

    Don't refer to absent, anonymous people. Avoid such references as "A lot of people here don't like it when you. . ." Don't allow yourself to be a conduit for other peoples' complaints. Instead, encourage others to speak for themselves.

* *Talk first about yourself, not about the other person.*

    Use a statement with the word "I" as the subject, not the word "you." This guideline is one of the most important and one of the most surprising. Consider the following examples regarding lateness:

    1. "You are frequently late for meetings."
    2. "You are very prompt for meetings."
    3. "I feel annoyed when you are late for meetings."
    4. "I appreciate your coming to meetings on time."

    Statements 1 and 2 are "you" statements. People become defensive around "you" statements and are less likely to hear what you say when it is phrased this way. Statements 3 and 4 are "I" messages and create an adult/peer relationship. People are more likely to remain open to your message when an "I" statement is used. Even if your rank is higher than the feedback recipient, strive for an adult/peer relationship. Use "I" statements so the effectiveness of your comments is not lost.

* *Phrase the issue as a statement, not a question.*

    Contrast "When are you going to stop being late for meetings?" with "I feel annoyed when you are late for meetings." The question is controlling and manipulative because it implies "You, the responder, are expected to adjust your behavior to accommodate me, the questioner." Most people become defensive and angry when spoken to this way. On the other hand, the "I" statement implies "I think we have an issue we must resolve together." The "I" statement allows the receiver to see what effect the behavior had on you.

* *Restrict your feedback to things you know for certain.*

    Don't present your opinions as facts. Speak only of what you saw and heard and what you feel and want.

* *Help people hear and accept your compliments when giving positive feedback.*

    Many people feel awkward when told good things about themselves and will fend off the compliment ("Oh, it wasn't that big a deal. Others worked on it as much as I did.") Sometimes they will change the subject. It may be important to reinforce the positive feedback and help the person hear it, acknowledge it, and accept it.

- **Know how to receive feedback**

    There may be a time when you receive feedback from someone who does not know feedback guidelines. In these cases, **help your critic refashion the criticism** so that it conforms to the rules for constructive feedback ("What did I say or do to dissatisfy you?"). When reacting to feedback:

    * *Breathe.*

        This is simple but effective advice. Our bodies are conditioned to react to stressful situations as though they were physical assaults. Our muscles tense. We start breathing rapidly and shallowly. Taking full, deep breaths forces your body to relax and allows your brain to maintain greater alertness.

    * *Listen carefully.*

        Don't interrupt. Don't discourage the feedback-giver.

    * *Ask questions for clarity.*

        You have a right to receive clear feedback. Ask for specific examples ("Can you describe what I do or say that makes me appear aggressive to you?").

    * *Acknowledge the feedback.*

        Paraphrase the message in your own words to let the person know you have heard and understood what was said.

    * *Acknowledge valid points.*

        Agree with what is true. Agree with what is possible. Acknowledge the other person's point of view ("I understand how you might get that impression") and try to understand their reaction.

        Agreeing with what's true or possible does not mean you agree to change your behavior. You can agree, for instance, that sometimes you jump too quickly to a conclusion without implying that you will slow down your conclusion-making process. Agreeing with what's true or possible also does not mean agreeing with any value judgment about you. You can agree that your reports have been late without thereby agreeing that you are irresponsible.

    * *Take time to sort out what you heard.*

        You may need time for sorting out or checking with others before responding to the feedback. It is reasonable to ask the feedback-giver for time to think about what was said and how you feel about it. Make a specific appointment for getting back to him or her. Don't use this time as an excuse to avoid the issue.

VI. Working Through Group Problems, Part 2: *General Guidelines*

It would be nice to say that if you follow the advice in this handbook, you will never run into problems. But we all know that simply isn't true. Though severe problems are rare, occasionally an individual's behavior disrupts the group: You should be prepared to deal with disruptive situations.

Generally, your best strategy is to

- **Anticipate and prevent group problems whenever possible**

    As noted previously, most problems can be anticipated or prevented if a group spends time developing itself into a team: getting to know each other, establishing ground rules, discussing norms for group behavior, agreeing to an improvement plan. If you do this when your team starts, you will save time, and prevent hassles, frustrations, and animosities.

- **Think of each problem as a group problem**

    A natural tendency is to blame individuals for causing problems. Remember, the 85/15 Rule: most problems are attributable to the system, not the individual. The truth is that many problems arise because the group lets them happen or even encourages them in some way. Examine each problem in light of what the group does to encourage or allow the behavior and what the group can do differently to encourage more constructive behavior. Assume the problem continues to exist because it somehow benefits the group. What could that hidden benefit be? How have group members contributed to the continuation of the problem?

- **Neither over-react nor under-react**

    Some behaviors are only fleeting disruptions in the group's progress. These are usually not a problem and sometimes even give a needed break in the activity. Other behaviors are very disruptive and impede, halt, or reverse the team's progress towards its goals. Some behaviors are chronic, occurring over and over again. The team leader should respond appropriately to the seriousness of the problem, ignoring fleeting disruptions, confronting chronic or serious disrup-

---

Guidelines for Reacting to Group Problems

- Anticipate and prevent group problems whenever possible.
- Think of each problem as a group problem.
- Neither over-react nor under-react. A leader's range of responses typically includes:
- Do nothing (non-intervention)
    * Off-line conservation (minimal intervention)
    * Impersonal group time (low intervention)
    * Off-line confrontation (medium intervention)
    * In-group confrontation (high intervention)
    * Expulsion from the group (**Do Not Use This Option**)

tions directly. Experienced leaders develop a range of responses to typical problems, each more direct than the previous one. This way they can "crank up" the response as a problem gets more disruptive and the team realizes the seriousness of the situation.

A leader's range of responses typically includes:

* *Do nothing (non-intervention)*

    Ignore the offensive behavior, particularly if it is not a chronic problem or doesn't seem to inhibit the group. Sometimes, the leader need not intervene because other group members will deal with the offending behavior. In such cases the leader is available to facilitate the discussion provoked when one member confronts another.

* *Off-line conversation (minimal intervention)*

    Talk to the disruptive members outside the group meeting, asking them what would increase their satisfaction with the group. Give constructive feedback.

* *Impersonal group time (low intervention)*

    At the start of a meeting, talk about general group process concerns without pointing out individuals, perhaps by going through a list previously written on a flipchart. Include the disruptive behavior on the list. During the critique at the end of the meeting, the group evaluates itself on each item on the list. It is usually difficult to deal with problems without referring to the offenders. Sometimes not referring to the specific offenders is awkward and phony. One way to get around this is to describe the context of the problem (such as, "Every time we talk about subject X, we get sidetracked"). Focus attention on how the group encourages the problem and what the group can do to discourage it. This approach treats all problems as group process problems rather than offenses by individuals.

* *Off-line confrontation (medium intervention)*

    Off-line confrontation is the same as off-line conversation except the leader is more assertive. Use it when other attempts have failed, especially when the disruptive behavior continues even when the group has tried to change. Sometimes this confrontation may lead to an informal "contract" regarding agreed-upon changes in the leader's and member's behavior. (For example, "I know you don't get along with Joe and I will do everything I can to avoid pairing you up on assignments. For your part I want you to stop being critical of him during team meetings.")

* *In-group confrontation (high intervention)*

    As a last resort, after other approaches have failed, the leader may deal with the offending behavior in the presence of the group. This disrupts the group's other business and exposes an individual's behavior to open critique in the group. This tactic can be effective; it can also be a disaster. The leader must prepare carefully for this intervention: how to word the confrontation, what reactions to anticipate, how to avoid defensiveness or hostility in the offending member. Use constructive feedback techniques, expressing feelings as "I statements." The purpose of high intervention is to change the offensive behavior, not to punish the offending member.

* *Expulsion from the group* (**do not use this option**)

   We believe that you should never kick anyone off a project team and recommend against expulsion for the following reasons: It can create a stigma that remains with the group and with the expelled member for a long time. The costs of expelling a member are ill will, creating an adversary, and creating an unfavorable impression of the group among others in the organization.

   What can a team leader do when highly disruptive behavior continues? One of the best strategies is to talk privately with the offending team member, and point out that disruptive behavior seems inconsistent with a commitment to help the team succeed. If the person would rather not attend meetings, find other ways to allow his or her input into the project.

VII. Working Through Group Problems, Part 3: *Ten Common Problems and What to Do About Them*

One way to deal with group problems, particularly those arising from unspoken issues, such as competing loyalties to the team and work groups, is to talk about them. Most problems, though, require a more structured solution. The following examples show how to use the guidelines for constructive feedback and working through common team problems.

1. Floundering

Teams commonly have trouble starting and ending a project or even different project stages. They flounder, wondering what actions to take next. At the beginning, they sometimes suffer through false starts and directionless discussions and activities. As the group progresses, team members sometimes resist moving from one phase or step to the next. At the end, teams may delay unnecessarily, postponing decisions or conclusions because "We need something else. We're not ready to finish this yet."

Problems at the beginning suggest the team is unclear or overwhelmed by its task. Start-up problems may also indicate group members are not yet comfortable enough with each other to engage in real discussion and decision making.

Floundering when trying to make decisions may indicate that the group's work is not the product of consensus, but some members are reluctant to say they don't support the group's conclusions. Floundering after completing one phase of a project could mean the group does not have a clear plan and does not know what steps to take next. Floundering at the end of the project usually indicates that the team members

> **Ten Common Group Problems**
> 1. Floundering
> 2. Overbearing participants
> 3. Dominating participants
> 4. Reluctant participants
> 5. Unquestioned acceptance of opinions as facts
> 6. Rush to accomplishment
> 7. Attribution
> 8. Discounts and "plops"
> 9. Wanderlust: digression and tangents
> 10. Feuding members

have developed a bond and are reluctant to separate. Or, perhaps, they are reluctant to expose their work to review and possible criticism from outsiders.

How a team leader can deal with floundering

- Get the group to look critically at how the project is being run.
- "Let's review our mission and make sure it's clear to everyone."
- "Let's go over our improvement plan and see what we have to do next."
- "What do we need to do so we can move on? What is holding us up?" (Data? Knowledge? Assurance? Support? Feelings?)
- "Are we getting stuck because we have previous business that is unfinished? Does anyone feel we have missed something or left something incomplete?"
- "Let's reserve time at the next meeting to discuss how we will proceed. Meanwhile, I suggest that each of us write down what we think is needed to move to the next stage."

2. Overbearing Participants

Some members wield a disproportionate amount of influence in a group. These people usually have a position of authority or an area of expertise on which they base their authority. Teams need authorities and experts because these are important resources. Most teams benefit from their participation. But the presence of an authority or an expert is detrimental when the person:

- Discourages or forbids discussion encroaching into his or her authority or expertise. ("You need not get involved in those technicalities. We are taking care of that. Let's move on to something else.")
- Signals the "untouchability" of an area by using technical jargon or referring to present specifications, standards, regulations, or policies as the ultimate determinants of future actions. ("What you don't understand is that PP85271 requires a bimordial interface between the cragstop and any abutting AC135.")

- Regularly discounts any proposed activity by declaring that it won't work, or citing instances when it was tried unsuccessfully here or in the past. Other members soon get the message that their suggestions will be seen as trite or naive. ("We tried that in Johnstown in 1968. It was a disaster! Steer clear of that solution.")

How a team leader can deal with overbearing participants

- Reinforce the agreement that no area is sacred, team members have the right to explore any area that pertains to the project.
- Get the authority to agree (before the project starts, if possible) that it is important for the group to make its own way, for all members to understand the process and operation. The expert may occasionally be asked to instruct the group, to share knowledge or a broader perspective.
- Talk to the authority off-line, and ask for cooperation and patience.
- Enforce the primacy of data and the scientific approach. ("In God we trust. All others must have data!")

3. Dominating Participants

Some members, with or without authority or expertise, consume a disproportionate amount of "air time." They talk too much. Instead of concise statements, they tell overlong anecdotes and dominate the meeting. Normal moments of silence that occasionally occur are an invitation for the dominator to talk. Their talk inhibits the group from building a sense of team accomplishment or momentum. Other members get discouraged and find excuses for missing meetings.

How a team leader can deal with dominating participants

- Structure discussion on key issues to encourage equal participation. For example, have members write down their thoughts and share them around the table.
- List "balance of participation" as a general concern to critique during the meeting evaluation.
- Practice gate-keeping: "We've heard from you on this, Joe. I'd like to hear what others have to say."
- Get the team to agree on the need for limits and focus in discussions, and the value of balanced participation.

4. Reluctant Participants

Many groups have one or two members who rarely speak. They are the opposites of the dominators. When invited to speak, these "underbearing" members commonly say "I *am* participating; I listen to everything that's said. When I have something to say, I'll say it."

Each of us has a different threshold of need to be part of a group ("tribal" instincts versus "loner" instincts) and a different level of comfort with speaking in a group (extrovert versus introvert). There is nothing right or wrong about being tribal or a loner, extroverted or introverted; these are just differences between people. Problems develop in a group when there are no built-in activities that encourage the introverts to participate and the extroverts to listen.

How a team leader can deal with reluctant participants

- Structure participation the same way as for dominating participants.
- When possible, divide the project task into individual assignments and reports.
- Act as a gatekeeper. "Does anyone else have ideas about this?" (done while looking at the reluctant participant); more directly, "Sam, what is your experience with this area?"

5. *Unquestioned Acceptance of Opinions as Facts*

Some team members express personal beliefs and assumptions with such confidence that listeners assume they are hearing a presentation of facts. This can be dangerous, leading to an unshakable acceptance of various "earth-is-flat" assertions.

Most team members are reluctant to question self-assured statements from other members. Besides not wanting to be impolite, they think they need to have data before they challenge someone else's assertions. Worse yet, the skeptic could be wrong and lose face with the team.

There is an ancient axiom of debate that says if a speaker presents something as fact without legitimate supporting evidence, the listener need not have evidence to respond with skepticism.

How a team leader can deal with unquestioned acceptance of opinions as facts

- "Is what you said an opinion or a fact? Do you have data?"
- "How do you know that is true?"
- "Let's accept what you say as possible, but let's also get some data to test it."
- Have the group agree on the primacy of the scientific approach.

6. *Rush to Accomplishment*

Many teams will have at least one "do something" member who is either impatient or sensitive to pressure from managers or other influential people or groups. This type of person typically reaches an individual decision about a problem and its solution before the group has had time to consider different options. They urge the team to make hasty decisions and discourage any further efforts to analyze or discuss the matter. Their nonverbal behavior, direct statements, and "throw away" expressions constantly communicate impatience.

Too much of this pressure can lead a group in a series of random, unsystematic efforts to make improvements. Like hunters shooting blindly at silent birds in a heavy fog, they are satisfied that they're "doing something" and pray that at least one shot will hit the target.

Teams must realize that improvements do not come easily, and rarely can they make significant gains overnight. Quality takes patience.

How a team leader can deal with a rush to accomplishment

- Remind team members of their prior agreement that the scientific approach will not be compromised or circumvented.
- Make sure he or she is not among those exerting the pressure.
- Confront the rusher, using the techniques of constructive feedback. Have examples of rushing and describes the effect of this impatience on the team's work.

7. Attribution

As individuals and groups, we tend to attribute motives to people when we disagree with or don't understand their opinion or behavior. Through attribution we try to bring order and meaning into apparent disorder and confusion.

However, attribution is a substitute for the hard work of seeking real explanations. It also creates resentment: it is perfectly normal to bristle when someone else tells you they know what makes you tick or tries to explain your motives.

Within a team, attribution can lead to hostility when aimed at another team member ("What you don't understand is . . ." or "He's just trying to take the easy way out.") When aimed at individuals or groups outside of the team ("They won't want to get involved. They're just waiting 'til they can collect their pension.") it can lead to misguided efforts based on erroneous attributions.

How a team leader can deal with attribution

- Reaffirm prior agreement on the primacy of the scientific approach.
- "That may well explain why they behave the way they do. But how do we know? What has anyone seen or heard that indicates this? Can we confirm that with data?"
- If the attribution is from one member to another, don't let it go by without checking it out. "Jim, I heard Sally describe your approach as 'catering to the other side.' How would you describe it?"

8. Discounts and "Plops"

We all have certain values or perspectives that are—consciously or unconsciously—important to us. When someone else ignores or ridicules these values, we feel discounted. This discounting can also cause hostility in a team, especially if it happens frequently.

For instance, there will be times in every team when someone makes a statement that "plops." No one acknowledges it, and the discussion picks up on a subject totally irrelevant to the statement, leaving the speaker to wonder why there was no response.

Discounts happen for many reasons. Perhaps the discounted member said something irrelevant to the team's discussion, or did not clearly state the idea. Perhaps the rest of the team missed the meaning in the statements. No matter what the reason, every member deserves the respect and attention from the team. Teams must help discounted members identify and articulate what is important to them.

How a team leader can deal with discounts and plops

- Include training in active listening and other constructive behaviors early in the team's life.
- Support the discounted person. "Nancy, it sounds like that is important to you and we aren't giving it enough consideration"; "I think what Jerry said is worthwhile and we should spend time on it before we move on"; "Bill, before we move on is there some part of what you said that you would like the group to discuss?"
- Talk off-line with anyone who frequently discounts, puts down, or ignores previous speakers' statements. Use the guidelines for constructive feedback.

9. Wanderlust: Digression and Tangents

The following scenario will probably sound familiar to anyone who has sat in on meetings: A group describing breakdowns in a work process is told of how one worker solved the problem. This reminds someone of how that same worker solved a problem in another process, which reminds someone else of an incident between that worker and his supervisor, which leads to a discussion of whatever happened to that supervisor, which leads to a discussion of retirement condominiums in Florida, and on and on. When the meeting ends, the team wonders where the time went.

Such wide-ranging, unfocused conversations are an example of wanderlust, our natural tendency to stray from the subject. Sometimes these digressions are innocent tangents from the conversation. But they also happen when the team wants to avoid a subject that it needs to address. In either case, the meeting facilitator is responsible for bringing the conversation back to the meeting agenda.

How a team leader can deal with wanderlust

- Use a written agenda with time estimates for each item; refer to the topic and time when the discussion strays too far.
- Write topics or items on a flipchart and post the pages on the wall where all members can refer to them throughout the discussion.
- Direct the conversation back on track: "We've strayed from the topic, which was ___. The last few comments before we digressed were ___."
- "We've had trouble sticking to this point. Is there something about it that makes it so easy to avoid?"

10. Feuding Team Members

Sometimes a group becomes a field of combat for members who are vying with each other. Usually, the issue is not the subject they are arguing about but rather the contest itself. Other members feel like spectators at a sporting match, and fear that if they participate in any disagreement between the pair, they will be swept into the contest on one side or the other. Usually these feuds predate the team, and in all likelihood will outlast it, too. The best way to deal with this situation is to prevent it by carefully selecting team members so that adversaries are never on the same team. If that is impossible, then bring the combatants together before the first meeting to work out some agreement about their behavior.

How a team leader can deal with feuding team members

- When confrontations occur during a meeting, get the adversaries to discuss the issues off-line. Offer to facilitate the discussion.
- Push them to some contract about their behavior (if you agree to X, I will agree to Y) or ground rules for managing their differences without disrupting the group.

CHAPTER 2

Participating in Work Groups

Members of the advertising division of Meyer Foods were gathered to review their hiring policies. At the beginning of the first meeting, Kareem, head of the division, began, "You know why I called you together. Each department has to review its hiring practices. So, let's get started." After a few seconds of silence, Kareem said, "Drew, what have you been thinking?"

"Well, I don't know," Drew replied. "I haven't really given it much thought."

"I'd like to contribute," Dawn said. "I just don't have much information."

"But I sent around a preliminary analysis of our practices with some questions for discussion," Kareem said.

"Oh, is that what that was," Byron said. "I read the part about the meeting, but I guess I didn't pay much attention to the material."

"Why don't we just say that we've given our guidelines careful thought and wish to keep them the way they are?" Dawn asked.

"But," replied Kareem, "I think the CEO is looking for some specific recommendations. They'd like us to comment on how we process minority and female applicants."

"Anything you think would be important would be OK with me," Byron replied.

"Well, how about if we each try to come up with some ideas for next time," Kareem suggested. "Meeting's adjourned."

As the group dispersed, Kareem overheard Drew say, "These meetings sure are a waste of time, aren't they?"

Perhaps you belong to a fraternal, business, governmental, or religious group. Or perhaps you have worked on a committee. Does this opening dialogue reflect the way your group meetings have gone? When group work is ineffective, it is easy to point the finger at the leader, but often, as is the case with this group, the responsibility for the "waste of time" lies squarely on the shoulders of the individuals involved. Because most of us spend some of our communication time in groups, we need to know how to participate in ways that maximize group effectiveness.

In this chapter, we consider characteristics of effective *work groups*—groups of two of more people using logical means, in public or in private, to solve a problem or arrive at a decision. Then we consider the specific roles group members play and a method for group problem solving. In the next chapter, we consider one of the most important group roles, leadership.

Characteristics of Effective Work Groups

Since work groups seek to achieve specific goals, it is relevant to ask what makes work groups effective. Research shows that effective groups generally have a good working environment, have an optimum number of members, show cohesiveness, are committed to the task, respect group rules, find ways to achieve consensus, are well prepared, and meet key role requirements.[1]

Good Working Environment

A good working environment is one that promotes group interaction. An important aspect of a good working environment is a seating arrangement that will encourage full participation. Seating can be formal or too informal for optimum interaction. Too formal would be a board of directors seating style, in which seating location is an indication of status. Imagine the long polished oak table with the chairperson at the head, the leading lieutenants at right and left, and the remaining people down the line. In this style, a boss-and-subordinate pattern emerges, which can inhibit group interaction. People are unlikely to speak until they are asked to do so. Moreover, no one has a good view of all the people present.

On the other hand, an excessively informal setting can also inhibit interaction. In an informal arrangement, people sit where they feel comfortable. People sitting in clusters may feel free to interact with one another, but it is unlikely that all the people in such an informal arrangement will interact as one group.

The ideal arrangement is the circle. Being seated in a circle increases participant motivation to speak. Contrast the perceived equality of participants seated in a circle with those seated at an oblong table where those at the ends will be perceived as having higher status—and thus be encouraged to lead. Or with those sitting on the corners who will tend to speak less than those on the ends or in the middle. In the circle arrangement, sight lines are better: Everyone can see everyone else. And, at least in terms of seating position, everyone has equal status. If the meeting place does not have a round table, the group may be better off without a table or with an arrangement of tables that makes a square.

From the beginning, it is important for the group to establish a climate that allows each person to participate. Anything suggesting that only one person is to be listened to or that some persons have ideas that are generally unworthy will hurt the group's efforts to achieve a balance of participation. People will not participate if they fear personal attack; if they believe that their ideas will be belittled, ridiculed, or discounted; or if they feel that no one will intervene to allow their ideas to be heard.

As a group deliberates, certain individuals will earn higher status than others. In a particular subject area, for instance, one person may be acknowledged as having better information, greater insight, or a more logical perspective. As a result, that person's comments will carry more weight in that area. But an effective group provides a climate in which everyone has an equal opportunity to earn higher status.

Optimum Number of Members

Effective groups contain enough members to ensure good interaction but not so many members that discussion is stifled. Because conventional wisdom dictates that "bigger is better," task forces created to examine major problems are almost always too large to work effectively. Having too many members causes several problems: Many people cannot or will not contribute, cohesiveness is nearly impossible to develop, and the decision is seldom a product of the group's collective thought.

Although optimum size depends on the nature of the task, groups consisting of five members are most desirable.[2] Why five? Groups with fewer than five members almost universally complain that they are too small and that there are not enough people for specialization. To be effective, a group needs certain skills. When the group contains only three or four members, chances are not all these skills will be present. Moreover, if one member of a group of three does not feel like contributing, you no longer have much of a group. Nevertheless, for small tasks the three-person group often works well. It's easier to get three people together than five or more. And if the task is relatively simple or within the expertise of the individuals, the three-person group may be a good choice.

When a group numbers more than seven or eight people, reticent members are even less likely to contribute. As the group grows larger, two, three, or four people may become the central spokespersons, with others playing more passive roles.[3]

In a group of any size, an odd number is better than an even number. Why? Although voting is not the best way of reaching a decision, if a group finds it necessary to resolve an issue on which it cannot achieve consensus, the odd number will prevent tie votes.

Cohesiveness

Cohesiveness means sticking together, pulling for one another, and being caught up in the task. Remember the Three Musketeers, who were all for one and one for all? They are the prototype of a cohesive group.

What determines the potential for group cohesiveness? At least three qualities seem particularly important. One is the attractiveness of the group's purpose. Members identify with one another when the groups' goals are particularly appealing. Social or fraternal groups, for example, build cohesiveness out of devotion to service or brotherhood. In a decision-making group, attractiveness is likely to be related to how important the task is to members. Suppose a church congregation forms a committee to consider how its outreach program can be made more responsible to community needs. The cohesiveness of the members of that committee will depend, at least in part, on the importance they attribute to this issue.

A second important quality necessary for cohesiveness is similarity of the needs and interests of members. Groups can be characterized as homogeneous or heterogenous. A *homogeneous group* is one in which members have a great deal in common. For example, a group of five women of the same age who are all strong feminists would be homogeneous. By contrast, a *heterogeneous group* is one in which various ages, levels of knowledge, attitudes, and interests are represented. A homogeneous group generally will achieve cohesiveness more quickly than a heterogeneous group because the members are more likely to identify with one another's needs and interests from the start.

A third important quality is reinforcement of interpersonal needs. William Schutz has identified three major interpersonal needs: affection (showing affection to others and receiving affection from others), inclusion (including others in activities and being included by others in their activities), and control (having a role in determining what will happen). Group cohesiveness seems directly related to the belief of individual members that they are liked, included, and respected. As people decide that they like one another, that they want to be around one another, and that their opinions will be respected, they begin to work more effectively as a unit.

Cohesiveness is difficult to develop in a one-meeting group, but it is and should be characteristic of ongoing groups. Cohesiveness is usually generated after initial meetings and should be well established during or before the group reaches its most productive stages.

Commitment to the Task

Whether the group is assigned a task or the group determines its task, members must be sufficiently committed to the group for it to succeed. When the task is deemed important and when the group believes that what it is doing will matter, members are much more inclined to devote their energies to the task.

When someone appoints you to a committee or asks you to serve on one, you have to decide whether you really want to be a part of that work group. If you aren't fully committed to the task described, you are better off declining. When people aren't committed, they miss meetings, avoid work, and fail to do what is expected of them.

Development of and Adherence to Group Rules

Rules are the guidelines for behavior that are established or are perceived to be established for conducting group business. They are the most powerful determiners of behavior in groups. Rules begin to be established at the onset of a group's deliberations, and they grow, change, and solidify as people get to know each other better.

Rules for a group may be formally spelled out in a group's operating guidelines (as in parliamentary procedures for organizational meetings), they may be adapted from proven social guidelines (such as "Don't talk about yourself in a decision-making group meeting"), or they may simply develop within a particular context. For instance, without any conscious decision, group members may avoid using common four-letter words during the meeting. When business has ended, conversation may become more earthy.

Although formally stated rules may be known to group members from the beginning, most group rules are learned through experience with a specific group, and because rules may vary from one group to the next, we have to constantly relearn them. Two particularly important areas of rule development are group interaction and group procedure. In one group, it may be acceptable to interrupt any speaker at any time; in another group, it may be forbidden for anyone to speak until he or she is recognized. Thus, Martha, who is used to raising her hand to be recognized at the business meetings of her social organization, may find herself unable to speak in a group meeting where the participants break in whenever they have a chance. In one group, it may be all right for someone to openly express anger or hostility toward a person or an idea; in another group, such displays may be frowned on. In one group, members' relative status may determine who speaks first, longest, or most often; in another group, the status of members may have no effect on interaction.

Rules help a group develop cohesiveness. As members conform to stated or implied guidelines of behavior, they find themselves relating to one another more effectively. One of the initial hurdles group members must surmount is *primary tension*—the anxieties of getting to know one another. As group members test out verbal and nonverbal behavior to see what will be accepted, they begin to become more comfortable with one another, primary tension is lessened, and the group is able to concentrate on its task.

Although rules are essential, some rules can be detrimental or destructive. Suppose that at the beginning of the first meeting, a few members of the group tell jokes and generally have a good time. If such behavior is allowed or encouraged, cutting up, making light of the task, and joke telling become a group norm. As a result, the group may become so involved in these behaviors that the task is delayed, set aside, or perhaps even forgotten. Participants may describe their experience by saying, "We don't do much, but it's fun." Even if some group members are concerned about such behavior, once it goes on for several meetings, it will be very difficult to change. As you participate in a group, you can try to be conscious of what rules seem to be in operation and whether or not those rules are helping the group's work. If you believe that certain rules are detrimental or destructive, make your position and the reasons for it known so that those rules do not become established and reinforced.

Consensus

If a decision is not a product of group thought and group interaction, the advantages of group decision making are lost. In addition, group members often feel more pleased about the process and more committed to the resulting decisions when such decisions are reached democratically, through group interaction.

Democratic decision making may be achieved through *consensus*, or total group agreement. After the group has discussed a point for a while, one member might pose a question that is phrased to capture the essence of the group's position. For example, someone might ask, "Are we in agreement that lack of direction is frustrating the efforts of department members?" If everyone agrees, the decision is reached by consensus. If the group does not agree, the group can continue to discuss the point until a statement can be made that incorporates differing viewpoints without compromising the principles behind them. But it takes the participation of most group members to arrive at a statement that represents the group position.

If consensus still cannot be reached, the group usually takes a vote. Suppose that after considerable discussion on the policy question "What measures should be taken to open lines of communication between the director and department employees?" it becomes obvious that the group cannot agree on whether to install a "gripe box" as one of the measures. The group should then take a vote. If in a seven-person group, the vote is six to one or five to two, the decision has been given solid support. If it is a four-to-three vote, however, there may be some questions about later group support of that decision. Nevertheless, the principle of majority rule is the only choice open.

Preparation

In most group deliberations, the better the quality of the information shared, the better the quality of the group decisions. And the quality of information is largely a function of how well prepared group members are when discussion begins.

Depending on the kind of problem being discussed, your preparation for group work may include one or more of the following:

1. *Read circulated information carefully before the meeting.* In some groups, the information necessary for decision making may be given to you before the meeting. But the whole point of starting a meeting with well-prepared members is short-circuited if you and other members of the group don't do the reading beforehand.

2. *Think about relevant personal experience.* Sometimes the topic to be considered is one that you have thought about or worked with before. For instance, if your group will be considering how to arrange available parking space so that it is equally distributed to administrators, faculty, and students, your own parking experiences may be useful to the group. Nevertheless, personal experience seldom constitutes complete preparation.

3. *Survey library sources.* Discussion of many questions requires solid, documented materials. Suppose your group will be considering changing college requirements. What are the requirements at similar colleges and universities? Your library should have catalogs from other schools that you can check. Or suppose you are considering instituting a class on media analysis. Your library has various magazines and journals that will have articles related to the issue. When you need to do library research, your reference librarian can suggest books, articles, government publications, newspapers, and other sources that contain useful data.

4. *Poll public opinion.* For some topics, a public opinion poll is appropriate. For instance, on the question of campus parking, you may be able to take advantage of the experience and opinions of current students. What do they think of the present system? What would they like to see done? Prepare a few well-worded questions, go to the parking lots, and

ask your questions. If a personal survey is not practicable, you may need to devise another means of eliciting responses from the relevant people. For the parking lot survey, you could put your survey questionnaire under the windshield wiper of every car and ask drivers to leave the completed questionnaires at the entry gate or drop them in the campus mail. Of course, in any survey, you need to make sure that you have polled a large enough group and that you have sampled different segments of the population before you attempt to draw any significant conclusions from your poll.

5. *Interview for information.* An effective but often overlooked means of preparation is the personal interview. One interview with a person with relevant expertise may be all that is needed for your subject, or you may have to interview several people.

Practice in Analyzing Group Characteristics

By Yourself

Select for analysis one of the most recent work groups in which you have participated. Which of the following had the greatest effect on group interaction or the quality of the group decision: environment, group size, presence or lack of cohesiveness, commitment to task, adherence to rules, methods of decision making, or group preparation? On what do you base your analysis?

Major Group Roles

Effective groups contain people who meet key role requirements. A *role* is a pattern of behavior that characterizes an individual's place in a group. Students of group dynamics have identified two key types of roles that are filled in productive groups: task roles and maintenance roles. *Task roles* pertain to the work a group must do to accomplish its goal; *maintenance* roles pertain to the group behaviors that keep the group working together smoothly.

In this section, we examine the major task and maintenance roles that are necessary for a group to function effectively; we also look at those negative roles that need to be kept to a minimum.

Task Roles

Some roles relate directly to the substance of the group's work. In effective groups, people will present information and opinions, ask for information and opinions, analyze data, create ideas, help keep the group focused on the topic, and record the group's key decisions.

Information or Opinion Giver. The information or opinion giver provides content for the discussion. Giving information actually constitutes about 50 percent of what is done in a group because without information (and well-considered opinions), the group will not have the necessary material from which to draw its conclusions.

Chances are everyone in the group will fill this role at some time during the discussion.

Playing the information-giving role well requires solid preparation. The more material you have studied, the more valuable your contributions will be. As information giver, you will want to draw material from several different sources, and you will usually bring a record of your sources with you to the discussion.

Effective information givers present information clearly and objectively without getting emotionally involved. For instance, in answer to the question of whether dormitory theft is increasing, you might say, "According to statistics gathered by the campus police, theft has increased by at least 10 percent each of the last three years." Since you always want to be sure that any related information is presented, you might then add, "I wonder whether anyone else has found any other data that indicate the levels of theft?" Raising such a question tells the group that you welcome discussion of the information and that, whether it is substantiated or disproven, you have no personal investment in it.

The following are examples of ways that information givers might introduce their material:

"When the Jones Corporation considered this problem, they found . . ."

"The other day I ran across these figures that relate to your point."

"According to the Controller's analysis, it doesn't necessarily work that way. He presented material that shows . . ."

Information Seeker. Information seeking is just the opposite of information giving. Instead of presenting information, you probe for information from others. Although it is very important to have information to present, it is also important to help the group recognize when more information is needed.

Information seeking serves two important functions in a group. The most obvious is asking for information when the data the group has are insufficient for drawing a conclusion. For instance, a group that is discussing whether to raise fees for a club will need to know how raising fees is likely to affect membership. To ensure that the group does not fall back on unsubstantiated opinion, one member might ask whether anyone has relevant information. If not, the group can note that this information is needed before a decision can be made on this point.

A second function information seeking serves is to clarify group procedure. Thus, it can be relevant to ask for information about where in the decision-making process the group is at the moment, whether or not they are in agreement, and what they should be doing next.

Analyzer. The analyzer probes both the content and the reasoning involved in the discussion. Analyzers know the steps a group must go through to solve a problem. They recognize when the group has skipped a point, has passed over a point too lightly, or has not considered relevant material. Analyzers help the group penetrate to the core of the problem they are working on.

First, analyzers probe the contributions of group members to determine whether information is accurate, typical, consistent, and otherwise valid. Suppose a group member reports that according to Paul Stewart, who oversees subscriptions to cable television, the number of new subscriptions dropped last month. An analyzer might ask such questions as "How many new subscriptions has the company been averaging each month over the past year? In how many months were new subscriptions below the average for this year? For last year? Has this drop been consistent?" The purpose of such questions is to test the data. If data are partly true, questionable, or relevant only to certain aspects of the issue, a different conclusion or set of conclusions might be appropriate.

Second, analyzers examine the reasoning of various participants. They make such statements as "Enrique, you're generalizing from only one instance. Can you give us some others?" or "Wait a minute, after symptoms, we have to take a look at causes," or "I think we're passing this possible solution too lightly. There are still questions about it that we haven't answered."

Idea Person. The idea person is an imaginative individual who thinks originally, rattles off alternative ideas, and often comes up with an idea that serves as the basis for the ultimate decision. Although everyone in the group may provide information, usually only one or two people are truly inventive. When others seem unable to see past tried-and-true solutions, the idea person suggests a new one, when others think they have exhausted the possibilities, idea people come up with still another. As we might expect, not all these ideas are necessarily "world beaters." The creative mind is constantly mining ideas, but only a few are golden. Nevertheless, a good idea person is indispensable, and groups should not discourage their more creative members from advancing ideas.

Expediter. The expediter keeps the group on track. Whether the group meets once or is ongoing, almost invariably some remarks will tend to sidetrack the group from the central point or issue. Sometimes apparent digressions are necessary to establish the background of the problem, enlarge its scope, or even give people an opportunity to air their feelings. Yet these momentary digressions can lead the group off on tangents that have little to do with the assignment. Expediters are the people who help the group stick to its agenda.

When the group has strayed, expediters will make statements like "I'm enjoying this, but I can't quite see what it has to do with resolving the issue," or "Let's see, aren't we still trying to find out whether these are the only criteria that we should be considering?" or "Say, time is getting away from us and we've considered only two possible solutions. Aren't there some more?"

Recorder. People's perceptions and memories differ. Consider that in a one-hour group discussion about 9,000 words will be spoken. Unless special effort is made to record the group's procedure and decisions, much valuable information can be lost.

The record of a formal group meeting is called the *minutes*. Minutes include major motions, key debates, and conclusions agreed on by the group. The recorder types the minutes and circulates them to group members prior to the next meeting. The minutes then become a public record of the group's activities.

A good record of group proceedings is necessary for the following reasons:

1. *To provide a formal statement of the group's decisions.* Statements such as "In the early portion of the discussion, the group decided to limit its

analysis to activity in the southeastern states where declines in sales have been noted" summarize what took place and apprise every group member of the decision. If some controversy arises later, the group can be reminded of the decision.

2. *To provide a record of all key information that serves as a basis for decisions.* Unless a group records the information that leads to decisions, the group's process is open to question. Others affected by the group's work cannot blindly accept that the group has done a comprehensive analysis of the question. A record of decisions shows others what was done.

3. *To protect against misunderstanding and misperception by individual members.* As time goes by, people recall less and less of what was said unless they are reminded of it. At the end of a day's meeting, members may be able to summarize key decisions and key information; three weeks later, however, the substance of a meeting is likely to be a blur. A precise record shows the exact wording of what the group agreed on.

4. *To serve as a running account of the group process.* An accurate record is also important to the group during discussion. It helps members find out where the group is, determine whether the discussion pertains to the group goal, and identify the foundation on which subsequent discussion should be built. Good discussion is a slow process, but anything that can be done to make the process more efficient without detracting from spontaneity should be encouraged. A written account keeps what is happening in front of the group and helps it avoid ambiguity.

Usually, the leader or another designated group member is responsible for keeping good records; occasionally, a person who is not a part of the group is solicited or hired to keep records. In either case, the recorder notes key comments of members, with special emphasis on decisions that the group has agreed on. Every person has the right to ask the recorder to read the last decision made or to read back a summary of information. As with any other skill, good recording takes a great deal of practice. You will find that when a person gets good at the job, the entire group prospers.

Maintenance Roles

Whereas task roles help the group deal with the content of discussion, maintenance roles help the group work together smoothly as a unit. In effective decision-making groups, people who fill maintenance roles will support one another, relieve tensions, control conflict, and give everyone a chance to talk.

Supporter. People participating in groups are likely to feel better about their participation when their thoughts and feelings are recognized. Sometimes, however, people get so wrapped up in the discussion or in their own ideas that they may neglect to recognize and reward positive contributions. Supporters help provide this recognition.

Supporters respond nonverbally or verbally when good points are made. Supporters give such nonverbal clues as a smile, a nod, or a vigorous head shake and make statements like "Good point, Ming," "I really like that idea, Nikki," "It's obvious you've really done your homework, Janelle," and "That's one of the best ideas we've had today, Drew."

Tension Reliever. According to folklore, all work and no play makes Jack a dull boy. When group members become immersed in their tasks, they sometimes get so involved and work so hard that they begin to wear themselves down. Nerves fray, vision clouds, and the machinery of progress grinds to a halt. Tension relievers recognize when the group process is stagnating or when the group is tiring. They have a sixth sense for when to tell a joke, when to take off on a digression, and when to get the group to loosen up a little before returning to the task. In some situations, a single well-placed one-liner will get a laugh, break the tension or the monotony, and jolt the group out of its lethargy. At other times, the group can be saved only with a real break—sometimes a minute or so will suffice; other times five, ten, or even fifteen minutes will be necessary.

Tension relieving adds nothing to the content of the discussion, but it does improve immeasurably the spirits of the participants. Of all the roles, this one is the most difficult to play consciously. When people have to make a conscious effort to be tension relievers, they are likely to fail. Although not every group has a person who fills the bill completely, most groups include at least one person who can meet it well enough to be helpful. Even if a group can accomplish its task without a tension reliever, it certainly is not as much fun. You will know, recognize, and be thankful for the person who plays this role well.

Harmonizer. The harmonizer brings the group together. It is a rare group that can expect to accomplish its task without some minor if not major conflict. Even when people get along well, they are likely to become angry over some inconsequential point in a heated discussion. Most groups experience some classic interpersonal conflicts caused by different personality types and by polarization. Norbert Kerr shows that when an issue is especially important, group members are likely to experience greater polarization and thus greater conflict.[4]

Harmonizers are responsible for reducing tensions and for straightening out misunderstandings, disagreements, and conflicts. They smooth ruffled feathers, encourage objectivity, and mediate between hostile or aggressively competing sides. A group cannot avoid some conflict, but if there is no one present to harmonize, participation can become an uncomfortable experience.

Harmonizers are likely to make such statements as "Brandon, I don't think you're giving Jana a chance to make her point," "Tom, Jack, hold it a second. I know you're on opposite sides of this, but let's see where you might have some agreement," "Lynne, I get the feeling that something Todd said really bugged you. Is that right?" or "Hold it, everybody, we're really coming up with some good stuff; let's not lose our momentum by getting into name-calling."

Gatekeeper. Gatekeepers help keep communication channels open. In an effective group, all the members should have something to contribute. To ensure balanced participation, those who tend to dominate need to be held in check, and those who tend to be shy need to be encouraged. The gatekeeper is the one who sees that Juanita is on the edge of her chair, eager to speak but unable to break in, or that Don is rambling a bit and needs to be directed, or that Larry's need to talk so frequently is making Cesar withdraw from the conversation, or that Betty has just lost the thread of the discussion. Gatekeepers assume responsibility for helping interaction by making statements like "Joan, I see you've got something to say here," or "You've made a really good point, Todd; I wonder whether we could get some reaction on it," or "Amir and Kristen, it sounds as if you're getting into a dialogue here; let's see what other ideas we have."

Gatekeepers can also be sensitive to social, cultural, and gender factors that may affect group members' participation. For example, even within the same culture, group members may bring very different backgrounds, vocabularies, and stores of information to the discussion. Thus, some members may not understand some of the terms, historical allusions, or other information that other speakers take for granted—and they may be too embarrassed to ask for clarification. The same point applies, only more so, when a group consists of people from different cultures.[5] Furthermore, some members may become frustrated because their ideas are not properly credited. (For a discussion of this point and its effect on women, see It's Her Idea, and He Gets the Credit. Why?)

Perspectives

It's Her Idea, and He Gets the Credit. Why?

In group meetings, your style of speaking can make the difference in whether you are heard, no matter how good your ideas are. Certain communication habits often put women at a disadvantage in groups.

Cynthia was a member of a committee to raise funds for a political candidate. Most of the committee members were focused in canvassing local businesses for support. When Cynthia suggested that they write directly to a list of former colleagues, friends, and supporters of the candidate, inviting them to join an honorary board (and inviting them to contribute), her suggestion was ignored. Later the same suggestion was made by another committee member, Barry. Suddenly, the group came alive, enthusiastically embracing and planning to implement "Barry's idea."

Some of the men I spoke to—and just about every woman—told me of the experience of saying something at a meeting and having it ignored, then hearing the same comment taken up when it is repeated by someone else (nearly always a man).

Many people (especially women) try to avoid seeming presumptuous at meetings by prefacing their statements with a disclaimer such as, "I don't know if this will work, but . . ." or "You've probably already thought of this, but. . . ." Such disclaimers are even found on e-mail—the electronic conversation medium. An example given by linguist Susan Herring to illustrate the tone of messages typical of women who took part in an on-line discussion began, "This may be a silly naive question, but. . . ."

Some speakers (again, including many women) may also speak at a lower volume, and try to be succinct so as not to take up more meeting time than necessary. Barbara and Gene Eakins examined tape recordings of seven university faculty meetings and found that, with one exception, the men spoke more often and, without exception, spoke longer. The men's turns ranged from 10.66 to 17.07 seconds, the women's from 3 to 10 seconds. The longest contribution by a woman was still shorter than the shortest contribution by a man.

Herring found the same situation in electronic meetings. In the e-mail discussion she analyzed, she found that men's messages were twice as long, on average, as women's. And their voices sounded very different. All but one of the five women used an "attenuated/personal" voice: "I am intrigued by your comment . . . Could you say a bit more?" The tone adopted by the men who dominated discussion was assertive ("It is obvious that . . ."; "Note that . . .").

All these aspects of how one speaks at a meeting mean that when two people say "the same thing," they probably say it very differently. They may speak with or without a disclaimer, loudly or softly, in a self-deprecating or declamatory way, briefly or at length, and tentatively or without apparent certainty. They may initiate ideas or support or argue against ideas raised by others. When dissenting, they may adopt a conciliatory tone, mitigating the disagreement, or an adversarial one, emphasizing it.

Before women decide to change their styles, though, they must realize the double bind they face. Geraldine Ferraro was called by Barbara Bush "the word that rhymes with witch." Ferraro's speech style was influenced by her Italian heritage, her New York City upbringing, and her working-class roots. Any woman who tries to become more "assertive" runs a risk of being sanctioned for being "too aggressive," just as men from the South may be seen as not masculine enough.

On the other hand, it may also be wise to decide that being seen as aggressive is a price worth paying for being listened to. Finally, we can all hope that if enough women adjust their styles, expectations of how a feminine woman speaks may gradually change as a result.

Source: Deborah Tannen, Talking From 9 to 5 (New York: Williams Morrow, 1994), pp. 277–289. © 1994 by Deborah Tannen, Ph. D. Reprinted by permission of William Morrow & Company, Inc.

Negative Roles

Just as the work group prospers when members fill the various task and maintenance roles, the group suffers when members play certain negative roles. The four most common negative roles that group members should try to avoid are those of aggressor, joker, withdrawer, and monopolizer.

Aggressor. Aggressors seek to enhance their own status by criticizing almost everything or blaming others when things get rough. The main purpose of aggressors seems to be to deflate the ego or status of others. One way of dealing with aggressors is to confront them. Ask them whether they are aware of what they are doing and of the effect their behavior is having on the group.

Joker. The behavior of jokers is characterized by clowning, mimicking, or generally disrupting by making a joke of everything. Jokers, too, are usually trying to call attention to themselves. The group needs to get jokers to consider the problem seriously; otherwise, they will be a constant irritant to other members. One way to proceed is to encourage them when tensions need to be released but ignore them when serious work needs to be done.

Withdrawer. Withdrawers refuse to be a part of the group. Sometimes they are withdrawing from something that was said; sometimes they are just showing their indifference. To get them involved in the group, try to draw them out with questions. Find out what they are especially good at, and rely on them when their skill is required. Compliments will sometimes bring them out of their shell.

Monopolizer. People who need to talk all the time are called monopolizers. Usually they are trying to make the impression that they are well read, knowledgeable, and of value to the group. They should, of course, be encouraged when their comments are helpful. However, when they are talking too much or when their comments are not helpful, the leader needs to interrupt them or draw others into the discussion.

Normal Group Behavior

You may be wondering about the proportion of time devoted in a "normal" group to the various functions described in this section. According to Robert Bales, one of the leading researchers in group interaction processes, 40 to 60 percent of discussion time is spent giving and asking for information and opinion; 8 to 15 percent of discussion time is spent on disagreement, tension, or unfriendliness; and 16 to 26 percent of discussion time is characterized by agreement or friendliness (positive maintenance functions).[6] Two norms we can apply as guidelines for effective group functioning, therefore, are (1) that approximately half of all discussion time is devoted to information sharing and (2) that group agreement far outweighs group disagreement.

Practice in Group Roles

By Yourself

Identify the role that is represented in each of the following examples as (A) information or opinion giver, (B) information seeker, (C) analyzer, (D) idea person, (E) expediter, (F) supporter, (G) tension reliever, (H) harmonizer, or (I) gatekeeper.

_____ 1. "Shelby, I get the feeling that you have something you wanted to say here."

_____ 2. "The last couple of comments have been on potential causes of the problem, but I don't think we've fully addressed the scope of the problem. If we've really identified the scope, perhaps we could draw a conclusion and then move on to causes."

_____ 3. "Antoine, that was a good point. I think you've really put the problem in perspective."

_____ 4. "Paul and Gwen, I know you see this issue from totally different positions. I wonder whether we might not profit by seeing whether there are any points of agreement; then we can consider differences."

_____ 5. "Well, according to the latest statistics cited in the *Enquirer*, unemployment in the state has gone back up from 7.2 to 7.9 percent."

_____ 6. "Sarah, you've given us some good statistics. Can we determine whether or not this is really an upward trend or just a seasonal factor?"

1.I 2.E 3.F 4.H 5.A 6.C

Problem Solving in Groups

Research shows that groups follow many different approaches to problem solving. Some groups move linearly through a series of steps to reach consensus, and some move in a spiral pattern in which they refine, accept, reject, modify, and combine ideas as they go along. Whether groups move in something approximating an orderly pattern or go in fits and starts, those groups that arrive at high-quality decisions are likely to accomplish certain tasks during their deliberations—namely, identifying a specific problem, arriving at some criteria that a solution must meet, identifying possible solutions to the problem, and determining the best solution or combination of solutions.

Defining the Problem

Groups are formed either to consider all issues that relate to a specific topic (a social committee, a personnel committee, or a public relations committee would be formed for this reason) or to consider a specific issue (such as the year's social calendar, criteria for granting promotions, or a long-range plan for university growth). Much of the wheel-spinning that takes place during the early stages of group discussion results from members not understanding their specific goal. It is the duty of the person, agency, or parent group that forms a particular work group to give the group a clear goal. For instance, a group may be formed for the purpose of "determining the criteria for merit pay increases" or "preparing guidelines for hiring at a new plant." If the goal is not stated this clearly, it is up to the group leader or representative to find out exactly why the group was formed and what its purpose is. If the group is free to determine its goal, it should move immediately to get the goal down on paper; until everyone in the group agrees on the goal, they will never agree on how to achieve it.

Regardless of the clarity of its goal, the group may still want to reword or in some way modify it. A group should consider several criteria before finalizing the wording of its statement of purpose.

1. *Is the problem phrased as a question?* The group discussion format is one of inquiry. A group begins from the assumption that answers are not yet known. Although some decision-making groups serve merely as rubber-stamping agencies, the group ideally has freedom of choice. Phrasing the group's purpose as a question furthers the spirit of inquiry.

2. *Does the question contain only one central idea?* The question "Should the college abolish its foreign language and social studies requirements?" is poorly phrased because it contains two distinct problems. Either one would make a good topic for discussion, but they cannot both be discussed at once.

3. *Is the wording of the question clear to all group members?* Sometimes a topic question contains wording that is so ambiguous that the group may waste time quibbling over its meaning. For instance, a group that is examining a department's curriculum might suggest the following question: "What should the department do about courses that aren't getting the job done?" Although the question is well intentioned and participants may have at least some idea about their goal, such vague wording as "getting the job done" can lead to trouble in the discussion. Instead of waiting until trouble arises, reword questions in specific terms before the group begins discussions. Notice how this revision of the preceding question makes its intent much clearer: "What should the department do about courses that receive low scores on student evaluations?"

4. *Does the question encourage objective discussion?* The phrasing of a question may drastically affect a group's decisions. Consider the following: "How should our sexist guidelines for promotions be revised?" What kind of objective discussion is likely to occur when, right from the start, the group has agreed that the guidelines are sexist? Moreover, such a phrasing suggests that being sexist is the only problem that new guidelines will have to resolve. With such wording, not only are the scales tilted before the group even gets into the issues involved, but also the group's thinking is given a single direction. The phrasing of the question should neither prejudice the group's thinking nor indicate which direction the group will go in even before discussion commences.

5. *Is the question appropriate for group consideration?* One of the most common criticisms of the group process is that it tends to waste time on tasks best dealt with by individuals. How can you tell whether your group should be discussing a particular question? Victor Vroom, an industrial psychologist, and his associates have suggested guidelines for evaluating the appropriateness of a question for group discussion.[7] Among the most important considerations are whether a high-quality decision is required and whether acceptance by members of the group is necessary to put the decision into practice. A high-quality decision is one that is well documented. Often high-quality decisions are too much for one person to handle; gathering the data alone may require hours of work by several people. Moreover, because vigorous testing is necessary at every stage of the decision-making process, a group is more likely to ask the right questions. Likewise, individuals within the organization are the ones who must carry out the decision. If group members are involved in the decision, they will be motivated to see that the decision is implemented.

Other conditions can indicate that an individual decision is more appropriate than group discussion. If one person has the necessary information and authority to make a good decision, if a solution that has worked well in the past can be applied to this situation, or if time is limited and immediate action is necessary, group discussion is less appropriate.

6. *Can the question be identified easily as one of fact, value, or policy?* How you organize your discussion will depend on the kind of question. Later, we discuss organization; for now, let's consider the three types of questions.

Questions of *fact* concern the truth or falsity of an assertion. Implied in such questions is the possibility of determining the facts by way of directly observed, spoken, or recorded evidence. For instance, "Is Smith guilty of stealing equipment from the warehouse?" is a question of fact. Either Smith committed the crime or he did not.

Questions of *value* concern subjective judgments of quality. They are characterized by the inclusion of some evaluative work such as *good, reliable, effective, or worthy.* For instance, advertisers may discuss the question "Is the proposed series of ads too sexually provocative?" In this case, "too sexually provocative" stands as the evaluative phrase. Another group may discuss the question "Is the sales force meeting the goals effectively?" Although we can establish criteria for "too sexually provocative" and "effectively" and measure material against those criteria, there is no way to verify our findings objectively. The answer is still a matter of judgment, not fact.

Questions of *policy* ask whether or not a future action should be taken. The question is phrased to invite a solution or to test a tentative solution to a problem or a felt need. "What should we do to lower the crime rate?" seeks a solution that would best address the problem of increased crime. "Should the university give equal amounts of money to men's and women's athletics?" seeks a tentative solution to the problem of how to achieve equity in the financial support of athletics. The inclusion of the word *should* in all questions of policy makes them the easiest to recognize and the easiest to phrase of all discussion questions. Most issues facing work groups are questions of policy.

If you are discussing either a question of fact or a question of value, the remaining steps of problem solving (analyzing the problem, determining possible solutions, and selecting the best solution) are not relevant to your discussions. What kind of a structure, then, is appropriate for discussing questions of fact and value?

Discussions of questions of fact focus primarily on finding the facts and drawing conclusions from them. For instance, in discussing the question "Is Smith guilty of stealing equipment from the warehouse?" the group would decide (1) whether facts can be assembled to show that Smith did take equipment from the warehouse and (2) whether his taking the equipment constituted stealing (as opposed to, say, borrowing or filling an order for equipment).

Discussions of questions of value follow a similar format. The difference is that with questions of value the conclusions drawn from the facts depend on the criteria or measures used to weigh the facts. For instance, in discussing the question "Who is the most effective teacher in the department?" the group would decide (1) what the criteria for an "effective teacher" are and (2) which teacher meets those criteria better than other teachers in the department.

Analyzing the Problem

Analysis of a problem entails finding out as much as possible about the problem and determining the criteria that must be met to find an acceptable solution. If you were discussing the question "What should be done to equalize athletic opportunities for women on campus?" these two aspects of your analysis might be phrased as follows:

1. What has happened on campus that signifies the presence of a problem for women? (Nature of the problem)
   A. Have significant numbers of women been affected?
   B. Do women have less opportunity to compete in athletics than men?
   C. Has the university behaved in ways that have adversely affected women's opportunities?
2. By what means should we test whether a proposed solution solves the problem? (Criteria)
   A. Does the proposed solution cope with each of the problems uncovered?
   B. Can the proposed solution be implemented without creating new and perhaps worse problems?

Determining Possible Solutions

For most problems, many possible solutions can be found. At this stage of discussion, the goal is not to worry about whether a particular solution is a good one or not but to come up with a list of potential answers.

One way to identify potential solutions is to brainstorm for ideas. *Brainstorming* is a free-association procedure; that is, it involves stating ideas as they come to mind, without stopping to evaluate their merits, until you have compiled a long list. In a good ten- or fifteen-minute brainstorming session, you may think of several solutions by yourself. Depending on the nature of the topic, a group may come up with a list of ten, twenty, or more possible solutions in a relatively short time.

Brainstorming works best when the group postpones evaluating solutions until the list is complete. If people feel free to make suggestions—however bizarre they may sound—they will be much more inclined to think creatively than if they fear that each idea will be evaluated on the spot. Later, each solution can be measured against the criteria. For the question on equalizing athletic opportunities for women, a framework for determining possible solutions might be outlined as follows:

3. What can be done to equalize opportunities? (Possible solutions)
    A. Can more scholarships be allocated to women?
    B. Can the time allocated to women's use of university facilities be increased to a level comparable with men's use?

Selecting the Best Solution

At this stage in the discussion, the group evaluates each prospective solution on the basis of how well it meets the criteria agreed on earlier. For the question on equalizing athletic opportunities for women, each solution would have to pass the following tests:

4. Which proposal (or combination) would work the best? (Best solution)
    A. How well would increasing women's scholarships solve each of the problems that have been identified? Would it create worse problems?
    B. How well would increasing women's time for use of facilities solve each of the problems that have been identified? Would it create worse problems?
    C. Based on this analysis, which solution is best?

Practice in Group Problem Solving

In Groups

Divide into groups of about four to six. Each group has ten to fifteen minutes to arrive at a solution to one of the following: (1) What should professors do to discourage cheating on tests? (2) What should the college or university do to increase attendance at special events? (3) What should be the role of students in evaluating their curriculum?

After discussion, each group should determine (1) what roles were operating in the group during the discussion; (2) who was filling those roles; (3) whether the group considered the nature of the problem, criteria, and possible solutions before arriving at a solution; and (4) what factors helped or hurt the problem-solving process.

Summary

Effective groups meet several criteria: They work in a physical and psychological setting that facilitates good interactions, they are of an optimum size, they work as a cohesive unit, they show a commitment to the task, they develop and adhere to rules that help the group work, their members interact freely to reach consensus, their members are well prepared, and they contain people who have enough expertise and aggregate skills to meet key role requirements.

Group members may perform one or more of the task roles of giving information, seeking information, analyzing, being an idea person, expediting, and recording. They may also perform one or more of the maintenance roles of supporting, tension relieving, harmonizing, and gatekeeping. They should try to avoid the negative roles of aggressor, joker, withdrawer, and monopolizer.

Questions for group discussion may be questions of fact, value, or policy.

Effective work groups discussing questions of policy define the problem, analyze the problem, determine possible solutions, and then select the best solution.

Suggested Readings

Brilhart, John K., and Galanes, J. *Effective Group Discussion*, 8th ed. Madison, WI: WCB Brown & Benchmark, 1995. A very popular textbook. Includes an intercultural perspective.

Sher, Barbara, and Gottlieb, Annie. *Teamworks!* New York: Warner Books, 1989. Based on the premise that a group of people working together can provide a system of support that will enable each person to accomplish more than they could on their own. Written in an easy-to-read style that is supplemented with countless experiences of real people.

Verderber, Rudolph F. *Working Together*. Belmont, CA: Wadsworth, 1982. Provides a thorough treatment of analyzing and resolving various types of discussion questions.

Notes

1. A great deal of relevant research is summarized in Marvin E. Shaw, *Group Dynamics: The Psychology of Small Group Behavior*, 3rd ed. (New York: McGraw-Hill, 1981). Cragan and Wright point out that very little research on these issues was done in the 1980s. See John F. Cragan and David W. Wright, "Small Group Communication Research of the 1980s: A Synthesis and Critique" *Communication Studies* 41 (Fall 1990): 216.
2. Paul Hare, *Handbook of Small Group Research*, 2d ed. (New York: Free Press, 1976), p. 214.
3. Shaw, p. 202.
4. For a review of research, see Norbert L. Kerr, "Issue Importance and Group Decision Making," in Stephen Worchel, Wendy Wood, and Jeffry A. Simpson, eds., *Group Process and Productivity* (Newbury Park, CA: Sage, 1992), pp. 69–74.
5. Arthur D. Jensen and Joseph C. Chilberg, *Small Group Communication: Theory and Application* (Belmont, CA: Wadsworth, 1991), pp. 367–371.
6. Robert F. Bales, *Personality and Interpersonal Behavior* (New York: Holt, Rinehart & Winston, 1971), p. 96.
7. V. H. Vroom and P. W. Yetton, *Leadership and Decision-Making* (Pittsburgh: University of Pittsburgh Press, 1973).

CHAPTER 3

Leadership in Groups

"Chapman, as you know, I'm concerned with the basic skills levels of the people we've been interviewing for jobs in manufacturing. The more I think about it, the more I believe we need to play a more active role in providing adult education that would not only be good for the community, but I think would benefit us in the long run. The reason I called you in here was to see whether you would take leadership in setting up a group whose goal it is to establish an adult literacy program that our company could sponsor. You can select the people you'd like to work with, and I'll give you full support."

Like Norm Chapman, you are likely to be called on to take a leadership role. As much as we may believe that we're up to the task, we are often uncertain exactly how we should go about exercising leadership in group decision making.

Our goal in this chapter is to show what it means to be the leader of a work group, how to proceed if you want to try for leadership, and what you are responsible for doing in the group after you get the job. Although much of this discussion is applicable to all leadership situations, we focus on the question of leadership in the decision-making or work-group context. Finally, we offer some guidelines for evaluating the process and outcomes of group communications.

What Is Leadership?

The definition of leadership varies from source to source, yet common to most definitions are the ideas of *influence* and *accomplishment*. Leadership means being in charge—exerting influence—and leadership results in reaching a goal.[1] Let's explore these two ideas.

1. *Leadership means exerting influence.* Influence is the ability to bring about changes in the attitudes and actions of others. Influence can be indirect (unconscious) or direct (purposeful). Many times we influence others without being aware of it. If you have a new hairstyle, or are wearing a

new suit, or have purchased a flashy new car, you may well influence someone who sees you to try your hairstyle or to buy a similar suit or car. In a group, a leader can influence members indirectly by serving as a role model. In this chapter, we look at what you can do consciously to help guide your group through the decision-making process.

The exercise of influence is different from the exercise of raw power. When you exercise raw power, you force the group to submit, perhaps against its will; when you influence others, you show them why an idea, a decision, or a means of achieving a goal is superior in such a way that they will follow your lead of their own free will. Members will continue to be influenced as long as they are convinced that what they have agreed to is right or is in their best interest as individuals or as a group.

2. *Leadership results in reaching a goal.* In the context of task or problem-solving discussions, reaching the goal means accomplishing the task or arriving at the best solution available at that time.

In an organizational setting, a leader is usually appointed or elected. In a decision-making group, however, the struggle for leadership often proceeds without benefit of election or appointment. In fact, those involved may not perceive that a struggle takes place. In groups in which one individual has strong urges to control and the others have equally strong urges to be controlled, leadership will be established with no struggle at all. In most decision-making groups, however, leadership is shared, switches back and forth, or develops into power struggles in which people exercise their need to lead.

Becoming a Leader

Many times problem-solving groups select their own leader. But even if one person is the selected leader, another person may emerge as the actual leader. What factors are involved in becoming a group leader? Leaders are likely to be selected or to emerge on the basis of perceived traits, style of leadership, and behavior in the group.

Leadership Traits

Are there certain traits that make one person a more likely candidate for leadership than another? Studies conducted over the years seem to substantiate portions of the trait perspective of leadership.[2]

Research findings suggest that leaders exhibit traits related to ability, sociability, motivation, and communication skills to a greater degree than do nonleaders.[3] With regard to ability, leaders have been found to exceed average group members in intelligence, scholarship, insight, and verbal facility. Leaders exceed group members in such aspects of sociability as dependability, activeness, cooperativeness, and popularity. In the area of motivation, leaders exceed group members in initiative, persistence, and enthusiasm. And leaders exceed average group members in the various communication skills we have focused on in this text. This does not mean that people with superior intelligence, those who are most liked, those with the greatest enthusiasm, or those who communicate best will necessarily be the leaders. However, it probably does mean that people are unlikely to be leaders if they do not exhibit at least some of these traits to a greater degree than do those they are attempting to lead.

Do you perceive yourself as having many of these traits? If so, you are a potential leader. However, because several individuals in almost any grouping of people have the potential for leadership, which one ends up actually leading others depends on factors other than having these traits. One of the most important of these factors is a person's leadership style.

Leadership Styles

Although there is no one "right" way to lead, different group situations do often require different leadership styles. Thus if you want to become a leader, you need to understand the various styles of leadership, and which is likely to be more appropriate at a particular time. Even though people will tend to lead a group with a style that reflects their own personality, leaders who want to be effective in all kinds of situations need to learn how to adjust their styles to the needs of the situation and the group.

What are the major leadership styles? Most recent studies look at leadership styles as either task-oriented (sometimes called authoritarian) or person-oriented (sometimes called democratic).

The *task-oriented* leader exercises more direct control over the group. Task leaders will determine the phrasing of the question. They will analyze the problem and decide how the group will proceed to arrive at the solution. They are likely to outline specific tasks for each group member and suggest the roles they desire members to play.

The *person-oriented* or democratic leader may suggest phrasings of the question, suggest procedure, and suggest tasks or roles for individuals. Yet in every facet of the discussion, the person-oriented leader encourages group participation to determine what actually will be done. Everyone feels free to offer suggestions to modify the leader's suggestions. What the group eventually does is determined by the group itself. Person-oriented leaders will listen, encourage, facilitate, clarify, and support. In the final analysis, however, it is the group that decides.

Pioneer work by Ralph White and Ronald Lippitt suggests the following advantages and disadvantages of each style: (1) More work is done under a task-oriented leader than under a person-oriented leader. (2) The least amount of work is done when no leadership exists. (3) Motivation and originality are greater under a person-oriented leader. (4) Task-oriented leadership may create discontent or result in less individual creativity. (5) More friendliness is shown in person-oriented groups.[4]

So which style is to be preferred? Research by Fred Fiedler suggests that whether a particular leadership style is successful depends on the situation: (1) How good are the leader's interpersonal relations with the group? (2) How clearly defined are the goals and tasks of the group? (3) To what degree does the group accept the leader as having legitimate authority to lead?[5] Some situations will be favorable to the leader on all dimensions: The leader has good interpersonal relations with the group, the goal is clear, and the group accepts the leader's authority. Some situations will be unfavorable to the leader on all dimensions: The leader has poor interpersonal relations with the group, the goal is unclear, and the group fails to accept the leader's authority. Then, of course, there are situations that are partly favorable and partly unfavorable to the leader on the various dimensions.

Fiedler proposes that task leaders are most effective in favorable or extremely unfavorable situations. In positive situations, in which the leader has good interpersonal relations, a clear goal, and group acceptance, the leader can focus entirely on the task. Conversely, in very negative situations, there will be little that the leader can do to improve member perceptions, so the leader may as well storm forward on the task. Where people-oriented leadership is likely to be most effective is in those moderately good or bad situations in which the leader has the most to gain by improving interpersonal relations, clarifying the goal, and building credibility with the group.

Let's consider two specific examples—one of a mostly favorable situation, and one of a moderately unfavorable situation. Suppose you are leading a group of employees who are meeting to determine the recipient of a merit award. If you have good interpersonal relations with the group, if the criteria for determining the award are clearly spelled out, and if the group accepts your authority, you are likely to be highly effective by adopting a task-oriented style of leadership. The group will understand what it is supposed to do and will accept your directions in proceeding to accomplish the task. If, on the other hand, your interpersonal relations with two of the group's other four members has been shaky, the group is not sure how it is supposed to go about making the decision, and at least two members of the group are undecided about your ability to lead, a person-oriented style of leadership is necessary. Before the group can really begin to focus on the task, you will need to build your interpersonal relations with at least two members of the group, work with them to clarify the goal, and engage in behaviors that will help build your credibility. So, it isn't a matter of which style is always best; it is a matter of what kinds of circumstances are present.

Are leaders likely to be equally adept at task- and person-oriented styles? Although it is possible, many people show more skill at one style or the other. Thus in many groups, even those with a designated leader, more than one person is needed to fulfill all the leadership roles within the group. Nevertheless, throughout this book, we have discussed the kinds of skills that can enable you to function well in either a task- or a people-oriented style.

Leadership Preparation

Although having certain leadership traits and being able to adapt leadership style to the needs of the group are important in determining who will lead, your chances of selection or emergence as a leader are increased if you behave in the following ways during group deliberations:

1. *Be knowledgeable about the group task.* Although the leader is not the primary information giver in a group, group members are more willing to follow when the leader appears to be well informed. The more knowledgeable you are, the better you will be able to analyze individual contributions.

2. *Work harder than anyone else in the group.* Leadership is often a question of setting an example. When others in the group see a person who is willing to do more than his or her fair share for the good of the group, they are likely to support that person. Of course, such effort may involve personal sacrifice, but the person seeking to lead must be willing to pay the price.

3. *Be personally committed to the group's goals and needs.* To gain and maintain leadership takes commitment to the particular task. When you lose that sense of commitment, your leadership may wane and be transferred to others whose enthusiasm is more attuned to a new set of conditions.

4. *Be willing to be decisive at key moments in the discussion.* When leaders are unsure of themselves or unwilling to make decisions, their groups may ramble aimlessly or become frustrated and short-tempered. Sometimes leaders must make decisions that will be resented; sometimes they must decide between competing ideas about courses of action. Any decisions leaders make may cause conflict. Nevertheless, people who are unwilling or unable to be decisive are not going to maintain leadership for long.

5. *Interact freely with others in the group.* One way to show potential for leadership is to participate fully in group discussions. This does not mean that you should dominate the group's deliberations, but it does mean sharing your ideas, feelings, and insights concerning both the content of the group's work and, when appropriate, the group process as well. Too often people sit back silently, thinking, "If only they would call on me for leadership, I would do a really good job." But there is no reason for a group to turn to an unknown quantity. Moreover, by participating fully in the early stages of group work, you can find out whether you are able to influence others before you try to gain leadership.

6. *Develop skill in maintenance functions as well as in task functions.* Effective leaders make others in their groups feel good, contribute to group cohesiveness, and take care to give credit where it is due. Although a group may have both a task leader and a maintenance leader, the primary leader is often the one who shows maintenance skills.

Gender Differences in Leader Acceptability

A question that has generated considerable research is whether the gender of a leader has any effect on a group's acceptance of leadership. Research suggests that gender does affect group acceptance, but not because women lack the necessary traits or abilities. Negative perceptions are largely a result of sex-role stereotypes and devaluing.

Sex-role stereotypes influence how leaders' behaviors are perceived. A persistent research finding is that the same messages are evaluated differently depending on the source of the message.[6] Thus, whereas some women's behaviors will be considered bossy, dominating, and emotional, men exhibiting essentially the same behaviors will be judged as responsible, as offering high-quality contributions, and as showing leadership. So the problem that women face is not that they don't possess or exhibit leadership characteristics, but that their efforts to show leadership are misperceived.

Moreover, sex-role stereotypes lead to devaluing cooperative and supportive behaviors that many women use quite skillfully. As Sally Helgesen points out, many female leaders are successful *because* they respond to people and their problems with flexibility and *because* they are able to break down barriers between people at all levels of the organization.[7]

As a result of male bias and devaluing of female skills, some women get discouraged in seeking leadership roles. But changes in perception are occurring as the notion of "effective" leadership changes. Thus, as women continue to show their competence, they will be selected as leaders more often. As Jurma and Wright have pointed out, research studies have shown that men and women are equally capable of leading task-oriented groups.[8] Patricia Andrews supports this conclusion, noting that it is more important to consider the unique character of a group and the skills of the person serving as leader than the sex of the leader. She goes on to show that a complex interplay of factors (including how much power the leader has) influences effectiveness more than gender does.[9]

Practice in Analyzing Leadership

By Yourself

1. What leadership traits do you believe you have?
2. What is your leadership style? Are you more of a task-oriented leader or a person-oriented leader? What are the strengths and weaknesses of your style?
3. Under which leadership style do you work best? Why?

Functions of Group Leadership

Becoming a leader and carrying out leadership functions are two different things. Many people reach the top of the leadership pole only to slide slowly to oblivion. The effective group leader prepares the meeting place, plans the agenda, introduces the topic and establishes procedures, ensures that all group members have a chance to contribute, asks appropriate questions, is sensitive to cultural differences, and summarizes the discussion as needed.

Preparing the Meeting Place

We have already talked about the importance of a good working environment. If the environment is not good, the leader needs to take responsibility for improving it. As leader, you are in charge of such physical matters as heat, light, and seating. Make sure the temperature of the room is comfortable. Make sure that lighting is adequate, and most important, make sure the seating arrangements will promote spirited interaction.

Planning the Agenda

Recall that an agenda is an outline of the topics that need to be covered at a meeting. Figure 3.1 shows a well-planned agenda for a group discussing the question "What should be done to integrate the campus commuter into the social, political, and extracurricular aspects of student life?"

You may prepare the agenda yourself or in consultation with the group. When possible, the agenda should be in the hands of group members several days before the meeting. How much preparing any individual member will do is based on many factors, but unless the group has an agenda beforehand, members will not have an opportunity for careful preparation. Too often, when no agenda is planned, the group discussion is a haphazard affair, often frustrating and usually unsatisfying.

March 1, 1996

To: Campus commuter discussion group

Fr: Janelle Smith

Re: Agenda for discussion group meeting

Date: March 8, 1996

Place: Student Union, Conference Room A

Time: 3:00 P.M. (Please be prompt.)

Please come prepared to discuss the following questions. Be sure to bring specific information you can contribute to the discussion of questions 1 through 4. We will consider question 5 on the basis of our resolution of the other questions.

Agenda for Group Discussion

Question: What should be done to integrate the campus commuter into the social, political, and extracurricular aspects of student life?

1. How many students commute?
2. Why aren't commuters involved in social, political, and extracurricular activities?
3. What criteria should be used to test possible solutions to the problem?
4. What are some of the possible solutions to the problem?
5. What one solution or combination of solutions will work best to solve the problem?

Figure 3–1. Agenda for a discussion group meeting. Note that the agenda is distributed a week in advance and that the date, time, place, and specific questions for discussion are clearly indicated.

Orienting Group Members

At the beginning of the group's first meeting, the leader needs to orient the group members. In a newly formed group, commitment may be low for some members, expectations may be minimal, and the general attitude may be skeptical. People may be thinking, "We know that many group sessions are a waste of time, so we'll take a wait-and-see attitude." A good leader will start the group process by answering such questions as Why are we here? Who got us together? What is our mission? To whom are we responsible? What kinds of responsibilities will each group member have? and How much will each member be expected to do? Some of these questions will already have been discussed with individuals, but the first meeting gives the leader a chance to put everything together.

Giving Everyone an Equal Opportunity to Speak

For the group process to work, group members need to be encouraged to express their ideas and feelings. Yet, without leader intervention, some people are likely to dominate and some people are likely to feel that they haven't been heard. For instance, in an eight-person group, left to its own devices, two or three people may tend to speak as much as the other five or six together; furthermore, one or two members may contribute little or nothing. At the beginning of a discussion, you must assume that every member of the group has something to contribute. You may have to hold in check those who tend to dominate, and you may have to work to draw reluctant members into the discussion.

Accomplishing this ideal balance is a real test of the gatekeeping skill of a leader. If ordinarily reluctant talkers are intimidated by a member of the group, they may become even more reluctant to participate. Thus, you may have to clear the road for shy speakers. For example, when Dominique gives visual or verbal clues of her desire to speak, say something like "Just a second, Lennie, I think Dominique has something she wants to say here." Then, instead of "Dominique, do you have anything to say here?" you may be able to phrase a question that requires more than a yes or no answer, such as "Dominique, what do you think of the validity of this approach to combating crime?" When people contribute a few times, it builds up their confidence, which in turn makes it easier for them to respond later when they have more to say.

Similar tact is called for with overzealous speakers. If garrulous yet valuable members are constantly restrained, their value to the group may diminish. For example, Lennie, the most talkative member, may be talkative because he has done his homework; if you turn him off, the group's work will suffer. After he has finished talking, try statements such as "Lennie, that's a very valuable bit of material; let's see whether we can get some reactions from other members of the group on this issue." Notice that a statement of this kind does not stop him; it suggests that he should hold off for a while.

Asking Appropriate Questions

Although the members of any group bring a variety of skills, information, and degrees of motivation to the group, they do not always operate at peak efficiency without help from the leader. Perhaps one of the most effective tools of leadership is the ability to question appropriately. This skill requires knowing when to ask questions and what kinds of questions to ask.

By and large, the leader should refrain from asking questions that can be answered yes or no. To ask group members whether they are satisfied with a point that was just made will not lead very far, for after the yes or no answer you must either ask another question to draw people out or change the subject. The two most effective types of questions are those that call for supporting information and those that are completely open-ended and give members complete freedom of response. For instance, rather than asking John whether he has had any professors who were particularly good lecturers, you could inquire, "John, what are some of the characteristics that made your favorite lecturers especially effective?"

Knowing when to ask questions is particularly important. Although we could list fifteen to twenty circumstances, let's focus on four essential purposes of questioning:

1. *To focus discussion.* Individual statements usually have a point; the point of each statement relates to a larger point being made; and the general discussion relates to an issue or to an agenda item. You can use questions to clarify speakers' points or to determine the relationship of the points to the issue or agenda item. For instance, to relate a statement to the larger topic in a discussion of marijuana use, you might ask, "Are you saying that the instances of marijuana use leading to hard-drug use don't indicate a direct causal relationship?" Or, in response to what has just been said, "How does that information relate to the point that Mary just made?" Or, to ask about an issue or an agenda item, "In what way does this information relate to whether or not marijuana is a health hazard?"

2. *To probe for information.* Many statements need to be developed, supported, or in some way dealt with. Yet often members of a group apparently ignore or accept a point without probing it. When the point seems important, the leader should do something with it. For example, to test the support for an assertion, you can say, "Where did you get that information, Miles?" or "That seems pretty important; what do we have that corroborates the point?" To test the strength of a point, you might ask, "Does that statement represent the thinking of the group?"

3. *To initiate discussion.* During a discussion, there are times when lines of development are apparently ignored, when the group seems ready to agree before sufficient scrutiny of a point. At these times, it is up to the leader to suggest a question for further discussion. For instance, "OK, we seem to have a pretty good grasp of the nature of the problem, but we haven't looked at any causes yet. What are some of the causes?"

4. *To deal with interpersonal problems.* Sometimes the leader can use questions to help members ventilate personal feelings. For example, "Ted, I've heard you make some strong statements on this point. Would you care to share them with us?" At times, a group may attack a person instead of the information that is being presented. Here you can say, "Juan isn't

the issue here. Let's look at the merits of the information presented. Do we have any information that runs counter to this point?"

Questions by themselves are not going to make a discussion. In fact, too frequent use of questions can hurt the discussion that is taking place. The effective leader, therefore, uses questions sparingly but incisively.

Dealing with Cultural Diversity

As John Brilhart and Gloria J. Galanes point out, every group discussion is "intercultural to some extent."[10] Thus it is important for a leader to recognize and accept differences within the group.

Most of us will see our group as comprised of individuals who, working hard enough together, can make changes. Thus we see things from an individualistic rather than a collectivist world view. According to Gudykunst and Kim, individualistic cultures promote self-realization for their members; collectivist cultures require that individuals fit into the group. How might such differences in views affect a group and its work? From a collectivist point of view, the group is comprised of members that sacrifice for the good of the group.[11] When a group does well, all members are praised; if a member stands out from the group, the group may feel an obligation to force the individual to conform. From an individualistic perspective, in contrast, a group is comprised of individuals, it is all right to praise an individual for his or her contribution to the group effort, and it is important for individuals to stand out.

To deal with such differences, Brilhart and Galanes suggest that before drawing inferences about group members when their behavior appears to be generally different, ask yourself whether you could be observing a cultural difference and, if so, try to adapt to different cultural practices.[12] Since this book is written from an individualist perspective, your task may prove to be even more difficult when you as a leader hold a collectivist perspective. Before a group with major cultural differences can work effectively, it is important for all members to recognize their differing perspectives and be willing to try to work through the differences.

Summarizing When Necessary

Often, a group talks for a considerable time, then takes a vote on how the members feel about the subject; A consensus is more likely to develop if the group moves in an orderly manner toward intermediate conclusions represented by summary statements that express the group's agreement. For instance, on the question "What should be done to lower the amount of employee theft?" the group should reach agreement on each of the following questions:

1. What is the problem?
2. What are the symptoms of the problem? (Draw intermediate conclusions; ask whether the group agrees.)

3. What are the causes? (Draw an intermediate conclusion on each cause separately or after all causes have been considered; ask whether the group agrees.)
4. What criteria should be used to test the solutions?
5. What is one criterion? (Draw conclusions about each criterion.)
6. What are some of the possible solutions? (Determine whether all worthwhile solutions have been brought up.)
7. How does each of the solutions meet the criteria? (Discuss each and draw conclusions about each; ask whether the group agrees.)
8. Which solution best meets the criteria? (The answer to this final question concludes the discussion; ask whether all agree.)

During the discussion, the group might draw six, eight, ten, or even fifteen conclusions before it is able to arrive at the answer to the topic question. The point is that the group is far more likely to agree on the final conclusion if each of the subordinate questions has been answered to the satisfaction of the entire group.

It is up to the leader to point up intermediate conclusions by summarizing what has been said and seeking consensus. Everyone in the group should realize when the group has arrived at some decision. If left to its own devices, a group may discuss a point for a while, then move on to another point before a conclusion is drawn. The leader must sense when enough has been said to reach a consensus. Then the leader must phrase the conclusion, subject it to testing, and move on to another area. Here are examples of phrases that can be used during the discussion.

"I think most of us are stating the same points. Are we really in agreement that . . ." (State the conclusion.)

"We've been discussing this for a while, and I think I sense an agreement. Let me state it, and then we'll see whether it does summarize the group's feeling." (State the conclusion.)

"Now we're getting into another area. Let's make sure that we are really agreed on the point we've just finished." (State the conclusion.)

"Are we ready to summarize our feelings on this point?" (State the conclusion.)

Practice in Exercising Leadership Responsibilities

In Groups

In groups of five, discuss a topic such as "What can be done to increase student motivation to keep classrooms free of litter?" Each person leads the group for approximately five minutes. After everyone has had a chance to lead, discuss efforts at giving people equal opportunity to speak, asking questions, and summarizing. Focus on behaviors that characterized successful efforts.

Evaluating Group Communication

You are likely to learn to increase your effectiveness in groups as you get feedback about individual and group performance. Groups can be evaluated on the quality of the decision, the quality of individual participation, and the quality of leadership.

The Decision

The questionnaire in Figure 3–2 gives you a framework for evaluating the quality of a group's decision. This questionnaire calls for you to consider three major questions:

1. *Did the group arrive at a decision?* That a group meets to discuss does not necessarily mean that it will arrive at a decision. As foolish as it may seem, some groups thrash away for hours only to adjourn without having come to a conclusion. Of course, some groups discuss such serious problems that a decision cannot be reached without several meetings. In such cases, it is important to ensure that the group adjourns with a

---

Group Decision Analysis

Analysis of group characteristics: _____

_____

Did the group arrive at a decision? Explain. _____

_____

What action was taken as a result of that discussion? Explain. _____

_____

Was the group decision a good one? Explain. _____

_____

Was quality information presented? _____

_____

Were the data fully discussed? _____

_____

Did interim conclusions reflect group discussion? _____

_____

Were conclusions measured against some set criteria? _____

_____

Did the group arrive at the decision by consensus? _____

_____

Did the group agree to support the decision? _____

_____

Figure 3–2. Form for evaluating group decisions

clear understanding of what the next step will be. When a group "finishes" its work without arriving at some decision, however, the result is likely to be frustration and disillusionment.

2. *What action will be taken as a result of the decision?* Problem-solving decisions imply implementation. If the group has "finished" without considering means for putting its decision into action, there is reason to question the practicality of the decision.

3. *Was the group decision a good one?* This may be the most difficult question to answer. Of course, whether a decision is good or bad is a value judgment. The questionnaire suggests six criteria for such an evaluation:

   a. Was quality information presented to serve as a basis for the decision?
   b. Were the data discussed fully?
   c. Did interim conclusions relate to information presented, or were they stated as opinions that had no relation to content?
   d. Was the final decision measured against some set of criteria or objectives?
   e. Did the decision seem to be the product of consensus, or was it determined by the persuasive or authoritarian power of the leader?
   f. Did the group agree to support the decision?

Individual Participation

Although a group will struggle without good leadership, it may not be able to function at all without members who are willing and able to meet the task and maintenance functions of the group.

Leadership

Although some group discussions are leaderless, no discussion should be without leadership. If there is an appointed leader—and most groups have one—evaluation can focus on that individual. If the group is truly leaderless, the evaluation should consider attempts at leadership by the various members or focus on the apparent leader who emerges from the group. Figure 3–4 contains a simple checklist for evaluating group leadership.

Practice in Analyzing Group Communication

In Groups

Divide into groups of about four to six. Each group should be given or should select a task that requires some research. Each group then has approximately thirty to forty minutes of class time for discussion. While group A is discussing, members of group B should observe and, after the discussion, analyze the proceedings. For practice in

> **Individual's Group Participation Checklist**
>
> For each of the following questions, rate the participant on a scale of 1 to 5: 1 = high; 2 = good; 3 = average; 4 = fair; 5 = poor.
>
> **Preparation**   1 2 3 4 5
> Seems to be well prepared   ☐ ☐ ☐ ☐ ☐
> Is aware of the problem   ☐ ☐ ☐ ☐ ☐
> Analyzes the problem   ☐ ☐ ☐ ☐ ☐
> Suggests possible solutions   ☐ ☐ ☐ ☐ ☐
> Tests each solution   ☐ ☐ ☐ ☐ ☐
>
> **Carrying Out Roles**
> As information or opinion giver   ☐ ☐ ☐ ☐ ☐
> As information seeker   ☐ ☐ ☐ ☐ ☐
> As analyzer   ☐ ☐ ☐ ☐ ☐
> As idea person   ☐ ☐ ☐ ☐ ☐
> As expediter   ☐ ☐ ☐ ☐ ☐
> As recorder   ☐ ☐ ☐ ☐ ☐
> As supporter   ☐ ☐ ☐ ☐ ☐
> As tension reliever   ☐ ☐ ☐ ☐ ☐
> As harmonizer   ☐ ☐ ☐ ☐ ☐
> As gatekeeper   ☐ ☐ ☐ ☐ ☐
>
> **Avoiding Negative Roles**
> As aggressor   ☐ ☐ ☐ ☐ ☐
> As joker   ☐ ☐ ☐ ☐ ☐
> As withdrawer   ☐ ☐ ☐ ☐ ☐
> As monopolizer   ☐ ☐ ☐ ☐ ☐
>
> Write an analysis of the person's group participation (two to five paragraphs) based on this checklist.

Figure 3–3. Form for evaluating individual participation

using the various questionnaires, some of the observers could be asked to do a decision analysis (Figure 3–2), some could be asked to do an individual member analysis (Figure 3–3), and some could be asked to do a leadership analysis (Figure 3–4). After the discussions, the observers could share their observations with the group. In the next class period, group B discusses and group A observes and analyzes. Sample questions for discussion include the following:

- What should be done to improve parking (advising, registration) on campus?
- What should be done to increase the participation of minorities in college or university teaching (governance, administration)?

Group Leadership Checklist

For each of the following questions, rate the participant on a scale of 1 to 5:
1 = high; 2 = good; 3 = average; 4 = fair; 5 = poor.

Preparation to Lead	1	2	3	4	5
Understands topic	☐	☐	☐	☐	☐
Works hard	☐	☐	☐	☐	☐
Shows commitment	☐	☐	☐	☐	☐
Interacts freely	☐	☐	☐	☐	☐
Is decisive	☐	☐	☐	☐	☐

Leading the Group					
Has group of optimum size	☐	☐	☐	☐	☐
Creates and maintains a suitable atmosphere	☐	☐	☐	☐	☐
Works to develop a cohesive unit	☐	☐	☐	☐	☐
Helps the group develop appropriate rules	☐	☐	☐	☐	☐
Has an agenda	☐	☐	☐	☐	☐
Promotes systematic problem solving	☐	☐	☐	☐	☐
Asks good questions	☐	☐	☐	☐	☐
Encourages balanced participation	☐	☐	☐	☐	☐
Refrains from dominating group	☐	☐	☐	☐	☐
Deals with conflict	☐	☐	☐	☐	☐
Arrives at decisions by means of consensus or voting	☐	☐	☐	☐	☐
Brings discussion to a satisfactory close	☐	☐	☐	☐	☐

Write an analysis (two to five paragraphs) based on this checklist.

Figure 3–4. Form for evaluating group leadership

Summary

Leadership means exerting influence to accomplish a goal. Although leaders may show higher levels of ability, sociability, motivation, and communication skills than others in the group, the presence of such traits does not guarantee that you will lead effectively.

How well you lead may depend on your style and how you put it into operation. Some leaders adopt the task-oriented style, focusing on what needs to be done and how to do it; others adopt the person-oriented style, focusing on interpersonal relationships of group members. As Fiedler's work has shown, how a leader performs depends on the interaction of task structure, leader-member relations, and position power. If you hope to earn the support of group members for leadership, you will want to be knowledgeable about the task, work harder than others in the group, be personally committed to group goals and needs, be willing to be decisive, interact freely with others in the group, and develop skill in maintenance and task functions.

Leaders have several specific functions. To lead a group well, you must prepare the meeting place, plan an agenda, introduce the topic and establish procedures, ensure that everyone has an equal opportunity to speak, ask appropriate questions, recognize the possibility of cultural differences, and summarize as needed.

Groups can be evaluated on the quality of the decision, the quality of individual participation, and the quality of leadership.

Suggested Readings

Bass, Bernard M. *Bass and Stogdill's Handbook of Leadership: Theory, Research, and Managerial Applications*, 3d ed. New York: Free Press, 1990. Provides reviews of historical and contemporary leadership theory and research. Focuses on the idea that leaders are agents of change.

Cohen, William A. *The Art of the Leader.* Englewood Cliffs, NJ: Prentice-Hall, 1990. Begins with the premise that many highly intelligent, well-educated, motivated people who want to be good leaders just don't know how to do it. Then focuses on specific methods of leadership that the author has learned from theory, observation, and his own experience, including his time as a reserve officer in the U. S. Air Force.

Covey, Stephen R. *Principle-Centered Leadership.* New York: Summit Books, 1991. Covey believes that leadership is the ability to apply principles, natural laws, and governing values that are universally valid to solving problems. He discusses application of leadership principles in interpersonal, managerial, and organizational settings.

Lawson, John D. *When You Preside,* 5th ed. Danville, IL: Interstate Printers and Publishers, 1980. Written as a handbook for leaders of many types of groups. A great deal of good, practical information.

Notes

1. See Bernard M. Bass, *Bass and Stogdill's Handbook of Leadership: Theory, Research, and Managerial Applications,* 3d ed. (New York: Free Press, 1990), pp. 19–20.
2. Ibid. See Chapter 5 for a review of studies up to 1970 and subsequent chapters for analysis of studies through the 1980s.
3. Marvin E. Shaw, *Group Dynamics: The Psychology of Small Group Behavior,* 3d ed. (New York: McGraw-Hill, 1981), p. 325.
4. Ralph White and Ronald Lippitt, "Leader Behavior and Member Reaction in Three 'Social Climates,'" in Dorwin Cartwright and Alvin Zander, eds., *Group Dynamics,* 3d ed. (New York: Harper & Row, 1968), p. 334. The point that groups are largely unproductive under laissez-faire leadership is reinforced by Bass, p. 559.

5. Fred E. Fiedler, *A Theory of Leadership Effectiveness* (New York: McGraw-Hill, 1967).

6. Doré Butler and Florence L. Geis, "Nonverbal Affect Responses to Male and Female Leaders: Implications for Leadership Evaluations," *Journal of Personality and Social Psychology* 58 (1990): 54.

7. Sally Helgesen, *The Female Advantage: Woman's Ways of Leadership* (New York: Doubleday, 1990).

8. William E. Jurma and Beverly C. Wright, "Follower Reactions to Male and Female Leaders Who Maintain or Lose Reward Power," *Small Group Research* 21 (1990): 110.

9. Patricia H. Andrews, "Sex and Gender Differences in Group Communication: Impact on the Facilitation Process," *Small Group Research* 23 (1992): 90.

10. John K. Brilhart and Gloria J. Galanes, *Effective Group Discussion,* 8th ed., Madison, WI: Brown & Benchmark, 1995, p. 107.

11. William B. Gudykunst and Young Yun Kim, *Communicating with Strangers: An Approach to Intercultural Communication,* 2d ed. (New York: McGraw-Hill, 1992), pp. 42–43.

12. Brilhart and Galanes, p. 107.

CHAPTER 4

Conflict in Interpersonal Relationships

Unit Objectives

After completing this chapter, you should be able to:

1. Define Interpersonal conflict
2. Distinguish between content and relationship conflict
3. Identify potentially negative and positive aspects of conflict
4. Explain the model of conflict resolution
5. Identify and explain at least six conflict strategies
6. Explain verbal aggressiveness and argumentativeness

In its most basic form, conflict refers to a disagreement. Interpersonal conflict, then, refers to a disagreement between or among connected individuals: for example, close friends, lovers, or family members. The word "connected" emphasizes the transactional nature of interpersonal conflict, the fact that each person's position affects the other person. The positions in conflict are to some degree interrelated and incompatible.

The Nature of Conflict

Conflicts can center on:
- goals to be pursued ("We want you to go to college and become a teacher or a doctor, not a disco dancer").
- allocation of resources, such as money or time ("I want to spend the tax refund on a car, not on new furniture").
- decisions to be made ("I refuse to have the Jeffersons over to dinner").

- behaviors that are considered appropriate or desirable by one person and inappropriate or undesirable by the other ("I hate it when you get drunk, pinch me, ridicule me in front of others, flirt with others, dress provocatively, and so on").

Myths About Conflict

One of the problems in studying and in dealing with interpersonal conflict is that we may be operating with false assumptions about what conflict is and what it means. For example, do you think the following statements are true or false?

- If two people engage in relationship conflict, it means their relationship is a bad one.
- Conflict hurts an interpersonal relationship.
- Conflict is bad because it reveals our negative selves—for example, our pettiness, our need to be in control, our unreasonable expectations.

As with most things, simple answers are usually wrong. The three assumptions above may all be true or may all be false. It depends. Conflict is a part of every interpersonal relationship, between parents and children, brothers and sisters, friends, lovers, coworkers.

It is not so much the conflict that creates the problem as the way in which you approach and deal with the conflict. Some ways of approaching conflict can resolve difficulties and actually improve the relationship. Other ways can hurt the relationship; they can destroy self-esteem, create bitterness, and foster suspicion.

Similarly, it is not the conflict that reveals your negative side but the fight strategies you use. Thus, if you attack the other person personally or use force, you reveal your negative side. But you can also reveal your positive self—your willingness to listen to opposing points of view, to change unpleasant behaviors, and to accept imperfection in others.

The Negatives and Positives of Conflict

Interpersonal conflict is inevitable because people are different and will necessarily see things differently. But it is neither good nor bad in itself. Rather, there are both negative and positive aspects to interpersonal conflict.

Negative Aspects

Conflict often leads to increased negative regard for the opponent, and when this opponent is someone you love or care for, it can create serious problems. One problem is that many conflicts involve unfair methods and focus largely on hurting the other person. If this happens, negative feelings are sure to increase. Conflict may also deplete energy better spent on other areas, especially when unproductive conflict strategies are used.

At times, conflict may lead you to close yourself off from the other individual. When you do this and hide your true feelings from an intimate, you prevent meaningful communication. Because the need for intimacy is so strong, one possible outcome is that one or both parties may seek this intimacy elsewhere. This often leads to further conflict, mutual hurt, and resentment—qualities that add heavily to the costs carried by the relationship. As these costs increase, the rewards may become more difficult to exchange. Here, then, is a situation in which costs increase and rewards decrease—a situation that often results in relationship deterioration and eventual dissolution.

POSITIVE ASPECTS

The major advantage of interpersonal conflict is that it forces you to examine a problem and work toward a potential solution. If productive conflict strategies are used, your relationship may well emerge from the encounter stronger, healthier, and more satisfying than before.

Conflict enables you to state what you each want and—if the conflict is resolved effectively—perhaps to get it. For example, let's say that I want to spend our money on a new car (my old one is unreliable), and you want to spend it on a vacation (you feel the need for a change of pace). Through our conflict and its resolution, we can learn what each genuinely wants: in this case, a reliable car and a break from routine. We may then be able to figure out a way for us each to get what we want. I might accept a good used car or a less expensive new car, and you might accept a shorter or less expensive vacation. Or we might buy a used car and take an inexpensive motor trip. Each of these solutions will satisfy both of us; they are win-win solutions—each of us wins, and each of us gets what we wanted.

Conflict also prevents hostilities and resentments from festering. Say I'm annoyed at your talking with your colleague from work for two hours on the phone instead of giving that time to me. If I say nothing, my annoyance and resentment are likely to grow. Further, by saying nothing I have implicitly approved of such behavior, and so it is likely that such phone calls will be repeated.

Through our conflict and its resolution, we stop resentment from increasing. In the process, we also let our own needs be known—that I need lots of attention when I come home from work and that you need to review the day's work and gain the assurance that it has been properly completed. If we both can appreciate the legitimacy of these needs, then solutions may be identified. Perhaps the phone call can be made after my attention needs are met, or perhaps I can delay my need for attention until you get closure about work. Or perhaps I can learn to provide for your closure needs and in doing so get my attention needs met. Again, we have win-win solutions; each of us gets our needs met.

Consider, too, that when we try to resolve conflict within an interpersonal relationship, we are saying in effect that the relationship is worth the effort; otherwise, we would walk away from such a conflict. Although there may be exceptions—as when we confront conflict to save face or to gratify some ego need—confronting a conflict usually indicates concern, commitment, and a desire to preserve the relationship.

Content and Relationship Conflicts

Using concepts developed earlier, we can make a distinction between content and relationship conflict. **Content conflict** centers on objects, events, and persons that are usually, but not always, external to the parties involved in the conflict. They include the many issues we argue and fight about every day—the value of a particular movie, what to watch on television, the fairness of the last examination or job promotion, and the way to spend our savings.

Relationship conflicts are seen in situations like these: a younger brother does not obey his older brother, two partners each want an equal say about vacation plans, and a mother and daughter each want the final word about the daughter's lifestyle. Here the conflicts are concerned not so much with external objects as with the relationships between the individuals, with such issues as who is in charge, the equality of a primary relationship, and who has the right to establish rules of behavior.

Content and relationship conflicts are always easier to separate in a textbook than they are in real life, where many conflicts contain elements of both. But if we can recognize which issues pertain to content and which to relationship, we will better understand the conflict and thus be able to manage it more effectively.

A Model of Conflict Resolution

We can explain conflict more fully and provide guidance for dealing with it effectively by referring to the model in Figure 4–1.

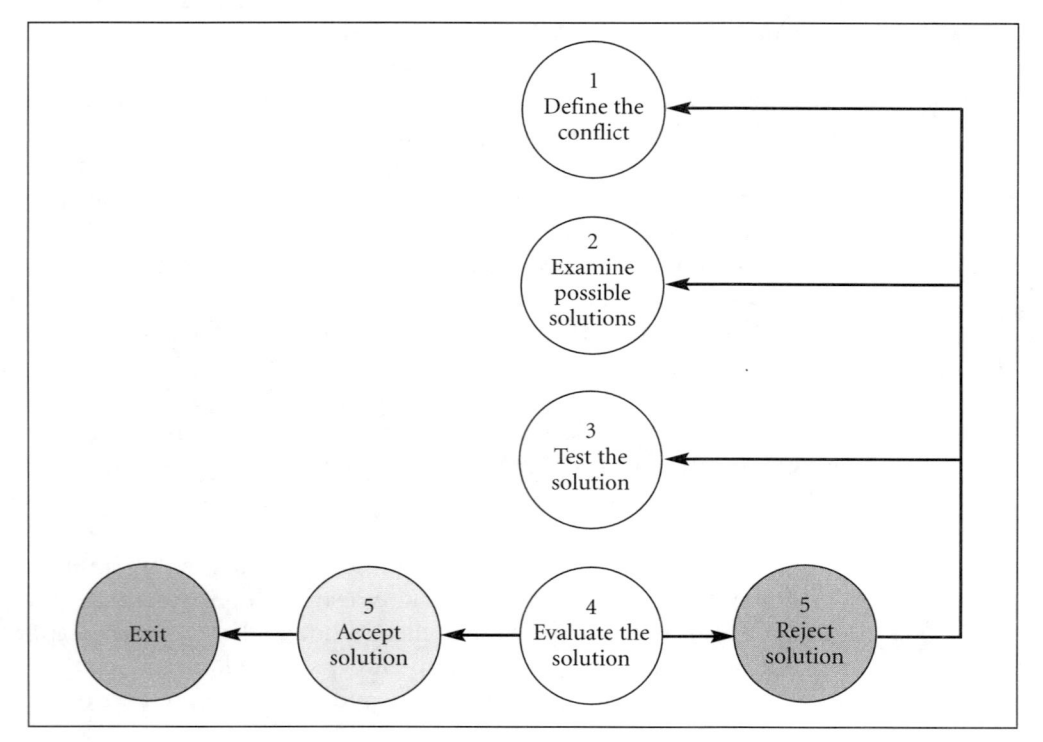

Figure 4–1. Stages in conflict resolution.

Define the Conflict

Define the obvious content issues (who should do the dishes, who should take the kids to school, who should take out the dog) as well as the underlying relationship issues (who has been avoiding household responsibilities, who has been neglecting responsibility toward the kids, whose time is more valuable).

Define the problem in specific terms. Conflict defined in the abstract is difficult to deal with and resolve. It is one thing for a husband to say that his wife is "cold and unfeeling" and quite another to say that she does not call him at the office, kiss him when he comes home, or hold his hand when they are at a party. These behaviors can be agreed upon and dealt with, but the abstract "cold and unfeeling" remains elusive.

Throughout this process, try to understand the nature of the conflict from the other person's point of view. Use your perspective-taking skills. Why is your partner disturbed that you are not doing the dishes? Why is your neighbor complaining about taking the kids to school? Why is your mother insisting you take out the dog?

Don't try to read the other person's mind. Ask questions to make sure you see the problem from the other person's point of view. Ask directly and simply: for example, "Why are you insisting that I take the dog out now when I have to call three clients before nine o'clock?"

Let us select an example and work it through the remaining steps. This conflict revolves around Pat's not wanting to socialize with Chris's friends. Chris is devoted to them, but Pat actively dislikes them. Chris thinks they are wonderful and exciting; Pat thinks they are unpleasant and boring.

Examine Possible Solutions

Most conflicts can probably be resolved through a variety of solutions. At this stage, try to identify as many solutions as possible.

Look for solutions that will enable both parties to win—to get something each wants. Avoid win-lose solutions, in which one wins and one loses. They will cause difficulty for the relationship by engendering frustration and resentment.

In examining these potential solutions, carefully weigh the costs and the rewards that each solution entails. Most solutions will involve costs to one or both parties (after all, *someone* has to take to dog out). Seek solutions in which the costs and the rewards will be evenly shared.

Once you have examined all possible solutions, select one and test it out. Among the solutions that Pat and Chris might identify are these:

1. Chris should not interact with these friends anymore.
2. Pat should interact with Chris's friends.
3. Chris should see these friends without Pat.

Clearly solutions 1 and 2 are win-lose solutions. In solution 1, Pat wins and Chris loses; in 2, Chris wins and Pat loses. Solution 3 has some possibilities. Both might win and neither must necessarily lose. Let's examine this solution more closely.

An especially interesting way to examine the solutions is to apply the critical-thinking hats technique, developed by the critical-thinking theorist Edward deBono (1987).

The technique, applicable to defining, analyzing, and evaluating problems and solutions, involves six "thinking hats." With each hat, you look at the problem from a different perspective.

- The **fact hat** focuses attention on the data, the facts and figures that bear on the problem. For example: *What are the relevant data in this conflict? How can Pat get more information on the rewards that Chris gets from these friends? How can Chris find out exactly what Pat doesn't like about these friends?*
- The **feeling hat** focuses attention on feelings, emotions, and intuitions concerning the problem. For example: *How do we feel about the problem? How does Pat feel when Chris goes out with these friends? How does Chris feel when Pat refuses to meet with them?*
- The **negative argument hat** puts you in the position of devil's advocate. For example: *How might this relationship deteriorate if Chris continues seeing these friends without Pat? How might the relationship deteriorate if Pat resists interacting with Chris's friends?*
- The **positive benefits hat** asks that you look at the upside. For example: *What opportunities might be gained if Chris sees these friends without Pat? What benefits might Pat and Chris derive from this new arrangement? What would be the best thing that could happen?*
- The **creative new idea hat** focuses attention on new ways of looking at the problem. For example: *In what other ways can you look at this problem? What other possible solutions might you consider?*
- The **control of thinking hat** helps you analyze what you have done and are doing. It asks you to reflect on your own thinking processes and to synthesize the results of your thinking. For example: *Have you adequately defined the problem? Are you focusing too much on insignificant issues? Have you given enough attention to the possible negative effects?*

Test the Solution

Test the solution mentally. How does it feel now? How will it feel tomorrow? Are you comfortable with it? Would Pat be comfortable with Chris's socializing with these friends alone? Some of Chris's friends are attractive; would this cause difficulty for Pat and Chris's relationship? Will Chris give people too much to gossip about? Will Chris feel guilty? Will Chris enjoy these friends without Pat?

Test the solution in practice. Put the solution into operation. How does it work? If it doesn't work, then discard it and try another solution. Give each solution a fair chance, but don't hang on to a solution when it is clear that it won't resolve the conflict.

Perhaps Chris might go out without Pat once to test this solution. How was it? Did these friends think there was something wrong with Chris's relationship with Pat? Did Chris feel guilty? Did Chris enjoy this new experience? How did Pat feel? Did Pat feel jealous? Lonely? Abandoned?

Evaluate the Solution

Did the solution help resolve the conflict? Is the situation better now than it was before the solution was tried? Share your feelings and evaluations of the solution.

Pat and Chris now need to share their perceptions of this possible solution. Would they be comfortable with this solution on a monthly basis? Is the solution worth the costs each will pay? Are the costs and rewards evenly distributed? Might other solutions be more effective?

Accept or Reject the Solution

If you accept the solution, you are ready to put it into more permanent operation. If you decide that this is not the right solution for the conflict, then you might test another solution or perhaps go back to redefine the conflict.

Let us say that Pat is actually quite happy with the solution. Pat was able to use that time to visit college friends. The next time Chris goes out with friends, Pat intends to go to wrestling with these people from college. Chris feels pretty good about seeing friends without Pat. Chris explains that they have both decided to see their friends separately and both are comfortable with this decision.

If, however, Pat or Chris were unhappy with this solution, they would have to try out another one or perhaps go back and redefine the problem and seek other ways to resolve it.

Throughout this process, avoid the common but damaging conflict strategies that can destroy a relationship. At the same time, use those strategies that will help to resolve the conflict and even improve the relationship.

Conflict Management Strategies

The following discussion focuses on unproductive strategies that should be avoided, as well as their productive counterparts.

Avoidance and Fighting Actively

Avoidance may involve actual physical flight: for example, leaving the scene of the conflict (walking out of the apartment or going to anther part of the office), falling asleep, or blasting the stereo to drown out all conversation. It may also take the form of emotional or intellectual avoidance, whereby you leave the conflict psychologically by not dealing with the issues raised. Men are more likely to use this strategy, coupled with denial that anything is wrong (Haferkamp 1991–92).

Nonnegotiation is a special type of avoidance. Here you refuse to discuss the conflict or to listen to the other person's argument. At times, this nonnegotiation takes the form of hammering away at one's own point of view until the other person gives in.

Instead of avoiding the issues, take an active role in your interpersonal conflicts. This is not to say that a cooling-off period is not at times desirable. It is to say, instead, that if you wish to resolve conflicts, you need to confront them actively.

Involve yourself on both sides of the communication exchange. Be an active participant as a speaker and as a listener; voice your own feelings and listen carefully to your partner's feelings.

Another part of active fighting involves taking responsibility for your thoughts and feelings. For example, when you disagree with your partner or find fault with her or his behavior, take responsibility for these feelings. Say, for example, "I disagree with . . ." or "I don't like it when you. . . ." Avoid statements that deny your responsibility; for example, "Everybody thinks you're wrong about . . ." or "Chris thinks you shouldn't. . . ."

Force and Talk

When confronted with conflict, many people prefer not to deal with the issues but rather to force their position on the other person. The force may be emotional or physical. In either case, however, the issues are avoided, and the person who "wins" is the one who exerts the most force. This is the technique of warring nations, children, and even some normally sensible adults.

More than 50 percent of both single and married couples reported that they had experienced physical violence in their relationship. If we add symbolic violence (for example, threatening to hit the other person or throwing something), the percentages are above 60 percent for singles and above 70 percent for marrieds (Marshall and Rose 1987). In another study, 47 percent of a sample of 410 college students reported some experience with violence in a dating relationship (Deal and Wampler 1986). In most cases, the violence was reciprocal—each person in the relationship used violence.

In cases in which only one person was violent, the research results are conflicting. For example, the study involving the college students found that in cases in which one partner was violent, the aggressor was significantly more often the female (Deal and Wampler 1986). Earlier research found similar sex differences (for example, Cate et al. 1982). These findings contradict the popular belief that males are more violent in heterosexual partnerships. One possible explanation for this is that in our society women are more likely to report it. . . . Aggression by women on the other hand, being "unnatural," would stand out more and be remembered more. Since women are stereotypically seen as less aggressive than men, it may take less aggression on the part of a woman for her to be labelled aggressive. This may then lead to an overreporting of the woman's aggressive acts. (Deal and Wampler 1986; also see Gelles 1981). Other research, however, has found that the popular conception of men being more likely than women to use force to achieve compliance is indeed true (Deturck 1987).

One form of relational force is, of course, rape. The studies in this area show alarming findings. According to Karen Kersten and Lawrence Kersten (1988), "forced sex on a date is probably one of the most common forms of all types of rape." In a study of force and violence on one college campus, more than half of the women students reported that they were verbally threatened, physically coerced, or physically abused; more than 12 percent indicated they had been raped (Barrett 1982; Kersten and Kersten 1988). In another investigation of sexual assault on college campuses, 45 percent of the women surveyed reported being victims of criminal sexual assault, criminal sexual abuse, and battery-intimidation (Illinois Coalition 1990). In yet another study, 42 percent of the men surveyed indicated they had engaged in coercive sexual relationships in which they were the coercing partners (Craig, Kalichman, and Follingstad 1989).

One of the most puzzling findings is that many victims of violence interpret it as a sign of love. For some reason, they see being beaten, verbally abused, or raped as a sign that their partner is fully in love with them. Many victims, in fact, accept the blame for contributing to the violence instead of blaming their partners (Gelles and Cornell 1985).

Equally puzzling but more frightening is the finding—from at least one study—that of the college-age men surveyed, 51 percent said they would rape a woman if they knew they would never get caught (Illinois Coalition 1990).

Findings such as these point to problems well beyond the prevalence of unproductive conflict strategies that we want to identify and avoid. They demonstrate the existence of underlying pathologies, which we are discovering are a lot more common than we previously thought when issues like these were never mentioned in college textbooks or lectures. Awareness is, of course, only the first step in understanding and eventually combating such problems.

The only real alternative to force is talk. Instead of using force, talk and listen. The qualities of openness, empathy, and positiveness for example, are suitable starting points.

Blame and Empathy

Because most relationship conflicts are caused by a wide variety of factors, any attempt to single out one or two for *blame* is sure to fail. Yet a frequently used fight strategy is to blame someone. Consider, for example, the couple who fight over their child's getting into trouble with the police. The parents may—instead of dealing with the conflict itself—blame each other for the child's troubles. Such blaming, of course, does nothing to resolve the problem or to help the child.

Often when you blame someone you attribute motives to the person. Thus, if the person forgot your birthday and this oversight disturbs you, fight about the forgetting of the birthday (the actual behavior). Try not to mind read the motives of another person: "Well, it's obvious you just don't care about me. If you really cared, you could never have forgotten my birthday!"

Perhaps the best alternative to blame is empathy. Try to feel what the other person is feeling and to see the situation as the other person does. Try to see the situation as punctuated by the other person and how this punctuation may differ from your own.

Demonstrate empathic understanding. Once you have empathically understood your opponent's feelings, validate those feelings when appropriate. If your partner is hurt or angry and you believe such feelings are legitimate and justified, say so: "You have a right to be angry; I shouldn't have called your mother a slob. I'm sorry. But I still don't want to go on vacation with her." In expressing validation, you are not necessarily expressing agreement on the issue in conflict; you are merely stating that your partner has feelings that you recognize as legitimate.

Silencers and Facilitating Open Expression

Silencers are conflict techniques that literally silence the other individual. Among the wide variety that exists, one frequently used silencer is crying. When a person is unable to deal with a conflict or when winning seems unlikely, he or she may cry and thus silence the other person.

Another silencer is to feign extreme emotionalism—to yell and scream and pretend to be losing control of oneself. Still another is to develop some "physical" reaction—headaches and shortness of breath are probably the most popular. One of the major problems with silencers is that you can never be certain whether they are strategies to win the argument or real physical reactions to which you should pay attention. Regardless of what we do, however, the conflict remains unexamined and unresolved.

Grant the other person permission to express himself or herself freely and openly; grant permission to be oneself. Avoid power tactics that suppress or inhibit freedom of expression. These tactics are designed to put the other person down and to subvert true interpersonal equality.

Gunnysacking and Present Focus

Gunnysacking—a term derived from the large burlap bag called a gunnysack—refers to the practice of storing up grievances so they may be unloaded at another time. The immediate occasion may be relatively simple (or so it might seem at first), such as someone's coming home late without calling. Instead of arguing about this, the gunnysacker unloads all past grievances. The birthday you forgot, the time you arrived late for dinner, the hotel reservations you forgot to make are all thrown at you. As you may know from experience, gunnysacking begets gunnysacking. When one person gunnysacks, the other person gunnysacks. The result is two people dumping their stored-up grievances on one another. Frequently, the original problem never gets addressed. Instead, resentment and hostility escalate.

Focus your conflict on the here-and-now rather than on issues that occurred two months ago (as in gunnysacking). Similarly, focus your conflict on the person with whom you are fighting and not on the person's mother, child, or friends.

Manipulation and Spontaneity

In *manipulation*, there is avoidance of open conflict. The individual attempts to divert the conflict by being especially charming (disarming, actually). The manipulator gets the other person into a receptive and noncombative frame of mind. The manipulator presents his or her demands to a weakened opponent. The manipulator relies on the tendency to give in to people who act especially nice.

Instead, try expressing your feelings with spontaneity. Remember that in interpersonal conflict there is no need to win a war. The objective is not to win but to increase mutual understanding and to reach a decision that both parties can accept.

Personal Rejection and Acceptance

In *personal rejection*, one person withholds love and affection. He or she seeks to win the argument by getting the other person to break down in the face of this withdrawal. The individual acts cold and uncaring in an effort to demoralize the other person. In withdrawing affection, for example, the individual hopes to make the other person question his or her own self-worth. Once the other is demoralized and feels less than worthy, it is relatively easy for the "rejector" to get his or her way.

Instead, express positive feelings for the other person and for the relationship between the two of you. Throughout any conflict, many harsh words will probably be exchanged, later to be regretted. The words cannot be unsaid or uncommunicated, but they can be partially offset by the expression of positive statements. If you are engaged in combat with someone you love, remember that you are fighting with a loved one and express that feeling: "I love you very much, but I still don't want your mother on vacation with us. I want to be alone with you."

Fighting Below and Above the Belt

Much like prize fighters in a ring, each of us has a "belt line." When you hit someone below it, you can inflict serious injury. When you hit above the belt, however, the person is able to absorb the blow. With most interpersonal relationships, especially those of long standing, you know where the belt line is. You know, for example, that to hit Pat with the inability to have children is to hit below the belt. You know that to hit Chris with the failure to get a permanent job is to hit below the belt. Hitting below the belt line causes all persons involved added problems. Keep blows to areas your opponent can absorb and handle.

The aim of relationship conflict is not to win and have your opponent lose. Rather, it is to resolve a problem and strengthen the relationship. Keep this ultimate goal always in clear focus, especially when you are angry or hurt.

Verbal Aggressiveness and Argumentativeness

An especially interesting perspective on conflict is emerging from the work on verbal aggressiveness and argumentativeness (Infante and Rancer 1982; Infante and Wigley 1986; Infante 1988). Understanding these two concepts will help in understanding some of the reasons why things go wrong and some of the ways in which you can use conflict to actually improve your relationships.

Verbal Aggressiveness

Verbal aggressiveness is a method of winning an argument by inflicting psychological pain, by attacking the other person's self-concept. It is a type of disconfirmation (and the opposite of confirmation) in that it seeks to discredit the individual's view of self. To explore this tendency further, take the accompanying self-test of verbal aggressiveness.

TEST YOURSELF
How Verbally Aggressive Are You?*

INSTRUCTIONS

This scale is designed to measure how people try to obtain compliance from others. For each statement, indicate the extent to which you feel it is true for you in your attempts to influence others. Use the following scale:

1 = almost never true
2 = rarely true
3 = occasionally true
4 = often true
5 = almost always true

_____ 1. I am extremely careful to avoid attacking individuals' intelligence when I attack their ideas.

_____ 2. When individuals are very stubborn, I use insults to soften the stubbornness.

_____ 3. I try very hard to avoid having other people feel bad about themselves when I try to influence them.

_____ 4. When people refuse to do a task I know is important, without good reason, I tell them they are unreasonable.

_____ 5. When others do things I regard as stupid, I try to be extremely gentle with them.

_____ 6. If individuals I am trying to influence really deserve it, I attack their character.

_____ 7. When people behave in ways that are in very poor taste, I insult them in order to shock them into proper behavior.

_____ 8. I try to make people feel good about themselves even when their ideas are stupid.

_____ 9. When people simply will not budge on a matter of importance, I lose my temper and say rather strong things to them.

_____ 10. When people criticize my shortcomings, I take it in good humor and do not try to get back at them.

_____ 11. When individuals insult me, I get a lot of pleasure out of really telling them off.

_____ 12. When I dislike individuals greatly, I try not to show it in what I say or how I say it.

_____ 13. I like poking fun at people who do things which are very stupid in order to stimulate their intelligence.

_____ 14. When I attack a person's ideas, I try not to damage their self-concepts.

_____ 15. When I try to influence people, I make a great effort not to offend them.

_____ 16. When people do things which are mean or cruel, I attack their character in order to help correct their behavior.

(continued)

> **Test Yourself** (continued)
>
> _____ 17. I refuse to participate in arguments when they involve personal attacks.
>
> _____ 18. When nothing seems to work in trying to influence others, I yell and scream in order to get some movement from them.
>
> _____ 19. When I am not able to refute others' positions, I try to make them feel defensive in order to weaken their positions.
>
> _____ 20. When an argument shifts to personal attacks, I try very hard to change the subject.
>
> SCORING
>
> To compute your verbal aggressiveness score, follow these steps:
>
> 1. Add the scores on items 2, 4, 6, 7, 9, 11, 13, 16, 18, 19.
> 2. Add the scores on items 1, 3, 5, 8, 10, 12, 14, 15, 17, 20.
> 3. Subtract the sum obtained in step 2 from 60.
> 4. To compute your verbal aggressiveness score, add the total obtained in step 1 to the result obtained in step 3.
>
> If you scored between 59 and 100, you are high in verbal aggressiveness; if you scored between 39 and 58, you are moderate in verbal aggressiveness; if you scored between 20 and 38, you are low in verbal aggressiveness.
>
> In computing your score, make special note of the characteristics the statements identify in connection with the tendency to act verbally aggressive. Note those inappropriate behaviors you are especially prone to commit. High agreement (4 or 5 on the scale) with statements 2, 4, 6, 7, 9, 11, 13, 16, 18, and 19 and low agreement (1 and 2 on the scale) with statements 1, 3, 5, 8, 10, 12, 14, 15, 17, and 20 will help you highlight any significant verbal aggressiveness you might have. Review previous encounters when you acted verbally aggressive. What effect did such action have on your subsequent interaction? What effect did it have on your relationship with the other person? What alternative ways of getting your point across might you have used? Might these have proved more effective?
>
> * From "Verbal Aggressiveness: An Interpersonal Model and Measure" by Dominic Infante and C.J. Wrigley, *Communication Monographs* 53, 1986, pp. 61–69. Reprinted by permission of the Speech Communication Association.

Character attack, perhaps because it is extremely effective in inflicting psychological pain, is the most popular tactic of verbal aggressiveness. Other tactics include attacking the person's abilities, background, and physical appearance; cursing; teasing; ridiculing; threatening; swearing; and using various nonverbal emblems (Infante et al. 1990).

Some researchers have argued that "unless aroused by verbal aggression, a hostile disposition remains latent in the form of unexpressed anger" (Infante, Chandler, and Rudd 1989). There is some evidence to show that people in violent marriages are more often verbally aggressive than people in nonviolent marriages.

Because verbal aggressiveness does not help to resolve conflicts, results in loss of credibility for the person using it, and increases the credibility of the target of the aggressiveness (Infante, Hartley, Martin, Higgins, Bruning, and Hur 1992), you may wonder why people act verbally aggressive. What, if anything, would lead you to act in a

TEST YOURSELF
How Argumentative Are You?*

INSTRUCTIONS

This questionnaire contains statements about controversial issues. Indicate how often each statement is true for you personally according to the following scale:

- 1 = almost never true
- 2 = rarely true
- 3 = occasionally true
- 4 = often true
- 5 = almost always true

_____ 1. While in an argument, I worry that the person I am arguing with will form a negative impression of me.

_____ 2. Arguing over controversial issues improves my intelligence.

_____ 3. I enjoy avoiding arguments.

_____ 4. I am energetic and enthusiastic when I argue.

_____ 5. Once I finish an argument, I promise myself that I will not get into another.

_____ 6. Arguing with a person creates more problems for me than it solves.

_____ 7. I have a pleasant, good feeling when I win a point in an argument.

_____ 8. When I finish arguing with someone, I feel nervous and upset.

_____ 9. I enjoy a good argument over a controversial issue.

_____ 10. I get an unpleasant feeling when I realize I am about to get into an argument.

_____ 11. I enjoy defending my point of view on an issue.

_____ 12. I am happy when I keep an argument from happening.

_____ 13. I do not like to miss the opportunity to argue a controversial issue.

_____ 14. I prefer being with people who rarely disagree with me.

_____ 15. I consider an argument an exciting intellectual challenge.

_____ 16. I find myself unable to think of effective points during an argument.

_____ 17. I feel refreshed and satisfied after an argument on a controversial issue.

_____ 18. I have the ability to do well in an argument.

_____ 19. I try to avoid getting into arguments.

_____ 20. I feel excitement when I expect that a conversation I am in is leading to an argument.

SCORING

1. Add your scores on items 2, 4, 7, 9, 11, 13, 15, 17, 18, and 20.
2. Add 60 to the sum obtained in step 1.
3. Add your scores on items 1, 3, 5, 6, 8, 10, 12, 14, 16, and 19.
4. To compute your argumentativeness score, subtract the total obtained in step 3 from the total obtained in step 2.

(continued)

> **Test Yourself** (continued)
>
> INTERPRETING YOUR SCORE:
> Scores between 73 and 100 indicate high argumentativeness.
> Scores between 56 and 72 indicate moderate argumentativeness.
> Scores between 20 and 55 indicate low argumentativeness.
>
> * From "A Conceptualization and Measure of Argumentativeness" by Dominic Infante and Andrew Rancer, *Journal of Personality Assessment*, 1982, Vol. 46, pp. 72–80. Copyright © 1982 Lawrence Erbaum Associates, Inc. Reprinted by permission of Lawrence Erbaum Associates, Inc. and the authors.

verbally aggressive manner? Acting verbally aggressive as a response to the other person's aggressiveness is the most frequently cited reason. Other reasons are dislike for the other person, anger, feeling unable to argue effectively, responding to a degenerating discussion, being taught to respond this way, being reminded of being hurt, and being in a bad mood (Infante, Riddle, Horvath, and Tumlin 1992).

Argumentativeness

Contrary to popular usage, the term "argumentativeness" refers to a quality to be cultivated rather than avoided. Argumentativeness is your willingness to argue for a point of view, your tendency to speak your mind on significant issues. It is the mode of dealing with disagreements that is the preferred alternative to verbal aggressiveness. Before reading about ways to increase your argumentativeness, take the accompanying self-test, "How Argumentative Are You?"

Generally, those who score high in argumentativeness have a strong tendency to state their position on controversial issues and argue against the positions of others. A high scorer sees arguing both as exciting and intellectually challenging and as an opportunity to win a kind of contest. Not surprisingly, high argumentatives also have greater resistance to persuasion and can generate a greater number of counterarguments to a persuasive appeal of another (Kazoleas 1993).

The person who scores low in argumentativeness tries to prevent arguments. This person experiences satisfaction not from arguing but from avoiding arguments. The low argumentative sees arguing as unpleasant and unsatisfying. Not surprisingly, this person has little confidence in his or her ability to argue effectively. The moderately argumentative person possesses some of the qualities of both the high argumentative and the low argumentative.

The researchers who developed this test note that both high and low argumentatives may experience communication difficulties. The high argumentative, for example, may argue needlessly, too often, and too forcefully. The low argumentative, in contrast, may avoid taking a stand even when it is necessary. Persons scoring somewhere in the middle are probably the more interpersonally skilled and adaptable, arguing when it is necessary but avoiding the many arguments that are needless and repetitive. People skilled in argumentativeness are also less likely than both low argumentatives and verbally aggressive people to experience marital violence (Infante, Chandler, and Rudd 1989).

Here are some suggestions for cultivating argumentativeness and for preventing it from degenerating into aggressiveness (Infante 1988):

- Treat disagreements as objectively as possible; avoid assuming that because someone takes issue with your position or interpretation, they are attacking you as a person.
- Avoid attacking the other person (rather than the person's arguments), even if the attack would give you a tactical advantage; center your arguments on issues rather than personalities.
- Reaffirm the other person's sense of competence; compliment the other person as appropriate.
- Avoid interrupting; allow the other person to state her or his position fully before you respond.
- Stress equality, and stress the similarities you have with the other person; emphasize areas of agreement before attacking the disagreements.
- Express interest in the other person's position, attitude, and point of view.
- Avoid presenting your arguments too emotionally; using an overly loud voice or interjecting vulgar expressions will prove offensive and eventually ineffective.
- Allow the other person to save face; never humiliate the other person.

Before and After the Conflict

If you are to make conflict truly productive, consider a few suggestions for preparing for conflict and for using it for relational growth.

Before the Conflict

Try to fight in private. When you air your conflicts in front of others, you create a variety of other problems. You may not be willing to be totally honest when third parties are present; you may feel you have to save face and therefore must win the fight at all costs. This may lead you to use strategies to win the argument rather than to resolve the conflict. You may become so absorbed by the image that others will have of you that you forget you have a relationship problem that needs to be resolved. Also, you run the risk of embarrassing your partner in front of others, and this embarrassment may create resentment and hostility.

Be sure you are each ready to fight. Although conflicts arise at the most inopportune times, you can choose the time to resolve them. Confronting your partner when she or he comes home after a hard day of work may not be the right time for resolving a conflict. Make sure you are both relatively free of other problems and ready to deal with the conflict at hand.

Know what you're fighting about. Sometimes people in a relationship become so hurt and angry that they lash out at the other person just to vent their own frustration. The problem at the center of the conflict (for example, the uncapped toothpaste tube) is merely an excuse to express anger. Any attempt to resolve this "problem" will be doomed to failure because the problem addressed is not what is causing the conflict. Instead, it is the underlying hostility, anger, and frustration that needs to be addressed.

Fight about problems that can be solved. Fighting about past behaviors or about family members or situations over which you have no control solves nothing; instead, it creates additional difficulties. Any attempt at resolution will fail because the problems are incapable of being solved. Often such conflicts are concealed attempts at expressing one's frustration or dissatisfaction.

After the Conflict

After the conflict is resolved, there is still work to be done. Learn from the conflict and from the process you went through in trying to resolve it. For example, can you identify the fight strategies that merely aggravated the situation? Do you or your partner need a cooling-off period? Can you tell when minor issues are going to escalate into major arguments? Does avoidance make matters worse? What issues are particularly disturbing and likely to cause difficulties? Can they be avoided?

Keep the conflict in perspective. Be careful not to blow it out of proportion to the extent that you begin to define your relationship in terms of conflict. Avoid the tendency to see disagreement as inevitably leading to major blowups. Conflicts in most relationships actually occupy a very small percentage of the couple's time, and yet, in recollection, they often loom extremely large. Also, don't allow the conflict to undermine your own or your partner's self-esteem. Don't view yourself, your partner, or your relationship as failures just because you had an argument or even lots of arguments.

Attack your negative feelings. Negative feelings frequently arise after an interpersonal conflict. Most often they arise because unfair fight strategies were used to undermine the other person—for example, personal rejection, manipulation, or force. Resolve to avoid such unfair tactics in the future, but at the same time let go of guilt, of blame, for yourself and your partner. If you think it would help, discuss these feelings with your partner or even a therapist.

Increase the exchange of rewards and cherishing behaviors to demonstrate your positive feelings and to show you are over the conflict and want the relationship to survive and flourish.

SECTION II

Problem Solving Tools

INTRODUCTION

In today's workplace, employers consistently call upon the problem solving and information literacy skills of their employees. Problem solving tools can be defined as the methods and procedures developed to increase the efficiency and/or effectiveness of the problem solving process. The use of such tools and procedures can increase the quality of solutions produced, assist in managing information in such a way that makes decision making easier and thinking explicit, and function to determine problem solving steps and strategies.

The problem solving strategies presented in this section are organized as follows: problem definition, idea generation, solution selection and solution implementation.

Through use of these strategies, or heuristics, problem solvers are more likely to find that such strategies assist them in asking the correct questions, storing appropriate and useful data, organizing, transforming and using information, and perhaps most importantly, in avoiding problem solving pitfalls.

Finally, problem solving tools assist students in both individual and team based environments. The use of problem solving heuristics in these environments allows for the transformation of information to all parties, thus promoting effective decisions and quality conclusions for the team. Moreover, such tools allow for the individual thinking process, which, when brought to the team environment, can produce group creativity and synergy.

CHAPTER 5

Problem Definition

> *The mere formulation of a problem is far more often essential than its solution, which may be merely a matter of mathematical or experimental skill. To raise new questions, new possibilities, to regard old problems from a new angle requires creative imagination and marks real advances in science.*
>
> —Albert Einstein

Often, the most difficult aspect of problem solving is understanding and *defining the real problem (sometimes also referred to as the underlying or root problem)*. In this chapter we address the first part of the heuristic, *problem definition*. A study that we conducted of experienced problem solvers in industry revealed some common threads that run through their problem definition techniques. We have classified these common threads into a number of steps that can help you understand and define the real problem.

The First Four Steps

The first four steps used by experienced problem solvers to understand and define the real problem are given in Table 3–1. You will observe that the first four steps focus on gathering information.

> **Table 3–1. What Experienced Problem Solvers Say**
> 1. Collect and analyze information and data.
> 2. Talk with people familiar with the problem.
> 3. If at all possible, view the problem first hand.
> 4. Confirm all findings.

Step 1. Collect and analyze information and data.

Learn as much as you can about the problem. Write down or list everything you can think of to describe the problem. Until the problem is well defined, anything might be important. Determine what information is missing and what information is extraneous. The information should be properly organized, analyzed and presented. It will then serve as the basis for subsequent decision making. Make a simple sketch or drawing of the situation. Drawings, sketches, graphs of data, etc. can all be excellent communication tools when used correctly. Analyze the data to show trends, errors, and other meaningful information. Display numerical or quantitative data graphically rather than in tabular form. Tables can be difficult to interpret and sometimes misleading. Graphing, on the other hand, is an excellent way to organize and analyze large amounts of data. The Case of the Dead Fish provides an interesting example of the use of graphical data to solve problems.

The Case of the Dead Fish

Research and information gathering are great tools in problem solving. We consider the case of a chemical plant that discharges waste into a stream that flows into a relatively wide river. Biologists monitored the river as an ecosystem and reported data of the number of dead fish in the river and the river level.

Graphs that show this type of information are called time plots and control charts. A time plot shows trends over a period of time (e.g., the level of a river over several days or weeks). A control chart is a time plot that also shows the acceptable limits of the quantity being displayed. For example, in the control chart of the river level, the upper and lower acceptable water levels would also be shown. If one of the acceptable limits is exceeded, this occurrence may yield some information about the timing of the problem and possible causes of it. We can then examine time plots of other pertinent quantities and look for additional clues about the problem.

From the use of graphs, we can see that the acceptable level of dead fish was exceeded on August 1 and 15. We look for anything that might have occurred on or between July 15th and August 1. We discover that on July 29 there was a large amount of chemical waste discharged into the river. Discharges of this size had not caused any problems in the past. Upon checking other factors, we see that there has been little rain and that the water level in the river, measured on August 1, had fallen so low it might not have been able to dilute the plant's chemical waste. Consequently, the low water level, coupled with the high volume of waste, could be suggested as a possible cause for the unusually large number of dead fish. However, to verify this, we would have to carry the analysis further. Specifically, we shall soon use one or more of the problem definition techniques discussed later in this chapter.

Step 2. Talk with people familiar with the problem.

Find out who knows about the problem. Ask penetrating questions by

- Looking past the obvious
- Challenging the basic premise
- Asking for clarification when you do not understand something

Our experience shows that seemingly naive questions (often perceived as "dumb") questions) can produce profound results by challenging established thinking patterns. This act of *challenging* must be an ongoing process.

You should also talk to other people about the problem. Verbalizing the problem to someone else helps clarify in your own mind just what it is you are trying to do. Try to find out who the experts in the field are and talk to them. Nonexperts are also a rich source of creative solutions, as evidenced by the following example.

Seeking Advice

Joel Weldon, in his tape "Jet Pilots Don't Use Rearview Mirrors," described a problem encountered by a major hotel a number of years ago. Since the hotel had become very popular, the elevators were very busy, and frequently caused backups in the lobby area. The manager and assistant manager were lamenting the problem in the lobby one day and were brainstorming about how to increase the elevator capacity. Adding additional elevator shafts would require removal of a number of rooms and a significant loss of income. The doorman, overhearing their conversation, casually mentioned that it was too bad they couldn't just add an elevator on the outside of the building, so as not to disturb things inside. A great idea! It occurred to the doorman because he was outside the building much of the time, and that was his frame of reference. Notice, however, that the doorman's creativity alone was not enough to solve the problem. Knowledge of design techniques was necessary to implement his original idea. A new outside elevator was born, and the rest is history. External elevators have since become quite popular in major hotels. Information, good ideas, and different perspectives on the problem can come from all levels of the organization. (*Chemtech.*, 13, 9, p. 517, 1983)

When equipment malfunctions, it is a *must* to talk to the operators because they know the "personality" of the equipment better than anyone.

Most organizations have employees who have "been around a long time" and have a great deal of experience, as illustrated in the following example.

Go Talk to George

Remember the leaking flowmeter discussed in Chapter 1? The solution that the company adopted was to replace the flowmeter at regular intervals. Let's consider a similar situation in which, immediately upon replacement, the flowmeter began to leak. List in order four people you would talk to.

- the person who installed the meter
- the technician who monitors the flowmeter
- the manufacturer's representative who sold you the flowmeter
- George

Who's George? Every organization has a *George*. George is that individual who has years of experience to draw upon and also has street smarts. George is an excellent problem solver who always seems to approach the problem from a different viewpoint—one that hasn't been thought of by anyone else. Be sure to tap this rich source of knowledge, when you are faced with a problem. Individuals such as George can often provide a unique perspective on the situation.

Step 3. View the problem first hand.

While it is important to talk to people as a way to understand the problem, you should not rely solely on their interpretations of the situation and problem. If at all possible, go inspect the problem yourself.

> **Viewing the Problem Firsthand**
>
> In the mid 1970s a company in the United Kingdom completed a plant to produce a plastic product (PVC). The main piece of equipment was a large reactor with a cooling jacket through which water passed to keep the reactor cool. When the plant was started up, the plastic was dark, nonuniform, and way off design specifications. The engineers in charge reviewed their design. They reworked and refined their model and calculations. They analyzed the procedure from every point of view on paper. They had the raw material fed to the reactor analyzed. However, they all came up with the same results—that the product should definitely meet the design specifications. Unfortunately, nobody examined the reactor firsthand. Finally after many days, one of the engineers decided to look into the reactor. He found that a valve had been carelessly switched to the wrong position, thereby diverting cooling water away from the reactor so that virtually no cooling took place. As a result the reactor overheated, producing a poor quality product. Once the valves were adjusted properly, a high quality plastic was produced.

Step 4. Confirm all key findings.

Verify that the information that you collected is correct. Cross check and cross reference data, facts, and figures. Search for biases or misrepresentation of facts. Confirm all important pieces of information and spot check others. Distinguish between fact and opinion. Challenge assumptions and assertions.

> **Confirm All Allegations**
>
> The authors of this book were involved in a consulting project for a pulp and paper company we will call Boxright. Several years ago, Boxright had installed a new process for recovering and recycling their "cooking" chemicals used in the papermaking process. Two years after the installation, the process had yet to operate correctly. Tempers flared and accusations flew back and forth between Boxright and Courtland Construction, the supplier of the recycling equipment. Courtland claimed the problem was that Boxright did not know how to operate the process correctly, while the company contended that the equipment was improperly designed. Boxright finally decided to sue Courtland for breach of equipment performance. Much data and information were presented by both sides to support their arguments. Courtland presented data and information from an article in the engineering literature that they claimed *proved* Boxright was not operating the process correctly. At this point it looked like Courtland had cooked our goose by presenting such data. However, before conceding the case we needed to confirm this claim. We analyzed this key information in detail, and to our glee found in the last few pages of the article it was stated that the data would not be expected to apply to industrial-size equipment or processes. When this information was presented, the lawsuit was settled in favor of the pulp and paper company, Boxright.

Defining the Real Problem

The four steps just discussed are all related to gathering information about the problem. This information lays the groundwork that will help us use the problem definition techniques discussed in this chapter.

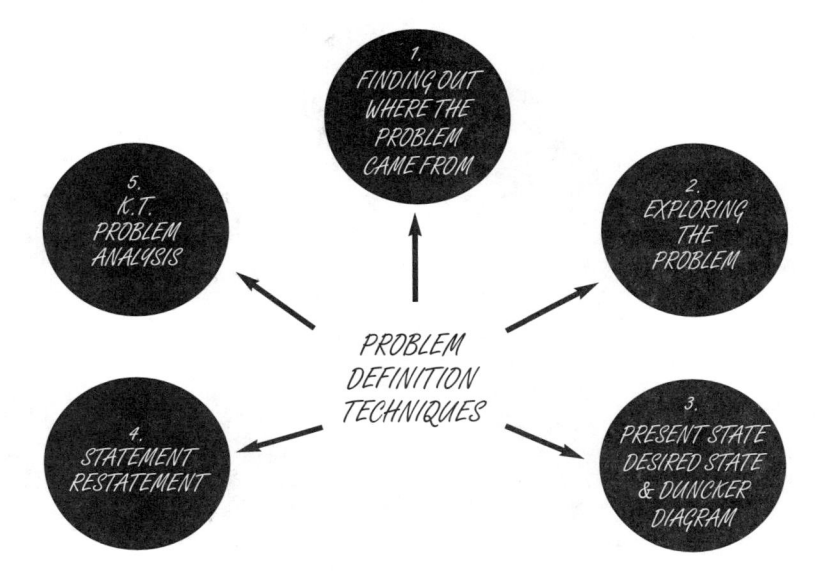

Problem Definition Techniques:
1. Finding Out Where the Problem Came From
2. Exploring the Problem
3. Present State, Desired State & Duncker Diagram
4. Statement Restatement
5. K.T. Problem Analysis

These techniques are used to help understand the problem so that we may define the real problem as opposed to the perceived problem.

Finding Out Where the Problem Came From

Many times you will be given a problem by someone else rather than discovering it yourself. Under these circumstances, it is very important that you make sure that the problem you were given reflects the true situation. This technique focuses on finding out who initiated the problem and ascertaining the validity of the reasoning used to arrive at the problem statement.

> **Find out where the problem statement came from.**
> - Where did the problem originate?
> - Who posed the problem statement in the first place, your supervisor, his/her supervisor, a colleague in your project group, or someone else?
> - Can that person explain the reasoning as to how they arrived at that particular problem statement?
> - Are the reasoning and assumptions valid?
> - Has that person considered the situation from a number of different viewpoints before arriving at the final problem statement?
> - Have you used *the first four steps* to gather information about the problem?

Try to detect any errors in logic as you trace the problem back to its origins. Distinguish opinion from fact and conclusions from evidence. **Never** assume that the problem statement you were given is correctly worded or has been thoroughly investigated.

Always check to be sure that the problem statement directs the solution to the true cause and does not seek merely to treat the symptoms. For example, it would certainly be better to find the cause of the off-taste in the hamburgers at a fast food chain rather than treating the symptoms by adding more spices to cover the off-taste. Make certain that time and energy are not wasted merely dealing with the symptoms.

Remember *The Case of the Dead Fish* in the river on p. 90? The dead fish example is a case where giving directions to treat the symptoms rather than discovering the real cause of the problem could have lead to a costly, unnecessary solution.

Finding Out Where the Problem Came From
The Case of the Dead Fish

The Situation: Stan Wilson is an engineer with six years of experience with his company. The instructions given by Stan's supervisor to solve the perceived problem: "Design a new waste treatment plant to reduce the toxic waste from the chemical plant." Stan and his team are requested to design treatment facilities to reduce the toxic chemical concentrations by a factor of 10. A quick back-of-the-envelope calculation shows that the plant could cost well over a million dollars. Stan is puzzled because the concentrations of toxic chemicals have always been significantly below governmental regulations and company health specifications.

Who posed the problem?

Stan approaches his supervisor to learn more about the reasons for the order. The supervisor informs Stan that it was not his decision, but upper management's.

Can reasons for arriving at the problem statement be explained?

The supervisor tells Stan it has something to do with the summer drought and a number of recent articles in the local newspaper about the unusually high number of dead fish that have turned up in the river in the last few weeks. He said that it was his understanding that the drought has brought the river to an extremely low level and that the discharge was no longer sufficiently dilute to be safe to the fish and other aquatic life. Consequently, to deflect the negative press and avoid possible lawsuits, the company has announced the planning of a new waste treatment facility.

Are the assumptions and reasoning valid?

Thus, Stan realizes that the decision to design and build a waste treatment plant is based on an *unusually large number of dead fish in the river*, and **not** *necessarily on the presence of high concentrations of toxic chemicals*. The company had decided to try to treat the symptoms (many dead fish) by removing toxic chemicals, thus solving the perceived problem, but not necessarily the true problem (how to prevent the fish from dying).

Has sufficient data/information been collected?

In the Explore Phase, we'll see how Stan initiated his own investigation into the case of the dead fish and eventually found the true cause of the problem.

> ### Finding Out Where the Problem Came From
> #### Sweet and Sour
>
> *The Situation:* (which has nothing to do with Chinese food): Natural gas (methane), which contains significant levels of hydrogen sulfide, is called a *sour gas*, while natural gas that does not contain hydrogen sulfide is called a *sweet gas*. Sour gas is particularly troublesome because it is extremely corrosive to the pipes and equipment used to transport it. Tom Anderson was the sour gas piping expert at a major oil company that was drilling an off-shore well in a gas field in the North Sea. Regions near the well being drilled were known to produce sour gas. Tom received a call from the head office. <u>The instructions given to solve the perceived problem:</u> *"Fly to Copenhagen to begin the design and installation of a piping system that would transport sour gas from the new well to the platform facility."*
>
> Laboratory tests were believed to have been carried out on gas samples from this well and it was assumed that the head office had reviewed these tests. An expensive piping system that would be resistant to corrosion by sour gas was designed and installed. When the gas well was brought on-line, it was found that the gas was sweet gas which did not require the corrosion resistant piping system that had cost several million dollars extra.
>
> Who was responsible for this blunder? Could this waste have been eliminated if Tom had found out where the problem had come from? Did the problem come from the lab or from the head office? What would have been the course of action regarding the type of piping installed,
>
> 1. **If** Tom, who was the piping expert, had asked the head office to explain why they wanted to install piping resistant to sour gas for *this* well, or,
> 2. **If** Tom had challenged their reasoning by asking what evidence they had that *this* well produced sour gas, or
> 3. **If** Tom had gathered more information by tracking down the laboratory results to learn how much sour gas was in the natural gas?
>
> **If** Tom had traced back the original source of the product to find out **where the problem came from**, this waste could have been eliminated.

A good rule of thumb is to treat the symptoms *only* if it is impossible or impractical to solve the real problem.

Exploring the Problem

This technique works well both for situations of analyzing incorrectly defined problems assigned to you and for formulating problem statements for new problems you uncover yourself. Once presented with a problem, we want to explore all aspects of the problem and its surroundings. This technique is a procedure that guides us to understand and define the real problem. Gathering information is also the key to the success of the exploration, and *the first four steps* (p. 89) are very helpful in this process.

> **Table 3–2. Exploring the Problem[2]**
> 1. Identify All Available Information.
> 2. Recall or Learn Pertinent Theories and Fundamentals.
> 3. Collect Missing Information.
> 4. Solve a Simplified Version of the Problem to Obtain a "Ballpark" Answer.
> 5. Hypothesize and Visualize What Could Be Wrong with the Current Situation.
> 6. Brainstorm to Guess the Answer.
> 7. Recall Past or Related Problems and Experiences.
> 8. Describe or Sketch the Solution in a Qualitative Manner or Sketch Out a Pathway That Will Lead to the Solution.
> 9. Collect More Data and Information.
> 10. After Using Some or All of the Activities Above, Write a Concise Statement Defining the Real Problem.

"Exploring the Problem" can also be used to build upon the results of the previous technique "Finding Out Where the Problem Came From."

> ### Exploring the Problem
> #### The Case of the Dead Fish
>
> Stan decides to initiate his own investigation into the dead fish problem over the weekend.
>
> 1. **Identify Available Information:** There is a toxic discharge from the plant, the river level is low, and there are a large number of dead fish in the river.
>
> 2. **Learn Fundamentals:** Stan calls a friend in the biology department at the local university and asks her about the problem of what could be causing the fish to die. She tells Stan that the extremely low water levels lead to significantly warmer water temperatures, and hence lower levels of dissolved oxygen in the water. These conditions make the fish susceptible to disease.
>
> 3. **Missing Information:** Secondly, she says that a fungus has been found in two nearby lakes that could be responsible for the death of the fish. Upon checking the recent daily temperatures, Stan learns that the day before the fish began dying was one of the hottest of the decade. Stan starts making phone calls to people upstream and downstream from the plant and learns that dead fish are appearing at the same unusually high rate everywhere, not just downstream of the plant.
>
> 5. **Hypothesis:** The fish were dying all over the area as a result of the fungus, and not from the plant discharge.
>
> *(continued)*

> **Exploring the Problem** (continued)
>
> 9. **More Information:** Upon examination of the dead fish, it was discovered that the fungus was indeed the cause of death, and that toxic chemicals played no role in the problem. Stan was glad that he had found out where the problem had come from and had explored the situation rather than blindly proceeding to design the treatment plant.
>
> 10. **Define the Real Problem:** Identify ways to cure the infected fish and prevent healthy fish from being infected.

We note from the above example that it is not always necessary to address all ten steps in Table 3–2 to fully explore the problem. However, as seen in the next example, each of the steps has a purpose and contributes to revealing the true problem.

> ### De-bottlenecking a Process
>
> Even though the following example is taken from an actual case history, don't worry if you don't know much about heat exchangers; just follow the reasoning. It is too good an example to pass up. <u>The situation:</u> A valuable product was being sold as fast as it could be manufactured in a chemical plant. Management tried to increase production but was unable to do so. Analysis of each step in the production line showed that the bottleneck was the refrigeration unit. This unit was a simple heat exchanger in which the hot liquid stream was cooled by passing it through a pipe which contacted a cold liquid stream. Heat flowed from the hot stream through the pipe wall into the cold stream. Unfortunately the refrigeration unit (i.e., heat exchanger) was not cooling the hot liquid stream to a sufficiently low temperature for it to be treated effectively in the next processing step. <u>The instructions given to solve the perceived problem:</u> *"Design and install a larger refrigeration unit."* The design of a larger refrigeration unit was started.
>
> **Explore Phase**
>
> 1. **Identify inputs/outputs:** Cold liquid stream not cooling hot product stream.
>
> 2. **Recall related theories and fundamentals:** The rate of cooling between the two streams is related to the temperature difference between the two streams, their flow rates, and the materials and condition of the unit.
>
> 3. **Collect missing information:** What is the size of the current refrigeration unit? What are the entering and exiting temperatures of the liquid streams?
>
> 4. **Carry out an order of magnitude calculation:** AH HA! The new unit need be no larger than the old one.
>
> 5. **Hypothesize and visualize what could be wrong with the current system:** Inefficient operation of current system? Could something be increasing the resistance to heat transfer (i.e., insulating)?
>
> *(continued)*

> **De-bottlenecking a Process** *(continued)*
>
> 6. **Guess the result:** Could scale (minerals deposited from the liquid) have built up on the inside of the unit acting as an insulating blanket? The buildup of scale on the pipe walls of the exchanger reduces the amount of heat that will transfer from the hot fluid to the cold fluid which severely degrades the ability of the exchanger to perform its intended task. The thicker the scale, the greater the resistance to heat transfer and the poorer the performance of the unit.
>
> 7. **Recall past problems, theories, or related experiences:** Scale greatly reduces the efficiency of the unit.
>
> 8. **Sketch solution or solution pathway:** Examine the unit for evidence of scale or fouling that may be reducing the heat transfer efficiency.
>
> 9. **Collect more data:** An examination of the heat exchanger showed it was indeed badly fouled.
>
> 10. **Define the real problem:** The scale on the pipe wall must be removed in order to cool the product stream effectively.

Using the Present State/Desired State Technique

How many times have you heard the statement "You can't get there from here?" The *Present State/Desired State* technique helps us verbalize where we are and where we want to go, so that an appropriate path can be found and we can indeed get there from here. The Present State/Desired State technique also helps us learn whether the solution goals (Desired State) are consistent with our needs (Present State).[3] When writing the Desired State statement, avoid using ambiguous and vague words or phrases like "best," "minimal," "cheapest," "within a reasonable time," "most efficient," etc. because these words mean different things to different people. Be quantitative where possible. For example, "The children's playground needs to be completed by July 1, 1994 at a cost under $100,000" *as opposed to* "The playground should be completed in a reasonable time at minimal cost." It is important that the Present State statement match the Desired State statement. In order for the Present State and Desired State to match, every concern in the Present State should be addressed in the Desired State. In addition, the Desired State should not contain solutions to problems that are not in the Present State. Sometimes a match exists, but it really doesn't get to the heart of the problem or allow many solution alternatives. Reworking the Present State and Desired State statements until they match is a technique that increases the probability of arriving at the true problem statement. Let us consider the following example of the Present State/Desired State Technique.

> ### Hitting 'Em Where They Aren't
>
> **The Situation:** During WWII, a number of aircraft were shot down while engaging in bombing missions over Germany. Many of the planes that made it back safely to base were riddled with bullet and projectile holes. The damaged areas were similar on each plane.
>
> **The instructions given to solve the perceived problem:** "Reinforce these damaged areas with thicker armor plating."
>
> | Present State | Desired State |
> |---|---|
> | Many bullets/projectiles penetrating aircraft. | Fewer planes being shot down. |
>
> **Discussion:** This is not a match because there are planes that are surviving that still have bullet holes. There is not a *one-to-one mapping* of all the needs of the present state being addressed and resolved in the desired state.
>
> | Present State | Desired State |
> |---|---|
> | Many bullets/projectiles penetrating aircraft. | Fewer bullet holes. |
>
> **Discussion:** These states are matched, but the distinction between the present state and the desired state is not clear enough. It may take only a single bullet hitting a critical area to down a plane.
>
> | Present State | Desired State |
> |---|---|
> | Many bullets/projectiles penetrating aircraft in critical and noncritical areas. | Fewer bullets/projectiles penetrating critical areas. |
>
> **Discussion:** These two statements now match and the distinction between them is sharp, opening up a variety of solution avenues such as reinforcing critical areas, moving critical components (e.g., steering mechanism) to more protected locations, providing redundant critical components, etc.
>
> Note: The original instructions given to solve the perceived problem would have failed. Reinforcing the areas where returning planes had been shot would have been futile. Clearly these were noncritical areas; otherwise these planes would have been casualties as well.

The Duncker Diagram

The Duncker Diagram helps obtain solutions that satisfy the criteria set up by the Present State/Desired State statements.[3] The unique feature of the Duncker Diagram is that it points out ways to solve the problem by making it OK *not* to reach the desired solution. Duncker Diagram solutions can be classified as General Solutions, Functional Solutions, and Specific Solutions (see Figure 3–1).

There are two types of General Solutions: 1) Solutions on the left side of the diagram that move from the present state to the desired state (i.e., we have to do something) and 2) solutions on the right side that show how to modify the desired state until it corresponds with the present state (make it OK **not** to do that *same* something). For example, suppose your *present state* was your current job and the *desired state* is a new job. The left hand side of the diagram would show the steps to reach the desired state of obtaining a new job (e.g., update resume, interview trips). The right side of the diagram show the steps that would make it OK to stay in your current job (e.g., greater participation in the decision making, salary increase). In addition, there could be a compromise solution in which both the Present State and Desired State are moved toward each other until there is a correspondence.

Functional Solutions are possible paths to the desired state (or modified desired state) that do not take into account the feasibility of the solution. We could solve the problem *only if* . . . we had more time, more personnel. . . . we won the lottery. . . . After arriving at each functional solution, one has to suggest feasible *Specific Solutions* to implement the functional solutions. For example in the job change situation, a functional solution on the right side of the diagram might be feeling more appreciated and a specific solution to feeling appreciated could be a salary increase or bonus, more verbal praise on a job well done, or a letter of commendation in your company personnel file. Representing the problem on a Duncker Diagram is a creative activity, and as

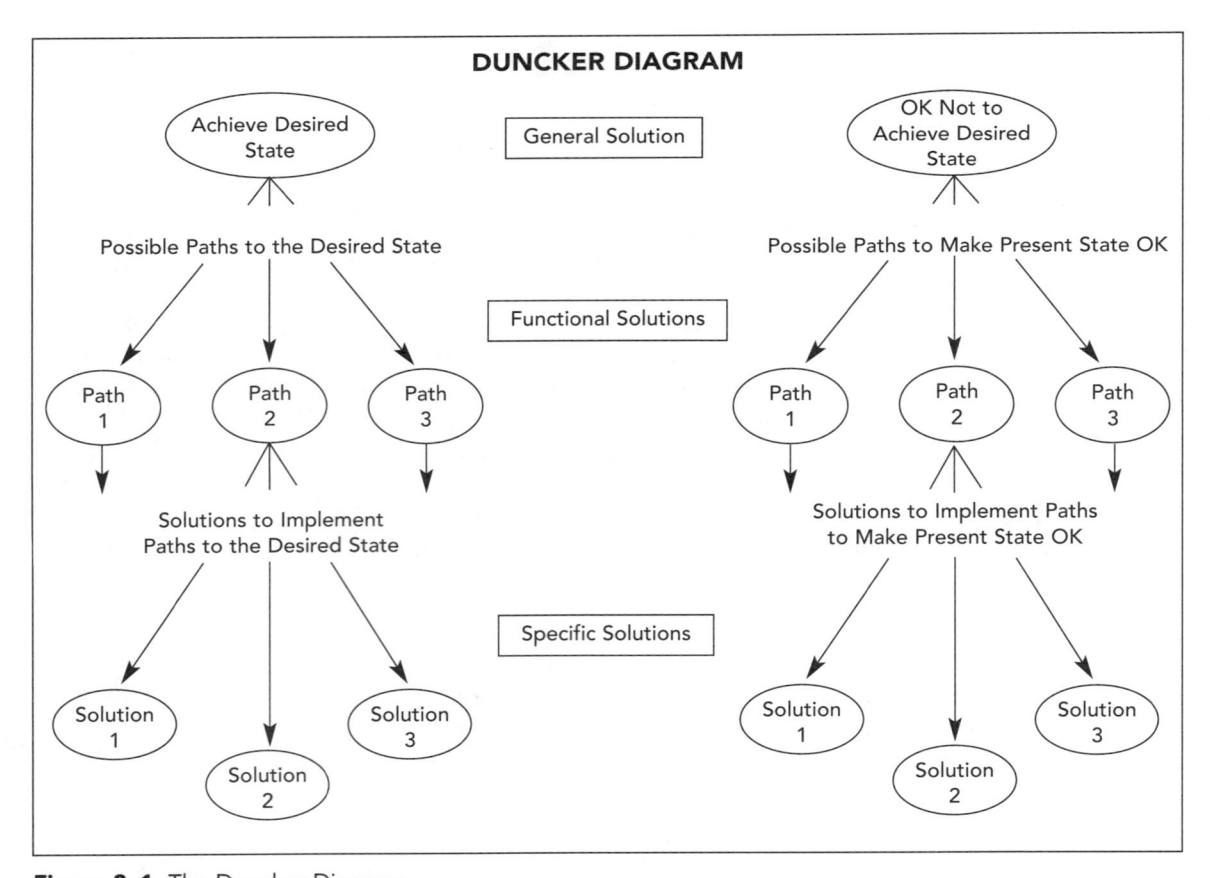

Figure 3–1. The Duncker Diagram

such, there is no right way or wrong way to do it. There is only more and less useful ways to represent the problem. Typically, the most difficult activity is choosing the appropriate desired state. This skill improves with practice.

Kindergarten Cop[†]

Linda Chen, who has been teaching elementary school for 25 years, has just finished a six-month leave of absence and is scheduled to return to teaching in February. She is dreading returning to teaching because the last few years have been extremely stressful and difficult, and she feels burned out teaching kindergarten. Students seem harder to control, Linda doesn't like the materials she is required to use in the classroom, and the parents don't seem to take much interest in their children's education. She also enjoyed the time she had to herself during her six-month leave and strongly feels she must continue to have more time to herself as she nears retirement which will be in five years if she is to receive full benefits. Consequently, Linda's *present state* is returning to teaching, and her *desired state* is not to return to teaching. Prepare a Duncker Diagram to analyze this situation.

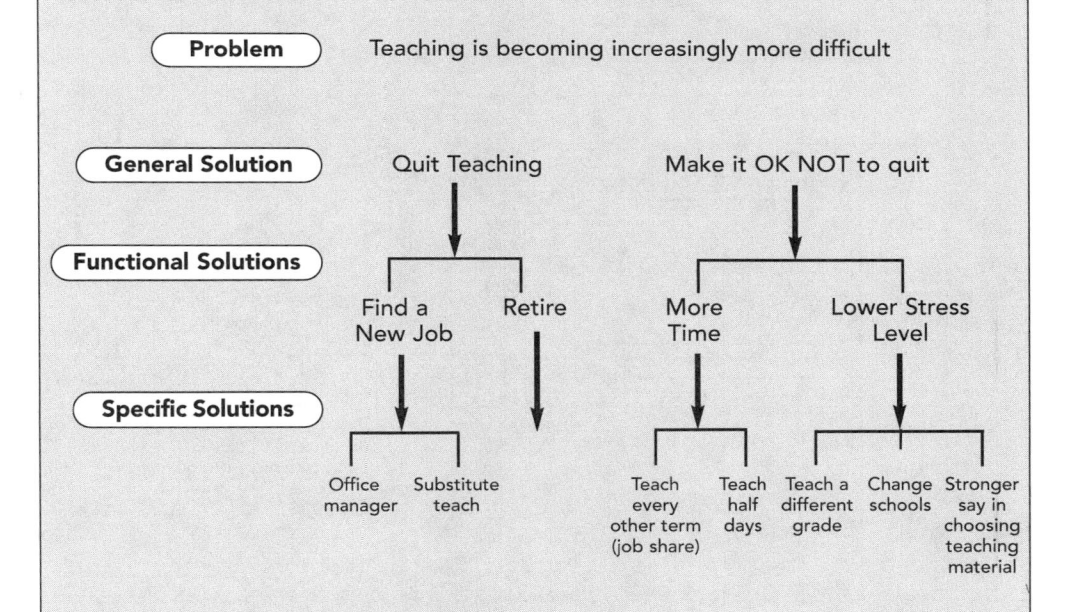

Problem: Teaching is becoming increasingly more difficult

General Solution: Quit Teaching | Make it OK NOT to quit

Functional Solutions: Find a New Job | Retire | More Time | Lower Stress Level

Specific Solutions:
- Office manager
- Substitute teach
- Teach every other term (job share)
- Teach half days
- Teach a different grade
- Change schools
- Stronger say in choosing teaching material

Recap: Upon analyzing her situation using a Duncker Diagram, Linda discovered the real problem was the high stress level brought on by the unruly classes she had the year before her six-month leave. Consequently, with the aid of a Duncker Diagram, she arrived at the conclusion that the *real* problem was she should find ways to lower her stress level at her workplace.

[†]Based on an actual case history.

Let us consider the application of the Duncker Diagram to the following To Market, To Market example.

To Market, To Market

The Situation: Toasty O's was one of the hottest selling cereals when it first came on the market. However, after several months, sales dropped. The consumer survey department was able to identify that customer dissatisfaction was expressed in terms of a stale taste. <u>The instructions given to solve the perceived problem:</u> *"Streamline the production process to get the cereal on the store shelves faster, thus ensuring a fresher product."* However, there wasn't much stack time that could be removed from the process to accomplish the goal. Of the steps required to get the product on the shelves (production, packaging, storage, and shipping), production was one of the fastest. Thus, plans for building plants closer to the major markets were considered, as were plans for adding more trucks in order to get the cereal to market faster. The addition of new plants and trucks was going to require a major capital investment to solve the problem.

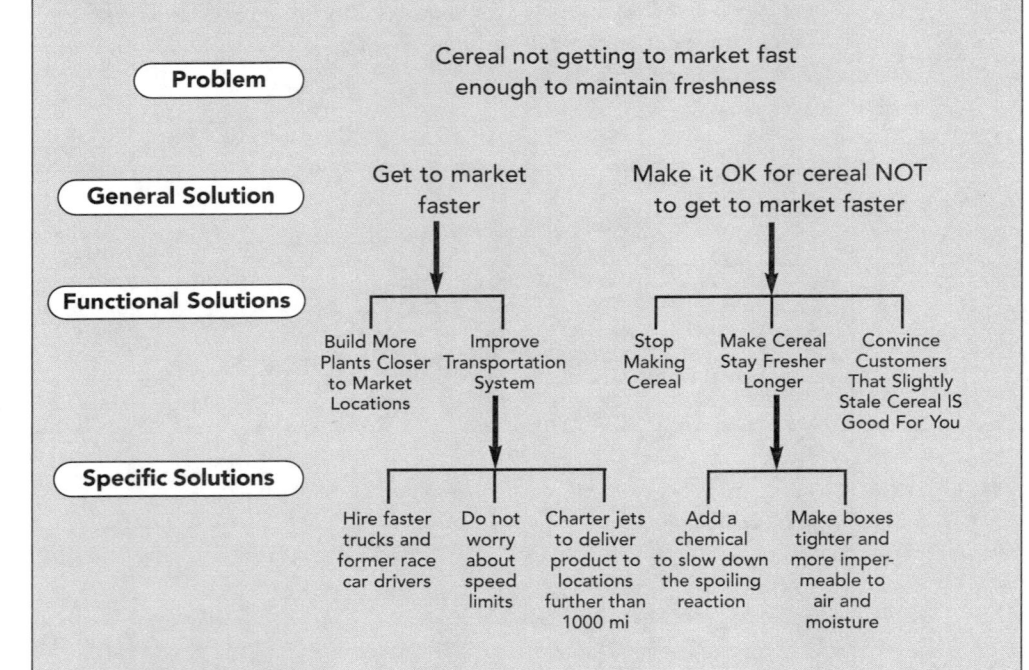

Problem: Cereal not getting to market fast enough to maintain freshness

General Solution:
- Get to market faster
- Make it OK for cereal NOT to get to market faster

Functional Solutions:
- Build More Plants Closer to Market Locations
- Improve Transportation System
- Stop Making Cereal
- Make Cereal Stay Fresher Longer
- Convince Customers That Slightly Stale Cereal IS Good For You

Specific Solutions:
- Hire faster trucks and former race car drivers
- Do not worry about speed limits
- Charter jets to deliver product to locations further than 1000 mi
- Add a chemical to slow down the spoiling reaction
- Make boxes tighter and more impermeable to air and moisture

The ***real problem*** was that the cereal was not staying fresh long enough, not that it wasn't getting to market fast enough. Keeping the cereal fresher longer was achieved by improved packaging and the use of additives to slow the rate of staling.

Using the Statement-Restatement Technique

This technique is similar to the Present State/Desired State technique in that it requires us to rephrase the problem statement. The *Statement-Restatement* technique was developed by Parnes,[4] a researcher in problem solving and creativity. Here, one looks at the fuzzy or unclear problem situation and writes a statement regarding a challenge to be addressed. The problem is then restated in different forms a number of times. Each time the problem is restated, one tries to generalize it further in order to arrive at the broadest form of the problem statement.

In restating the problem it is important to inject new ideas, rather than changing only the word order in the restated sentence. The following problem restatement *triggers* should prove helpful in arriving at a definitive problem statement.

As an illustration of the use of these triggers, consider *trigger 3* below. Instead of asking "How can my company make the biggest profit?" ask "How can my company lose the most money?" In finding the key activities or pieces of equipment which, when operated inefficiently, will give the biggest loss, we will have found those pieces that need to be carefully monitored and controlled. This trigger helps us find the *sensitivity* of the system and to focus on those variables that dominate.

It is often helpful to *relax constraints* on the problem, modify the criteria, and idealize the problem when writing the restatement sentence (see trigger 4). Also, does the problem statement change when different time scales are imposed (i.e., are the long-term implications different from the short-term implications)? As one continues to restate and perhaps combine previous restatements, one should also focus on tightening up the problem statement, eliminating ambiguous words, and moving away from a fuzzy, loose, ill-defined statement.

Table 3–3. Problem Statement Triggers

1. Vary the stress pattern—try placing emphasis on different words and phrases.
2. Choose a term that has an explicit definition and substitute the explicit definition in each place that the term appears.
3. Make an opposite statement, change positives to negatives, and vice versa.
4. Change "every" to "some," "always" to "sometimes," "sometimes" to "never," and vice versa.
5. Replace "persuasive words" in the problem statement such as "obviously," "clearly," and "certainly" with the argument it is supposed to be replacing.
6. Express words in the form of an equation or picture, and vice versa.

Using the Triggers

Original Problem Statement: Cereal not getting to market fast enough to maintain freshness.

Trigger 1
- *Cereal* not getting to market fast enough to maintain freshness.
  (Do other products we have get there faster?)
- Cereal not *getting* to market fast enough to maintain freshness.
  (Can we make the distance/time shorter?)
- Cereal not getting to *market* fast enough to maintain freshness.
  (Can we distribute from a centralized location?)
- Cereal not getting to market fast enough to maintain *freshness*.
  (How can we keep cereal fresher, longer?)

Trigger 2
- *Breakfast food that comes in a box* is not getting to *the place where it is sold* fast enough to keep it from *getting stale*.
  (Makes us think about the box and staleness . . . what changes might we make to the box to prevent staleness?)

Trigger 3
- How can we find a way to get the cereal to market *so slowly* that it will *never* be fresh?
  (Makes us think about how long we have to maintain freshness and what controls it?)

Trigger 4
- Cereal is not getting to market fast enough to *always* maintain freshness.
  (This change opens new avenues of thought. Why isn't our cereal *always* fresh?)

Trigger 5
- The problem statement implies that we obviously want to get the cereal to market faster to maintain freshness.
  Thus, if we could speed up delivery freshness would be maintained. Maybe not! Maybe the store holds it too long. Maybe it's stale before it gets to the store.
  (This trigger helps us challenge implicit assumptions made in the problem statement.)

Trigger 6
- Freshness is inversely proportional to the time since the cereal was baked, i.e.,

$$(\text{Freshness}) = \frac{k}{(\text{Time Since Baked})}$$

Makes us think of other ways to attack the freshness problem. For example, what does the proportionally constant, *k*, depend upon?

The storage conditions, packaging, type of cereal, etc. are logical variables to examine. How can we change the value of *k*?

The total time may be shortened by reducing the time at the factory, the delivery time, or the time to sell the cereal (i.e., shelf time). So, again, this trigger provides us with several alternative approaches to examine to solve the problem? Reduce the time *or* change (increase) *k*.

> **Making an Opposite Statement**
>
> The Situation: To many people, taking aspirin tablets is a foul-tasting experience. A few years ago, a number of companies making aspirin decided to do something about it. <u>The instructions given by the manager to his staff to solve the perceived problem were:</u> "*Find a way to put a pleasant-tasting coating on aspirin tablets.*" Spraying the coating on the tablets had been tried, with very little success. The resulting coating was very nonuniform and this led to an unacceptable product. Let's apply the triggers to this problem.
>
> **Trigger 1** Emphasize different parts of statement
> 1. **Put** coating **on** tablet.
>
> **Trigger 3** Make an opposite statement
> 2. **Take** coating **off** tablet.
>
> This idea led to one of the newer techniques for coating pills. The pills are immersed in a liquid which is passed onto a spinning disk. The centrifugal force on the fluid and the pills causes the two to separate, leaving a nice, even coating around the pill.

An example from reliable, although undocumented, sources that elucidates the need to find the real problem is one related to the early research on the reentry of space capsules to the earth's atmosphere. It was evident that available materials would not withstand the temperatures from frictional heating by the atmosphere. Consequently, a directive went out to find a material to withstand the temperatures encountered on reentry. Application of the Statement-Restatement technique to this problem is shown in the gray box on the next page.

The real problem here was to protect the astronauts (restatement 3) rather than find a material that would withstand high temperatures. Once the real problem was found, an appropriate solution to the capsule reentry problem soon followed.

> ### Wanted: Exotic Materials, or . . .?
>
> ***The Situation:*** In the 1960s scientists recognized that there was no available material that would survive the high temperatures generated on the capsule's surface during reentry to the earth's atmosphere. <u>Consequently, a government directive went out to</u> "*find a material able to withstand the temperatures encountered on reentry.*" By the early 1970s no one had produced a suitable material that satisfied the directive, yet we had sent astronauts to the moon and back. How had this achievement been possible? The **real problem** was to protect the astronauts upon reentry, rather than to find a material that would withstand such high temperatures. Once the real problem was determined, a solution soon followed. One of the scientists working on the project asked a related question: How do meteors eventually reach the earth's surface without disintegrating completely? Upon investigation of this problem, he found that although the surface of the meteor vaporized while passing through the atmosphere, the inside of the meteor was not damaged. This analogy led to the idea of using materials on the outside of the capsule that would vaporize when exposed to the high temperatures encountered during reentry. Consequently, the heat generated by friction with the earth's atmosphere during reentry would be dissipated by the vaporization of a material that coated the outside of the space capsule. By sacrificing this material, the temperatures of the capsule's underlying structural material remained at a tolerable level to protect the astronauts. Once the real problem was uncovered, the scientists solved the problem by using analogies and transferring ideas from one situation to another.
>
> **Statement-Restatement**
>
> The statement-restatement technique might have been used as follows:
>
> *Statement 1:* Find a material that will withstand the high surface temperature of the capsule resulting from frictional heating upon reentry into the earth's atmosphere.
>
> *Restatement 1:* Find a way to slow the reentry into the earth's atmosphere or to redesign the capsule so that the capsule surface temperature will be lower.
>
> *Restatement 2:* Find a way to cool the capsule or absorb the frictional energy during reentry so that the surface temperature will be lower.
>
> *Restatement 3:* Find a way to protect the astronauts on their reentry into the earth's atmosphere.
>
> *Restatement 4:* Find a disposable material that could surround the capsule and could be sacrificed to absorb the frictional heating.

Evaluating the Problem Definition

Now that we have used one or more of the preceding techniques to define the problem, we need to check to make sure we are going in the right direction. Consequently, we need to evaluate the problem definition before proceeding further. The following checklist could help us in this evaluation.

- Have all the pieces of the problem been identified?
- Have all the constraints been identified?

- What is missing from the problem definition?
- Have you challenged the assumptions and information you were given to formulate the problem?
- Have you distinguished fact from opinion?

The Next Four Steps

We now extend the first steps experienced problem solvers recommend and continue Table 3–1 in Table 3–4.

Step 5. Determine if the problem should be solved.

Having defined the real problem, we now need to develop criteria by which to judge the solution to the real problem. One of the first questions experienced engineers ask is: Should the problem be solved? The first step is to determine if a solution to an identical or similar problem is available. A literature search may determine if a solution exists.

How do experienced problem solvers go about deciding if the problem is *worth* solving? Perhaps it is just mildly irritating and consequently may be ignored altogether. (For instance, suppose the garage door at your plant's warehouse facility is too narrow for easy access by some of the delivery vehicles. They can pass through, but the clearance is very tight. This is an annoying problem, but if the fix is quite costly, you could probably "live with it.") Questions you should ask early in the process are: What are the resources available to solve the problem? How many people can you allocate to the problem, and for how long a time? How soon do you need a solution? Today? Tomorrow? Next year? These are key questions to keep in mind as you take your first steps along the way to a problem solution. The quality of your solution is often, but not always, related to the time and money you have to *generate it and carry it through*. In some instances it may be necessary to extend deadlines in order to obtain a quality solution.

Table 3–4. What Experienced Problem Solvers Say

The First Four Steps of Experienced Problem Solvers
1. Collect and analyze information and data.
2. Talk with people familiar with the problem.
3. If at all possible, view the problem firsthand.
4. Confirm all findings.

The Next Four Steps
5. Determine if the problem should be solved.
6. Continue to gather information and search the literature.
7. Form simple hypotheses and quickly test them.
8. Brainstorm potential causes and solution alternatives.

It may not be possible to completely address the cost issue until we are further along in the solution process. The cost will depend on whether or not the solution will be a permanent one or if it will be a temporary or patchwork solution. Sometimes *two* solutions are required. One to treat short-term symptoms to keep the process operating and one to solve the real problem for the long term. Be aware of these two mindsets in the problem-solving process. In some cases the **No's** in the figure on deciding if the problem should be solved can be changed to **Yes's** by *selling* the project to management. This change can be achieved by showing that the problem is an important one and is relevant to the operation of the company.

Step 6. Continue to gather information and search the literature.

Gather as much information as possible by reading texts and literature related to the problem to learn the underlying fundamental principles and peripheral concepts. Literature searches are particularly helpful. Perhaps a closely related problem has already been solved. George Quarderer of Dow Chemical Company appropriately describes the idea of reinventing the wheel by his statement, *"Four to six weeks in the laboratory can save you an hour in the library."* The message is clear: Doing a bit of research into the background of the problem may save you hours of time and effort.

Search out colleagues who may have useful information and pertinent ideas. Have them play **"What if . . . ?"** with you; that is, "What if you did this?" or "What if I applied this concept?" Also have them play the devil's advocate and deliberately challenge your ideas. This technique stimulates creative interactions.

Step 7. Form simple hypotheses and quickly test them.

Returning to the Dead Fish example, an experienced problem solver could hypothesize that there was something else present in the water that was killing the fish. This hypothesis could be tested in the laboratory by analyzing samples of river water or by performing post-mortem examinations on the dead fish. These tests may have uncovered the presence of the fungus, thereby quickly defining the problem.

Step 8. Brainstorm potential causes and solution alternatives.

This last "first step" brings us to the close of the first phase of the creative problem-solving process and is really the first step of the second phase of the process: Generating Solutions to Problems. Techniques to generate solutions will be discussed in the next chapter.

Which Techniques to Choose

We do not expect the reader to apply every technique to every situation. In fact, when 400 problem solvers were surveyed to which two techniques presented in this chapter were the most useful, *the choices were virtually equally divided among those presented in this chapter.* In other words, different techniques work better for different individuals and different situations, and it is a personal choice. The main point is to be organized as well as creative in your approach to problem definition.

> **Summary**
>
> In this chapter we have discussed the necessity for defining the real problem. We have presented the eight steps that experienced problem solvers first use to attack problems. They are
>
> - Collect and analyze information and data.
> - Talk with people familiar with the problem.
> - If at all possible, view the problem firsthand.
> - Confirm all findings.
> - Determine if the problem should be solved.
> - Continue to gather information and search the literature.
> - Form simple hypotheses and quickly test them.
> - Brainstorm potential causes and solution alternatives.
>
> Five problem definition techniques were presented to help you zero in on the true problem definition. They are
>
> - *Find Out Where the Problem Came From*
>   - Use the first four steps to gather information.
>   - Learn who defined the problem initially.
>   - Challenge reasoning and assumptions made to arrive at the problem statement given to you.
>
> - *Explore the Problem*
>   - Recall or learn the fundamental principles related to the problem.
>   - Carry out an order-of-magnitude calculation.
>   - Hypothesize what could be wrong.
>   - Guess the result.
>
> - *Present State/Desired State*
>   - Write a statement of where you are and a statement of what you want to achieve and make sure they match.
>
> - *Duncker Diagram*
>   - Devise a pathway that makes it OK not to solve the problem posed to you.
>
> - *Statement-Restatement*
>   - Use the six triggers to restate the problem in a number of different ways.

References

1. Kepner, C. H., and B. B. Tregoe, *The New Rational Manager,* Princeton Research Press, Princeton, NJ. 1981.
2. Woods, D. R., *A Strategy for Problem Solving,* 3rd ed., Department of Chemical Engineering, McMaster University, Hamilton, Ontario, 1985; *Chem. Eng. Educ.,* p. 132, Summer 1979, *AIChE Symposium Series,* 79 (228), 1983.
3. Higgins, J. S., et al., "Identifying and Solving Problems in Engineering Design," *Studies in Higher Education,* 14, No. 2, p. 169, 1989.
4. Parnes, S. J., *Creative Behavior Workbook,* Scribner, New York, 1967.

Further Reading

Copulsky, William, "Vision → Innovation," *Chemtech,* 19, p. 279, May 1989 Interesting anecdotes on problem definition and vision related to a number of popular products.

DeBono, Edward, *"Serious Creativity,"* Harper Business, a division of Harper Collins Publishers, New York, 1993. Summary of 20 years of creativity researched by deBono. Many useful additional problem definition techniques are presented.

Exercises

1. Make a list of the most important things you learned from this chapter. Identify at least three techniques that you believe will change the ways you think about defining and solving problems. Which problem definition techniques do you find most useful? Prepare a matrix table listing all the problem definition techniques discussed in this chapter. Identify those attributes that some of the techniques have in common and also those attributes that are unique to a given technique.

	Attribute 1	Attribute 2	Attribute 3
Technique A	X		X
Technique B		X	
Technique C	X	X	

2. Write a sentence describing a problem you have. Apply the triggers in the *Statement-Restatement Technique* to your problem.

Perceived Problem Statement _____
_____
_____

Restatement 1 _____
_____
_____
_____

Restatement 2 _____
_____
_____
_____

Final Problem Statement _____
_____
_____
_____

Next apply the Duncker Diagram to this same problem. (Use the Duncker Diagram work sheet on page 59.)

3. Carry out a *Present State/Desired State* analysis on "I want a summer internship but no one is hiring" and then prepare a Duncker Diagram to solve the problem.

4. You have had a very hectic morning, so you leave work a little early to relax a bit before you meet your supervisor, who is flying into a nearby airport. You have not seen your supervisor from the home office for about a year now. He has written to you saying that he wants to meet with you personally to discuss the last project. Through no fault of yours, everything went wrong: The oil embargo delayed shipment of all the key parts, your project manager met with a skiing accident, and your secretary enclosed the key files in a parcel that was sent, by mistake, to Japan via sea mail. Your supervisor thinks that you have been so careless on this project that you would lock yourself out of your own car.

As you are driving through the pleasant countryside on this chilly late fall afternoon, you realize that you will be an hour early. You spot a rather secluded roadside park about 200 m away. A quiet stream bubbles through the park, containing trees in all their autumn colors. Such an ideal place to just get out and relax. You pull off into the park, absentmindedly get out and lock the car, and stroll by the stream. When you return, you find the keys are locked in the car. The road to the airport is not the usual route; there are cars about every 10 to 15 minutes. The airport is 9 km away; the nearest house (with a telephone) is 1 km away. The plane is due to arrive in 20 minutes. Your car, which is not a convertible, is such that you cannot get under the hood or into the trunk from the outside. All the windows are up and secured. Apply the Duncker Diagram and one other problem-solving technique to help decide what to do. (D. R. Woods, McMaster University)

5. You are driving from Cambridge to London on the M11 motorway (expressway). You are scheduled to give a very important slide presentation at 1 PM. The drive normally takes 1 hr and 30 minutes but this morning you left at 10:30 AM to insure you had sufficient time. Suddenly your car stalls on the motorway halfway between Cambridge and London. What do you do? Apply two or more problem definition techniques to help answer this problem. (From J. Higgins and S. Richardson, Imperial College, London)

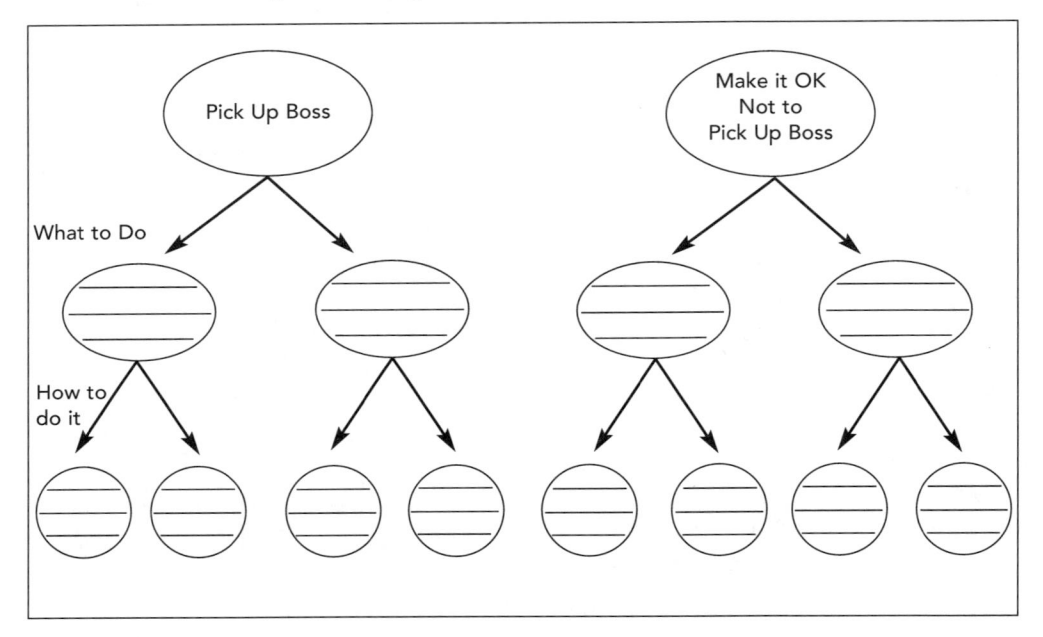

6. A propellant used in an air bag system is the chemical sodium azide. It is mixed with an oxidizing agent and pressed into pellets which are hermetically sealed into a steel or aluminum can. Upon impact, ignition of the pelletized sodium azide generates nitrogen gas that inflates the air bag. Unfortunately, if it contacts acids or heavy metal (e.g., lead, copper, mercury and their alloys), it forms toxic and sensitive explosives. Consequently, at the end of an automobile's life, a serious problem surfaces when an automobile with an undetonated airbag is sent to the junk yard for compacting and shredding, whereby it could contact heavy metals. The potential for an explosion during processing represents a serious danger for those operating the scrap recycling plant. Apply two or three problem definition techniques to this situation. (*Chemtech*, 23, p. 54, 1993)

7. Pillsbury, a leader in the manufacture of high-quality baking products, had its origins in the manufacture of flour for the baking industry. However, at the time Charles Pillsbury purchased his first mill in Minneapolis, the wheat from Minnesota was considered to be substandard when compared to the wheat used in the St. Louis mills, then the hub of the milling industry. Part of the problem was that winter wheat, commonly used in high-grade flour, could not be grown in Minnesota because of the long and cold winters. Consequently, the Minnesota mills were forced to use spring wheat which had a harder shell. At the time, the most commonly used milling machines used a "low grinding" process to separate the wheat from the chaff. The low grinding process refers to using stone wheels. A stone wheel rests directly on the bottom wheel, with the wheat to be ground placed between them. With harder wheats, a large amount of heat was generated, discoloring and degrading the product quality. Thus, the flour produced from the Minnesota mills was discolored, inferior, and had less nutritional value and a shorter shelf life. The directions given could have been "Order more river barges to ship winter wheat up the Mississippi from St. Louis to Minneapolis." Apply two or more problem definition techniques to the situation. (Adapted from "When in Rome" by Jane Ammeson, *Northwestern Airlines World Traveler,* 25, No. 3, p. 20, 1993.)

8. *Late Baggage.* An airline at the Houston Airport tried to please the passengers by always docking the plane at a gate within a one to two minute walk to the airport entrance and baggage claim and by having all the bags at baggage claim within eight to ten minutes. However, many complaints were received by the airline about the time it took to get the bags to the claim area. The airline researched the situation and found that there was virtually no way they could unload the bags to the transport trucks, drive to the unloading zone, and unload the bags any faster. However, the airline didn't change the baggage unloading procedure, but did change another component of the arrival process and the complaints disappeared. The airline did not use mirrors to solve the problem as was the case for the slow elevators. (a) What was the real problem? (b) Suggest a number of things that you think the airline might have done to eliminate the complaints. Apply two or more problem-solving techniques. (*The Washington Post,* p. A3, Dec. 14, 1992)

9. In 1991, 64% of all commercial radio stations in the country lost money. In order for a radio station to remain solvent it must have significant revenue from advertisers. Advertisers, in turn, target the market they consider desirable (i.e., income, spending, interest), and for the past several years this target has been the age group from 25 to 54. Along with the revenue loss, the number of radio stations playing the Top 40 songs (i.e., the 40 most popular songs of that week) has decreased by a factor of 2 in the past three years, as did the audience for the Top 40 songs. Many stations tried playing a blend of current hits with hits of 10 and 20 years ago; however, this blend irritated the younger listeners and also did not seem to solve the economic problem. Apply two or more problem definition techniques to this situation. (Adapted from *The International Herald Tribune,* p. 7, March 24, 1993.)

10. ***The situation:*** Sara is a freshman away at college preparing for her first final exams. She is homesick, stressed out, and would like to go home for the weekend to visit her parents, but her car is not working.

Present State	Desired State
Sara's car is not working.	At home with her parents.

Discussion: These states do not match and this mismatch confuses the problem. Which problem should she be attacking? The malfunctioning car? The visit?

First Revision.

Present State	Desired State

Continue in this manner until the states match.

11. ***The situation:*** FireKing is a small manufacturer of rich looking fireproof filing cabinets and wanted to increase its market share of 3%. While the designs were elegant, the cabinets were also the heaviest ones on the market and in people's minds, this meant the highest quality. However, higher weight meant higher shipping and transportation costs which made them very expensive. FireKing asked the following question, "How can we make our product lighter so as to have a competitive price?" However, some executives believed a lighter product might hurt the image of quality. Apply one or more problem definition techniques to this situation. (David Turczyn)

12. ***The situation:*** A new method for killing roaches was developed by Bug-B-Gone Company which was more effective than any of the other leading products. In fact, no spraying was necessary because the active ingredient was in a container that is placed on the floor or in corners and the roach problem would disappear. This method has the advantage that product does all the work. The user does not need to search out and spray the live roaches. The product was test marketed to housewives in some southern states. Everyone who saw the effectiveness test results agreed the new product was superior in killing roaches. However despite a massive ad campaign, the standard roach sprays were still far outselling the new product. Apply one or more problem definition techniques to this situation. (David Turczyn)

13. ***The situation:*** A pneumatic conveyor is a device that transports powdered solids using air in the same manner that money is transported from your car at a bank's drive-through window. In the figure below, the solids are "sucked" out of the storage hopper and conveyed by air into the discharge hopper.

The instructions given to solve the perceived problem: *"Find an easier way to clean a pneumatic conveying system when it plugs and interrupts operation."*

First Revision.

Present State	Desired State
Conveying system plugs, interrupting operation.	The system is easily and rapidly cleaned.

Continue in this manner until the states match.

14. ***The situation:*** A major American soap company carried out a massive advertising campaign to expand its market into Poland. The T. V. commercials featured a beautiful woman using the company's soap during her morning shower. Thousands of sample cakes were distributed door to door throughout the country. Despite these massive promotional efforts, the campaign was entirely unsuccessful. Polish television had been used primarily for communist party politics, and commercials were relatively rare. What is aired is usually party line politics. Apply one or more problem definition techniques to this situation. (Christina Nusbaum)

15. ***The situation:*** Employees are allowed to take merchandise out of the department store on approval. The original procedure required the employee to write an approval slip stating the merchandise taken. However, some employees were abusing the system by taking the clothing and destroying the slip, thereby leaving no record of the removed merchandise. Apply one or more problem definition techniques to this situation. (Maggie Michael)

DUNCKER DIAGRAM WORKSHEET

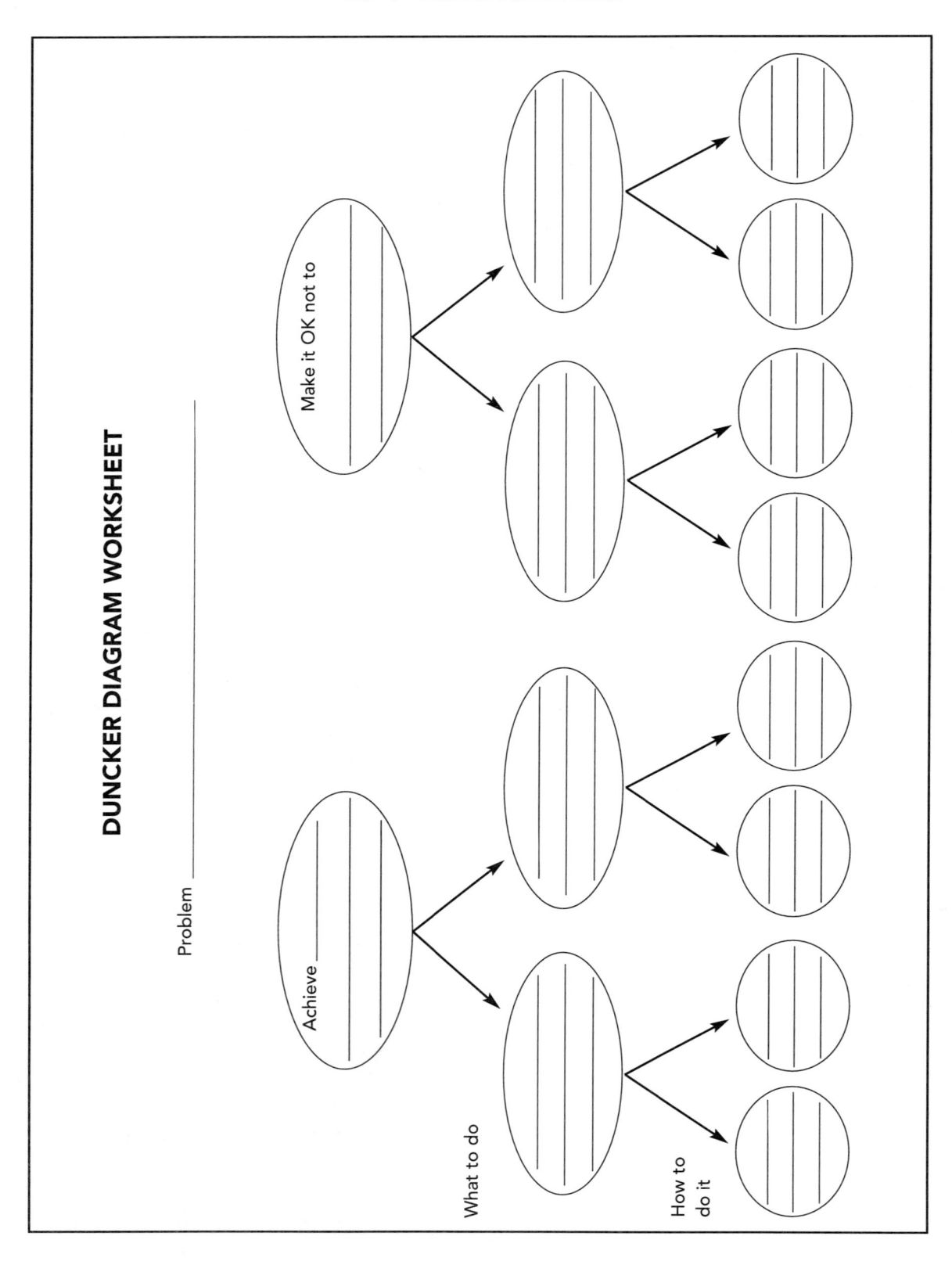

Problem _____

Achieve _____

Make it OK not to _____

What to do

How to do it

CHAPTER 6

Generating Solutions

> *Nothing is more dangerous than an idea, when it is the only one you have.*
>
> —Emile Chartier

Once you have defined the problem you want to make sure you generate the best solution. Sometimes problems may seem unsolvable or they may appear to have only one solution, which as Emile Chartier points out is quite dangerous. This is a situation where you can use the idea generation technique in this chapter to lead you to find the best solutions. Perseverance is perhaps the most notable characteristic of successful problem solvers, so you shouldn't become discouraged when solutions aren't immediately evident. Many times mental blocks hinder your progress toward a solution. The first step to overcoming these blocks is to recognize them, and then use blockbusting techniques to move forward toward the best solution.

Common Causes of Mental Blocks

- Defining the problem too narrowly.
- Attacking the symptoms and not the real problem.
- Assuming there is only one right answer.
- Getting "hooked" on the first solution that comes to mind.
- Getting "hooked" on a solution that almost works (but really doesn't).
- Being distracted by irrelevant information, called "mental dazzle."
- Getting frustrated by lack of success.
- Being too anxious to finish.
- Defining the problem ambiguously.

What is the nature of these mental blocks and what causes them? Some common causes of blocks have been summarized by Higgins et al.:[1]

There is a direct correlation between the time people spend "playing" with a problem and the diversity of the solutions generated. Don't be afraid to "play" with the problem. Let's look at how easy it is to have a conceptual block to a problem. Try this exercise *before* reading the several solutions provided.

> **The Nine Dot Problem**
> Draw four or fewer straight lines (without lifting the pencil from the paper) that will cross through all nine dots. (Adams,[2] pp. 16–20)
>
> • • •
> • • •
> • • •

This puzzle is very difficult to solve if the imaginary boundary created by the eight outer dots is not crossed. Another common assumption that is not part of the problem statement is that the lines must go through the centers of the dots. Two possible solutions are provided below.

> **Two Solutions to the Nine Dot Problem**

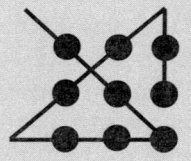

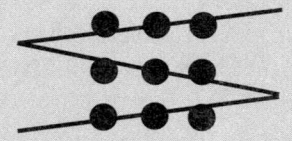

Several other creative solutions to the nine dot problem exist. These include rolling up the piece of paper such that it is cylindrical in shape and then drawing one line around the cylinder that passes through all nine dots, or photoreducing the nine dots and then using a thick felt pen to connect them with a single line. Another suggestion is to crumple up the piece of paper and stab it with a pencil (this is a statistical approach that may require more than one attempt to hit all the dots).

The purpose of this exercise is to show that putting too many constraints (either consciously or unconsciously) on the problem statement narrows the range of possible solutions. Normally, novice problem solvers will not cross a perceived imaginary limit—a constraint that is formed unconsciously in the mind of the problem solver—even though it is not part of the problem statement. Whenever you are faced with a problem, recall the nine dots to remind yourself to challenge the constraints.

Recognizing Mental Blocks

Conceptual Blockbusting by James L. Adams[2] focuses on the cultivation of idea-generating and problem-solving abilities. The first step to becoming a better problem solver is to understand what conceptual blocks are and how they interfere with problem solving. A conceptual block is a mental wall that prevents the problem solver from correctly perceiving a problem or conceiving its solution. The most frequently occurring conceptual blocks are perceptual blocks, emotional blocks, cultural blocks, environmental blocks, intellectual blocks, and expressive blocks.

A. **Perceptual Blocks** are obstacles that prevent the problem solver from clearly perceiving either the problem itself or the information needed to solve it. A few types of perceptual blocks are

- *Stereotyping*

    Survival training teaches individuals to make full use of all the resources at their disposal when they are faced with a life-threatening situation. For example, if you were stranded in the desert after the crash of your small airplane, you would have to make creative use of your available resources to survive and be rescued. Consider the flashlight that was in your tool kit. The *stereotypical* use for it would be for signaling, finding things in the dark, etc. But how about using the batteries to start a fire, the casing for a drinking vessel for water that you find in the desert cacti, or the reflector as a signaling mirror in the daylight, etc.

- *Limiting the problem unnecessarily*

    The nine dot problem above is an example of limiting the problem *unnecessarily*. The boundaries of the problem must be explored and challenged.

- *Saturation or information overload*

    Too much information can be nearly as big a problem as not enough information. You can become overloaded with minute details and be unable to sort out the critical aspects of the problem. Air traffic controllers have learned to overcome this block. They face information overload regularly in the course of their jobs, particularly during bad weather. They are skilled in sorting out the essential information to ensure safe landings and takeoffs for thousands of aircraft daily.

B. **Emotional Blocks** interfere with your ability to solve problems in many ways. They decrease the amount of freedom with which you explore and manipulate ideas, and they interfere with your ability to conceptualize fluently and flexibly. Emotional blocks also prevent you from communicating your ideas to others in a manner that will gain their approval. Some types of emotional blocks include:

- *Fear of risk taking*

    This block usually stems from childhood. Most people grow up being rewarded for solving problems correctly and punished for solving problems incorrectly. Implementing a creative idea is like taking a risk. You take the risk of making a mistake, looking foolish, losing your job, or in a student's case, getting an unacceptable grade.

- *Lack of appetite for chaos*

    Problem solvers must learn to live with confusion. For example, the criteria for the best solution may seem contradictory. What may be best for the individual may not be best for the organization or group.

- *Judging rather than generating ideas*

    This block can stem from approaching the problem with a negative attitude. Judging ideas too quickly can discourage even the most creative problem solvers. Wild ideas can sometimes trigger feasible ideas which lead to innovative solutions. This block can be avoided by approaching the problem with a positive attitude.

- *Lack of challenge*

    Sometimes, problem solvers don't want to get started because they perceive the problem is too trivial and can be easily solved. They feel that the problem is not worthy of their efforts.

- *Inability to incubate*

    Rushing to solve the problem just to get it off your mind can create blocks.

C. **Cultural Blocks** are acquired by exposure to a given set of cultural patterns, and environmental blocks are imposed by our immediate social and physical environment. One type of cultural block is the failure to consider an act that causes displeasure or disgust to certain members of society.

Rescuing a Ping Pong Ball

Two pipes, which serve as pole mounts for a volleyball net, are embedded in the floor of a gymnasium. During a game of ping pong, the ball accidentally rolls into one of the pipes because the pipe cover was not replaced. The inside pipe diameter is 0.06" larger than the diameter of a ping-pong ball (1.50") which is resting gently at the bottom of the pipe. You are one of a group of six people in the gym, along with the following objects:

A 15' extension cord	A file
A carpenter's hammer	A wire coat hanger
A chisel	A monkey wrench
A bag of potato chips	A flash light

List as many ways as you can think of (in five minutes) to get the ball out of the pipe without leaving the gym, or damaging the ball, pipe, or floor.

Comment: A common solution to the problem is to smash the handle of the hammer with the monkey wrench and to use the splinters to obtain the ball. Another less obvious solution is to urinate in the pipe. Many people do not think of this solution because of a cultural block, since urination is considered a "private" activity in many countries.

Other types of mental blocks are

D. **Environmental Blocks:** Distractions (phones, easy intrusions) are blocks that inhibit deep prolonged concentration. Working in an atmosphere that is pleasant and supportive most often increases the productivity of the problem solver. On the other hand, working under conditions where there is a lack of emotional, physical, economical, or organizational support to bring ideas into action usually has a negative effect on the problem solver and decreases the level of productivity. Ideas for establishing a working environment that enhance creativity were presented in Chapter 2.

E. **Intellectual Blocks:** This block can occur as a result of inflexible or inadequate uses of problem-solving strategies. Lacking the necessary intellectual skills to solve a problem can certainly be a block as can lack of the information necessary to solve the problem. For example, attempting to solve complicated satellite communications problems without sufficient background in the area would soon result in blocked progress. Additional background, training, or resources may be necessary to solve a problem. Don't be afraid to ask for help.

F. **Expressive Blocks:** The inability to communicate your ideas to others, in either verbal or written form, can also block your progress. Anyone who has played a game of charades or Pictionary™ can certainly relate to the difficulties that this type of block can cause. Make sketches, drawings, and don't be afraid to take time to explain your problem to others.

As we have just seen, there are many types and causes of mental blocks. If you find your problem-solving efforts afflicted by one of them, what can you do? Try one of the blockbusting techniques that we present next!

Blockbusting

A number of structured techniques are available for breaking through mental roadblocks.[3] Collectively, they are referred to as blockbusting techniques. Goman identifies a number of blocks to creativity and offers some suggestions on how to overcome these blocks.[4] The table on the next page summarizes these blocks and blockbusters.

In regard to Goman's fifth Blockbuster, Raudelsepp has presented definitive ways you can increase your creativity by learning new attitudes, values, and ways of approaching and solving problems by heeding the principles[5] on page 127.

Dr. Edward deBono, the international creativity authority, is serious about the need for creative thinking.[6] In his book *Serious Creativity*, deBono, the father of lateral thinking, takes the opportunity to summarize 25 years of research into creative thinking techniques.

Remember, one of the first steps in the problem solving process recommended by experienced problem solvers was the gathering of information. deBono cautions problem solvers in this regard. For example, when one begins working on a new problem or research topic, it is normal to read a>>>ll the information available on the problem. To fail to do this may mean "reinventing the wheel" and wasting much time. However, during the course of information gathering, you may destroy your chances of obtaining an original and creative solution if you are not careful. As you read, you will be exposed to all the existing assumptions and prejudices that have been developed by previous workers or researchers. Try as you may to remain objective and orig-

> ### Goman's Blockbusters
>
> | Block | Blockbuster |
> |---|---|
> | *1. Negative Attitude*
Focusing attention on negative aspects of the problem and possible unsatisfactory outcomes hampers creativity. | *1. Attitude Adjustment*
List the positive aspects and outcomes of the problem. Realize that with every problem there is not only a danger of failure but an opportunity for success. |
> | *2. Fear of Failure*
One of the greatest inhibitors to creativity is the fear of failure and the inability to take a risk. | *2. Risk Taking*
Outline what the risk is, why it is important, what is the worst possible outcome, what your options are with the worst possible outcome, and how you would deal with this failure. |
> | *3. Following the Rules*
Some rules are necessary, such as stopping at a red light, while other rules hinder innovation. | *3. Breaking the Rules*
Practice trying new things. Take a different route to work, try a new food, go somewhere you've never gone. |
> | *4. Overreliance on Logic*
Relegate imagination to the background because of a need to proceed in a step-by-step fashion. | *4. Internal Creative Climate*
Turn the situation over to your imagination, your feelings, your sense of humor. Play with insights and possibilities. |
> | *5. You Aren't Creative*
Believing that you are not creative can be a serious hinderance to generating creative solutions. **Believing that you can't do something is a self-fulfilling prophesy.** | *5. Creative Beliefs*
Encourage your creativity by asking "what if" questions; daydream; make up metaphors and analogies. Try different ways of expressing your creativity. |

inal, your innocence will have been been lost. deBono recommends reading enough to familiarize yourself with the problem and get a "feel" for it. At this point you may wish to stop and organize some of your own ideas before proceeding with an exhaustive review of the literature. In this way you can best preserve your opportunities for creativity and innovation.

Have you ever heard the old saying: *"If it ain't broke, don't fix it?"* deBono claims the attitude reflected by this statement was largely responsible for the decline of American industry. American managers operated in a strictly reactive mode, merely responding to problems as they arose. Meanwhile, the Japanese were fixing and improving things that weren't problems. Soon, the American "problem fixers" were left behind. To survive in today's business culture, proactive thinking, as opposed to reactive thinking, is required. This shift in thinking patterns requires creativity.

deBono summarizes a number of lateral thinking techniques that he popularized to improve creative thinking. These include random stimulation and the Six Thinking Hats. We will discuss random stimulation in this chapter. The Six Thinking Hats is an application of creative thinking that deBono advocates for many situations. The

Improving Your Creative Abilities

- *Keep track of your ideas at all times.* Many times ideas come at unexpected times. If an idea is not written down within 24 hours it will usually be forgotten.
- *Pose new questions to yourself every day.* An inquiring mind is a creatively active one that enlarges its area of awareness.
- *Keep abreast of your field.* Read the magazines, trade journals, and other literature in your field to make sure you are not using yesterday's technology to solve today's problems.
- *Learn about things outside your specialty.* Use cross-fertilization to bring ideas and concepts from one field or specialty to another.
- *Avoid rigid, set patterns of doing things.* Overcome biases and preconceived notions by looking at the problem from a fresh view point, always developing at least two or more alternative solutions to your problem.
- *Be open and receptive to ideas (yours and others).* Rarely does an innovative solution or idea arrive complete with all its parts ready to be implemented. New ideas are fragile; keep them from breaking by seizing on the tentative, half-formed concepts and possibilities and developing them.
- *Be alert in your observations.* This principle is a key to successfully applying the Kepner-Tregoe strategies discussed in the next chapter. Be alert by looking for similarities, differences, as well as unique and distinguishing features in situations and problems. The larger the number of relationships you can identify, the better your chances will be of generating original combinations and creative solutions.
- *Adopt a risk taking attitude.* Fear of failure is the major impediment to generating solutions which are risky (i.e., small chance of succeeding) but would have a major impact if they are successful. Outlining the ways you could fail and how you would deal with these failures will reduce this obstacle to creativity.
- *Keep your sense of humor.* You are more creative when you are relaxed. Humor aids in putting your problems (and yourself) in perspective. Many times it relieves tension and makes you more relaxed.
- *Engage in creative hobbies.* Hobbies can also help you relax. Working puzzles and playing games help keep your mind active. An active mind is necessary for creative growth.
- *Have courage and self-confidence.* Be a paradigm pioneer. Assume that you can and will indeed solve the problem. Persist and have the tenacity to overcome obstacles that block the solution pathway.
- *Learn to know and understand yourself.* Deepen your self-knowledge by learning your *real* strengths, skills, weaknesses, dislikes, biases, expectations, fears, and prejudices.

hats are a device that help you look at a situation from many different viewpoints. As you imagine yourself wearing each different hat, you should assume the characteristics associated with that particular hat.

There are a variety of techniques that can be used to generate creative ideas. We will now begin to explore some of them.

Brainstorming

Brainstorming, one of the oldest techniques to stimulate creativity, is a familiar and effective technique for generating solutions. It provides an excellent means of getting the creative juices flowing. Recent surveys of people working in industry show that brainstorming is routinely used as an effective tool not only for one or two individuals discussing a problem in an informal setting but also in more formal large-group problem-solving sessions. Typically, the initial stages of idea generation begin with an unstructured free association of ideas to solve the problem (brainstorming). During this activity, lists of all possible solutions are generated either in group discussions or individually. The lists should include wild solutions or unusual solutions without regard to their feasibility. When brainstorming in groups, people can build upon each other's ideas or suggestions. This triggering of ideas in others is key to successful group brainstorming. Another critical component of group brainstorming is to maintain a positive group attitude. No negative comments or judgments are allowed during this stage of the solution process. Reserve evaluation and judgment until later. The more ideas that are generated, the better chance there is for an innovative, workable solution to the problem at hand. Nothing will kill a brainstorming session faster than negative comments. These comments must be kept in check by the group leader or the session will usually reduce to one of "braindrizzling."

Comments That Reduce Brainstorming to Braindrizzling

- That won't work.
- That's too radical.
- It's not our job.
- We don't have enough time.
- That's too much hassle.
- It's against our policy.
- We haven't done it that way before.
- That's too expensive.
- That's not practical.
- We can't solve this problem.

We conducted some brainstorming exercises with a number of groups of students. Some of the exercises were free-format in nature, totally unstructured, where the only guideline used was to generate as many ideas as possible. An example of an unstructured session is shown on the next page.

Usually the ideas flow quickly at first and then slow abruptly after several minutes. The process has hit a "roadblock." These roadblocks hinder our progress toward a solution. Now let's use some other blockbusting techniques to help overcome some mental blocks and generate additional alternatives.

> **Problem Statement:** How could the roles of basketball be changed so that players under 5′9″ tall might be more competitive?
>
> **Ideas Generated:**
>
> - Lower the height of the basket.
> - Two separate baskets.
> - Platform tennis shoes.
> - Tall players can't block.
> - Tall players can't rebound.
> - Tall players can't dribble.
> - Tall players can't jump.
> - No fouls on short players.
> - Tall players can't look at the basket.
> - Tall players can't use the backboard.
> - Play in zero gravity.
> - Some players on each team under 5′9″.
> - Short players' baskets count.
> - Taller players are not allowed outside the key.
> - 3-point shot line closer for shorter players.
> - Tall players can guard only tall players.
> - Tall players have to wear weighted shoes.
> - Short players can use trampoline.
> - Tall players must use a heavier ball.
> - Make tall players run (winded) before game.
> - Tall players wear uniforms with itching powder.
> - Allow players to pick other players up.
> - Short players wear spikes.
> - Tall players must carry a small child on their backs.
> - Tall players wear glasses restricting peripheral vision.
> - Short and tall teams: Short teams have more players.

Osborn's Checklist

Osborn's Checklist techniques are used to generate additional alternatives that are related to those previously obtained. It is useful to help a group build on one another's ideas (i.e., piggyback). The checklist is shown in an abbreviated format in the following table.[7]

> **Osborn's Checklist for Adding New Ideas**
>
> | | |
> |---|---|
> | **Adapt?** | How can this (product, idea, plan, etc.) be used as is? What are other uses it could be adapted to? |
> | **Modify?** | Change the meaning, material, color, shape, odor, etc.? |
> | **Magnify?** | Add new ingredient? Make longer, stronger, thicker, higher, etc.? |
> | **Minify?** | Split up? Take something out? Make lighter, lower, shorter, etc.? |
> | **Substitute?** | Who else, where else, or what else? Other ingredient, material, or approach? |
> | **Rearrange?** | Interchange parts? Other patterns, layouts? Transpose cause and effect? Change positives to negatives? Reverse roles? Turn it backwards or upside down? Sort? |
> | **Combine?** | Combine parts, units, ideas? Blend? Compromise? Combine from different categories? |

> **Continuing with the basketball example...**
>
> **Adapt?** Smaller players can foul as many times as they want (rule adaptation). Assists by smaller players count as points.
>
> **Modify?** Raise baskets for taller players (modify court). Tall players stay inside 3 point line.
>
> **Magnify?** Short player's baskets worth 4 points (magnify score)
>
> **Minify?** Tall player's shots worth 1 point (minify score).
>
> **Rearrange?** Separate leagues for taller and shorter players (rearrange grouping).

Random Stimulation

Random Stimulation is a technique which is especially useful if we are stuck or in a rut.[8] It is a way of generating totally different ideas than previously considered and can "jump start" the idea generation process and get it out of whatever current rut it may be in.

The introduction of strange or "weird" ideas during brainstorming should not be shunned but instead should be encouraged. *Random Stimulation* makes use of a random piece of information (perhaps a word culled from the dictionary or a book) (e.g., eighth word down on page 125), or a random finger placement on one of the words in the sample list below. This word is used to act as a trigger or switch to change the patterns of thought when a mental roadblock occurs. The random word can be used to generate other words that can stimulate the flow of ideas.

> **Examples of Random Stimulation Words**
>
> all, albatross, airplane, air, animals, bag, basketball, bean, bee, bear, bump, bed, car, cannon, cap, control, cape, custard pie, dawn, deer, defense, dig, dive, dump, dumpster, ear, eavesdrop, evolution, eve, fawn, fix, find, fungus, food, ghost, graph, gulp, gum, hot, halo, hope, hammer, humbug, head, high, ice, icon, ill, jealous, jump, jig, jive, jinx, key, knife, kitchen, lump, lie, loan, live, Latvia, man, mop, market, make, maim, mane, notice, needle, new, next, nice, open, Oscar, opera, office, pen, powder, pump, Plato, pigeons, pocket, quick, quack, quiet, rage, rash, run, rigid, radar, Scrooge, stop, stove, save, saloon, sandwich, ski, simple, safe, sauce, sand, sphere, tea, time, ticket, treadmill, up, uneven, upside-down, vice, victor, vindicate, volume, violin, voice, wreak, witch, wide, wedge, x-ray, yearn, year, yazzle, zone, zoo, zip, zap

> **Example of Random Stimulation**
>
> **Problem: Continuing the basketball example**
> *Random word or concept*
> **Humbug**—What ideas come to mind?
> **Humbug** → Scrooge → mean → rough → more relaxed foul rules for short players.
> **Jealous** → rage → short players may **taunt** tall players to distract them.

> **Industrial Example of Random Stimulation**
>
> **Problem: Make toxic holding tank safe.**
> A large tank to hold toxic waste from a certain process is to be built. The problem is that the tank must be safe.
> Choose a random word: Airplane
>
> *Airplane*—An airplane flies over the toxic waste tank. What if a plane were to crash into this tank causing it to rupture? Now use this idea to find a feasible concern. If a plane may crash into the tank, what about a forklift or a waste delivery truck? ?This is a real concern that we must deal with. To make a long story short, it was decided to build a fence and dike around the tank to serve as a protection barrier. The benefit of random stimulation is that it allows the generation of a reasonable alternative that may not have been considered before.

For example, in the 5'9" basketball player brainstorming session, the word *humbug* was chosen at random from a book. *Humbug* brought to mind (i.e., led to (→)) the word *scrooge* which led to (→) *mean* which led to (→) *rough*, which resulted in the idea of *more relaxed foul rules for short players*. The goal of the pattern change allows the problem to be viewed from new perspectives not previously considered.

Other People's Views

When approaching a problem that involves the thoughts and feelings of others, a useful thinking tool is *Other People's Views,* or OPV.[8] The inability to see the problem from various viewpoints can be quite limiting. Imagining yourself in the role of the other person allows you to see complications of the problem not considered previously. For example, consider an argument between the new store manager and an employee. The issue is the employee's desire to take two weeks vacation during the store's busiest period, the Christmas season. The manager's main concern is having enough help to handle the sales volume. The employee, however, has made reservations for an Antarctic cruise, one year in advance (with the former manager's approval), and stands to lose a lot of money if he has to cancel them. The problem does not have a solution yet, but by using OPV each person can see what the other person stands to gain or lose from the vacation, and each has a better understanding of the types of compromises the other person might be willing to make. Automotive engineers must be aware of many viewpoints to design a successful vehicle. They must consider the views of the consumers, the marketing personnel, management, the safety department, the financial people, and the service personnel. Failure to consider any of these groups' views could result in a failed product. Examples using this technique are shown below.

Example of Other People's Views

Problem:	**Continuing the basketball example**
Owners:	They like to win and fill the arena with fans. Game must be exciting. It must have some advantages for the coaches to want to have shorter players. Maybe consider a maximum cumulative height for the team, so that teams with very small players can have more very tall players, and a better chance of winning.
Fans:	They like fast, exciting games with good ball handing, shooting, and slam dunks. Maybe we *do* need to lower the basket.
Short Players:	Want big bucks and to play in the pros.
Tall Players:	Don't want the game changed.

Another Example of Other People's Views

Problem:	**Space capsule burns open entering the atmosphere.**
Project Manager:	Complete the project on time.
NASA Accountant:	Solve problem but keep cost low.
Engineer:	New material should not interfere with capsule performance.
Materials Scientist:	Find a material that can handle the high temperature on reentry.
Astronaut:	Doesn't care about the capsule, wants to return alive.
Final solution:	Allow the surface of the capsule to be destroyed, protecting the astronauts.

The Case of the Putrid Pond

Problem Statement: A very large (500,000 sq. ft. = 10 football fields) sludge pond is part of a waste treatment plant. The liquid in the pond is very viscous and sticky. From time to time, unwanted floating objects (dead animals, branches, etc.) appear on the pond and must be removed. Unfortunately, covering the pond is not an option. Devise ways to solve the problem.

Brainstorming

Use a crane.
Large net over the pond.
Use a hovercraft.
Use a helicopter.
Build rail system above sludge pond.
Build a fence around the pond.

Osborn's Checklist

Modify
Change treatment process to eliminate sludge.
Add chemical to break down branches and dead animals.
Change properties of pond, so things sink, then dredge.

Substitute
Build in desert/change location.
Substitute many tanks for pond.
Anaerobic digesters.

Magnify-Minify
Shallow pond so people can wade.
Make narrow and deep, then cover.

Rearrange
Grinder to cut everything up.
De-vegetate surrounding countryside.
Bring in vultures and scarecrows.

Other People's Views

Animals — Food around the side of the pond.
Electric fence.
Add obnoxious odor to keep animals away.

Pigeons — Scarecrow/predatory bird.
Large fans around the side to blow birds in opposite direction.

Plant Manager — Change the law → it is OK to have dead animals in the pond.
Mechanical arm that grabs stuff from the pond.

Random Stimulation

Latvia — Run process in different country; remote location for plant.

Custard Pie — Food → eat → algae → inject bacteria that digest floating debris.

Ski — Ski chair lift system across the pond to reach down and to pick off dead animals.

Futuring

Futuring is a blockbusting technique that focuses on generating solutions which currently may not be technically feasible but could be in the future. In futuring we ask questions such as: What are the characteristics of an ideal solution? What currently existing problem would make our jobs easier when solved, or would solve many subsequent problems, or would make a major difference in the way we do business? One of futurist Joel Barker's key ideas is that you should be bold enough to suggest alternatives that promise major advances, yet may only have a small probability of success.

The rules for futuring are relatively simple: Try to imagine the ideal solution without regard to whether or not it is technically feasible. Then begin by making statements such as . . . "If (this) _____ happened, it would completely change the way I do business." The University of Michigan's College of Engineering Commission on Undergraduate Education used futuring exercises to help formulate the goals and directions of engineering education for the 1990s and into the twenty-first century. The members of the commission were asked, "What do you see the student doing in 1999?" Some answers included: "I see the students using interactive computing to learn all their lessons. There are animations of processes where the students can change operating parameters and get instant visual feedback on their effect." "I see lecture halls where the lecturer is a hologram of the most authoritative and dynamic professor in the world on that particular topic." In futuring, you visualize the idealized situation that you would like to have and then work on devising ways to attain it.

How to Use Futuring

- Examine the problem carefully to make sure the real problem has been defined.
- Now, imagine yourself at some point in the future after the problem has been solved. What are the benefits of having a solution?
- "Look around" in the future. Try to imagine an ideal solution to the problem at hand without regard to technical feasibility. Remember, in the future, anything is possible.
- Make statements such as: "If only (this) _____ would happen, I could solve . . . ."
- Dare to change the rules! The best solutions to some problems are contrary to conventional wisdom.

Futuring—Sludge Pond Problem Revisited

- We don't have sludge in the future.
- Genetic engineering—dead plants and animals decay instantaneously.
- No waste products in the future.
- Change pond to gaseous or solid state.
- Use sludge as energy source.
- Use sludge as building material.
- Grow vegetation on pond.
- Heat source to boil.
- High frequency sound source that keeps animals away.
- Use sludge for roads.

Futuring—Useful Products from Cheese Waste

The waste products from cheese and yogurt plants are quite acidic and consequently cannot be discharged directly into lakes or rivers. This waste must be treated so that it can be safely discharged from the plant. One suggestion is to build a waste treatment facility that will neutralize the acid and kill the bacteria in the waste. It is important to keep the cost of the treatment materials, as well as the capital cost of the facility, at a minimum so that we do nit severely impact the profits of the yogurt and cheese making. Let's try an exercise in futuring.

Let's imagine ourselves in the future, with a booming yogurt- and cheese-making business. Why is our plant doing so well? Our plant is very successful because there are no wasted materials in our operation. Al our "waste" streams are being put to good use. What are we using them for? The main waste stream contains sugar and protein. What could we be using those for? Protein is an essential dietary requirement. We could be separating the protein and using it for human consumption (food additives) or animal feed supplements (more likely). What about the sugar? Could it be sold to someone as a raw material for another process? What kind of process? Sugars can be fermented, can't they? Perhaps we could be using the sugar to produce ethanol for a profit. What's left after removing the protein and the sugar? Could this material be landfill? But, landfilling is placing the material in the ground. Could we place it in the ground for a profit? What about placing it on the surface of the ground? Maybe it could be used as a fertilizer? Or perhaps as a biodegradable de-icing product for use on the roads? The de-icing idea is already being used in some cities.

Summary

- *Define the Real Problem:*   The problem is not how to treat the waste but more generally what to do with it.
- *Imagine the Future:*   Plant is profitable and has no adverse environmental impact.
- *Generate Solutions:*   Success due to no waste production. All byproducts are recycled or sold.

Organizing Brainstorming Ideas: The Fishbone Diagram

Fishbone diagrams are a graphical way to organize and record brainstorming ideas. The diagrams look like a fish skeleton (hence their name). To construct a fishbone diagram the following procedure is used:

1. Write the real problem in a box (or circle) to the right of the diagram. Draw a horizontal line (the backbone) extending from the problem to the left side:

2. Brainstorm potential solutions to the problem.
3. Categorize the potential solutions into several major categories and list them along the bottom or top of the diagram. Extend diagonal lines from the major categories to the backbone. These lines form the basic skeleton of the fishbone diagram.
4. Place the potential solutions related to each of the major categories along the appropriate line (or bone) in the diagram.

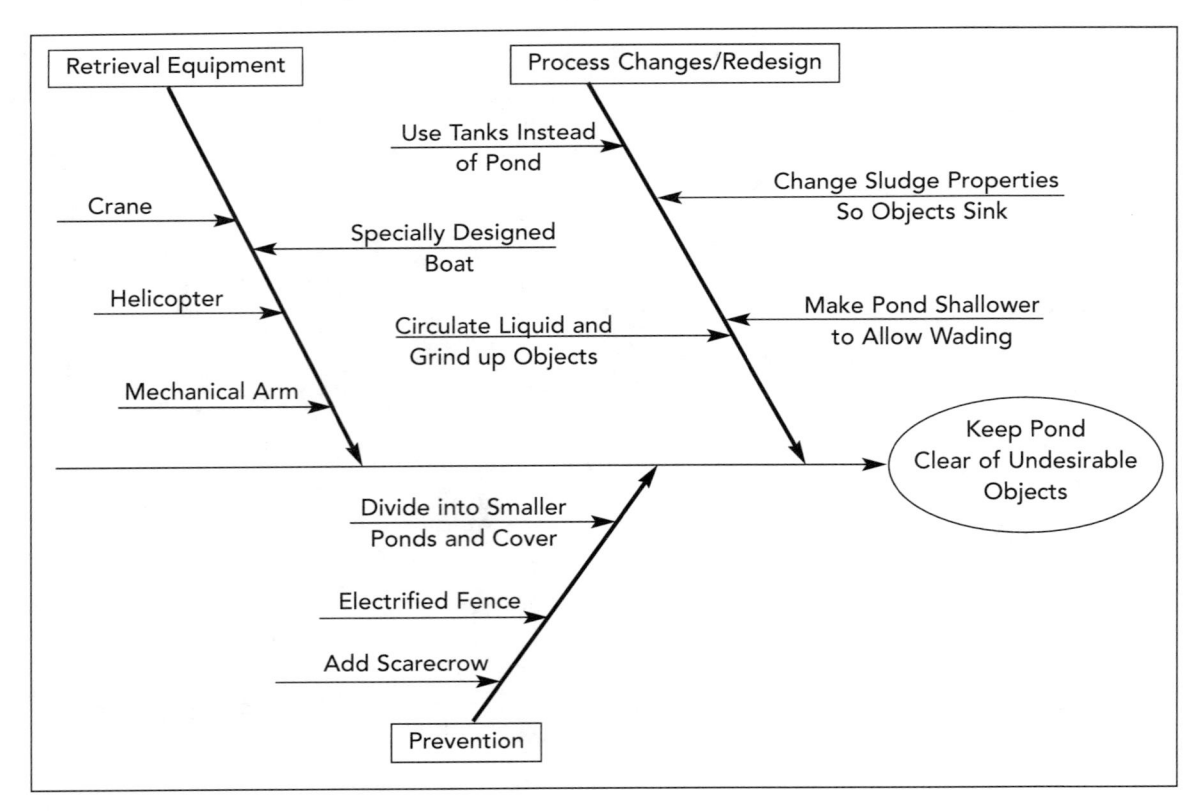

A fishbone diagram for organizing the ideas for the putrid pond problem is shown below. The most difficult task in constructing a fishbone diagram is deciding the major categories to use for organizing the options. In this example, we have selected "Retrieval Equipment," "Process Changes/Redesign," and "Prevention." The ideas that are generated fall nicely into these categories. Other common categories used in fishbone diagrams are personnel, equipment, method, materials, and environment. This activity of sorting and organizing the information is a very valuable effort in the solution process.

From the fishbone diagram, we can evaluate the solutions that have been generated. We have put a structure to the solutions, organizing them and allowing us to "attack" the problem from a number of different fronts if we choose. These diagrams can be very helpful in visualizing all the ideas that you have generated.

Brainwriting

Two or more individuals are required in order to carry out an interactive brainstorming session. However, when there is no one to interact with, a technique being used by many companies is that of brainwriting. In brainwriting you follow the same procedure as brainstorming (e.g., free association, Osborn's checklist, random stimulation, futuring). Write down your ideas as fast as you generate them, never pausing or stopping to evaluate the idea. Also keep a notebook handy to write down ideas, because they often come at unusual times. After you have completed your list, organize your ideas (solutions) in a fishbone diagram.

Analogy and Cross-Fertilization

It is well documented that a number of the most important advances in science, engineering, art, and business come from cross-fertilization and analogies with other disciplines. Here ideas, rules, laws, facts, and conventions from one discipline are transferred to another discipline. When we use analogies, we look for analogous situations/problems in other related and unrelated areas. Consequently, it is important that you read and learn about things outside your area of expertise. Generating ideas by *analogy* works quite well for many individuals. One recent example is that of Shockblockers™ Shoes developed by the U. S. Shoe Corporation (*Washington Post*, p. A47, December 18, 1992). The company wanted to develop shoes that absorb the shocks associated with walking. The company looked around to find out what other paraphernalia were used to protect the body from external contact. Ultimately they studied the materials inside a professional football helmet and eventually used the same shock absorbing foam in the soles in their new line of Shockblockers™ Shoes.

Remember the reentry of the space capsule problem in Chapter 5? One of the scientists used an analogy with a meteor entering the earth's atmosphere and asked why it did not burn up as a result of frictional heating. The answer was that the surface of the meteor was in a molten state and was being vaporized upon entering the earth's atmosphere. The frictional heat generated during reentry was dissipated into the heat of vaporization of the meteor surface. Consequently, the analogy between the space capsule and the meteor led to the use of a sacrificial material on the capsule surface that vaporized and thus dissipated the frictional heating.

In order to practice generating ideas by analogy and cross-fertilization, you might ask what each of the following pairs would learn from one another if they went to lunch or dinner together that would improve themselves, and/or the way they perform their job:

A beautician and a college professor.
A policeman and a software programmer.
An automobile mechanic and an insurance salesman.
A banker and a gardener.
A choreographer and an air traffic controller.
A maitre d' and a pastor.

> ### Dinner at Antoine's
>
> Let's consider a dinner meeting between a beautician and a college professor. The beautician could provide the professor with tips on the importance of having and maintaining a good physical appearance. Beauticians, also typically good conversationalists and listeners, could share these skills to help the professor establish a more effective rapport with the students. The professor would be better able to understand and respond to student concerns and problems. The professor might also pick up some tips on managing a small business which would be helpful in organizing and managing a research group.
>
> College professors, on the other hand, are usually involved in research and are up on the latest developments in their field. The beautician could benefit from a discussion of these topics and be encouraged to obtain the newest beauty information and perhaps experiment with some new ideas. For example, new chemical/color treatments could be studied/explored using hair samples. The beautician could learn how to carry out an experiment by treating samples of hair with a new curling product for varying lengths of time to determine the optimum treatment procedure for different types of hair.

Many other combinations of professions would also provide growth experiences for both participants. The cross-fertilization of ideas from one group to another is a powerful method for adapting ideas from one discipline or profession to solve problems in another. Many times managers will bring together a small group of people from diverse backgrounds (ethnic, cultural) to interact and look at a problem and solution from many vantage points.

There are four steps you can use to solve problems by analogy:[4] 1) State the problem, 2) generate analogies (this problem is like trying to . . .), 3) solve the analogy, and 4) transfer the solution to the problem. When generating analogies, apply the same rules you did in brainstorming. For example in the case of the stale cereal, one could say, "Keeping the cereal fresh is like preserving raw fish in the tropics without a refrigerator and without cooking." How could one preserve fish? Add lemon/lime juice to make seviche (pickled fish). What could be added to the cereal to keep it fresh?

> ### A Cold Winter's Day
>
> **The Situation:** A large office building in the city was not as energy efficient as the building's owners would have liked. As a result, in order to keep their heating bills down, the building was kept colder than the occupants preferred, and many complaints were received.
>
> **Step One:** State Problem (*What is the situation?*)
> Occupants of building are too cold. Utilities bills are too high. Too many complaints.
>
> **Step Two:** Generate Analogies (*What else is **like** this situation?*) *Generate as many possibilities as you can, then choose one to work with:* Being cold in the office is like . . .
> Being too cold at a football game.
> Being too cold on a camping trip.
> Being too cold in a car that hasn't warmed up in the winter.
> Being too cold in bed at night.
>
> **Step Three:** Solve the Analogy
> When you are too cold on a camping trip, you build a campfire which serves as a source of both heat and light.
>
> **Step Four:** Transfer the Solution to the Problem
> Instead of building a campfire in the office, rent or buy a portable space heater. Use a readily available source of heat and light to solve the building's energy problems. Install a heat recovery system to recover waste heat from the florescent lights to warm the offices and improve the energy efficiency. (This is a practice that is used in modern energy-efficient office buildings.)

Incubating Ideas

The incubation period is very important in problem solving. Working on a solution to a problem to meet a deadline often causes you to pick the first solution that comes to mind and then "run with it," instead of stopping to think of alternative solutions.

Once the generation of ideas has halted (or you collapse from the effort), an incubation period may be in order. Little is truly understood about mental incubation, but the basic process involves stopping active work on the problem and letting your subconscious continue the work. Everyone has, at one time or another, been told to "sleep on a problem," and maybe the solution will be apparent in the morning. This incubation or subconscious work has been described as a mental scanning of the billions of neurons in the brain in search of a novel or innovative connection to lead to a possible solution.[9] A number of members of the National Academy of Engineering were asked, "What do you do when you get stuck on a problem?" Some of the responses were

- "Communicate with other people. Read articles. Try new techniques *after a period of digestion*. Follow a lead if it looks promising. Keep pursuing."

- "Ask questions about all the circumstances. *Go home and think.* Go to your arsenal of past experiences. Identify factors related to the problem. Read, write and exchange ideas."
- "I write down everything that I must know to have a solution and everything that I know about the problem so far. Then I usually *let it sit overnight,* and think about it from time to time. While it is sitting I often review the recent literature on similar problems and often get an idea on how to proceed."
- "When I can afford the liberty of doing so, I will *put the problem down and do something else for awhile.* My mind keeps working on the problem, and often I will think of something while trying not to."

The common thread that runs through these responses is the notion of an incubation period. If the solution to the problem is not an emergency, incubation is a useful (in)activity to consider.

Closure

The goal of this chapter was to present techniques to help you general creative solutions. Mental blocks and techniques to remove them (blockbusting techniques) were presented. Blockbusting techniques help break preconceived notions about the problem situation. Many times it is advantageous to take a break when working on a problem to let your ideas incubate while your subconscious works on it. However, don't turn the responsibility over to your subconscious completely by saying, "Well, my subconscious hasn't solved the problem yet."

Summary

- Be able to recognize the different mental blocks when they appear (Perceptual, Emotional, Cultural, Environmental, Intellectual, and Expressive Blocks).
- Use Goman's Blockbusters:

  Attitude Adjustment, Risk Taking, Breaking the Rules, Internal Creative Climate, and Creative Beliefs.
- Use Osborn's Checklist to generate new ideas: Adapt, Modify, Magnify, Minify, Rearrange, Combine.
- Use *Random Stimulation* and *Other People's Views* to generate new ideas when you are stuck in a rut.

  Telegraph → wire → electricity → light bulb → new ideas
- Remove all technical blocks to envision a solution in the future.
- Use a fishbone diagram to help organize the ideas/solutions you generate.
- Use analogy and cross-fertilization to bring ideas, phenomena, and knowledge from other disciplines to bear on your problem.
- Let the problem incubate so that your mind keeps working on it while you are doing other things.

References

1. Higgins, J.S., et al., "Identifying and Solving Problems in Engineering Design," *Studies in Higher Education,* 14, No. 2, p. 169, 1989.
2. Adams, James L., *Conceptual Blockbusting: A Guide to Better Ideas,* W. H. Freeman and Company, San Francisco, 1974.
3. Van Gundy, A.B., *Techniques of Structured Problem Solving,* 2nd ed., Van Nostrand Reinhold, New York, 1988.
4. Goman, Carol K., *Creativity in Business—A Practical Guide for Creative Thinking,* Crisp Publications, Inc., 1200 Hamilton Ct., Menlo Park, CA 94025, 800-442-7477, 1989.
5. Raudelsepp, E., *Chemical Engineering,* 85, p. 95, July 2, 1979.
6. deBono, Edward, *Serious Creativity,* Harper Business, a division of Harper Collins Publishers, New York, 1993.
7. Felder, R.M., "Creativity in Engineering Education," *Chemical Engineering Education,* 22(3), 1988.
8. deBono, E., *Lateral Thinking,* Harper & Row, New York, 1970.
9. Reid, R.C., "Creativity?," *Chemtech,* 17, p. 14, January 1987.

Further Reading

Adams, James L., *Conceptual Blockbusting, A Guide to Better Ideas,* 3rd ed., Addison-Wesley Publishing Co., Inc., Stanford, CA, 1986.

von Oech, Roger, *A Whack on the Side of the Head, How You Can be More Creative,* revised edition, Warner Books, New York, 1990.

Exercises

1. Keep a journal of all the good ideas you generate.
   A._____
   B._____
   C._____
2. a) Make a list of the worst business ideas you can think of (e.g., a maternity shop in a retirement village, a solar-powered night-light, *reversible* diapers).
   A._____
   B._____
   C._____
   b) Take the list you generated in part (a) and turn it around to make them viable concepts for entrepreneurial ventures, (e.g., reversible diapers–blue on one side and pink on the other).

A. _____
B. _____
C. _____

3. Apply Goman's four steps of generating solutions to problems by analogy to a problem you have.

   1. State the Problem.

      _____
      _____
      _____

   2. Create Analogies: This situation is like . . .

      1. _____
      2. _____
      3. _____

   3. Solve the Analogy.

      1. _____
      2. _____
      3. _____

   4. Transfer the Solution.

      1. _____

      2. _____

      3. _____

4. Rent a video. Watch half the movie with a friend(s). Stop the movie and each of you "create" your own ending. Watch the rest of the movie and discuss the results. Whose ending was better? Why?

5. Suggest 50 ways to increase spectator participation at a) professional basketball games. Examples: Have a drawing at each game and the people in the randomly selected seats get to play for two minutes. Give the fans one arrow each to shoot at the basketball in midair to try to block the shot. Suggest 50 ways for spectator participation in professional b) football, c) baseball, d) hockey.

6. Suggest or devise 50 different ways to cross a lake of molasses.

7. You are a passenger in a car without a speedometer. Describe 20 ways to determine the speed of the car.

8. An epidemic on a chicken farm created a thousand tons of dead chickens. The local landfill would not accept the dead chickens. It is also against the law to bury the chickens and the local authorities are insisting the matter be dealt with immediately. Suggest ways to solve the farmer's problems. (*Chemtech*, 22, 3, p. 192, 1992)

GENERATING SOLUTIONS / 143

9. A reforestation effort in Canada is running into trouble in a particular region. In one nursery alone, 10 million seedlings were eaten by voles. The voles even consumed the varieties of seedlings chosen for the unpalatable phenol/condensed tannin secondary metabolite they contain. The voles overcame this unpalatability by cutting the branches, stripping the bark, and then leaving them for a few days before eating. This process caused the unpleasant components to decline to acceptable levels. Suggest 15 ways to solve the reforestation problem in this nursery. (*Chemtech*, 21, p. 324, 1991)

10. Kite flying is a growing hobby around the world. (They are very entertaining; it is not unusual to find kites that fly at altitudes of more than 2,000 feet.) Suggest 50 ways kites can be used for purposes other than entertainment.

11. a) Rearrange four pencils to make six equal triangles.

    b) Remove six pencils to leave two perfect squares and no odd pencils.

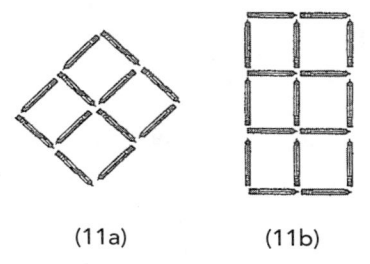

    (11a)   (11b)

12. a) Rearrange three balls so that the triangle points up instead of down.

    b) Moving one black poker chip only, make two rows of four.

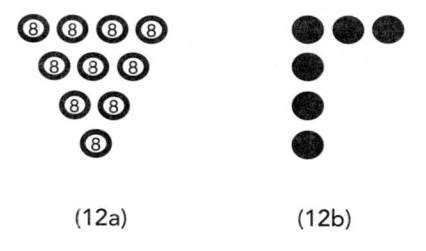

    (12a)   (12b)

13. Apply a variety of brainstorming techniques to one or more of the following situations

    a) Suggest ways to measure the pressure over the top of the carbonated liquid in a 2-liter bottle. This might be required to determine the necessary pressure rating for a bottle. How could you measure the pressure inside a balloon?

    b) A coin collector has a coin that she suspects is zinc. Suggest ways to determine nondestructively and precisely whether the coin is zinc. (Be specific.)

    c) Imagine yourself in the year 2020. What would an automobile look like? What would be some of the selling features?

d) Suggest some ways to prevent the problem of driving under the influence of alcohol in the future.

e) What features would be nice to have on a television, ten years from now? How about on a computer?

Prepare a fishbone diagram of any one of the above brainstorming examples.

14. Choose two people from different professions (e.g., repairman, florist, dentist, accountant, policeman, hockey coach, car designer, custodian, bell hop, cruise ship activity director, cub scout leader) and make a table similar to the one below of what they could learn from one another that would enrich each others lives. (Matt Latham, Sue Stagg)

Pastor gives to a Maitre d'
1) ideas to rapidly assess people's needs.
2) suggestions on how not to take every problem he hears personally (thick skinned).
3) importance of good physical appearance.
4) suggestions on how far you can push people (in terms of views and ideals).
5) ideas on offering suggestions and advice.
6) ideas on how to be more self-reliant (scheduling).

Maitre d' gives to a Pastor
1) knowledge to calm upset individuals/crowd control.
2) understanding and dealing with people, approachability.
3) memory techniques to remember frequent customers.
4) an appreciation of having a boss and someone watching what you do.
5) ideas on how to learn to be happy with your job and yourself.

15. Make a list of several ways you can improve your creative abilities. Describe how you would implement some techniques from the table on page 66.

A. _____   C. _____
   _____   _____
   _____   _____

B. _____   D. _____
   _____   _____
   _____   _____

16. Fifty-seven sticks are laid out to form the equation. Remove eight sticks to make the answer correct. Do not disturb any sticks other than the eight to be removed. First list any perceived constraints that you initially thought could be blocks to solving this problem. (Source: *Brain Busters* by Phillip J. Carter and Ken A. Russel, Sterling Publishing, Inc., New York, 1992)

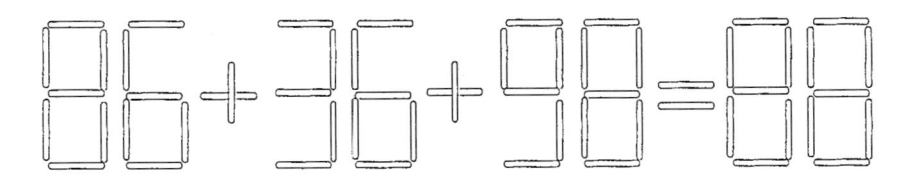

$$86 + 36 + 98 = 88$$

17. Carry out a futuring exercise to visualize
    a) A telephone call in the year 2010.
    b) Eating a meal with your family in the year 2050.
    c) A homework assignment in the year 2025.
    d) A homework assignment in the year 2125.

CHAPTER 7

Deciding the Course of Action

Once the real problem(s) is defined and we have generated a number of possible solutions, it is time to make some decisions. Specifically, we must

- Decide which problem to work on first
- Choose the best alternative solution
- Decide how to successfully implement the solution

An organized process for making these essential decisions is the Kepner-Tregoe (K.T.) Approach, which is described in *The New Rational Manager*.[1,2]

```
                    Situation Analysis
                    (Where are we?)
                    /       |       \
                   /        |        \
        Problem          Decision         Potential
        Analysis         Analysis      Problem Analysis

         Past             Present          Future

        What is         How to correct    How to prevent
       the fault?        the fault?       future faults?
```

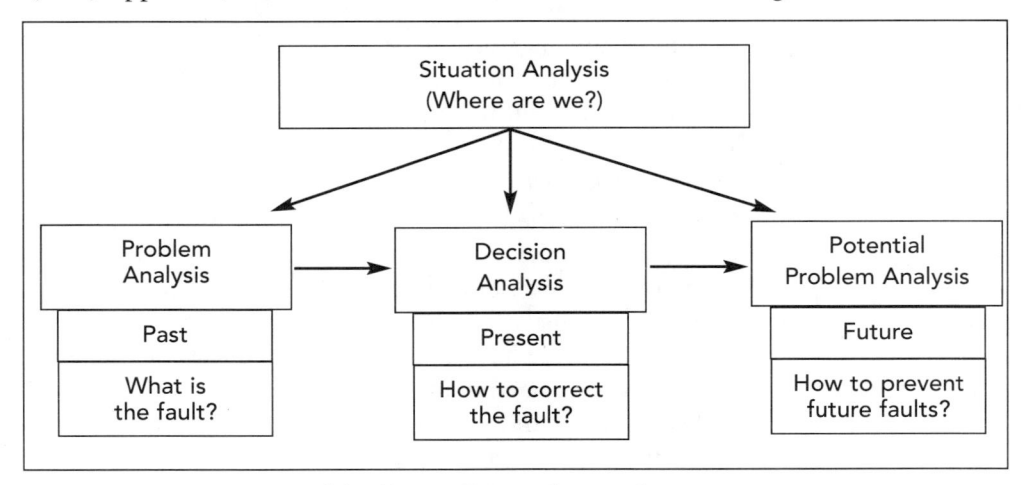

Figure 5–1. Components of the Kepner-Tregoe Approach

K.T. *Situation Analysis* not only helps us decide which problem to work on first; it also guides us with respect to what is to be done. Do we need to learn the cause (Problem Analysis, PA), make a decision (Decision Analysis, DA), or plan for success (Potential Problem Analysis, PPA)? That is, in situation analysis we also classify the problem into one of these analysis groups. In *Problem Analysis* the cause of the problem or the fault is unknown and we have to find it. What is it that happened in the *past* that is causing the current trouble? In *Decision Analysis* the cause of the problem has been found and now we need to decide what to do about it. The decision at the *present* time is how to correct the fault. In *Potential Problem Analysis* we want to ensure the success of the decision and anticipate and prevent *future* problems from occurring.

Situation Analysis

In many situations, a number of problems arise at the same time. In so cases they are interconnected; in other cases, they are totally unrelated, and it is "just one of those days." When these situations occur, Kepner-Tregoe (K.T.) Situation Analysis can prove useful in helping to decide which problem receives the highest priority.

We first make a list of all of the problems and then try to decide which problem in this group should receive attention first. Each problem will be measured against three criteria: (1) timing, (2) trend, and (3) impact, each of which will be evaluated as being of a high (H), moderate (M), or low (L) degree of concern. We also decide what type K.T. analysis is to be carried out: PA, DA, or PPA.

Evaluation Criteria

1. *Timing:* How urgent is the problem? Is a deadline involved? What will happen if nothing is done for a while? For example, if one of the five ovens in a bakery is malfunctioning and the other four ovens could pick up the extra load, it may be possible to wait on this problem and address more urgent problems, so we would give the problem an L rating (low degree of concern). On the other hand, if the other four ovens are operating at maximum capacity and a major order must be filled by the evening, the rating for *timing* would be H (high degree of concern) because the problem must be solved now.

2. *Trend:* What is the problem's potential for growth? In the bakery example, suppose the malfunctioning oven is overheating, getting hotter and hotter, and cannot be turned off. Consequently the *trend* is getting worse, and you have a high degree of concern (an H) about a fire starting. You also could have a high degree of concern if you are getting further and further behind on your customer's orders. On the other hand, if the oven is off and you can keep up with the orders with four ovens, the *trend* is a low degree of concern (L).

3. *Impact:* How serious is the problem? What are the effects on the people, the product, the organization, and its policies? In the bakery example, suppose you cannot get the oven repaired in time to fill the order of a major client. If, as a result, you could subsequently lose the client's business, then the *impact* is a high degree of concern (H). On the other hand, if you can find a way to fill all the orders for the next few days, then the *impact* of one malfunctioning oven is a moderate degree of concern (M).

Deciding the Course of Action / 149

We now consider several examples and solutions to help illustrate the K.T. approach to prioritizing problems. First let's consider the problem below.

K.T. Situation Analysis of:
You know it's a really bad day when . . .

Project	Timing	Trend	Impact	Process
1. Get dog off leg	H	H	H	DA
2. Repair car	L	L	M	PA
3. Put out fire	H	H	H	DA
4. Ensure papers in briefcase will not be destroyed	M	M	H	PPA
5. Prepare for touchdown of tornado	M	H	H	DA/PPA

1. It is necessary to get the dog off your leg now (High Priority). The trend is getting worse because there are more and more lacerations (High Priority) and the impact is that you can do nothing else until the dog is off your leg (High Priority). The process is to decide how to get the dog off your leg (DA).

2. Repairing the car can wait (Low Priority) and it is not getting worse (Low Priority), but if it is not repaired soon it could have impact on your job by your not being able to visit clients (Moderate Priority). The problem is to find out what is wrong with the car (PA).

3. Putting out the fire receives high priority in all three categories. The problem is to decide (DA) how to do it: Get the hose or fire extinguisher; call the fire department; and/or make sure everyone is out of the house.

4. If you rush off to handle the other projects in this list, you need to make sure your months of work, which includes signed documents in your briefcase, are protected. The process is one of Potential Problem Analysis (PPA) and of making sure your signed papers (which your clients now wish they had not signed) are in a safe place.

5. While the tornado looks somewhat close in the picture, it may be used to represent a tornado in the area, and thus may only be a tornado warning. So this hazard could merit Decision Analysis/Potential Problem Analysis.

First Day on the Job . . . Trial by Fire

Sara Brown just became manager of Brennan's Office Supply Store. The Brennan Company owns ten such stores in the Midwest. Sara's store, which is located in the downtown area on a busy street, has an inventory of over one million dollars and over 20,000 square feet of floor space. On her first day of work, Sara is inundated with problems. A very expensive custom-ordered desk that was delivered last week received a number of scratches during unpacking, and the stockroom manager wants to know what he should do. She just discovered that the store has not yet paid the utility bills that were due at the end of last month, and she realizes that the store has been habitually late paying its bills. The accounts receivable department tells her that it has had an abnormally high number of delinquent accounts over the past few months, and it wants to know what action should be taken. There is a large pile of boxes in the storeroom from last week that have yet to be opened and inventoried. The impression she has been getting all morning from the 30 employees is that they are all unhappy and dislike working at the store. To top things off, shortly after lunch, a large delivery truck pulls up to the front of the store and double-parks, blocking traffic. The driver comes into the store and announces that he has a shipment of 20 new executive desks. Where does Sara want them placed? The employees tell Sara that this shipment was not due until next week and there isn't any place to put them right now. Outside she hears horns of the angry drivers as the traffic jam grows. What should Sara do?

SITUATION ANALYSIS

Major concern	Subconcern	Timing	Trend	Impact	Process
Space	Unopened Boxes	L	L	L	DA
	20 New Desks	H	H	H	DA
Personnel	Employee Morale	M	M	H	PA
Finances	Money Owed	M	M	H	DA
	Money Due	M	M	M	PA
Quality	Scratched Desk	L	L	M	DA/PPA

While boxes on the floor may be an eyesore and awkward to step around, it is not necessary we do anything about them immediately (L in timing). The situation is not getting worse by having them there (L in trend), and the impact of not having them opened and the contents shelved is low. The process to address this subconcern is decision analysis—we have to decide who is to open the boxes and when to do it. What to do about the 20 new desks has to be decided (DA) immediately and thus is a high degree of concern. The impact of not accepting or accepting and storing such a large order is a high degree of concern. A traffic jam is beginning to form and is getting worse while Sara is deciding what to do so the trend is a high (H) degree of concern. The employee morale needs to be addressed in the very near future. It is believed that lack of care and sloppiness were factors in damaging the custom-ordered desk, so its impact has a high degree of concern. The morale, while low, could get worse and therefore the trend is a moderate (M) degree of concern. We don't know why the morale is low so we need to carry out a problem analysis (PA) to learn the problem. Sara needs to pay the utility bills fairly soon or the electrical power to the store could be shut off, which would cause a high degree of concern in the impact category. Sara needs to find out why the money due her has not been paid (Problem Analysis). Nothing needs to be done with the scratched desk immediately, but we do need to decide what to do in the not too distant future (DA). We also need to plan how to unpack the desks and other items more carefully (Potential Problem Analysis).

The Pareto Analysis and Diagram

When it is evident that there is more than one problem to be dealt with, a Pareto Analysis is another helpful tool for deciding which problems to attack first. This tool is commonly used in industry for quickly deciding which problem to attack first. The Pareto Analysis shows the *relative* importance of each individual problem to the other problems in the situation. Pareto Analysis draws its name from the Pareto Principle which states that 80% of the trouble comes from 20% of the problems. Thus, it helps to highlight the *vital few* concerns as opposed to the *trivial many*. The defects to investigate first for corrective action are those that will make the large impact. As an example, let's consider the problems that the Toasty O's plant had with their product last year. The problems were classified as follows:

		Number of Boxes
A.	Inferior printing on boxes (smeared/blurred)	10,000
B.	Overfilling boxes (too much weight)	30,000
C.	Boxes damaged during shipping	2,000
D.	Inner wrapper not sealed (stale)	25,000
E.	No prize in box	50,000

The data are shown graphically below:

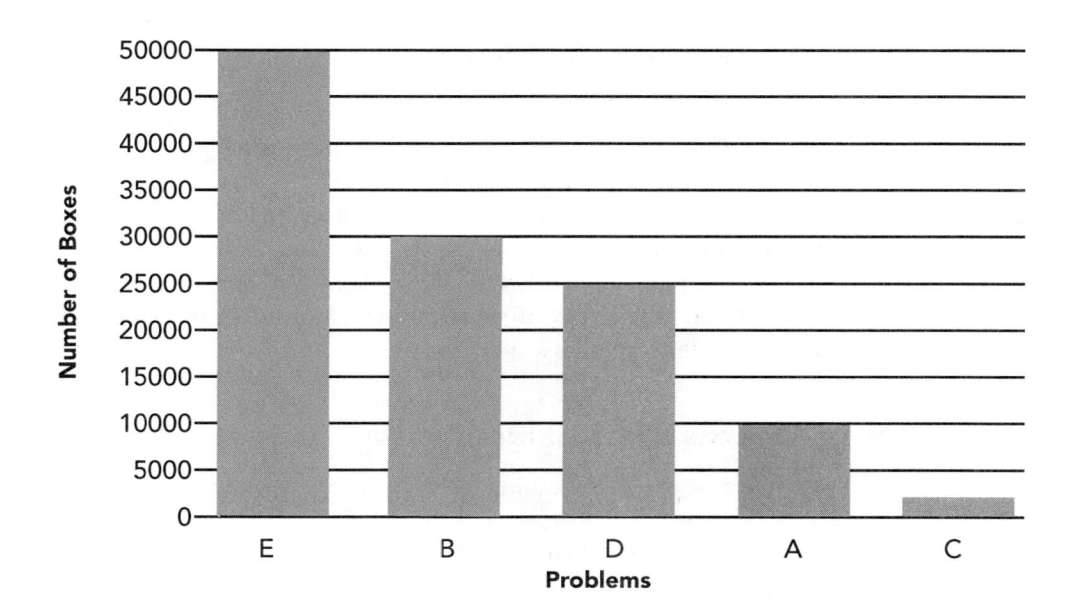

When the bar graph has the frequencies arranged in a descending order, the resulting figure is called a Pareto Diagram. Based on the number of boxes affected, the Toasty O's plant would probably attack the problem in the following order E-B-D-A-C. But, if they reexamine the data in terms of lost revenue instead of the number of boxes affected, a different picture of the problems emerges.

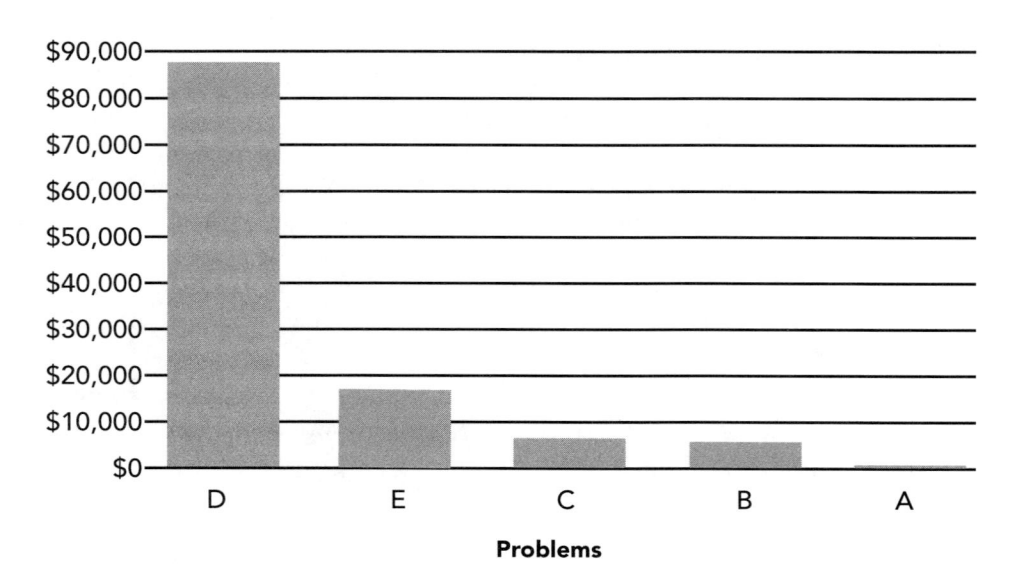

Boxes		Lost Revenue($)
A. Inferior printing on boxes (smeared/bluffed)	10,000	$100
B. Overfilling boxes (too much weight)	30,000	$6,000
C. Boxes damaged during shipping	2,000	$7,000
D. Inner wrapper not sealed (stale)	25,000	$87,500
E. No prize in box	50,000	$17,500

From this graph it is clear that we can make the biggest impact on the problem situation by attacking the stale cereal problem (D) first, followed by E-C-B-A. When a Pareto Diagram is made, care should betaken to "weight" the problems using the most relevant quantity to the particular situation. In this case (and in many others) the impact on plant revenue is the key parameter. Pareto Diagrams are merely a useful, convenient way to organize and visualize problem data to help decide which of multiple problems to attack first.

K.T. Problem Analysis and Troubleshooting

Our studies on problem-solving techniques in industry revealed that one of the major differences between experienced problem solvers and novice problem solvers was their ability to ask the right questions. Experienced problem solvers have learned to ask questions that will penetrate to the heart of the problem and to interview as many people as necessary who might have useful information about the problem. A technique that facilitates asking the proper questions is Kepner-Tregoe (K.T.) Problem Analysis. In this technique, *distinctions* are made between

- What *is* the problem and what *is not* the problem?
- Where did the problem occur? Where is everything OK?

- When did the problem first occur? When was everything OK?
- What is the magnitude (extent) of the problem?

This analysis is most useful in *troubleshooting operations* where the cause of the problem or fault is not known. Problems that lend themselves to K.T. Problem Analysis are ones in which an undesirable level of performance can be observed and compared with the accepted standard performance. For example, consider the following case in which a company ordered and received a new shipment of company stationery with the logo printed at the top. A few days later, it was noticed the logo was easily smeared. This smearing had never been observed before. In the K.T. analysis, Table 7-1, the deviation is that the printing quality was unacceptable and hence a problem must be precisely identified, described, and located.

Table 7–1. The Four K.T. Dimensions of a Problem

		IS	IS NOT	DISTINCTION	CAUSE
What:	Identify:	What is the problem?	What is not the problem?	What is the distinction between the **is** and the **is not**?	What is a possible cause?
Where:	Locate:	Where is the problem found?	Where is the problem not found?	What is distinctive about the difference in locations?	What is a possible cause?
When:	Timing:	When does the problem occur?	When does the problem not occur?	What is distinctive about the difference in the timing?	What is a possible cause?
		When was it first observed?	When was it last observed?	What is the distinction between these observations?	What is a possible cause?
Extent:	Magnitude:	How far does the problem extend?	How localized is the problem?	What is the distinction?	What is a possible cause?
		How many units are affected?	How many units are not affected?	What is the distinction?	What is a possible cause?
		How much of any one unit is affected?	How much of any one unit is not affected?	What is the distinction?	What is a possible cause?

Copyright Kepner-Tregoe, Inc., 1994. Reprinted with permission.

The basic premise of K.T. Problem Analysis is that there is always something that distinguishes what the problem **IS** from what it **IS NOT**. The cause of the problem is usually a change that has taken place to produce undesirable effects. Things were OK, now they're not. Something has changed. (The printing company changed to a glossier paper.) The possible causes of the problem (deviation) are deduced by examining the differences found in the problem. (It is difficult to impregnate glossy paper with ink using the current printing process.) The most probable cause of the problem is the one which best explains all the observations and facts in the problem statement. (The ink is not penetrating the paper and thus it wipes off when used.)

The real challenge is to identify the distinction between the *IS* and the *IS NOT*. Particular care should be taken when filling in the distinction column. Sometimes the distinction statement should be rewritten more than once in order to sharpen the statement to specify the distinction exactly. For example, in one problem analyzed by the K.T. method, the statement "two of the filaments were clear (OK), and two were black (not OK)" was sharpened to "two filaments were clear and two were covered with carbon soot." This *sharpening* of the distinction was instrumental in determining the reason for the black filament. Think in terms of dissimilarities. What distinguishes *this* fact (or category) from *that* fact (or category)? By examining the distinctions, possible causes are generated. This step is the most critical in process and usually requires careful analysis, insight, and practice to ferret out the differences between the *IS* and *IS NOT*. From the possible causes, we try to ascertain the most probable cause. The most probable cause is the one that explains each dimension in the problem specification. The final step is to verify that the most probable cause is the true cause. This may be accomplished by making the appropriate change to see if the problem disappears.

In addition to what, when, where, and to what extent, it can sometimes be beneficial to add who, why, and how. For example,

Who was involved?

Who was not involved?

Why is it important?

Why is it not important?

How did you arrive at this conclusion?

Troubleshooting is an important skill for problem solvers. Some guidelines for troubleshooting have been given by Woods.[3] The problem solver should also separate people's observations from their interpretations of what went wrong. A common mistake is to assume that the most obvious conclusion or the most common is always the correct one. (This is, however, a good place to start, though not necessarily to stop.) A famous medical school proverb that relates to the diagnosis of disease is: "When you hear hoofbeats, don't think zebras." In other words, look for common explanations first. Finally, the problem solver should continually reexamine the assumptions and discard them when necessary.

Fear of Flying. . . .

A new model of airplane was delivered to Eastern Airlines in 1980. Immediately after the planes were in operation, the flight attendants developed a red rash on their arms, hands, and faces. It did not appear on any other part of the body and the rash occurred only on flights that were over water. Fortunately, it usually disappeared in 24 hours and caused no additional problems beyond that time. When the attendants flew other planes over the same routes, no ill effects occurred. The rash did not occur on all the attendants of a particular flight. However, the same number of attendants contacted the rash on each flight. In addition, a few of those who contracted the rash felt ill, and the union threatened action because the attendants were upset, worried, and believed some malicious force was behind it. Many doctors were called in, but all were in a quandary. Industrial hygienists could not measure anything extraordinary in the cabins. Carry out a K.T. Problem Analysis to see if you can learn the cause of the problem. (*Chemtech*, 13(11), 655, 1983)

	IS	IS NOT	DISTINCTION
What:	Rash	Other illness	External contact
When:	New planes used	Old planes used	Different materials
Where:	Flights over water	Flights over land	Different crew procedures
Extent:	Face, hands, arms	Other parts	Something contacting face, hands and arms
	Only some attendants	All attendants	Crew duties

We now look at all the distinctions and see that a) something contacting the arms and face could be causing the rash, b) the rash occurs only on flights over water, and that the use of lifevests are demonstrated on flights over water, and c) the lifevests on the new plane are made of new materials or of a different brand of materials and that usually three flight attendants demonstrated the use of the lifevests. The new life preservers had some material in or on them that was the rash-causing agent!

Oh, Nuts!!!*

The Nuts'n'Bolts Auto Parts Company manufactures and distributes auto parts throughout the United States. Over a period of several months, they have been receiving a large number of complaints about corroded bolts from consumers. Virtually all of the complaints were received between June and August. There were a few complaints during some of the other months, but almost none in January and February.

In addition to its manufacturing plant in Detroit, Nuts'n'Bolts has four major distribution centers in Atlanta, Phoenix, Denver, and Houston, where shipments from Detroit are stored in warehouses. There seems to be a strong geographical pattern to the complaints with respect to where shipments originated. A majority of the complaints came from shipments from the regions in Houston and Atlanta. Virtually no complaints came from the centers at Denver and Phoenix. Sampling indicates that not every part from any given shipment is corroded; only some of the parts, some of the time, from certain geographical locations. Also, due to excellent quality control, virtually no product leaves the plant with any signs of corrosion.

The parts are packaged in cardboard boxes, with cardboard placed in between layers of bolts to act as a shock absorber. A few years ago paper was supplied exclusively by Wolverine Paper, whose plant is located near Lake Superior in Michigan. The newly appointed manager in the Nuts'n'Bolts packaging department noted that Wolverine Paper was overcharging for their product and decided to look into other suppliers.

The best price offered by far (almost 20% cheaper than the next lowest bid) was from Acadia Paper, located in Maine. Research into how Acadia was able to provide such a low bid yielded the following information. The plant was intended to produce high-grade paper, but the water intake for the mill is located in a tidal basin, allowing seawater to enter the processing water supply. Because of this, only low-grade paper can be produced at the plant. In order to get rid of their excess low-grade paper, Acadia began offering packaging paper well below the "market price."

The manager also set up a contract with Badger Paper, whose plant is located near Lake Michigan in Wisconsin. Badger had recently been fined by the Environmental Protection Agency for dumping excessive waste in Lake Michigan. As a result, several changes in Badger's production were made to stay within the EPA's waste limits. This resulted in a decrease in the overall paper quality. In addition to these two suppliers, Nuts'n'Bolts still purchased some of its paper from Wolverine Paper Co. Current prices offered by the paper companies determine which company's paper ends up as packaging material for any batch of product.

A confounding factor is that Nuts'n'Bolts has noticed that the quality of the steel to make bolts provided by Heavy Metal has decreased substantially after several key personnel retired. On one occasion Heavy Metal tried to supply materials that arrived exhibiting excessive amounts of corrosion. The president of Nuts'n'Bolts had the shipment sent back to Heavy Metal and threatened to pull the account. After this, there were two other similar incidents of corroded Heavy Metal materials reported. Use a K.T. Problem Analysis to find the cause of the corrosion.

*Based on a true industrial problem. Developed in collaboration with Michael Szachta and Professor Brymer Williams, University of Michigan, 1992.

(continued)

Oh, Nuts!!! *(continued)*

Solution

K.T. Problem Analysis
Problem Statement: What causes the corrosion in the product?

	Is	Is Not	Distinction	Probable Cause
What	Corroded product	Non-corroded product	Corrosion	Salt
Where	In Atlanta and Houston	Denver and Phoenix	Type of climate	Effect of humidity on corrosion
	Badger or Acadia Plant	Wolverine Plant	Salt in Acadia No salt in Badger or Wolverine	Tidal basin contamination
When	Summer	Winter	Temperature and humidity	Moist paper
	After new paper companies added	Before new paper companies added	Different paper companies process	Salt in paper
Extent	Some of the product	All of the product	Different paper for packaging	Different paper companies
	All bolts in shipment	All bolts in all boxes	Something contacting surface of all bolts	Packaging material

Probable cause: Salt in paper is moving onto parts through water from humid air.

Analysis

In many problems, as in this one, there is an overload of information. A key step in the solution process is to sort out the relevant information from the extraneous facts. For example, in this problem it would be easy to assume that the steel company is responsible for the corroded parts, but this fact does not explain why complaints occur in the summer and why in only certain regions of the country. The only major change recently is the switch in paper companies. But which of the paper companies is causing the problem and how? Wolverine Paper can be eliminated as the cause, since there had never been a problem with them before and no major changes have occurred in their production process. The change in Badger Paper's process could be the cause of the problem, but Acadia Paper seems the most likely candidate, since salts, which are known to cause corrosion, are in the paper already. This fact explains how the salt gets to the parts, but not why only certain geographical locations are affected during certain times of the year.

Because the problem occurs mostly in the summer time, we might suspect that temperature, in combination with the paper type, would be the cause of the

(continued)

> **Oh, Nuts!!!** *(continued)*
>
> corrosion problem, but the problem doesn't occur in Phoenix, which eliminates temperature as an independent factor. Therefore, we must look at another major change in the affected areas: The arrival of summer brings not only an increase in temperature but an increase in humidity. The paper absorbs the water in the air during humid days, creating a medium through which the salt in the paper is able to contact the metal parts. Once this has occurred, the salts then act to corrode the product.
>
> As we can see, the use of the Kepner-Tregoe Problem Analysis is beneficial in determining which parts of a problem statement are relevant, thereby facilitating solution of the problem. This problem was adapted from an actual scenario. Unfortunately, because of the problems with their paper, Acadia Paper Co. went out of business.

Decision Analysis

In this section, we will discuss *how to choose the best solution* from a number of alternatives that have been formulated to solve the problem. The K.T. Decision Analysis is a logical algorithm for choosing between different alternatives to find the one that best fulfills all the objectives. The first step is to write a concise *decision statement* about what it is we want to decide and then to use the first four steps discussed in Table 5-1 to gather information.

> **Choosing a Paint Gun***
>
> A new auto manufacturing plant is to be built and you are asked to choose the electrostatic paint spray gun to be used on the assembly line. The industry standard gun is Paint Right. While experience has shown that Paint Right performs adequately, its manufacturer is located in Europe, making service slow and difficult. In addition, because Paint Right dominates the market, its price is significantly inflated. Two American companies are eager to enter the market with their products: New Spray and Gun Ho.
>
> **Decision statement:** Choose an electrostatic paint spray gun. The paint guns available are Paint Right, New Spray, and Gun Ho.
>
> *Based on a true industrial problem developed in collaboration with Corinne Falender.

Next we specify the objectives of the decision and divide these objectives into two categories: **musts** and **wants**. The musts are mandatory to achieve a successful solution and they have to be measurable. Next we evaluate each alternative solution against each of the musts. If the alternative solution satisfies all the musts, it is a "go"; if it does not satisfy any one of the musts, it is a "no go," that is, it should not be considered further. In the paint gun example, laboratory experiments showed that Gun Ho could not control the flow of paint at the level required, and thus it was dropped from consideration.

After learning which alternatives satisfy the musts, we proceed to make a list of the objectives we would want to satisfy. The wants are desirable but not mandatory and give us a comparative picture of how the alternatives perform relative to each other.

We list each want, and then assign it a *weight* (1–10) to give us a sense of how important that want is to us. If a want is extremely important, it should be given a weight of 9 or 10. However, if it is only moderately important, such as the "durability of the paint gun," the weight should be a 6 or 7. The next step is to evaluate each alternative against the wants and give it a *rating* (0–10) as to how well it satisfies the want. If the alternative fulfills all possible aspects of a want, it would receive a rating of 10. On the other hand, if it only partially fulfilled the want, it might receive a 4 or 5 rating. For example, in *Choosing a Paint Gun*, the plant personnel are quite experienced at using the current Paint Right spray gun, so it receives a rating of 9 for the experience want. We then multiply the weight of the want by the rating to arrive at a score for the want for that alternative. For the "experience" want, the score is 4 × 9 = 36. We do this evaluation for every want and add up the scores for each alternative. The alternative with the highest total score is your tentative first choice.

Assigning weights is indeed a subjective task. However, comparing all the wants two at a time can help to arrive at a consistent assignment of weights. Returning to the paint gun example, there are three pairs of the wants that we can compare: Want 1 with Want 2, Want 2 with Want 3, and Want 3 with Want 1. Let's first compare *ease of service* with *durability* and decide *ease of service* is more important. Next we compare *durability* with *experience* and decide that *durability* is more important. Finally, we compare *experience* with *ease of service*. If we would decide that *experience* is more important than *ease of service*, then we would have an inconsistency that we would have to resolve:

{Ease of Service}	is more important than	{Durability}
{Durability}	is more important than	{Experience}
{Experience}	is more important than	{Ease of Service}

This is like saying, "I like red better than blue, and blue better than green, but I like green better than red." There is an inconsistency that doesn't make sense. The weights and the ordering must be reconsidered in view of the overall picture, so that the final values assigned are consistent.

This situation is obviously easy to avoid with so few wants to consider (three in the paint gun example). However, with a larger list to consider, things become more difficult, and inconsistencies can arise. There is a story that the U.S. Army was taking a survey regarding the food preferences of enlisted men. The men were provided with a long list of food and asked to indicate their preference for the foods, on a scale of 1–10 (10 = like very much, 1 = dislike very much). As a test of the consistency of the information, the Army put several foods on the long list more than one time. Cauliflower was placed on the list twice, once following ice cream, and once following asparagus. The cauliflower entry following ice cream was scored a 3, while the cauliflower entry following asparagus scored a 7. This is clearly inconsistent. The score given to cauliflower was influenced by the foods surrounding it on the list. After ice cream, a real favorite, it scored quite low, while after asparagus, it scored much higher. The warning here is clear: The assessments of the weights for the wants in a decision analysis, while very subjective, must be checked for internal consistency if the decision is to be valid.

While identifying weights and scoring may at first seem somewhat subjective, it is an extremely effective technique for those who can dissociate themselves from their personal biases and arrive at a logical evaluation of each alternative. If the alternative you "feel" should be the proper choice turns out to have a lower score than the tentative first choice, then you should reexamine the weight you have given to each want. Analyze your instincts to better understand which wants are really important to you. After this rescoring, if your alternative still scores lower than the others, perhaps your "gut feeling" may be incorrect.

Course of Action: The first step is to break down the important qualities of paint guns, and to decide what you **must** have and what you **want** to have. From your experience and discussions with other paint personnel, you determine that you have two **musts**: 1) adequate control over paint flow rate, and 2) acceptable paint appearance. Also, you identify four **wants**: 1) easy service, 2) low cost, 3) long-term durability, and 4) plant personnel with experience in using the product. Plant records show that Paint Right is able to meet both musts. You then run laboratory experiments with New Spray and Gun Ho to determine whether each of them is also able to meet both musts. The four wants are then weighted, and ratings assigned for each gun that satisfies the musts (as carefully as possible).

Solution

Musts		Paint Right		New Spray		Gun Ho
Adequate flow control		Go		Go		No Go
Acceptable appearance		Go		Go		Go

Wants	Weight	Rating	Score	Rating	Score	
Easy Service	7	2	14	9	63	
Low cost	4	3	12	7	28	**NO**
Durability	6	8	48	6	36	**GO**
Experience	4	9	36	2	8	
Total			110		135	

New Spray was chosen to replace Paint Right.

The last step is to explore the risks associated with each alternative. We take the top-scoring alternatives and make a list of all the things that could possibly go wrong if we were to choose that alternative. We then try to evaluate the *probability* (0–10) that the adverse consequence could occur and the *seriousness* (0–10) of this consequence *if* it were to occur. The product of these two numbers can be thought of as the *threat* to the success of the mission. It is important not to let the numerical scores in the decision table obscure the seriousness of an adverse consequence. In some cases, the second highest scoring alternative may be selected because the adverse consequences of selecting the highest scoring alternatives are too threatening.

Several years ago, a graduating senior from the University of Michigan used K.T. Decision Analysis to help him decide which industrial job offer he should accept. John had a number of constraints that needed to be met. Specifically, his fiancée (now his wife) was also graduating in chemical engineering at the same time and they both

K.T. Decision Analysis—Job Offer

Objectives **Musts**	Dow Corning		ChemaCo		TrueOil	
In Midwest	Midland, MI	GO	Toledo, OH	GO	Detroit, MI	GO
Located w/in 40 miles of spouse's position	Another major company is also in Midland	GO	Industrialized N. Ohio	GO	Southeastern Michigan	GO
Non-transfer policy **Transfer**	Major plant in Midland	GO	Major plant in Toledo	GO **NO GO**	**Must** **NO GO**	

WANTS	Weight	Rating/Score		Rating/Score			
Near home town (Traverse City, MI)	8	150 miles	10	80	400 miles	5	40
Attitude of interviewer	5	Knowledgeable & positive	8	40	Knowledgeable & positive	8	40
Large company	6	Medium size	6	36	Small size	3	18
Salary & benefits	9	Good	6	54	Very good	8	72
Plant safety	10	Good (silicone)	7	70	Mainly oil derivatives (OK)	5	50
Education assistance program	10	Tuition aid	8	80	Tuition aid	8	80
Encourage advanced degree	10	Very positive	9	90	Positive	8	80
Stability of industry	4	Silicone (very good)	9	36	Oil (excellent)	10	40
Company image	4	Known	5	20	Unknown	3	12
Type of position	10	Process engineer	9	90	Pilot plant design & operation	10	100
Advancement policy	7	From within	10	70	From within	10	70
Return on stockholder investments	3	Excellent (#2 in nation)	10	30	Excellent (#4 in nation)	10	30

wanted to remain reasonably close to their hometown in Michigan. In addition, as a part of a dual-career family, he needed a guarantee that the company would not transfer him. After interviewing with a number of companies, he narrowed his choices to three companies, Dow Corning, ChemaCo, and TrueOil.

The first thing John did was to identify the **musts** that had to be satisfied. These criteria are shown in K.T. Decision Analysis—Job Offer above. Upon evaluating each company to learn if it satisfied all the musts, he found that TrueOil did not satisfy the non-transfer *must*. Consequently, it was eliminated from further consideration. Next all the wants were delineated and a weight assigned to each criterion. The remaining two companies were then evaluated against each want and a total score was obtained for each company. Dow Corning scored 696 points, and ChemaCo. 632 points; the apparent best choice was Dow Corning.

However, before making the final decision, the adverse consequences of the first and second choices needed to be evaluated. The results of the adverse consequence analysis are shown in the following table. The adverse consequences analysis ranked both choices in the same order as before, thus the apparent first choice became the final choice.

Adverse Consequences
Job Offer Analysis

	Probability of Occurrence (P)	Seriousness (S)	P×S
Alternative—Dow Corning			
Wife working in same company	5	7	35
Midland is not very exciting	6	3	18
High rent	4	6	<u>24</u>
Total			77
Alternative—ChemaCo.			
Wife working in same company	3	7	21
Must work nights	6	8	48
High rent	5	6	<u>30</u>
Total			99

Both John and his wife are working at Dow Corning in Midland, Michigan. (Only the names of the other companies have been changed in this real-life example.)

Cautions

The assigning of weights and scores is indeed very subjective. One could easily abuse this decision-making process by giving higher weights/scores to a predetermined favored project. Such a biased weighting would easily skew the numbers and sabotage the decision-making process. The user is urged to refer to Kepner and Tregoe's book to become aware of certain danger signals that guarantee acceptance of a certain alternative and that blackball all others. This biasing could result from "loaded" want objectives, listing too many unimportant details which obscure the analysis, or a faulty perception of which objectives can guarantee success. Consequently, it is very important to keep an open mind when making your evaluation.

Missing Information

The most difficult decisions are those where you don't have all the necessary information available upon which to base the decision. Under these conditions it could be helpful after you have prepared a K.T. Decision table to look at the extremes of the missing information and to perform a "What if . . . ?" analysis. For example, just suppose in the job offer scenario, Dow Corning had not yet decided the type of position John would have with the company. John could assume the best case (his desired position of process engineer) which he would rate at 9.0, and the worst case in his opinion (e.g., traveling sales representative on the road full time) which would give a low rating of 1.0. With this assumption, the total score for Dow Corning would drop to 616 which is now below the score of ChemaCo. We see that this "want" requires a key piece of information and that John must obtain more information from Dow Corning before he can accept their offer. If Dow Corning could not tell John which type of job he would have, they might at least be able to tell him which type of job he might *not* have (e.g., traveling sales representative). If they cannot do the latter, John could have been "forced" to choose ChemaCo. On the other hand, if all other factors are positive, John could decide to *take a risk* and choose Dow Corning with the chance he will be able to secure the desired position upon hiring or shortly after being hired.

Potential Problem Analysis

Having made our decision, we want to plan to ensure its success. We need to look into the future to learn what could go wrong and make plans to avoid these pitfalls. To aid us in our planning, Kepner and Tregoe have suggested an algorithm that can be applied not only to ensuring the success of our decision but also when analyzing problems involving safety. The K.T. Potential Problem Analysis (PPA) approach can decrease the possibility of a disastrous outcome. As with the other K.T. approach, a table is constructed: The PPA Table delineates the potential problems and suggests possible causes, preventive actions, and contingent actions.

K.T. Potential Problem Analysis			
Potential Problem	Possible Causes	Preventive Action	Contingent Actions
A.	1.		
	2.		
B.	1.		
	2.		

In analyzing potential problems, identify how serious each problem would be if it were to occur and how probable it is to occur. Would the problem be fatal to the success of the decision (a must), would it hurt the success of the decision (a want), or would the problem only be annoying? First, we identify all the *potential problems* that could occur and the *consequences* of each occurrence. Be especially alert for potential problems when (1) deadlines are tight, (2) you are trying something new, complex, or unfamiliar, (3) you are trying to assign responsibility, and (4) you are following a critical sequence. Next, list all the *possible causes* that could bring about each problem and develop *preventive actions* for each cause. Finally, develop a *contingent action* (last resort) to be undertaken if your preventive action fails to prevent the problem from occurring. Establish early warning signs to trigger the contingency plan. Do not, however, proceed with contingency plans rather than focusing on preventive actions.

Ragin' Cajun Chicken*

Wes Thompson is a manager of a Burgermeister restaurant, which specializes in fast food hamburgers. He has just been notified by the corporation that a new chicken sandwich, called Ragin' Cajun Chicken, will be introduced into Burgermeister restaurants in two weeks. This surprised Wes because he has never heard anything about the new sandwich from the company or from advertisements. The memo says that plans for a national advertising campaign have unfortunately been delayed until after the introduction of the sandwich.

The memo also says that next week, Wes's restaurant will receive a shipment of 500 Ragin' Cajun Chickens. These are shipped frozen and have a shelf life of three months in the freezer. The notification also stresses the importance of proper handling of the uncooked chicken. In order to prevent cross-contamination by salmonella, the bacteria present in some raw chicken, specially marked tongs will be used to handle only uncooked chicken.

With the shipment of the chicken, Wes's restaurant will receive a new broiler to be used exclusively for the new sandwich. It is important that the broiler operate at least at 380°F to ensure that the chicken will be fully cooked in the five-minute preparation time.

Potential Problem	Consequence	Possible Cause	Preventive Action	Contingent Action
People don't buy sandwich	Restaurant loses money	Customers don't know about sandwich	Make own signs for sandwich	Have cashiers suggest chicken to customers
		Too expensive	Compare unit cost with competition	Run promotional specials
		Food too spicy	Inform customers of mild variety	Run promotional specials
Bacteria in food	Illness, lawsuits	Employees don't handle raw chicken properly	Train employees	Perform periodic inspections
		Improper use of broiler	Train employees	Perform periodic inspections
		Chicken stored too long	Set up dating system	Inspect and discard chicken if necessary
		Freezer not cold enough	Perform temperature checks	Inspect and discard chicken if necessary

(continued)

Ragin' Cajun Chicken *(continued)*

Potential Problem	Consequence	Possible Cause	Preventive Action	Contingent Action
Substandard sandwich quality	Customers complain; no return business	Wrong items on sandwich	Have cashiers double-check accuracy	Provide free remade sandwiches for affected customers
		Sandwich sits too long under heat lamps	Mark discard times on sandwiches	Inspect sandwiches before serving
Substandard service quality	Customers complain; no return business	Sandwich preparation takes too long	Always have chicken precooked	Have sandwiches premade

*Developed in collaboration with Michael Szachta, University of Michigan, 1993.

    Wes thought that it was very important that the transition run smoothly when Ragin' Cajun Chicken would be added to the menu in two weeks. To prevent any problems, he noted concerns in four areas and constructed the previous PPA table.

    Of the 10 possible causes for potential problems noted in the table, four occurred. With the strategy in place, possible disaster was averted. Wes noticed the following problems:

- Most customers were unaware of the new menu item. Wes made signs announcing the new sandwich and asked his cashiers to suggest the chicken sandwich (i.e., "Would you care to try our new Ragin' Cajun Chicken today?"). Sales of the sandwich increased dramatically because of this.

- Wes held a special training session for all the employees to explain how critical the proper handling and preparation of the chicken is. Afterwards, Wes also performed periodic inspections and noticed that employees weren't following his instructions (use special tongs and wash hands after handling raw chicken). After a week of inspections, the new operating procedures were being followed by all employees. Fortunately, no cases of food poisoning were reported.

- At the training session, Wes also explained the broiler operating procedures. Once the Ragin' Cajun Chicken was placed on the menu, Wes observed how employees operated the new broiler. Thanks to his observation, an explosion that might have been caused by improper lighting of the broiler was avoided.

- Early on, there were several complaints about improperly made sandwiches. This problem was solved by having cashiers double-check the accuracy of the order before serving the sandwich. This double-checking helped improve the communication between cashiers and cooks, and higher accuracy in sandwich preparation was noticed in all sandwiches.

Lemon-Aid
Buying a Used Car—Not a Lemon

Potential Problem	Possible Causes	Preventive Action	Contingency Plan
1. Buying a car that has improperly aligned front and back wheels.	Car in accident	Pour water on dry pavement and drive through to determine if front and rear wheel tracks follow the same path or are several inches off	Don't buy car.
2. Body condition not what it appears to be (concealed body damage).	Car in an accident or body rusted out	Use a magnet along rocker panels, wheel wells, and doors to check for painted plastic filler to which the magnet won't stick. Look under insulation on doors and trunk for signs the car was a different color.	Offer much lower price.
	Car was in a flood, window/trunk leak	Take a deep whiff inside car and trunk. Does it smell moldy? Look for rust in spare tire well.	
3. Car has suspension problems.	Hard use, poor maintenance	Check tire treads for peaks and valleys along the outer edges.	Require suspension be fixed before buying.
4. Leaking fluids.	Poor maintenance	Look under hood and on the ground for signs of leaking fluids.	Require seals be replaced before buying.
5. Odometer not correct.	Tampered with or broken	Check windows and bumpers for decals or signs of removed decals indicating a lot of traveling. Look for excessive wear on accelerator and brake pedals. Check the title.	Offer much lower price.
6. Car ready to fall apart.	Car not maintained during previous ownership	Check fluid levels (oil, coolant, transmission, brake). Check to see if battery terminals are covered with sludge. Check for cheap replacement of oil filters, battery, etc.	Don't buy car.

© Copyrighted April, 1993 Chicago Tribune Company. All rights reserved. Used with permission.

Summary

Situation Analysis				
Problems	Timing (H,M,L)	Trend (H, M, L)	Impact (H, M, L)	Process (PA, DA, or PPA)
1.				
2.				
3.				

Problem Analysis				
	IS	IS NOT	Distinction	Probable Cause
What				
Where				
When				
Extent				

Decision Analysis							
Alternative:		A		B		C	
Musts	1.		GO		GO		GO	
	2.		GO		NO GO		GO	
Wants	WT	Rating	Score	Rating	Score	Rating	Score
1.					NO GO		
2.							
		Total A=		Total B=		Total C=	

Potential Problem Analysis			
Potential Problems	Possible Causes	Preventive Actions	Contingency
A.	1.		
	2.		
B.	1.		
	2.		

Copyright Kepner-Tregoe, Inc., 1994. Reprinted with permission.

References

1. Kepner, C.H., and B.B. Tregoe, *The Rational Manager*, 2nd ed., Kepner-Tregoe, Inc., Princeton, NJ, 1976.
2. Kepner, C.H., and B.B. Tregoe, *The New Rational Manager*, Princeton Research Press, Princeton, NJ, 1981.
3. Woods, D.L., *A Strategy for Problem Solving*, 3rd ed., Department of Chemical Engineering, McMaster University, Hamilton, Ontario, 1985; *Chem. Eng. Educ.*, p. 132, Summer 1979; *AIChE Symposium Series*, 79 (228), 1983.

Further Reading

Kepner, C.H., and B.B. Tregoe, *The New Rational Manager*, Princeton Research Press, Princeton, NJ, 1981. Many more worked examples on the K.T. Strategy.

Keith, Lawrence A., "Report Results Right!," Parts I and 2, *Chemtech*, p. 35 1, June 1991, and p. 486, August 1991. Guidelines to help prevent drawing the wrong conclusions from your data,

Exercises

Situation Analysis

1. *The Exxon Valdez.* It is 12:45 AM in the morning, March 24, 1989; you have just been alerted that the Exxon Valdez tanker has run aground on the Bligh Reef and is spilling oil at an enormous rate. By the time you arrive at the spill, 6 million gallons of oil have been lost and the oil slick extends well over a square mile.

    A meeting with the emergency response team is called. At the meeting it is suggested that a second tanker be dispatched to remove the remaining oil from the Exxon Valdez. However, the number of damaged compartments from which oil is leaking is not known at this time and there is concern that if the tanker slips off the reef, it could capsize if the oil is only removed from the compartments on the damaged side.

    The use of chemical dispersants (i.e., soap-like substances) which would break up the oil into drops and cause it to sink is suggested. However, it is not known if there is sufficient chemical available for a spill of this magnitude. The marine biologist at the meeting objected to the use of dispersants, stating that once these chemicals are in the water, they would be taken up by the fish and thus be extremely detrimental to the fishing industry.

    The use of floatable booms to surround and contain the oil also brought about a heated discussion. Because of the spill size, there is not enough boom material even to begin to surround the slick. The Alaskan governor's office says the available material should be used to surround the shore of a small village on a nearby island. The Coast Guard argues that the slick is not moving in that direction and should be used to contain or channel the slick movement in the fjord. The Department of Wildlife says the first priority is the four fisheries that must be protected by the boom or the fishing industry will be depressed for years, perhaps generations to come. A related issue is that millions of fish were scheduled to be released from the fisheries into the oil contaminated fjord two weeks from now. Other suggestions as to where to place the boom material were also put forth at the meeting.

Carry out a K. T Situation Analysis on the Exxon Valdez Spill as discussed above,

2. *The Long Commute.* The Adams family of four lives east of Los Angeles in a middle-class community. Tom Adams' commute to work is 45 miles each way to downtown L.A. and he is not in a car or van pool. He has been thinking about changing to a job closer to his home but has been working for over a year on a project that, if successfully completed, could lead to a major promotion. Unfortunately, there is a major defect in the product which has yet to be located and corrected. Tom must solve the problem in the very near future because the delivery date promised to potential customers is a month away.

   Tom's financial security is heavily dependent on this promotion because of rising costs at home. Both children need braces for their teeth, he is in need of a new car (it broke down twice on the freeway this past fall), the house is in need of painting, and there is a water leak in the basement that he has not been able to repair.

   Sarah, Tom's wife, a mechanical engineer, has been considering getting a part-time job, but there are no engineering jobs available in the community. Full-time positions are available in Northern L.A., but this would pose major problems with respect to chauffeuring and managing the children. There are a couple of day-care centers in the community, but rumor has it they are very substandard. In addition, last year, their son, Alex was accepted as a new student by the premier piano teacher in the area and there is no public transportation from their home to his studio. Melissa is very sad at the thought of giving up her YMCA swimming team and her girl scout troop, which both meet after school.

   Carry out a K. T. Situation Analysis on the Adams family's predicaments.

3. Make up a situation similar to Exercises 1 and 2 and carry out a K.T. Situation Analysis.

Problem Analysis

4. *Off-Color Tooth Paste.* After Crest™ tooth paste had been on the market for some time, Procter & Gamble, its manufacturer, decided to offer a mint-flavored version in addition to the original, wintergreen-flavored product.

In the course of developing the new mint-flavored product, a test batch of mint product was produced by the same pilot unit used to produce wintergreen-flavored product. The pilot equipment uses a tank and impeller device to mix the mint flavor essence with the rest of the ingredients to form the finished product (which is a very viscous solution).

Some of the pilot plant product was packed into the familiar collapsible tubes for further testing. Tubes used in testing the mint flavor were identical to those used for the wintergreen-flavored product. In the packing operation, toothpaste is pumped through lines into the as-yet unsealed ends of brand new tubes. After filling, the open tube ends are heat-sealed.

To assess storage stability, some of the filled tubes were randomly separated into several groups and each group was stored in a constant temperature room. Storage temperatures varied from 40°F to 120°F. Early sampling of the stored product showed nothing unusual. However, several months into the test, a technician preparing to test the product from one of the stored tubes noted that the first 1/4" of paste squeezed onto a toothbrush was off-color. The rest of the product in the tube met the color specification. Nothing like this had ever been seen with the original formula.

Further testing showed that one had to squeeze more product out of those tubes that had been stored at higher temperatures and/or stored for longer times before a product that met color specs would exit the mouth of the tooth paste tube. Tubes stored for a period of time at 40°F contained no off-color product while tubes stored for the same length of time at higher temperatures produced off-color paste. The only exception to these results was a single tube, stored above 40°F. A leakage of off-color product was around the base of the cap on this tube, but the product inside the tube met color specs. While other tests showed the off-color product to be safe and effective in cleaning teeth, consumers clearly would not accept a color change in a product expected to have the same color from the first squeeze to the last. Moreover, such a change could have been an early warning of more serious problems to come. This phenomenon had to be understood and eliminated before the new flavor could be marketed.

Accordingly, various possible remedies were tested: caps and tubes made of different materials, different mixing methods, etc. None of these had any effect on the off-color problem. All raw materials, including the new mint flavor essence, were checked and found to meet specs. A subsequent batch of the wintergreen product was made and tested for storage stability, and as usual, no off-color problems occurred.

Carry out a K. T. Problem Analysis to learn the cause of the off-color tooth paste.

5. *Chocolate Covered Bacteria.* Chocolate butter paste is the primary ingredient used by number of major bakeries for a wide variety of pastries. The paste is a very viscous liquid that is manufactured by *Cocomaker Industries* in a major populous city in the Midwest. *Cocomaker* supplies customers as close as Dolton, and as faraway as Chicago, which is a long drive. The paste flows from the production line into five-gallon drums, which are placed immediately into refrigerated trucks for shipment to the respective customers. Until February, all the trucks were the same size and the drums were stacked in rows three drums wide, four drums high, and eight drums deep. However, now two other small customers each requiring 20 drums per day were added in the Chicago area, which, along with an increased order by the Chicago customer Hoyne, necessitated the purchase of a larger truck. The new truck could fit five drums across, four drums high, and eight drums deep. The truck would stop at the two smaller additions, Bell Bakery and Clissold Bakery, just before and just after stopping at Hoyne Industrial Bakers in Chicago proper.

With the increased market in the Chicago area, *Cocomaker* is running at close to maximum capacity. Because the ingredients of the paste are mixed by static mixers, the pumps are currently operating at their maximum capacity and the plant is operating 20 hours per day. In November, *Cocomaker* was successful in luring two nearby customers, Damon Bakery and Oakley Bakery, away from one of its competitors. By increasing plant operation to 24 hours per day, all orders could be filled.

As the Christmas season approaches, the usual seasonal demand for the chocolate butter paste poses a problem of meeting demands not encountered in previous years. It was decided that if the processing temperature were increased by 20 degrees, the paste could be sufficiently less viscous, and production demands could be met with the current pump limitations. However, the increased capacity began to generate problems as Christmas approached. The pumps began failing on a regular basis: a strike at the supplier of the shipping containers caused *Cocomaker* to buy from a new container supplier, which claimed to carry only sturdier containers at a 10% increase in price; the safety officer had an emergency appendectomy; and most troubling, Hoyne Industrial Bakeries have been calling about an unacceptable bacteria count in shipments for the last five days. As a result, buyers of their product may have been getting ill. An immediate check of the bacteria levels show that they are at the same acceptable levels they have always been when leaving *Cocomaker*. You call Mr. Hoyne and tell him that the plant levels show that the paste is within bacteria specifications. Two days later you receive a call from Hoyne saying that they hired an independent firm and they reported the bacteria levels are well above an acceptable level. You call Damon, Bell, Clissold, and Oakley bakeries and ask them to check their bacteria count; they report back that everything is within specifications most often reported. A spot check of other customers shows no problems. You receive a call from Hoyne saying they are starting legal and governmental actions to close you down.

Carry out a K. T. Problem Analysis to learn the cause of the problem.

6. *Toxic Water.* Sparkling mineral water is the primary product of Bubbles, Inc., based in France, which serves three major markets in Europe, North America, and Australia. The water is collected from a natural spring and filtered through a parallel array of three filter units, each containing two charcoal filters. The filtration process is needed to remove trace amounts of naturally occurring contaminants. The filtered water is stored in separate tank farms, one for each market, until it is transported by tanker truck to one of the three bottling plants that serve the company's markets.

When the water arrives at the bottling plant, it is temporarily placed in 3500 m^3 storage tanks until it can be carbonated to provide the effervescence that is the trademark of the producer. Some of the water is also flavored with lemon, cherry, or raspberry additives. The sparkling water is then packaged in a variety of bottle sizes and materials from 10 oz. glass bottles to 1 liter plastic bottles. The European market receives its shipments directly by truck, usually within three days. Product bound for North America or Australia is shipped first by truck to the waterfront and then by freighters to their overseas destinations.

Business has been good for the last several months, with the North American and European markets demanding as much sparkling water as can be produced. This situation has required additional plastic bottle suppliers to keep up with the increased demand. It has also forced regularly scheduled maintenance for the Australian and North American markets to be delayed and rescheduled because of the high demand for the product. There is also, of course, a larger demand placed on the spring that supplies the mineral water for the process.

Unfortunately, all news is not good for Bubbles, Inc. The bottling plant for the Australian market is currently several weeks behind schedule due to a shipment lost at sea. This catastrophe has required that water from the company's reserve springs, which are located many miles from the bottling plant, be used to augment the water supplied by the regular spring so that the bottling plant can operate at an even higher level of production. The availability of water from the reserve springs is hindered by their remoteness, but the water from these springs does not require filtration. In addition, contract negotiations are going badly and it appears there will be a strike at all of the bottling plants. Recent weather forecasts indicate that relief from the drought that has already lasted three months is not likely.

Worst of all, the North American and Australian markets are complaining that all shipments of the sparkling water in the last six weeks have contained benzene in unacceptably high concentrations. You know that benzene is often used as an industrial solvent but is also found naturally. A quick survey of the bottling plant managers shows that the North American-bound products currently packaged and awaiting shipment have benzene concentrations in excess of acceptable concentrations. However, the managers of the bottling plants that service the Australian and European markets report that no significant level of benzene was detected in the bottles currently stored. The North American and Australian markets have already begun recalling the product, with the European market pressuring for a quick solution and threatening to recall products as a precautionary measure. (Adapted from *Chemtech*, "When the Bubble Burst," p. 74, Feb. 1992)

Carry out a K. T. Problem Analysis to learn the cause of the problem.

7. Currently there are many platforms in the Gulf of Mexico that collect the oil from a number of wells and then pump it through a single pipeline from the platform to shore. Most of these wells have always been quite productive and consequently the oil flows through the pipeline lying on the ocean floor at a reasonable rate. When the oil comes out of the wells it is at temperatures of approximately 145°F, and by the time the oil reaches shore the temperature in most pipelines is around 90°F. The temperature of the water on the ocean floor for the majority of the platforms within two miles of shore is approximately 42°F. However, the water depth increases as you move away from shore and the temperature of the water on the ocean floor decreases.

Recently two new platforms (A and B) were erected in the Gulf Coast farther out from shore than the others. About a year and a half after they both came on stream a disaster occurred on Platform A. No oil was able to be pumped to shore through the pipeline from Platform A. However, Platform B was operating without any problems. When the crude composition at the well head was analyzed it was found to be the same weight percent composition (e.g., or asphaltenes, waxes, gas) as that found in all the well heads on all other platforms. The only difference between Platform A and Platform B was that the production rate of Platform A was much less than that of Platform B. However, the production rate from Platform A was still greater than many of the platforms near the shore line.

Carry out a K. T. Problem Analysis to learn the reason for the plugging of the pipeline.

Decision Analysis

8. *Buying a Car.* You have decided you can spend up to $12,000 to buy a new car. Prepare a *K.T. Decision Analysis* table to decide which car to buy. Use your local newspaper to collect information about the various models, pricing, and options and then decide on your musts (e.g., air bag) and your wants (e.g., quadraphonic stereo, CD player). How would your decision be affected if you could spend only $9,000? What about $18,000?

9. *Choosing an Elective.* You need one more three hour nontechnical course to fulfill your degree requirements. Upon reviewing the course offerings, and the time you have available, you note the following options:

- Music 101   Music Appreciation—2 hours
- Art 101   Art Appreciation—3 hours
- History 201   U.S. History; Civil War to Present—3 hours
- Art 203   Photography—3 hours
- Geology 101   Introductory to Geology—3 hours
- Music 205   Piano Performance—2 hours

Music 101 involves a significant amount of time outside of class listening to classical music. The student reaction to the class has been mixed; some students learned what to listen for in a symphony, while others did not. The teacher for this class is knowledgeable but boring.

Art 101 has the students learn the names of the great masters and how to recognize their works. The lecturer is extremely boring and you must go to class to see the slides of the great art works. While the course write-up looks good, it misses the mark in developing a real appreciation of art. However, it is quite easy to get a relatively good course grade.

History 201 has an outstanding lecturer that makes history come alive. However, the lecturer is a hard grader and C is certainly the median grade. In addition, the outside reading and homework are enormous. While some students say the work load is equivalent to a five-hour course, most all say they learned a great deal from the course and plan to continue the interest in history they developed during this course.

Art 203 teaches the fundamentals of photography. However, equipment and film for the course are quite expensive. Most of the time spent on the course is outside of class looking for artistic shots. The instructor is very demanding and bases his grade on artistic ability. Some students say that no matter how hard you work, if you don't develop a "photographic eye" you might not pass the course.

Geology 101 has a moderately interesting lecturer and there is a normal level of homework assignments. There are two major out-of-town field trips that will require you to miss a total of one week of class during the term. The average grade is B and there is nothing conceptually difficult nor memorable about the course.

Music 205 requires you pass a tryout to be admitted to the class. While you only spend 1/2 hour a week with your professor, many, many hours of practice are required. You must have significant talent to get a C or better.

Prepare a K.T Decision Analysis Table to decide which course to enroll in.

10. *The Centralia Mine Fire.* Centralia, Pennsylvania, a small community situated in the Appalachian mountain range, was once a prosperous coal mining town. In 1962, in preparation for the approaching Memorial Day parade, the landfill of Centralia was set afire in order to eliminate odors, paper buildup, and rats. Unfortunately, the fire burned down into the passageways of the abandoned mine shafts under the town. Although repeated efforts were made to stop the blaze, the fire could not be put out. By 1980, after burning for 18 years, the fire had grown in size to nearly 200 acres, with no end in sight.

Mine fires are especially difficult situations because they are far below the surface of the earth, bum very hot (between 400°F and 1000°F), and give off both toxic and explosive gases, as well as large volumes of steam when the heat reaches the water table. Anthracite coal regions have very porous rock, and consequently, a significant amount of combustion gas can diffuse directly up through the ground and into people's homes. Subsidence, or shifting of the earth, is another serious condition arising from the fire. When the coal pillars supporting the ceilings of mines' passageways burn, large sections of earth may suddenly drop 20 or 30 feet into the ground.

Clearly, the Centralia mine fire has very serious surface impact and must be dealt with effectively. Several solutions to the mine fire are described below. Perform a K. T. Decision Analysis to decide which is the most effective method to deal with the fire. Consider such issues as cost, relocation of the town of Centralia, and potential success of extinguishing the fire.

Solution Options

1. *Completely excavate the fire site*—Strip mine the entire site to a depth of 435 feet, digging up all land in the fire's impact zone. This would require partial dismantling of Centralia and nearby Byrnesville for upwards of ten years, but available reclamation techniques could restore the countryside after this time. This method guarantees complete extinction at a cost of $200 million. This cost includes relocation of families, as well as the restorative process.

2. *Build cut-off trenches*—Dig a trench to a depth of 435 feet, then fill with a clay-based noncombustible material. Behind the trench, the fire burns unchecked, but is contained by the barrier. Cost of implementation would be about $15 million per 1000 feet of trench, and total containment of the fire would require approximately 7000 feet of trench. Additionally, partial relocation of Centralia would be required for three years, costing about $5 million.

3. *Flood the mines*—Pump 200 million gallons of water per year into the mine at a cost of $2 million annually for 20 years to extinguish the fire. Relocation of the townspeople is not necessary, but subsi-

dence and steam output should be considered, as well as the environmental impact and trade-offs of the large quantities of acidic water produced by this technique.

4. *Seal mine entrances to suffocate fire*—Encase the entire area in concrete to seal all mine entrances. then allow the fire to suffocate due to lack of air. This would require short-term relocation of the towns and outlying areas, and suffocation itself would probably take a few years owing to the large amount of air in the shafts and in the ground. Although this method has never been attempted, the cost is estimated to be about $100 million.

5. *Use fire extinguishing agents*—Pump halons (gaseous fluorobromocarbons) into the mines to extinguish the blaze. The cost for this method would be on the order of $100 million. Relocation may be necessary.

6. *Do nothing*—Arrange a federally funded relocation of the entire area and allow the fire to burn unchecked. Approximately $50 million would be required to relocate the town.

(This problem developed by Greg Bennethum, A. Craig Bushman, Stephen George, and Pablo Hendler, University of Michigan, 1990)

11. You need energy for an upcoming sports competition. You have the following candy bars available to choose from: Snickers™, MilkyWay™, Mars Bar™, Heath Bar™, Granola Bar. Which do you choose? Prepare a K.T. Analysis Table.

12. Prepare a K.T. Decision Analysis Table on selecting an apartment to move into next term (year). Consult your local newspaper to learn of the alternatives available.

Potential Problem Analysis

13. *Sandy Beach.* There was a minor oil spill on a small sandy resort beach. The CEO of the company causing the beach shoreline to be soiled with oil said: "Spare no expense, use the most costly method, steam cleaning, to remove the oil from the sand." (Adapted from *Chemtech,* August 1991, p. 481)

    Carry out a K.T. Potential Problem Analysis on the direction given by the CEO.

14. *Laboratory Safety.* The procedure in a chemistry laboratory experiment called for the students to prepare a 1.0 dm^3 aqueous solution of 30 g of sodium hydroxide. By mistake the student used 30 g of sodium hydride dispersion which reacted violently with water, evolving heat and hydrogen gas which caught fire. The sodium hydride, which was available for a subsequent experiment, was a commercial product. The container bore

a warning of the hazard of contact with water, but this warning was not visible from the side showing the name of the compound. (Adapted from *ICE Prevention Bulletin,* 102, p. 7, Dec. 1991)

Carry out a Potential Problem Analysis that, if followed, would have prevented this accident.

15. *Safety in the Plant.* A reactor approximately 6 feet in diameter and 20 feet high in an ammonia plant had to be shut down to repair a malfunctioning nozzle. The nozzle could be repaired only by having a welder climb inside the reactor to carry out the repair. During welding, the oxygen concentration was regularly monitored. Four hours after the welding was completed, a technician entered the reactor to take pictures of the weld. The next day he was found dead in the reactor. (Adapted from *ICE Prevention Bulletin,* 102, p. 27, Dec. 1991)

    Prepare a Potential Problem Analysis Table that could have prevented this accident.

16. *New Chicken Sandwich.* Burgermeister has been serving fast food hamburgers for over 20 years. To keep pace with the changing times and tastes, Burgermeister has been experimenting with new products in order to attract potential customers. Product development has recently designed a new Cajun chicken sandwich to be called Ragin' Cajun Chicken (see example on page 164). The developers have spent almost nine months perfecting the recipe for this new product.

    One of the developers got the idea for a new product while in New Orleans during last year's Mardi Gras. Product Development has suggested that the sandwich be placed on Burgermeister's menu immediately, in order to coincide with this year's Mardi Gras festivities. A majority of the time spent developing the Ragin' Cajun Chicken sandwich was dedicated to producing an acceptable sauce. Every recipe was tasted by the developers, who found early recipes for sauces to be too spicy. Finally, they agreed on the seventy-eighth recipe for sauce (Formula 78) as the best choice.

    After converging on a sauce, the Development Team focused on preparation aspects of the new sandwich. Several tests confirmed that the existing equipment in Burgermeister restaurants could not be used to prepare Ragin' Cajun Chicken. Instead, a new broiler would have to be installed in each of the 11,000 Burgermeister restaurants, at a cost of over $3,000 per unit. The new broiler would keep the chicken moist while cooking it, as well as killing any salmonella, the bacteria prevalent in chicken.

    While testing cooking techniques for the new broiler, one of developers became very ill. A trip to the hospital showed that the developer had food poisoning from salmonella. Tests determined that the source of the bacteria was a set of tongs that the developer used to handle both the raw and the cooked chicken.

Next, the Development Team decided how the sandwich would be prepared. When the Ragin' Cajun Chicken sandwich was prepared using buns currently used for other Burgermeister sandwiches, the sandwich received a very low taste rating. After experimenting, researchers found that a Kaiser roll best complemented the sandwich. Early cost estimates showed that Kaiser rolls will cost twice as much as the buns used currently for hamburgers, and are fresh half as long.

You are an executive in charge of product development for Burgermeister. Based on the information above, perform a Potential Problem Analysis, considering what could go wrong with the introduction of this new sandwich.

(Developed in collaboration with Mike Szachta. The University of Michigan, 1992)

17. *Choices.* Carry out a Potential Problem Analysis for
    a) A surprise birthday party.
    b) A camping trip in the mountains.
    c) The transportation of a giraffe from the Detroit Zoo to the Los Angeles Zoo.
    d) An upcoming laboratory experiment.
    e) The transport of nuclear waste from the reactor to the disposal site.

CHAPTER 8

Implementing the Solution

Many people get stalled in the problem-solving process because they analyze things to death and never get around to acting. In this chapter we will present a number of techniques that will facilitate the *implementation* process. Figure 8–1 identifies the phases of the implementation process.

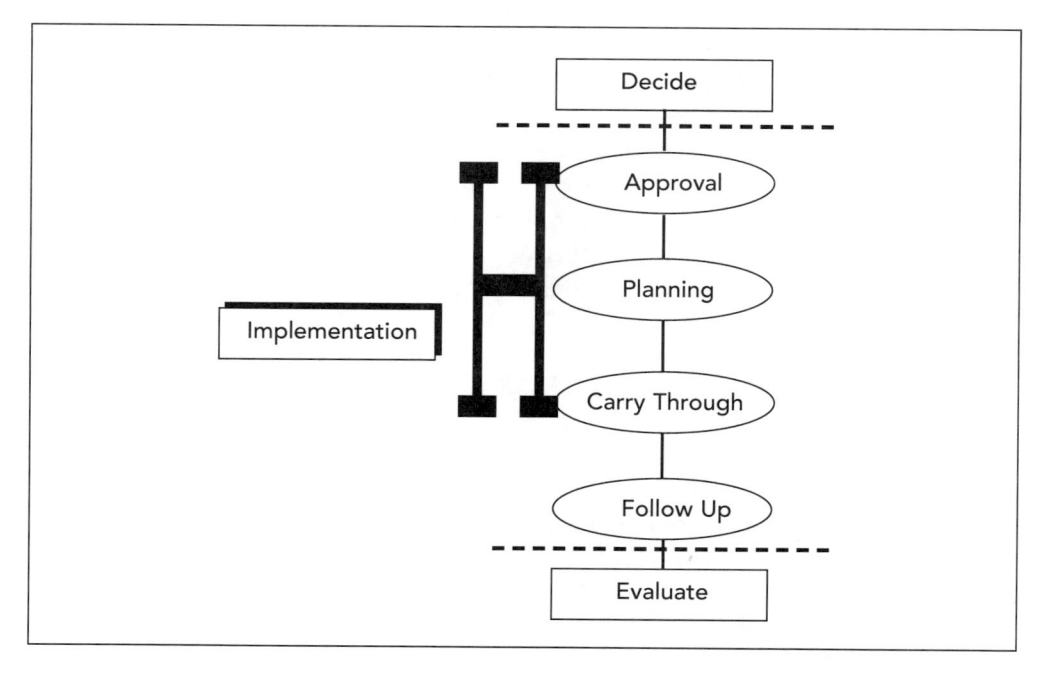

Figure 8–1. Implementing the Solution

Each of these phases will be discussed in this chapter.

Approval

In some situations, the first step in the implementation is to get approval from your organization to proceed with the chosen solution. Many times it may be necessary to *sell your ideas* so that your organization will provide the necessary resources for you to successfully complete your project. This process may include the preparation of a document or presentation describing 1) what you want to do, 2) why you want to do it, 3) how you are going to do it, 4) how your project will greatly benefit the organization and/or others. The following short checklist can help sell your ideas.

- Avoid technical jargon—keep the presentation clear and to the point.
- Make the presentation in a logical and orderly manner.
- Be concise; avoid unnecessary minute details.
- Anticipate questions and be prepared to respond to them.
- Be enthusiastic about your ideas or nobody else will be.

Planning

Now that you have the resources for the process, it is time to plan what to do, what order to do it in, and when to do it. The most important aspect of *implementing* is the planning stage. Here we look at allocations of time and resources, anticipate bottlenecks, identify milestones in the project, and identify and *sketch the pathway through to the finished solution.* After examining the various parts of the solution which are to be implemented, criteria are needed to decide which part to work on first. A modified K.T. Situation Analysis will help to identify the critical elements of the solution and to prioritize them in order to prepare a meaningful plan. Gantt Charts, Development Charts, Budgets and Critical Path Management[1] will be used to effectively allocate our time and resources. Finally, we proceed to identify what could go wrong and devise ways to prevent these roadblocks from occurring (K.T. Potential Problem Analysis). Market surveys are often used as a part of K.T. PPA to anticipate the possible success or failure of a product or process (e.g., chicken ripple chip ice cream).

To aid us in our planning, we draw on two topics previously discussed: K.T. Situation Analysis, and K.T. Potential Problem Analysis.

Allocation of Time and Resources

Having been presented with a problem, situation, or opportunity, we need to allocate our time and resources to the various steps to bring about a successful solution. The Gantt and Deployment charts, Critical Path Management, along with budgeting of personnel and money, can be used to arrive at an efficient and effective allocation. Additionally, a popular tool for scheduling daily activities is the personal organizer (e.g., the Franklin Day Planner™) used by executives and students alike to keep track of important appointments and commitments.

GANTT CHART

One of the most common ways used to allocate specific blocks of time to the various tasks in a project is the *Gantt Chart*. A Gantt Chart is a bar graph that shows when a specific task is to begin and how long it will take to complete. For the sake of discussion, suppose we have a time constraint of one year to solve the problem and we are to allocate time to each of the five building blocks of the problem-solving process. January (J), February (F), and March (M) will be spent working the problem definition and mid-March to May will be devoted to generating solutions. Note that we have suggested that time be taken to evaluate our progress at four different points along the way to check that all criteria are fulfilled: 1) after completion of the definition of the problem, 2) after deciding the course of action, 3) during the course of action, and 4) at the end of the project.

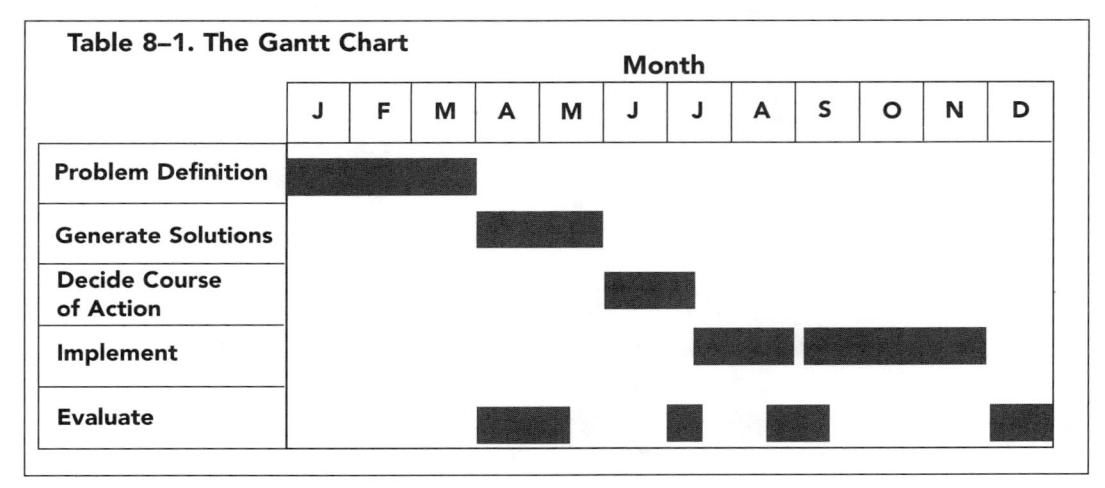

Table 8–1. The Gantt Chart

	J	F	M	A	M	J	J	A	S	O	N	D
Problem Definition	██	██	██									
Generate Solutions				██	██	██						
Decide Course of Action						██						
Implement							██	██	██	██	██	
Evaluate				██	██		██		██			██

Note that at least 25% of the time has been devoted to the problem definition phase. Many, if not most, of the consequences of incorrectly defined problems would not have occurred if more time had been spent defining the problem rather than hurrying to start a solution. Most experts agree that the project is half completed once the real problem is defined, written down, and communicated.

We now return to the heat exchanger problem discussed in Chapter 5 in which it was learned that the **real problem** was to remove the scale from the heat exchanger rather than designing and building a larger heat exchanger. Typically there can be scale on the inside and on the outside of the heat exchanger tubes. If we have an organic liquid on the outside of the tubes and water inside the tubes, the scales on either side of the tube will be different in nature. The organic scales are tar-like and the water scales are usually mineral salts.

As shown in the Gantt Chart below, a day and a half (all day Monday and Tuesday morning) are devoted to disassembling the heat exchanger. Two and a half days, Tuesday noon through Thursday, are allotted to remove the scale and get the lab results. Each of the remaining tasks in the process is scheduled in a similar manner.

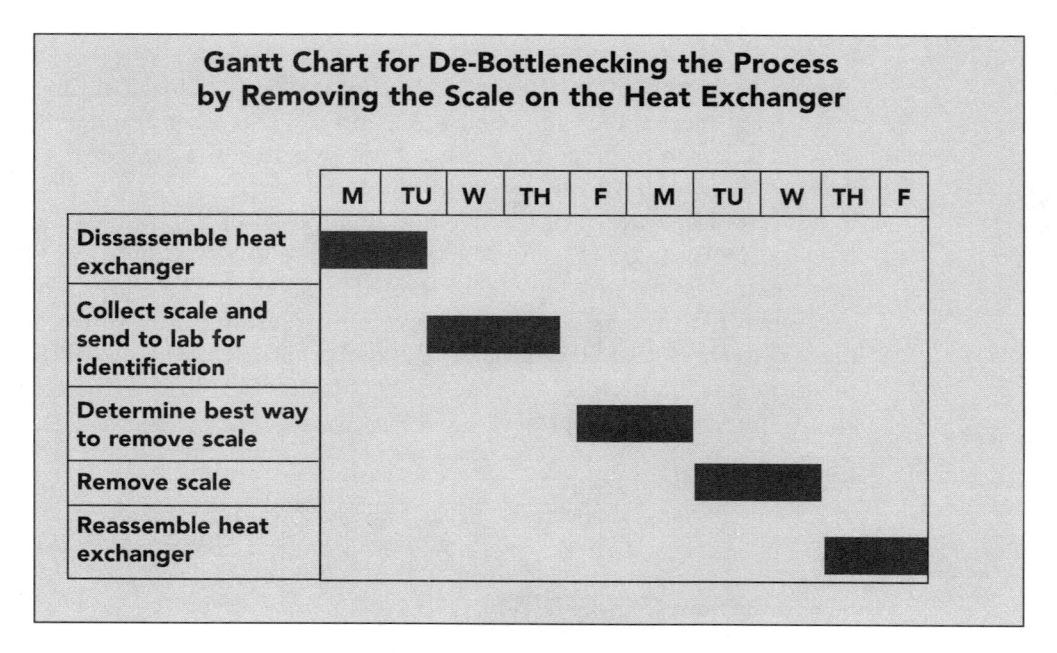

Gantt Chart for De-Bottlenecking the Process by Removing the Scale on the Heat Exchanger

	M	TU	W	TH	F	M	TU	W	TH	F
Dissassemble heat exchanger	■	■								
Collect scale and send to lab for identification			■	■						
Determine best way to remove scale					■	■				
Remove scale							■	■		
Reassemble heat exchanger									■	■

Coordination and Deployment

Most often groups of individuals will work together as a team to solve a problem. Under these circumstances, coordination among various team members is imperative to achieving an efficient solution in the time allotted. The use of a *Deployment Chart* will help guide the team through the solution by assigning different team members either major or minor responsibilities to each of the tasks.

For example, let's again consider the example of cleaning the scale (fouling) from the heat exchanger in order for it to operate more efficiently. Cesar and Stan will disassemble and reassemble the equipment. Linda will analyze the scale to determine the type and amount. Sheila will help Linda with the analysis and will also be the one responsible for seeing that the scale is properly removed. The remaining tasks and assignments are shown in the Deployment Chart for cleaning the heat exchanger on page 184.

An example of the use of a Gantt Chart that most people can relate to is the preparation of a Thanksgiving turkey dinner.

Thanksgiving Dinner

Our extended family consists of 25 people who will be attending our celebration. Let's consider our dinner menu:

		Time requirements
Main Course:	Roasted turkey (of course) with dressing (stuffing)	clean (1/2 hr), stuff (1/2 hr), cook (7 hrs at 350°F), cool and slice (1 hr)
Vegetable:	Green beans with mushroom sauce	prep. time (30 min), microwave (30 min)
Potato:	Sweet potato casserole	prep. time (30 min), cook (2 hrs at 350°F)
Sauce:	Jellied cranberry sauce	open can, slice, serve
Dessert:	Pumpkin Pie	prep. time (3/4 hrs), cook (1 hr at 425°F)
Beverages:	Coffee, Tea, Milk, Water, White wine	prep. time (minimal)

Clearly, the successful preparation and serving of the Thanksgiving meal will require substantial planning and coordination by the cook. A Gantt Chart will help us organize our time and resources (stove, microwave, etc.). We'd like to sit down to eat at 4 PM. The longest "lead-time" item is the turkey, which requires 9 hours to prepare. Thus, using the turkey as a yardstick, we must begin our preparations by at least 7 AM (a long day for the cook!). Let's try to fit this into a Gantt Chart for the preparation of the entire meal.

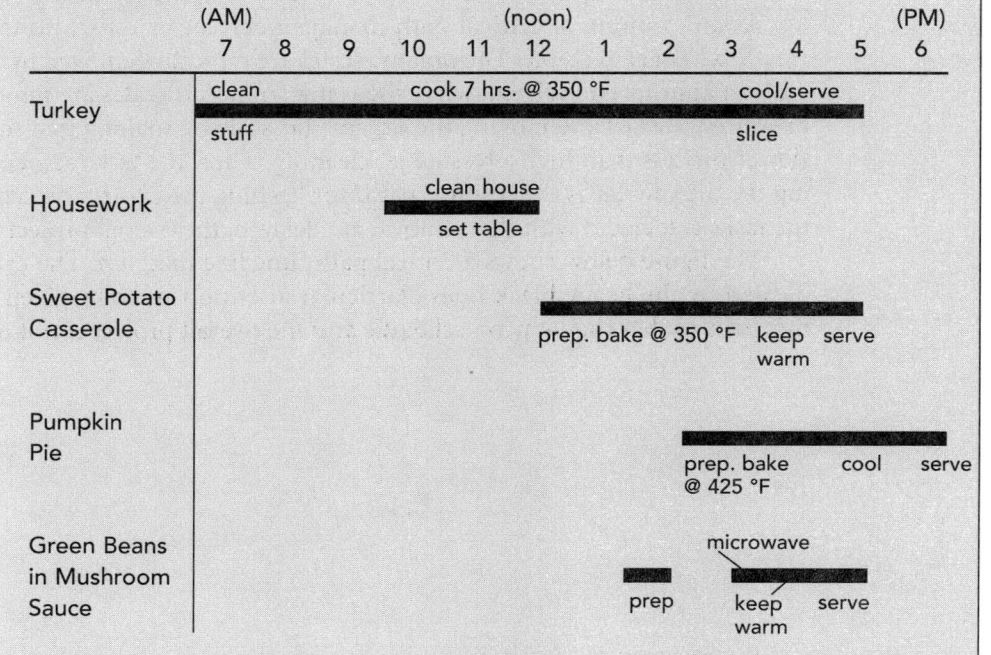

	(AM)					(noon)					(PM)
	7	8	9	10	11	12	1	2	3	4	5	6

Turkey: clean, stuff — cook 7 hrs. @ 350 °F — cool/serve, slice

Housework: clean house, set table

Sweet Potato Casserole: prep. bake @ 350 °F, keep warm, serve

Pumpkin Pie: prep. bake @ 425 °F, cool, serve

Green Beans in Mushroom Sauce: prep, microwave, keep warm, serve

The Gantt Chart shows the hectic nature of the Thanksgiving dinner preparations clearly. Any time conflicts should be apparent from the chart.

Deployment Chart for De-bottlenecking the Process by Removing the Scale on the Heat Exchanger

Task	Stan Wilson	Linda Brown	Cesar Reda	Sheila Strong
1. Disassemble heat exchanger	X		X	
2. Analyze the fouling to determine type and extent of scale		X		Advisor
3. Determine best way to remove scale	Everyone			
4. Arrange for scale to be removed		Advisor		X
5. Reassemble heat exchanger and put back on stream	X			X

Critical Path

We use critical path management to identify the critical points in the process. These critical points are readily identified by determining which tasks will cause a substantial delay in the implementation of the solution if the schedule is not met.

As an example of critical path management, let us return to the Cleaning the Heat Exchanger example. The organic scales are typically removed by dissolving them with an appropriate solvent, while the water (mineral) scales are removed with high-pressure water jets. Removing the organic tar scale by soaking in a solvent is a much slower process than high-pressure jet cleaning. Thus, the tasks associated with cleaning the organic tar is the "critical path" for keeping the project on schedule. If any of the tasks associated with this removal are delayed, the overall project will be delayed.

The figure below shows a critical path time line diagram. The critical path is indicated by the heavy black lines. Particular attention must be given to the tasks on this path so that they stay on schedule and the overall project is not delayed.

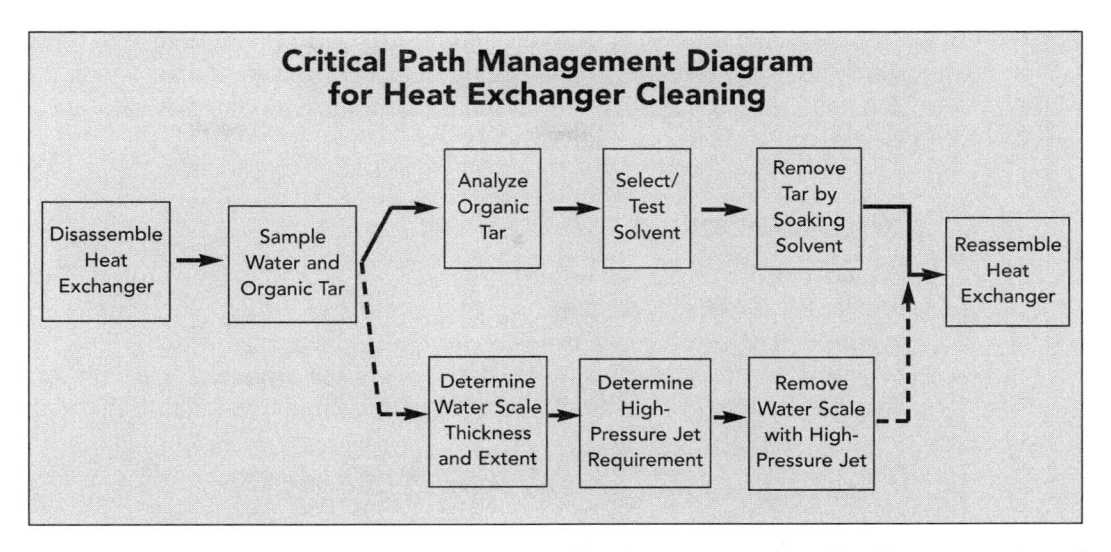

Critical Path Management Diagram for Heat Exchanger Cleaning

Disassemble Heat Exchanger → Sample Water and Organic Tar → Analyze Organic Tar → Select/Test Solvent → Remove Tar by Soaking Solvent → Reassemble Heat Exchanger

Sample Water and Organic Tar ⇢ Determine Water Scale Thickness and Extent → Determine High-Pressure Jet Requirement → Remove Water Scale with High-Pressure Jet ⇢ Reassemble Heat Exchanger

Another example of the use of critical path management is for the preparation of the annual Thanksgiving dinner. For the meal to be served on time (and to keep the guests happy) there are several critical steps in the preparation that must be completed in a timely manner or substantial delays will result. In the figure below, for example, the bold lines and boxes indicate the critical path. It refers to items that require a fair amount of time to complete. If the schedule "slips," the meal will be delayed. For example, the turkey requires approximately eight hours to clean, stuff, and cook. If the preparation of the turkey is delayed, chances are the serving time will be delayed too. The sweet potato casserole also requires a long time to complete (more than 3.5 hours), so it is critical that it is completed on schedule, or the meal will be delayed. Noncritical path items, such as setting the table, cleaning the house, and preparing the pie for baking, can be done as time permits after the critical items are completed.

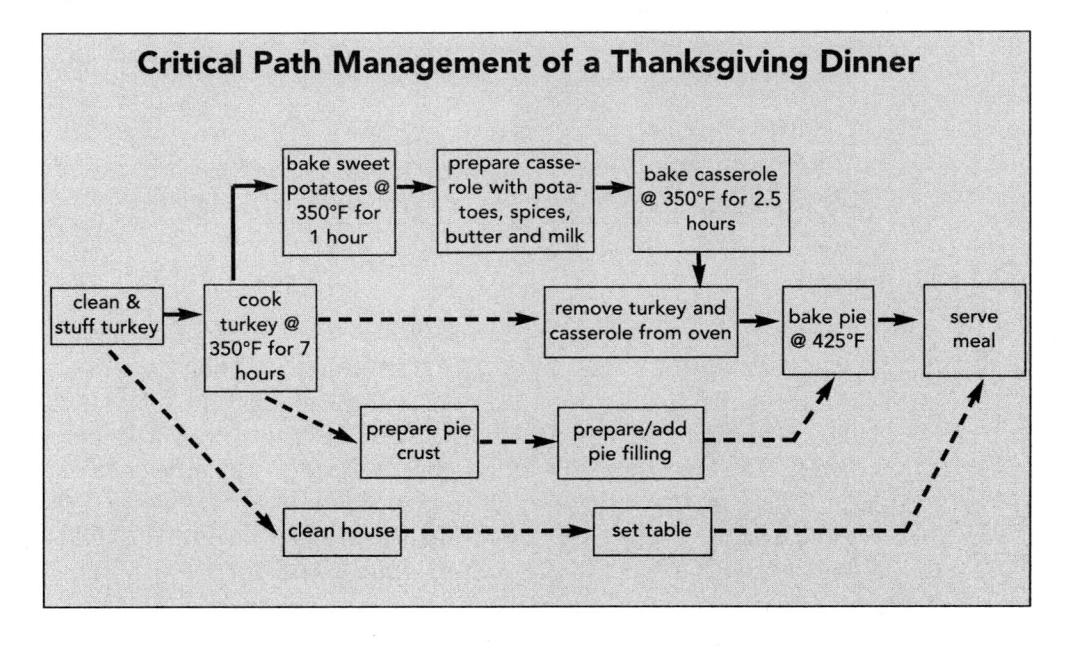

Critical Path Management of a Thanksgiving Dinner

clean & stuff turkey → cook turkey @ 350°F for 7 hours → bake sweet potatoes @ 350°F for 1 hour → prepare casserole with potatoes, spices, butter and milk → bake casserole @ 350°F for 2.5 hours → remove turkey and casserole from oven → bake pie @ 425°F → serve meal

cook turkey ⇢ prepare pie crust ⇢ prepare/add pie filling ⇢ bake pie

clean & stuff turkey ⇢ clean house ⇢ set table ⇢ serve meal

A word of caution is in order here. If noncritical path items are completed too slowly, they can become critical path items. Thus, making a critical path diagram is a dynamic process. The diagram should be continually updated as tasks are completed, viewing the project as a whole.

Necessary Resources

We must also estimate the resources necessary to complete the project. The resources usually fall into five categories: available personnel, equipment, travel, supplies, and overhead. The contingency funds are to cover unexpected expenses (e.g., extra lumber, more expensive dishwasher). At the start of the project, it is usually important to obtain an estimate of the total cost by preparing a budget similar to that shown below.

Proposed Budget

Personnel	Months/Rate	Cost	% of Total
Tom Smith, Project Director	6 mos @ $5000/mo	$ 30,000	
Bill Wade, Engineer	12 mos @ $3500/mo	42,000	
Secretary	2 mos @ $2250/mo	4,500	
Subtotal–Salaries		76,500	44%
Fringe Benefits 24% of Salaries		18,360	10%
Total Salary and Benefits		$ 94,860	
Equipment			
Fabrication in machine shop			
Parts and Labor		$ 10,000	6%
Travel			
Attend Professional Meeting		$ 1,140	0.7%
Supplies			
Chemicals, etc.		$ 4,000	2.3%
Subtotal		$110,000	
Overhead 58%		$ 63,800	37%
TOTAL BUDGET		$173,800	100%

Carry Through

The Carry Through Phase is an essential step in a successful solution process. In this phase, the various people involved in the problem-solving process act upon the plans they have formulated. Here they may carry out a design, fabricate a product, carry out experiments, make calculations, prepare a report, cook a dinner, go on an activity, etc. There are some instances in which the *Implementation* phase and the *Deciding the Course of Action* phase are intertwined. For example, it may be necessary to collect experimental or other data (implement a plan) before the right decision can be made. Great care should be taken with this phase. All the planning in the world will not save a poor job of carrying through the chosen solution. Table 8–2 provides a check list of things to monitor in the Carry Through Phase.

> **TABLE 8–2. Carry Through Check List**
> - Find the limits of your solution by making different simple models or assumptions that would clearly both
>   * overestimate the answer, and
>   * underestimate the answer.
> - Make an educated guess of what your solution will look like.
> - Construct a quick test or experiment to see if the solution you have decided upon will work under the simplest conditions.
> - Continue to learn as much as you can about the solution you have chosen. Read the literature and talk to your colleagues.
> - Continue to challenge and/or validate the assumptions of the chosen solution. Make sure no physical laws are violated.
> - Plan your computer experiments (i.e., simulations) as carefully as you would plan your experiments in the laboratory.

Revealing the Solution

A procedure for *carrying through* a solution that has many facets or components is one that is adapted from Bloom's Taxonomy. In this procedure, the activities are arranged from the most difficult (synthesis) to the easiest (comprehension). The description of these activities carried out is as follows: Evaluation, Synthesis, Analysis, Application, Comprehension, and Knowledge.

Evaluation: Evaluation is an *ongoing* process throughout the entire problem-solving process. Qualitative and quantitative judgments about the extent to which the materials and methods satisfy the external and internal criteria should be made.

Synthesis: This activity is the putting together of parts to form a new whole. Synthesis enters into problem solving in many ways. Given a fuzzy situation, synthesis is the ability to formulate (synthesize) a problem statement and/or the ability to propose a method of testing hypotheses. At the end of this activity we have *defined* the problem, *generated* a number of potential solutions and decided on which solution to implement.

Once the various parts are synthesized, each part (problem) now uses the intellectual skill described in *analysis* to continue toward the complete solution.

Analysis: This activity is the process of breaking the problem into parts such that a hierarchy of subproblems or ideas is made clear, and the relationship among these ideas is made explicit. In analysis, one identifies missing, redundant, and contradictory information.

Once the analysis of a problem is completed, the various subproblems are then reduced to problems requiring the use of *application skills.*

Application: This activity recognizes *which set* of principles, ideas, rules, equations, or methods should be applied, given all the pertinent data.

Once the principle, law, or equation is identified, the necessary knowledge is recalled, and the problem is solved as if it were a comprehension problem.

Comprehension: This activity involves understanding, manipulation, and/or extrapolation of the knowledge (i.e., principle, equation) we identified in the *Application Step* to solve a given problem. That is, given a familiar piece of information, such as a scientific principle, can the problem be solved by recalling the appropriate information and using it in conjunction with manipulation, translation, or interpretation of the equation or scientific principle?

Knowledge: Knowledge is remembering previously learned material. It is used in each step of Bloom's method of unraveling. Here we ask, "Can the problem be solved simply by defining terms and by recalling specific facts, trends, criteria, sequences, or procedures?"

The main advantage of using Bloom's Method is that it allows us to unravel the solution. That is, completion of each step (e.g., analysis) uncovers the next step to be worked on (e.g., application). Of course, additional knowledge must be injected into each step along the way.

As an example of this "unraveling" procedure, let's apply the adaptation of Bloom's Method to unravel a problem and see how it works. The Carry Through Process actually begins after we have defined the problem and synthesized a solution.

Shipping Gas

Your company has purchased a gas field in the coastal waters off Louisiana in order to have a supply of methane gas for your chemical plant on the western coast of Florida. Use Bloom's taxonomy to unravel a plan to get the gas from the field to the chemical plant.

Synthesis

The first problem statement is: *"Find a way to transport the gas from Louisiana to Florida."* We begin this task by generating ways to accomplish the transportation. The techniques in Chapter 6 will greatly aid us in addressing this first task. Some of the ways this might be accomplished are to build a pipeline from the field to the plant, to ship by rail, or to ship by sea. A K.T. Decision Analysis shows that building a pipeline is too expensive and that the plant is not anywhere near a rail line. Consequently, the transport of the gas will take place by liquefying the gas and then shipping it to the chemical plant by boat. The next statement is: *"Design a system that will liquefy 2000 lbs of methane per hour for shipment by boat from Louisiana to Florida."*

Evaluate

Before proceeding further to carry out a detailed design and sizing of the various pieces of equipment, we need to pause and evaluate the overall scheme. That is, we need to stop and do a preliminary evaluation of the proposal to ship compressed methane to the Florida plant. In the next chapter, we discuss the various items to consider in the **evaluation** phase. For example, is this scheme reasonable? What does a Potential Problem Analysis reveal?

(continued)

Shipping Gas *(continued)*

Analysis

In the analysis step we break the problem into parts and then examine each part. In order to liquify the methane, it must be compressed and cooled. The liquid methane will then be pumped into the ship. After shipping, the methane will be off-loaded at the plant in Florida.

In this example, an analysis reveals the parts are a compressor, a heat exchanger, a pump, and a ship. Having recognized that we need a compressor to liquefy the gas, we collect information to learn what pressure and temperature are necessary to liquefy and transport the methane. Next we determine which type of compressor we should use. Should it be a centrifugal or a reciprocating pump?

The gas enters the compressor at 200 psi and 110°C, and is to be compressed to 1000 psi. In order to design the heat exchanger, we must know the temperature of the gas as it leaves the compressor and enters the heat exchanger. Other points to be addressed at the analysis stage are the number of pumps required, and whether interstage cooling is required between the pumps. (K.T. Decision Analysis was used and a reciprocating pump operating close to adiabatic conditions was chosen.)

Application

We are going to use a reciprocating pump compressor and we need to know the temperature exiting the pump before we can design the heat exchanger. In the application stage, we recall the laws that apply and what assumptions are reasonable.

For adiabatic operation we recall (or look up) the pressure-volume relationship for a gas compressed adiabatically:

$$P\underline{V}^\gamma = \text{constant}$$

We also recall the ideal gas law: $P\underline{V}^\gamma = RT$

where

P = pressure, kPa, $\underline{V}$ = specific volume, m³/mol, T = temperature, K
γ = ratio of specific heats = C_p/C_v, R = Ideal Gas Constant, (m³•kPa)/(mol•K)

Note: We could also have considered departures from ideal gas law behavior.

Comprehension

Here we manipulate the equations in order to predict the exit temperature from the compressor.

$$T_2 = T_1 \left[\frac{P_2}{P_1} \right]^{1-\frac{1}{\gamma}}$$

$$T_2 = 383\,\text{K} \left[\frac{1000}{200} \right]^{1-\frac{1}{1.2}} = (383\,\text{K})(1.31) = 501\,\text{K} = 228°\text{C}$$

Evaluation

Are the numbers reasonable? A check of related problems in thermodynamics texts shows that this is indeed a reasonable number.

Follow Up

Flexibility is an essential trait for problem solvers to have in order to deal with the inevitable changes that occur during projects. Finally, in the *Follow Up Phase,* we monitor not only our progress with respect to time deadlines but also with respect to meeting solution goals that do indeed solve the problem. In this phase we periodically check the progress of the *Carry Through Phase* to make sure it is

- following the solution plan
    - *meeting solution goals
    - *fulfilling solution criteria
- proceeding on schedule
- within budget
- of acceptable quality
- still relevant to solving the original problem

It is important to check these points to make sure the solution is "on track" and satisfying all the necessary goals. Be sure to check periodically that the problem is still correctly defined during the implementation phase. Sometimes a change in conditions can occur during implementation that will invalidate the solution.

Problem Statements That Change With Time

Sometimes it may feel as if you are shooting at a moving target, as the desired goals change over the course of the project. A change in the problem statement could be the result of changing market conditions, the introduction of a competing product or services, reduced financing, or other factors. If during the *Carry Through Phase* some part, or perhaps all of the project cannot be accomplished, the problem statement must be modified. This type of information is only learned *after* we begin the solution. For example, during the course of your product development, your competitor markets a more advanced model than you were designing for nearly the same price. Consequently, you are now faced with several alternatives, which include cutting your price to significantly undercut that of the new product, or improving your design to surpass that of your competitor.

SECTION III

Logical Reasoning Tools

INTRODUCTION

Logical reasoning is the activity of determining what we should and should not believe. Because of the fact that truth is the criterion by which we determine what to believe, meaning we only want to believe that which is true, the function of logical reasoning is essentially the evaluation truth claims. The reason why this is important is that, as individuals, we can not experience everything directly and rely on other people for much of our information about the world. One problem is that we cannot always trust the accounts of the world that are presented to us for obvious reasons. People may wish us to believe certain things, not because they are true, but because it would benefit them if we believe their claims, or they might simply have gotten their information from unjustified sources. Furthermore, we ourselves may generate certain beliefs from our observations of the world that are unjustified. The objective of logical reasoning is therefore to test the integrity of our beliefs and those presented to us by others by determining their level of justification. If a belief is not sufficiently justified then we should not believe it, if it is sufficiently justified then we should believe it.

A great deal of logical reasoning is simply a matter of learning the vocabulary and concepts necessary to talk and think about thinking. Although we all think everyday, most of us do not think about thinking very often so that we lack the necessary vocabulary and concepts to do so. Learning the vocabulary and concepts necessary to evaluate truth claims is thus the first and most important step in logical reasoning. The main concept that must be learned is that of the argument. Arguments are representations of the basic units of thought. When we argue with someone, we are trying to get them to believe something based on the reasons we present to them. Arguments are therefore attempts to justify specific beliefs, and we evaluate arguments in terms of truth and validity. Truth is the criterion by which we evaluate the content of an argument, and validity is the criterion by which we evaluate its structure. Once we are able to evaluate arguments, logical reasoning is simply a question of adopting the proper attitude toward the continual development of our thinking process as well as practicing this unfamiliar activity of self-evaluation of the content and structure of our beliefs until it becomes habitual.

CHAPTER 9

Foundations of Arguments

What Is a Critical Thinker and When Do You Need to Be One?

> *A critical thinker understands the structure of an argument, whether that argument is presented by a politician, a salesperson, a talk-show host, a friend, or a child.*

This chapter will cover:

- The structure of an argument
- The three parts of an argument: issues, reasons, and conclusions

We live in what has been called the Information Age because of the many messages that we receive daily from newspapers, magazines, radio, television, books, and the Internet.

Sometimes we turn to this information for its entertainment value, such as when we watch a situation comedy, listen to music, read the sports page, or participate online in a chat room. But in a democratic society, in which the people are asked to vote on candidates and political propositions, we also need to use print and electronic sources to help us make decisions about the direction our community, state, and nation will take.

We need to know how to understand and evaluate the information that comes our way. This book will give you tools for coming to rational conclusions and making responsible choices.

> *A critical thinker is someone who uses specific criteria to evaluate reasoning and make decisions.*

When you learn to communicate well in a formal situation, your skill usually transfers to informal situations as well. For example, if you learn to make an effective informative speech in the classroom, you will also feel better about introducing yourself at parties or making a spontaneous toast at your brother's wedding. The same principle applies to critical thinking skills.

When you can listen to a presidential debate and make good judgments about what each candidate has to offer, you may also be more thoughtful about less formal arguments that are presented, such as which breakfast cereal is best for you or which car you should buy. You will be better prepared to deal with sales pitches, whether written, televised, or personal.

The methods of discernment and decision making that you will learn apply to choosing a viewpoint on a political issue or to choosing a career, a place to live, or a mate.

In short, critical thinkers do not just drift through life subject to every message that they hear; they think through their choices and make conscious decisions. They also understand the basics of both creating and presenting credible arguments.

The Structure of Argument

"The aim of argument, or of discussion, should not be victory, but progress."

Joseph Joubert, *Pensees* (1842)

When most people hear the word *argument,* they think of a disagreement between two or more people that may escalate into name-calling, angry words, or even physical violence.

Our definition of argument is different. When critical thinkers speak about arguments, we are referring to a **conclusion** that someone has (often called a claim or position) about a particular **issue**. This conclusion is supported with **reasons** (often called premises). If an individual has a conclusion but offers no reasons why he has come to that conclusion, then he has only made a statement, not an argument.

Political slogans, often found on billboards or in television advertisements, are good examples of conclusions that should not be relied upon because supporting reasons are not offered. If you see a billboard that proclaims, "A vote for Johnson is a vote for the right choice," you are encountering a conclusion with no evidence, which does not constitute an argument.

Critical thinkers withhold judgment on such a claim until they have looked at evidence both for and against Johnson as a candidate.

An argument has three parts: the *issue,* the *conclusion,* and the *reasons.*

The Issue

The issue is the question that is being addressed. It is easiest to put the issue in question form so that you know what is being discussed. When you listen to a discussion of a political or social issue, think of the question being addressed.

Examples of Issues:

- Should North, Central, and South Americans work together to combat acid rain?
- Should air traffic controllers be given periodic drug tests?
- Should we have a flat tax rate?
- Are the salaries paid to professional athletes too high?

The same method of "issue detection" will be useful in understanding commercial appeals (ads) and personal requests.

More Examples of Issues:

- Is Alpo the best food for your dog?
- Should you marry Leslie?
- Should you subscribe to the *Wall Street Journal?*

Another way to isolate the issue is to state, "The issue is whether _____."

- The issue is whether aspirin can prevent heart disease.

Issues can be about facts, values, or policies. Factual issues concern whether something is true or false, as in the following examples:

- Does aspirin prevent heart disease?
- Are smog-control devices effective in preventing pollution?
- Do we have enough money to buy a new car?

Issues about values deal with what is considered good or bad or right or wrong, as, for example:

- Is there too much violence on television?
- Is marriage better than living together?
- Are salaries of executives of major corporations too high?

Policy issues involve taking action; often, these issues emerge from discussions of facts and values. If we find that, in fact, smog-control devices are effective in preventing pollution and if we value clean air, then we should support policies that enforce the use of these devices. If aspirin prevents heart disease and we value a longer life, then we should ask a doctor whether we should take aspirin. If we do have enough money for a new car and we value a car more than other items at this time, then we should buy the new car.

Every decision that we need to make, whether it involves public or private matters, will be made easier if we can define exactly what it is that we are being asked to believe or do. Discourse often breaks down when two or more parties get into a heated discussion over different issues. This phenomenon occurs regularly on talk shows.

For example, a recent television talk show featured the general topic of spousal support, and the issue was "Should the salary of a second wife be used in figuring alimony for the first wife?" The lawyer who was being interviewed kept reminding the guests of this issue as they proceeded to argue instead about whether child support should be figured from the second wife's salary, whether the first wife should hold a job, and even whether one of the first wives was a good person.

A general rule is that the more emotional the reactions to the issue, the more likely the issue will become lost. The real problem here is that the basic issue can become fragmented into different sub-issues so that people are no longer discussing the same question.

When you listen to televised debates or interviews, note how often a good speaker or interviewer reminds the audience of the issue. Also notice how experienced spokespersons or politicians will often respond to a direct, clearly defined issue with a preprogrammed answer that addresses a *different* issue, one they can discuss more easily.

If a presidential candidate is asked how he is going to balance our federal budget, he might declare passionately that he will never raise taxes. He has thus skillfully accomplished two things: he has avoided the difficult issue and he has taken a popular, vote-enhancing stand on a separate issue.

Exercise

Purpose: To be able to identify issues.

1. Read an essay or an editorial, study an advertisement, listen to a radio talk show, or watch a television program about a controversial issue. Decide whether the issue is primarily one of fact, value, or policy. Define the issue and see if the speakers or writers stay with the issue.

   In particular, try to find an example of a person who is asked to respond to one issue and instead gives an answer to a different issue. Check to see whether the interviewer reminds the speaker that he or she has not answered the question.

2. By yourself, or as a class, come up with as many current issues as you can. Think of both light and serious issues; consider campus, community, social, national, and international concerns. Now, look at your list of issues and choose three that really concern you. Then, try to choose three about which you are neutral. Finally, answer these questions:

   a. What is it about the first three issues that makes you concerned?
   b. Why are you neutral about some issues?
   c. Do you believe there are issues on the list that should be more important to you? Why or why not?

The Conclusion

Once an issue has been defined, we can state our conclusion about the issue. Using some examples previously mentioned, **we can say yes or no to the issues presented:** yes, I believe air traffic controllers should be tested for drug use; yes, I want to subscribe to the *Wall Street Journal;* no, I will not marry Leslie at this time, and so on. We take a stand on the issues given.

The conclusion can also be defined as the position taken about an issue. It is a claim supported by evidence statements. These evidence statements are called reasons or premises.

We often hear the cliché, "Everyone has a right to his or her opinion." This is true, in the legal sense—North Americans do not have "thought police" who decide what can and cannot be discussed. When you are a critically thinking person, however, your opinion has *substance.* That substance consists of the reasons you give to support your opinion. Conclusions with substance are more valuable and credible than conclusions offering no supporting evidence.

The term *conclusion* is used differently in different fields of study. The definition given here applies most correctly to the study of argumentation. In an argumentative essay, the thesis statement will express the conclusion of the writer. In Chapter 11, you will note a related definition of conclusion used by philosophers in the study of deductive and inductive reasoning. In addition, the term *conclusion* is used to describe the final part of an essay or speech.

How can we locate the conclusion of an argument? Try the following methods when you are having trouble finding the conclusion:

1. Find the issue and ask yourself what position the writer or speaker is taking on the issue.
2. Look at the beginning or end of a paragraph or an essay; the conclusion is often found in one of these places.
3. Look for conclusion indicator words: *therefore, so, thus, hence*. Also, look for indicator phrases: *"My point is," "What I am saying is," "What I believe is."* Some indicator words and phrases are selected to imply that the conclusion drawn is the right one. These include: *obviously, it is evident that, there is no doubt (or question) that, certainly,* and *of course.*
4. Ask yourself, "What is being claimed by this writer or speaker?"
5. Look at the title of an essay; sometimes the conclusion is contained within the title. For example, an essay might be called "Why I believe vitamins are essential to health."

You may hear people discussing an issue, and someone says, "I don't know anything about this, but . . ." and proceeds to state an opinion about the issue. This comment is sometimes made as a means of continuing a conversation. Critical thinkers take a stand only when they know something about the issue; they give reasons why they have come to a certain conclusion. Of course, a critical thinker is open to hearing new evidence and may change his or her opinion on issues as new information becomes available.

Exercise

Purpose: To be able to isolate conclusions.

Take your list of issues from Question 2 in the previous exercise. Choose four issues and, in a simple declarative sentence, write your conclusion for each one.

Example:
Issue: Should air traffic controllers be given periodic drug tests?
Conclusion: Yes, air traffic controllers should be given periodic drug tests.

The Reasons

> *"Everything reasonable may be supported."*
> Epictetus, *Discourses* (2nd century)

Reasons are the statements that provide support for conclusions. Without reasons, you have no argument; you simply have a statement of someone's opinion, as evidenced in the following limerick:

> I do not like thee, Doctor Fell
> The reason why I cannot tell
> But this I know, I know full well
> I do not like thee, Doctor Fell.

Reasons are also called *evidence, premises, support,* or *justification.* You will spend most of your time and energy as a critical thinker and responsible writer and speaker looking at the quality of the reasons used to support a conclusion.

Here are some ways to locate the reasons in an argument:

1. Find the conclusion and then apply the "because trick." The writer or speaker believes _____ (conclusion) because _____. The reasons will naturally follow the word *because.*

2. Look for other indicator words that are similar to *because: since, for, first, second, third, as evidenced by, also, furthermore, in addition.*

3. Look for evidence supporting the conclusion. This support can be in the form of examples, statistics, analogies, reports of studies, and expert testimony.

There is a world of difference between supporting a political candidate because his policies make sense to you and supporting the same candidate because he or she looks like a good person. Information in the following chapters will give you skills to help you decide how a reason supports a conclusion.

Critical thinkers focus their attention first on the issue being discussed, second, on the conclusions taken, and third, on the reasons given to support or justify the conclusions.

Example:
I believe student athletes should be paid (conclusion) **because**:

- they are committed to certain hours and demands on their time
- they are making money for their schools

Exercise

Purposes: To be able to use reasons to support a conclusion. To use knowledge gained in this chapter to both analyze and construct basic arguments.

1. Write a short rebuttal to the above example, using reasons to support your conclusion.

2. Take your conclusions from the exercise on conclusions and support each conclusion with at least three reasons. This exercise can be done alone or in classroom groups, in writing or as a short speech. You might also have one group present the "pro" side of an issue and another group the con.

3. Get the editorial page of your favorite newspaper (including your campus paper) and list the issue, conclusion, and reasons given for each editorial. Use this format:

    The issue (question) is:

    The conclusion of this writer is:

    The reasons he/she gives are:

    Then evaluate the editorial by answering the following questions:

    a. Was the writer clear about the reasons given for the conclusion?

    b. Were there other reasons that could have been included in the argument?

    c. Did the writer express any understanding for an opposing viewpoint? If so, how? If not, can you articulate an opposing viewpoint for the editorial?

    d. Were you convinced by the editorial? Why or why not?

4. Read the following editorials, essays, letters, and writings. Then, isolate the issues discussed, the conclusions of the writers, and the reasons given for the conclusions. Answer the following questions:

a. Are the reasons given adequate to support the conclusions? If not, what other reasons could have been given?

b. Do you agree or disagree with the conclusions? If you disagree, what are your reasons for disagreeing?

War on Drugs Fails; We Need New Approach
by Daryl A. Bergman

The war on drugs is an abysmal failure. A fresh and bold approach is needed—beginning with the legalization of marijuana and the registration of drug addicts. It's also necessary to look to other countries such as Holland that have been successful curbing drug associated crime through the legalization of marijuana. The legalization of pot would:

- Eliminate the stepping stone to harder drugs.
- Eliminate the crime associated with large dollar street transactions.
- Provide taxes to step up law enforcement efforts (meth labs, heroin smuggling) and rehab programs.
- Free space in jails housing non-violent criminals, saving incarceration costs.

The registration of addicts would:
- Eliminate the use of dirty needles, decreasing victims of AIDS, Hepatitis B and C and associated health care costs.

Let's move forward to save our children.

Cause, Not the Effect
by Patrick Burns

The real problem we face is that society never directly addresses the problems, only the symptoms.

Gun control opponents and gun control advocates have spent millions discussing the effects of the availability of guns. That's not the concern, the concern is what is done with the guns. Switzerland has issued a machine gun to every male of military age. Most of the homes in that country are fully armed, yet no one reads of their terrible gun connected crimes.

Nearly ninety percent of all crimes in the U.S. are connected in some fashion to drugs or alcohol. If substance abuse were solved, isn't it logical that the crimes connected to it would decrease? And would there still be this battle about gun control?

As long as our society continues to placate and enable by providing access to harmful substances, then we will also reap violence and murder.

Let us focus on the source of our problems, not on the specific symptoms.

Is it because as a society, we are so selfish as to be unwilling to eradicate such harmful substances and thereby give up our momentary fixes? Such short-term thinking leads to the long-term problems we face today.

Drug use is increasing at an alarming rate. How is that going to improve our society? Think about it.

Nothing Positive in Airbag News
by Jack Hagerty

While it is always gratifying to be able to say "I told you so," there can be nothing positive about the current revelations of the tragedy concerning airbags.

I have been an opponent of airbags (which are not technically air bags but sodium azide bags, that being the chemical which explodes to fill the bag with gas) since the beginning. Most people don't realize how old the concept is, having been developed in automotive research laboratories of several universities in the 1960s. The government tried to mandate airbags in the early 1970s, but the industry successfully resisted for more than 10 years before succumbing and introducing them on the driver's side in the late 1980s.

Why should I object to a device that has proven life-saving potential? Well, outside of the current headlines about children and small adults being killed, the answers are many. First is the psychological aspect. I've dealt with explosive devices long enough both professionally and as a hobby (I am president of the largest hobby rocketry club in Northern California) to feel uncomfortable driving around with an armed pyrotechnic device aimed at my face! Beyond that, though, are the many technical shortcomings of airbags:

- Airbags are designed for a single type of crash: the single-impact, straight frontal collision. They provide no protection from multiple-impact, side-impact, corner-impact, rear-impact or roll-over collisions.
- Airbags have a limited range of operation. Despite the way they look in commercials, airbags are not big satiny pillows that balloon up gently to catch you; they explode with tremendous violence and then deflate—all in less than 1/10 of a second. This means that they are ineffective at speeds below 35 MPH (because the bag deflates before you reach it) and over 65 MPH (because you hit the steering wheel or dashboard before the bag inflates).
- Airbags do not work well unless you are right in front of them, so all manufacturers require that you wear a seat belt to hold you in position—and refer to the bag as a "supplemental" restraint system.
- Airbags are designed to work with the "average" adult which, of course, is the problem associated with the current headlines.
- Even with people satisfying all of the above criteria, there have been many documented classes of injury associated with airbags: abrasive burns of the face and hands due to the friction from the bag hitting the skin, bronchitis caused by the release powder (which coats the bag to keep it from sticking to itself) being rammed down the throat, and eyeball trauma.

To be fair, seat belts can also cause damage ranging from minor bruising to torn chest muscles and dislocated shoulders, but I know of no case where someone was killed by a belt in an accident that they would have otherwise survived had they not been wearing the belt.

Properly fastened 3-point seat belts of the type found in every car prior to the introduction of airbags provide protection superior to airbags in all types of crash situations and speeds, except single frontal impact within the speed range of the airbag, where they are roughly equal. Seat belts can be adjusted to property fit anyone from a small child (one old enough to be out of the child safety seat) to the largest adult.

- Finally, there is the issue of disposal. Only a tiny fraction of all bags installed are ever deployed, and since we are pumping them into the automotive population at the rate of some tens of millions per year, how do we get rid of them? Ever see the "care" with which your average wrecking yard disassembles a car, usually with a torch? Add to that the fact that sodium azide is incredibly toxic and a known carcinogen and it makes me not want to visit auto salvage yards anymore.

When the flaws in the system began to appear (e.g. no protection in side and corner impacts) the response was typical bureaucratic defensiveness. Rather than admit that the program doesn't work, they are mandating more of what doesn't work in the form of side airbags, which are beginning to appear in the doors of higher-end cars. In addition, they want to require warning labels on the dashboards of new cars, and automakers are having to send letters to the tens of millions of owners of airbag-equipped cars warning them that the device installed to protect them may actually kill them. It seems sometimes that the madness never ends.

In summary, then, we have a government-mandated system that is both flawed and of limited effectiveness. It replaced an existing belt system that was superior in every way, being cheaper, simpler, and more effective. The problem is that seat belts require active involvement on the part of the occupant to actually put them on.

Air bags were designed to protect those too lazy or ignorant to protect themselves. The irony is that it turns out that manually fastened seat belts are required anyway for the airbags to have even their minimal effectiveness, so what's the point?

For my personal cars I have a 1974 Alfa Romeo and a 1984 Saab, both bought new and kept in perfect running condition. Until airbags disappear from the U.S. automotive scene, I have bought my last new car.

Chapter Highlights

1. Critical thinking about information is necessary in order for us to make clear decisions as citizens, consumers, and human beings.
2. An argument consists of issues, conclusions, and reasons.
3. The issue is the question that is raised; our decisions are made easier if we can define the issues on which we are asked to comment or act.
4. The conclusion is the position a person takes on an issue.
5. Reasons, often called premises, provide support for conclusions; reasons are acceptable or unacceptable on the basis of their relevance and quality.

Articles for Discussion

These two articles give differing viewpoints on the same issue. Read both and then consider the questions that follow.

Talk-show Host Angers Disabled Community
Hand Deformity Inherited from Mom Sparks L.A. Dispute
by Michael Fleeman
Associated Press, September 2, 1991

LOS ANGELES—Aaron James Lampley, all 7 pounds, 14 1/2 ounces of him, was only a few hours old when a local radio station dedicated a show for the second time to the circumstances and controversy surrounding his birth.

In addressing the matter again, KFI-AM last week refueled a dispute that pitted the station against activists for the disabled and raised questions about freedom of speech and society's treatment of the disabled.

Aaron Lampley was born Wednesday morning, with ectodactyly, which leaves the bones in the feet and hands fused. His mother, local TV anchorwoman Bree Walker Lampley, also has the condition and knew the child had a 50 percent chance of inheriting it.

Her other child, a daughter, has the condition as well.

Before the boy's birth, KFI outraged the KCBS-TV anchorwoman and advocates for people with disabilities with a July 22 call-in show in which host Jane Norris asked whether it was fair for Walker Lampley to give birth when the child had a "very good chance of having a disfiguring disease."

Critics of the show said it smacked of bigotry and illustrated societal prejudice and lack of understanding toward the disabled. KFI said the matter was handled properly and that radio talk shows are appropriate forums for controversial issues.

In KFI's second visit to the subject, this time with Norris acting as guest on Tom Leykis' afternoon show, Norris accused Walker Lampley of orchestrating a campaign to discredit her and contended she had a First Amendment right to discuss the matter.

"I was supportive of Bree's decision," Norris said on the show. "All I did, and have done, is voice my opinion of what would be right for me. I thought I handled the topic sensitively, but all [Walker Lampley has] seen fit to do is slander me."

Norris' statements did nothing to cool the situation.

"They came on the air supposedly to set the record straight. In our view, she set the record even more crooked," said Lillabeth Navarro of American Disabled for Access Power Today.

"This is like a bunch of thugs ganging up on the disability community. It just rained forth what caused us to be outraged to begin with."

Navarro said activists planned a protest at KFI studios.

The demonstration is part of a grass-roots campaign organized in part by a media consulting firm hired by Walker Lampley and her husband, KCBS anchorman Jim Lampley.

The company, EIN SOF Communications, gives the disability rights community a public voice. The firm has sent tapes of the Norris show to disability rights groups and is helping to file a complaint with the Federal Communications Commission.

In the original show, Norris said she wasn't intending to dictate what Walker Lampley should have done. But she said she couldn't have made the same decision if she were in Walker Lampley's position.

Norris said there were "so many other options available," including adoption and surrogate parenting, and "it would be difficult to bring myself to morally cast my child forever to disfigured hands."

Throughout the show, Norris seemed to take issue with people who disagreed with her.

After a caller named Jennifer from Los Angeles said, "I don't really see why it's your business," Norris responded, "Well, I think it's everybody's business. This is life. These things happen in life. What's your problem? Do you have a problem talking about deformities?"

Norris also repeatedly referred to Walker Lampley's condition, ectodactyly, as a disease, even though it is a genetically caused disability.

Walker Lampley and her husband, in interviews before their child was born, said Norris' first program was an attack on the handicapped and Walker Lampley personally, and was full of errors and poorly chosen remarks.

"I felt assaulted and terrorized," Walker Lampley said. "I felt like my pregnancy had been robbed of some of its joy."

She added, "I felt disappointed that someone would be so insensitive."

Radio Show on Rights of Disabled Defended
Crippled Woman's Pregnancy Debated
Associated Press

LOS ANGELES—The chairman of the Equal Employment Opportunity Commission said a local radio station shouldn't be disciplined for a talk show that debated whether a disabled TV anchorwoman should give birth.

Chairman Evan J. Kemp, who is disabled and confined to a wheelchair, said he was "appalled and sickened" by the majority of callers to the KFI program who said KCBS anchor Bree Walker Lampley had no right to become pregnant and should abort if she did.

However, Kemp said the right of free speech should protect KFI from any Federal Communications Commission action.

Kemp's statements were published in the Los Angeles *Times*.

Lampley, who was pregnant at the time of the July 1991 broadcast, lodged a complaint to the FCC and asked for an investigation. The newswoman, her husband, co-anchor Jim Lampley, and more than 20 organizations for the disabled asked the agency to examine whether the station and its owner, Cox Broadcasting Corp., should lose their license, be fined or reprimanded.

The couple charged the broadcast was not a thorough discussion, but rather an attack on Lampley's integrity without inviting them to appear and harassed callers who attempted to express contrary views.

Lampley gave birth five weeks after the broadcast to a boy who had the same genetic condition as his mother—ectodactylism, in which the bones of the hands and feet are fused. There was a 50 percent chance that the baby would have the condition.

Kemp said he was not speaking out as chairman of the Washington, D.C.-based EEOC, but as a "severely disabled person" with a rare polio-like disease—Kugelberg-Welander—that may be inherited.

He said he plans to write to the FCC to defend grass-roots discussions and radio talk shows such as the KFI program as necessary forums.

Questions for Discussion

1. The author of the first article states that this controversy "raised questions about freedom of speech and society's treatment of the disabled." What were the questions—that is, issues—that were raised?

2. Take one of the issues raised by the talk show controversy and discuss how well it was defended by those mentioned in the articles.

3. Comment on the following excerpt from the first article. What is your opinion of the host's response to the caller?

   After a caller named Jennifer from Los Angeles said, I don't really see why it's your business," Norris responded, "Well, I think it's everybody's business. This is life. These things happen in life. What's your problem? Do you have a problem talking about deformities?"

4. Are there any issues discussed by radio and television talk shows that you consider inappropriate? Are certain groups targeted for criticism and others left alone, or is every topic fair game? Give examples to support your answer.

5. Each article used a different subheading to explain the controversy. The first article's subheading reads: "Hand Deformity Inherited from Mom Sparks L.A. Dispute." The second article's subheading reads: "Crippled Woman's Pregnancy Debated." How do these different subheadings frame the issue? To what extent do you think they are fair and accurate statements about the controversy?

Ideas for Writing or Speaking

1. Consider the following quote from the first article: "Critics of the show said it smacked of bigotry and illustrated societal prejudice and lack of understanding toward the disabled. KFI said the matter was handled properly and that radio talk shows are appropriate forums for controversial issues." The framers of our Bill of Rights did not anticipate the phenomenon of broadcast media. Based on your understanding of the freedom of speech, are there any issues that should not be discussed in a public forum? Does sensitivity to the feelings of a particular group make some topics less desirable for public discussion? State your conclusion and support it with reasons.

2. Take a stand on one of the issues involved in these articles. Write an essay or give a short speech, expressing your viewpoint and supporting it with reasons.

3. Imagine that you are a program director for a radio talk show. What guidelines would you give your talk-show hosts? Give reasons for each guideline. Share your guidelines in a group or write them in essay form.

4. Write or speak on the following: Given the power of talk-show hosts to influence large numbers of people, do you believe there should be stricter licensing requirements for this profession, as there are for doctors, lawyers, and accountants, in order to ensure a uniform code of journalistic conduct? If so, why? If not, why not?

More Ideas for Writing or Speaking

1. Think about an issue that really interests you; it might be an issue currently being debated on your campus, or a community or national problem. The editorial pages of campus, community, or national newspapers may give you more ideas to help you choose your issue.

    In the form of an essay or a brief speech, state the issue and your conclusion and give at least three reasons to support your conclusion.

2. Letter or speech of complaint: Practice using your knowledge about the structure of argument by writing a letter of complaint or doing a classroom "complaint speech."

    Constructive complaining is an important life skill. Use this letter or speech to express your dissatisfaction. Choose the most relevant aspects of the problem to discuss. A clear statement of the issue, your conclusion, and reasons distinguishes "whining" from complaining. Whereas "whining" could be characterized as a long string of feelings expressed vehemently about random aspects of a problem, a true complaint describes the nature of the problem in an organized fashion. Sincerely expressed feelings then add richness to the clear and organized content.

    To make the complaint clear, be sure to support your ideas with examples, illustrations, instances, statistics, testimony, or visual aids. To make your feelings clear, you can use vivid language, humor, sarcasm, understatement, exaggeration, irony, and dramatic emphasis.

    Examples of topics for the complaint speech/essay: a letter or speech to a city planning commission about excessive airport noise, a letter to a supervisor about a change in salary or working conditions, a complaint to neighbors about reckless driving in the neighborhood, a complaint to housemates about sharing the workload, a letter or speech to insurance agents about rates for college students.

CHAPTER 10

Values and Ethics
What Price Ethics and Can You Afford Not to Pay?

> *A critical thinker understands the value assumptions underlying many arguments and recognizes that conflicts are often based on differing values.*

This chapter will cover:
- Value assumptions
- Conflict between value assumptions
- Ethics in argumentation
- Ethical decision making

In the last chapter, we discussed the structure of argument, including issues, conclusions about issues, and reasons used to support conclusions. This chapter and the next will cover the assumptions underlying arguments that influence all of us as we consider claims and take positions on issues.

Assumptions are ideas we take for granted; as such, they are often left out of a written or spoken argument. Just as we can look at the structure of a house without seeing the foundation, we can look at the structure of an argument without examining the foundational elements. To truly understand the quality of a house or an argument, we need to understand the foundation upon which it is built.

Assumptions made by speakers and writers come in two forms: value assumptions and reality assumptions. *Value assumptions* are beliefs about how the world should be and *reality assumptions* are beliefs about how the world is. We will look at reality assumptions in the last chapter. In this chapter, we will focus on value assumptions that form the foundations of arguments; we will also examine ethical considerations in argumentation and decision making.

Consider the values expressed in the following newspaper column. Compare the answers given to the question "What fictional character do you admire most?" What are the different values represented by the choices? Do you think the careers chosen by the respondents reflect their values?

Question Man: Fictional Character You Admire Most?
by Kris Conti
San Francisco Chronicle, January 28, 1990

Female, 23, curatorial assistant:
   Howard Roark of *The Fountainhead,* for never compromising his standards. His self-centeredness and arrogance was a problem, but I admired the fact that he had standards and lived by them. It seems that standards are fairly loose, sort of ad hoc. People go by the situation they're in rather than a set of standards that they follow. I admire someone who has ideals.

Female, 31, bank teller:
   Scrooge. He was a cad but when he had a chance to turn his life around he did. I admire his ability to turn his life around, because it's hard to change. He finally found that being rich is not what makes you happy. That being a true giver and a caring person are very rich qualities, and you can be happy in spite of poverty and adversity.

Male, 28, office manager:
   Bugs Bunny. I admire the way he outsmarts his rivals and talks his way out of adverse situations. He always gets the best of any situation. Of course, in the cartoon universe, it doesn't matter how, so it's not applicable in the nonanimated universe. Who's going to discuss morals once you throw the law of physics and gravity out the window?

Male, 38, nuclear industry engineer:
   Mr. Spock. He always has the answer. Whatever the problem is, he's always got the solution. He's witty. He's got a great sense of humor. It's just a subtle-type humor. I love that his character is very intelligent. Everything to him has a logic. It has to be logical. It has to click for him in a logical, rational way or it isn't happening.

Female, 25, Salvation Army program assistant:
   Cinderella. She overcame through all the hardships she had to face and kept that spirit of endurance and forgiveness. She just kept plugging away and was humble. She served her stepsisters and stepmother and didn't gripe. We could all be a little more serving. Not to the point of being oppressed, but be more serving like she was.

© *San Francisco Chronicle*. Reprinted by permission.

Value Assumptions and Conflicts

Have you ever noticed how some issues are really interesting to you while others are not? Your interest in a particular question and your opinion about the question are often influenced by your **values,** those ideals, people, or things you believe are important and that you hold dear.

Value assumptions are beliefs about what is good and important, that form the basis of opinions on issues.

These assumptions are important for the critical thinker because:

1. Many arguments between individuals and groups are primarily based on strongly held values that need to be understood, and, if possible, respected.

2. An issue that continues to be unresolved or bitterly contested often involves cherished values on both sides. These conflicting value assumptions can be *between* groups or individuals or *within* an individual.

Almost everyone in a civilized society believes that its members, especially young and defenseless members, should be protected. That's why we never hear a debate on the pros and cons of child abuse—most of us agree that there are no 'pros' to this issue. Similarly, we don't hear people arguing about the virtues of mass murder, rape, or burglary.

Our values, however, do come into the discussion when we are asked to decide how to treat the people who do engage in these acts. Some issues having a value component would be:

Should we have and enforce the death penalty?
Should rapists receive the same penalties as murderers?
Should we allow lighter sentences for plea bargaining?

Although most of us value order and justice, we often disagree on how justice is best administered, on what should be done to those who break the law.

You can see that the question of the death penalty centers on a conflict about the priorities of justice and mercy, two values cherished by many. Of course, a good debate on this issue will address such factual (not value-based) issues as whether the death penalty is a deterrent to crime and whether the penalty is fairly administered throughout the country.

Keep in mind, however, that most people who argue passionately about this issue are motivated by their values and beliefs concerning justice and mercy. Often these values are shaped by significant personal experiences. In fact, we generally hear arguments involving values by persons who are deeply concerned about an issue. Both sides of arguments involving values are likely to be persuasive because of the conviction of their advocates.

In coming to thoughtful conclusions on value-based arguments, the critical thinker needs to decide which of two or more values is best. In other words, the thinker must give one value or set of values a higher priority than the other.

Examples

We often hear arguments about the legalization of drugs, gambling, or prostitution. People may claim that legalizing these activities would lessen crime, improve public health, and direct large sums of money to the government and out of the hands of dealers, bookies, and pimps. Those who oppose legalization of these activities may have equally impressive arguments about the problems the community would face if these activities were legalized. We need to understand the root of this argument as a disagreement about which is more important:

1. Cleaning up the crime problems caused by underground activities linked to illegal vices, that is, the value of taking care of the immediate problem, or
2. Maintaining our standards of healthy living by discouraging and making it a crime to engage in activities that we as a culture deem inappropriate and harmful, that is, the value of honoring cultural standards and long-term societal goals.

If most people in our society believe that taking drugs, gambling, and prostitution are morally wrong, then no list of advantages of legalizing them would be persuasive. Thus, the argument starts with understanding whether the conclusion is based upon values; relative societal benefits have a much lower priority for those who believe we cannot condone harmful activities.

Think of a decision you might be facing now or in the future, such as whether you should work (or continue working) while attending school, which career you should choose, or which person you should marry. An internal conflict about a decision often involves an impasse (being stuck) between two or more values.

Let's say you are undecided about continuing to work. You want to devote yourself to school because in the long run you can get a better job (long-term goal). On the other hand, you'd really like the money for an upgraded lifestyle—a car or better car, money to eat out, and nicer clothes.

Your career decision may involve a conflict between the value of serving others in a field such as nursing or teaching and the value of a secure and substantial salary (such as you might find in a business career) that would help you to provide better for your future family.

You might think of getting serious with one person because he or she has good prospects for the future and is ambitious, but another person is more honest and has cared for you in both good and bad times. In this case, the conflict is between security (or materialism) and loyalty.

Exercise

Purpose: To isolate value conflicts and to understand how different conclusions can be based on conflicting values.

Try to isolate the various value conflicts in these personal and social problems. You can do this on your own, with others, or as a classroom exercise. Some of the issues may involve more than one set of conflicting values.

Note especially how sometimes both values are important and we as persons or as citizens need to make tough decisions for which there are no easy answers. Creating policies for difficult problems means giving one value a higher priority than another.

The first one is done for you as an example.

1. Should teenagers be required to obtain the approval of their parents before they receive birth control pills or other forms of contraception?

The conflict in this issue is between the value of individual freedom and privacy on one side and parental responsibility and guidance on the other.

2. Should birth parents be allowed to take their child back from adoptive parents after they have signed a paper relinquishing rights?
3. Should you give your last $40.00 of the month to a charity that feeds famine-stricken families or use it for some new jeans you've needed?
4. Should air traffic controllers be given tests for drug use?
5. Should persons be hired for jobs without regard to maintaining an ethnic mix?
6. Should prisoners on death row be allowed conjugal visits?
7. Should superior athletes receive admission to colleges regardless of their grades or SAT scores?
8. Should criminals be allowed to accept royalties on books they've written about the crimes they committed?

An important issue involving conflicting value priorities is that of equal opportunity in educational and employment opportunities. In the 1970s, affirmative action policies were initiated in universities in an attempt to create a more level playing field for those who had been disadvantaged and discriminated against. Affirmative action has been a controversial topic in the 1990s; some people believe that it has achieved its original purpose and others believe that efforts to dismantle equal opportunity policies will take us back to segregationist conditions of the past. There are even those who contend that affirmative action is discriminatory to some minorities; Joan Beck, writing in the *Chicago Tribune*, made these observations before mandated affirmative action was removed from the University of California:

Do Colleges Treat Asian-American Applicants Fairly?
by Joan Beck
Chicago Tribune, August 24, 1989

It almost sounds like a replay of 1970s affirmative action battles. But it has an Oriental twist.

This time, it's Asian-Americans complaining that they aren't getting a fair deal in admissions to top-level colleges, even though their share of student slots far exceeds their percentage in the population.

The case they make is opening up old conflicts about quotas and goals, about affirmative action and excellence, about whites versus minorities, and about racism and equal opportunity in America.

The uneasy accommodations of the '80s in college admissions may be coming apart at the top, for the curious reason that too many Asian-Americans are—or are perceived to be—too smart. . . .

... Berkeley, which has been extremely aggressive—and successful—in recruiting minority students, has been under fire for several years for discriminating against Asian-Americans in its admissions choices. The university has used slightly higher standards for them than for other applicants and turned down some who would have gotten in had they been white or members of another minority.

What few people are saying out loud is that increasing the number of Asian-Americans in the most selective schools will necessarily come at the expense of white students. Berkeley's student body is now 48.5 percent white—giving whites less representation on campus than in the population of the state as a whole.

The real problem is not racism, but the convoluted, complex policies most colleges have adopted to avoid it. They're trying to remedy centuries-old problems with preferential treatment for some minorities that, in effect, penalizes whites and now Asian-Americans.

Colleges are essentially attempting to reconcile competing values: Academic excellence, affirmative action and a diverse student body. The results, inevitably, are controversial admissions decisions.

Neither grades nor test scores are completely reliable measures of academic ability, for example. "Diversity" is difficult to define, requires flexible admissions standards and hurts the well-qualified students who are left out in the process.

(Colleges traditionally have bent admission standards for promising athletes, children of alumni and well-connected families, perhaps even a trombone player needed by the marching band, and for other reasons.)

If racial and ethnic "diversity" in the student body of a prestigious college is an acceptable goal, then Asian-Americans don't have a legitimate complaint; they are very well represented, indeed.

But by traditional standards of academic merit, they do have a justifiable case—even if the criteria are expanded to include such qualities as leadership, extracurricular activities and volunteer work. So does every applicant who loses out to a candidate who brings nontraditional qualifications such as the ability to overcome racial, cultural, physical or economic disadvantage and whose admission to college can be seen as furthering vital national goals.

There is no easy resolution to these issues. And there won't be until race and ethnicity are no longer so divisive.

© Copyrighted Chicago Tribune Company. All rights reserved. Used with permission.

Decisions made about which values take priority in college admissions have a real and lasting impact on people's lives. Consider the following two articles, which show contrasting effects of affirmative action. What do you believe is the most equitable way to resolve the competing values represented by this issue?

Affirmative Action Triumphs
The Untold Stories
by Paul Rockwell
Oakland, California

Eva Jefferson Paterson is Executive Director of the Lawyers Committee for Civil Rights, one of California's most brilliant attorneys. She is an African-American and a beneficiary of affirmative action.

She recently told a personal, uplifting story to a crowd of 3,000 cheering University of California, Berkeley, students.

"I got into Boalt Law School (U.C. Berkeley) through an affirmative action proram, a program that gave me the opportunity to study law. (She was a classmate of Lance Ito.) Affirmative action gave me an opportunity, but I cracked the books, did the work, and passed the tests."

Ms. Eva Paterson passed the bar exam on the first round. On her indefatigable speaking tours, she often gets applause and laughter when she mentions that Pete Wilson failed the bar exam twice. (He finally passed.)

"Never apologize for affirmative action," she tells the crowd, "I am proud of affirmative action because I am qualified."

Stories of hope abound. The Eva Paterson story is not unique. California is full of thousands of affirmative action triumphs—stories of opportunity, realized potential, and achievement rarely told on the public airwaves.

When Pete Wilson launched his anti-immigrant, anti-affirmative action campaign, no doubt he expected affirmative action beneficiaries would be cowed into hiding and silence.

How wrong Wilson was!

Not only are women and communities of color coming together, affirmative action beneficiaries and participants are speaking out in public. At long last we can listen to real people whose opportunities were expanded, whose own lives were enhanced, and whose humble communities were served, by affirmative action.

Antonia Hernandez, well-known defender of Latino rights, is president of the Mexican-American Legal Defense and Education Fund. Class-action suits, redistricting cases are some of her legal triumphs.

It was affirmative action that helped change the course of her life. Her family lived in La Cruces and worked in the cotton fields, until her uncle brought the entire family to Los Angeles, "all crunched up" in an old Chevrolet.

"I was," she writes, "an immigrant kid out of East Los Angeles. Without affirmative action I would not have had an opportunity to go to U.C.L.A. and explore horizons that were never opened to my parents. Huppies—upwardly mobile Hispanics—do not acknowledge sometimes that affirmative action has opened doors for them. They feel uncomfortable with what they perceive as a negative tag. We need to openly say we are examples of the success of affirmative action.

"I am a kid out of Garfield High School in East Los Angeles. I am a pretty bright individual and I had decent grades. I was just dirt-poor. My parents lived in the projects and I dreamed of going to Cal State L.A. because it was just across the street. That is as far as my dreams would take me. I am sure that I was judged by standards other than just grades or test scores. They saw in me a burning determination, the drive, the willingness to work. They gave me a break, but I am not the only one. It happened to thousands of Latinos who went to medical school, to architectural school."

Were public standards lowered to make room for Antonia Hernandez? Or was the public, which pays for the University system, better served by giving her an opportunity?

Standards were not lowered, Ms. Hernandez says. "That is the beauty of affirmative action. It gives the flexibility to find new standards that are more relevant, more current, taking into account our past and present history of exclusion." Universities enable individuals to build personal careers. But public universities also serve a larger public purpose. Improving legal services in the Hispanic communities is a noble goal.

Ronald W. Johnson is director of financial aid at U.C.L.A. He worked 15 years at U.C. Davis. As a young African-American he came to California from Brooklyn, New York, and he has dedicated the last 21 years of his life to higher education.

"I know for certain," he writes, "that were it not for affirmative action, many doors would have been closed. My accomplishments weren't given to me because of who I knew or who my father knew. They weren't handed to me because of how well I played sports. I earned my accomplishments through hard work, integrity and intelligence. But I knew I had a lot to be thankful for, most of which were the many doors of opportunity that opened for me to show my attributes. . . .

"I know that all of my qualifications have nothing to do with my race, but rather with who I am as a person. But what if I had never had the opportunity to show others my skills to manage? What if I had never had the opportunity to show others my ability to lead? My future, and the future of those lives I have touched, would never be realized. Whether its due to racism, closed doors, or perhaps the non-existence of affirmative action, the results would have been the same—lack of opportunity."

Affirmative action programs are not unique to women and people of color. White males are beneficiaries of many types of special programs, including programs that make exceptions to strict meritocracy. Albert Vetere Lannon lives in San Francisco. He writes: "The fact is that we older white men are beneficiaries of affirmative action. I'm a tenured teacher now, but seven years ago, I was a high school dropout. I entered San Francisco State University at age 50 through the re-entry program, a form of affirmative action. I graduated with honors and am working on a master's degree in history.

"Affirmative action benefited me directly, and I am now able to give something back to the society that gave me a hand."

Stories of hope, of opportunities that serve a higher public purpose, are rare in our cynical media. But the stories of Eva Paterson, Antonia Hernandez, Ronald Johnson, and Albert Lannon manifest the real significance of affirmative action. Affirmative action is one way to discover and realize human potential, and affirmative action is good for America.

Paul Rockwell, formerly assistant professor of philosophy at Midwestern University, is a writer and children's librarian in the San Francisco Bay Area. He is chair of "Angry White Guys for Affirmative Action."

The Backlash of Affirmative Action
by Martin Geraghty
Chicago Tribune, October 21, 1996
Martin Geraghty is Senior Vice-President of Collins Tuttle & Co., Inc.

It's in her eyes, mainly. That's where you see Debbie's 11 years of pent-up bitterness at the injustice of affirmative action. She's listened for years to the lie that mandatory racial and gender discrimination benefits women. She knows the names and faces of the feminist elites whom TV adores. They've been babbling for years at her about how it's really good for her and for all other women to deprive Gerry, her husband, of the promotion he earned in 1985. And she turns away.

Gerry, my brother-in-law, has always wanted to be a cop. He earned a bachelor's degree in criminology 20 years ago. He finally got his sergeant's badge and his white shirt in March. But for 11 years, Debbie watched him seethe at the cruelty of a system that tested first his skills and then his great heart. When Harold Washington was mayor, Gerry took a sergeant's exam that was indisputably non-biased, fair to all, racially (and every other way) neutral. Out of nearly 4,000 officers who took it, he scored in the top 15 percent.

Soon he would be promoted. Soon the extra $700 per month would take some of the strain off his family's finances. Soon the decision Gerry and Debbie made when they adopted the first of their two sons would be justified. Yeah, they could have used the extra money from Debbie's excellent job with the insurance company, but little Brian (and a couple of years later, his baby brother David) deserved a mom at home. So that's where Debbie stayed.

Now most folks agree that babies, and bigger kids, are better off in the presence of a mom who'll talk to them and play with them and read to them and drop whatever she's doing to find a toy or wipe a nose or kiss a bump. But to do that all day, every day, a mom usually has to hook on with a male. If that male is white (which happens in quite a few cases) the notion of affirmative action as "good for women" gets turned on its head.

At its most basic level, affirmative action says to women: "If you have babies and turn over their daily care to someone else so you can work, we'll penalize others (white mates and all who depend on them) in your favor. But if you marry a white male, we'll victimize you by depriving him of simple justice."

It's easy today to find overwrought racial and feminist activists who'll slander America as "most racist . . . most bigoted . . . most sexist . . . worse than ever before . . . etc." But this great land, its values twisted by a misguided need to balance every conceivable scale, is the only nation in history where active discrimination against its majority population is not only permitted—it's required.

Racial discrimination has always been ugly. It's bad when it arises out of personal human meanness or ignorance. But Jim Crow laws earlier in this century, and affirmative action today, have been even more pernicious because of the official sanction they've enjoyed. The victim must not only endure; he must know that his own government, with society's assent, is the agent of his suffering.

And make no mistake. Every affirmative action decision is a cruel zero-sum game with a victor and a victim. Luckily for the elites who so casually espouse affirmative action, it falls most heavily on the white, working-class male who works where racial and gender nose-counting is easier to do.

The elites who prattle on about "redressing wrongs" and "200 years of injustice" find it very easy to ignore the folks who will bear the cost of that redress. But until they have looked Gerry, and especially Debbie, in the eye and tasted the pain of affirmative action, they are hollow saints, casually, painlessly bestowing on one group of victims what rightfully belongs to a new set of victims.

© Copyrighted Chicago Tribune Company. All rights reserved. Used with permission.

Questions for Discussion

1. What are the competing values that businesses, government agencies, and colleges are attempting to reconcile with their employment and admissions policies? In what ways can these values be reconciled?

2. What values are most important, in your mind, when considering college admissions and job advancement policies? Should these values be the same for private universities and corporations as for state-supported universities and government agencies?

3. Do you believe that there comes a time when inequities in a society have been addressed or do you believe that we will always need to have policies in place that assure diversity in admissions and hiring?

Ideas for Writing or Speaking

Part A: List some values you hold. These can be character traits, such as honesty, fairness, and compassion. You can also list such concerns as peace, freedom of speech, family ties, ethnic identity, health, wealth, competition, or cooperation.

To isolate some of your values, consider the professions that interest you. If you want to be a high school coach, you may value sports, young people, and/or education. If you want to be an artist, you may value beauty and creativity.

Also, consider how you spend your free time. Different values may be expressed by those who spend time reading science fiction, shopping, volunteering at a nursing home, socializing, or working on a political campaign.

Try to list at least three values reflected in your life.

Part B: Choose a controversial issue and take a position on this issue; your position should reflect a value you hold. Examples of controversial topics with a value dimension include capital punishment, surrogate parenting, homelessness, nuclear power, active and passive euthanasia, socialized medicine, welfare, immigration, and environmental policies. You might look up issues that are currently being considered by the Supreme Court; many of the court's rulings establish the precedence of one value over another.

After you have chosen an issue and taken a position reflecting your values, arrange your ideas in the following manner:

1. Give several reasons to support your position. Give both moral and fact-based reasons. Use examples and evidence to strengthen your reasons.

2. State some good reasons why you think a person might believe the opposite of what you believe. For example, if you are against compulsory drug testing for athletes, state why someone might argue in favor of it.

3. Conclude by indicating if and how your initial belief was changed by considering the opposite viewpoint. Or, conclude by stating why your initial belief was not changed, despite your fair consideration of the arguments against your belief.

Ethics—An Important Dimension of Values

> *"Without civic morality communities perish; without personal morality, their survival has no value."*
> Bertrand Russell, "Individual and Social Ethics,"
> *Authority and the Individual* (1949)

For our purposes, we will examine ethics as one dimension of values. **Ethics**, sometimes called morals, are standards of conduct that reflect what we consider to be right or wrong behavior. Many conflicts about values involve an ethical dimension, that is, we are asked to choose whether one action or policy is more ethical than another.

Look at the difference in the following value conflicts:

Should you take a job that pays more but has evening hours you value for studying or should you take a job that pays less but gives you the hours that you want?

If you arrive home and notice that a cashier at a store gave you too much change, should you go back to the store and return the money?

Note that in the first example you need to decide what you value more—the extra money or the working hours you want. There is no ethical (good–bad) dimension to this decision; you can still study even if you take the job with the less desirable hours.

The second dilemma is about your personal standards of right and wrong, or good and evil. Do you inconvenience yourself by making a trip to the store or sending the money back because you believe it is wrong to take what does not belong to you? Or do you believe that if you didn't intend to take the money, you are not responsible? What are your standards of right and wrong, especially regarding relationships with others?

Philosophers and theologians have grappled with theories of ethical behavior for centuries. Several schools of thought about ethics have emerged. Some of the more common are listed below. Note the substantial similarity among the principles listed.

Libertarianism

VALUE ASSUMPTION:

The highest value is to promote the liberty of all.

PRINCIPLES:

Behavior is considered ethical when it both allows for one's individual freedom and does not restrict the freedom of others.

Examples:

Honesty is important because dishonesty restricts the freedom of others. Education is good because it increases personal freedom.

Violence, oppression, and poverty are bad because they restrict freedom.

Freedom of speech and assembly are important; restrictions on the right of any group to speak and assemble threaten the rights of other groups.

Reporters should not have to reveal sources of information because that would restrict the freedom of the press.

Utilitarianism

VALUE ASSUMPTION:

The highest value is that which promotes the greatest general happiness and minimizes unhappiness.

PRINCIPLES:

Behavior is judged according to its utility (usefulness) in creating the greatest human well-being. Actions are considered in terms of "happiness" consequences.

Examples:
Giving to others is good when it makes people, including the giver, happy. Giving would be discouraged if it caused greater unhappiness in the long run, as in the case of giving treats to children who throw tantrums.

National policies should consider the happiness consequences for the majority of the people affected by the policy. Taxing the rich might be better than taxing the middle-class, since more people are middle-class and would feel the pinch of taxes to a greater degree.

Societal rules that maximize the possibilities of individuals flourishing and prospering involve all of our "enlightened self-interest." Selfishness and greed are bad when they don't make it probable for most people to be happy.

Freedom of assembly for "hate groups" might be restricted because of the strife and unhappiness they would cause to a larger number of citizens.

Hardship and difficulty may be necessary in order to achieve desired results in the long run; people may derive happiness from intensive labor, as when a sports team trains and works for an ultimate victory or when a student works hard for a good grade.

Egalitarianism

VALUE ASSUMPTION:

The highest value is equality. Justice and fairness are synonymous with equality.

PRINCIPLES:

Behavior is ethical when the same opportunities and consequences apply to all people. We should treat others as we wish to be treated

Examples:
Since people are equal, discrimination of any kind is unethical. People should not take more than their fair share; they should give to those who have not received their fair share.

Punishment for crimes should be exacted in a fair manner; the poor and unknown should not be given harsher sentencing than the rich and famous.

If the justice system allows for unequal or unfair treatment of certain individuals or groups, then the system needs to be changed to ensure fairness for all citizens.

Judeo-Christian Principles

VALUE ASSUMPTION:

The highest values are to love God and to love one's neighbor.

PRINCIPLES:

Ethical behavior is based on biblical principles found in the Ten Commandments and other prescriptions, and on the desire to please and honor God.

Examples:
Since all people are created by God, all should be treated with love and respect.

People should not steal, cheat, lie, or envy because these acts are contrary to biblical principles; they are not loving to others and they dishonor God.

When values conflict, resolution comes by doing the most loving, God-honoring act. For example, some Christians lied to SS officers about hiding Jewish people during the Nazi occupation; had they turned them over to the officers, the Jewish people would have been sent to concentration camps and/or killed.

Universal Ethical Norms or Universal Action-Guiding Principles

VALUE ASSUMPTION:

Universal ethical principles exist and are self-evident (prima facie) and obvious to rational individuals of every culture.

PRINCIPLES:

Individuals should act in accordance with these principles for the betterment of the individual and the society

Examples:
A modern system of prima facie principles has been developed by Michael Josephson, of the Josephson Institute. His list includes honesty, integrity, fidelity, fairness, caring and respect for others, accountability, and responsible citizenship. Implications of these values are that individuals should not steal, should be responsible enough to avoid

drinking when working or driving and should be informed voters and contributors to the larger society.

Values cited above are to be honored and values such as materialism and self-centeredness are to be discouraged.

One Bandit's Ethic

Harper's Magazine, January 1992

We all have personal standards. Consider this list of personal rules that Dennis Lee Curtis, an armed robber in Rapid City, South Dakota, was carrying in his wallet when he was arrested in June of 1991.

1. I will not kill anyone unless I have to.
2. I will take cash and food stamps—no checks.
3. I will rob only at night.
4. I will not wear a mask.
5. I will not rob minimarts or 7-Eleven stores.
6. If chased by cops on foot I will get away. If chased by a vehicle I will not put the lives of innocent citizens on the line.
7. I will rob only seven months out of the year.
8. I will enjoy robbing from the poor to give to the poor.

© 1992 by *Harper's Magazine.* All rights reserved. Reprinted from the January 1992 issue by special permission.

Exercises

Purposes: To discover how policy debates are influenced by ethical standards, and to discover personal standards and principles that determine how ethical dilemmas are resolved.

1. Review the systems of ethics just discussed. Individually, or in groups, come up with examples of situations where the principles of one of these systems clashes with the principles of another. You may want to bring in recent local or campus controversies, such as the one detailed in the following excerpt from a college newspaper.
   Discuss the conflicting value principles represented by your examples.

Example:
In the following case, a murder was committed on campus and a newspaper photographer took pictures of the scene. The police wanted these pictures to help them identify the suspects; the photographer did not want to turn his work over to the police because he felt that would compromise the freedom of the press. Can you see that this issue involves a conflict between libertarianism (freedom of the press) versus utilitarianism (the police concern about promoting the general welfare by identifying and prosecuting criminals)?

Staffer Gets Subpoenaed

by Steve Logan
Advocate, October 11, 1996

Police services Lt. Paul Lee delivered a subpoena to *Advocate* photographer Soren Hemmila Thursday morning to appear in Superior Court in Martinez at 1:30 p.m. Tuesday.

Lee delivered the subpoena through District Attorney William Clark and the San Pablo Police Department in connection with photographs taken of the scene after Christopher Robinson's murder on campus September 25.

Hemmila and the *Advocate* have refused to turn over unpublished photos, taken shortly after the murder, to the San Pablo Police Department.

California's shield law is designed to help news organizations protect sources and information from outside forces, including law enforcement agencies. The law also states a journalist cannot be held in contempt of court for refusing to turn over unpublished work.

Hemmila believes the photographs are protected by the shield law.

The *West County Times* reported Thursday that San Pablo police believe the photos could give them important information in prosecuting the case of the three suspects who have already been taken into custody and charged with Robinson's murder.

Hemmila said he arrived on the crime scene just as the police were putting up yellow tape. Among the photographs taken, but not published, included shots of the crowd in the background.

Hemmila said San Pablo Det. Mark Harrison first came to ask for the negatives "nicely," on Monday.

"I don't like being part of the investigation in this case," Hemmila said Thursday after receiving the subpoena. "I'm willing to do what it takes to protect our rights."

The subpoena said the photographs will be helpful to the police in three ways. Section one said the credibility of an eyewitness who commented in last Friday's story which ran in the *Advocate* needs to be evaluated.

Section two said the photographs will show the crime scene closer to the time of the shooting, which will allow the prosecution to evaluate the weight of the physical evidence which included expended casings at the scene.

Section three said the photographs may show whether the attack was "planned, a surprise attack, or a chance encounter that turned violent."

Hemmila said it would set a bad precedent if the *Advocate* turned over the photos.

"If we make it a [practice] to turn over the negatives to police agencies, they'll expect it in the future and they'll expect it from other publications.

"I don't want the public to think that journalists are part of law enforcement or acting in their behalf."

   2. Consider your own definition of ethical behavior; it may fit into one of the schools of thought outlined in this chapter or it may be a combination of several approaches. Then, using your own principles, try to be completely "ethical" for one week. As often as possible, ask yourself "What is the best way to respond to this situation?" Keep a daily record of your ethical challenges. Then, report your successes and failures in dealing with these situations.

Here are some examples of common ethical dilemmas: should you defend a friend who is being criticized by another friend? Should you give to a homeless person who approaches you? Should you tell the truth to someone even if it hurts their feelings? Should you tell your instructor that several students cheated when she answered a knock at the classroom door? Should you tell callers your roommate isn't home if she asks you to? Should you complain about rude treatment in a store? Should you copy a friend's tape of your favorite music rather than buying your own copy?

Your own situations will be unique. If time permits, share some ethical dilemmas that you encountered with the rest of the class.

3. Consider the following situations alone or with a group:

   a. You and your friend are taking the same required history class; you are taking it on Mondays and Wednesdays and your friend is taking it Tuesday evening. You have given up much of your social life to study for this class because the tests are hard. One Monday after the midterm, your friend calls you and wants to know what was on the test since he partied too hard over the weekend and didn't study. You have a good memory and could tell him many of the questions. Do you tell him what was on the test?

   b. You go to a garage sale and notice a diamond ring that is being sold for $10.00. You know that the ring is worth far more than that. What do you do?

   c. The manager of the fast-food restaurant where you work is selling food that is not fresh or prepared according to the standards of the company. You have complained to him, but he has done nothing despite your complaints. You need this job, and the location, hours, and pay are perfect for you; in fact, this boss has tailored your working hours to your class schedule. Nevertheless, you are concerned about public safety. What do you do?

   d. You are a member of a city council and you have a serious problem of homelessness in your city. A businessman offers you $100,000 in aid for the homeless if you will let him build an office building over a popular park. How do you vote?

Ideal Values versus Real Values

If you completed the last exercises, you may have realized that ethical behavior is easier to discuss than it is to carry out. We have complex needs and emotions, and situations are also complicated. Even with good intentions, we sometimes find it difficult to choose ethical behavior.

Because of the difficulty of living up to our standards, most of us can make a distinction between our ideal values and our real values. An **ideal value** can be considered a value that you believe to be right and good, but have not put into practice in your life. A **real value** is a value that you consider to be right and good and actually act upon in your life. As critical thinkers, it is important for us to understand and be honest about our own behavior and to distinguish our words from our actions.

People may say they value good citizenship; they believe people should be informed about candidates and issues and express their viewpoints by voting, but they may continue to vote without studying issues and candidates. In some cases, the value of citizenship is only an ideal. For the value to be real, it must be carried out in the life of the individual claiming that value. Consider the following dialogue from Dr. Laura Schlessinger's book *How Could You Do That?*:

> Stephanie, twenty-one, is a virgin and had planned to stay that way until she's married. But now she finds herself very attracted to somebody ... did I say "very"? She'd hoped that her values, the rules, would protect her from temptation. Now she is set adrift without a paddle because she discovered that values don't function like an automatic, invisible protective shield.
>
> "Just in case I start dating him, do you have any advice on how to stay a virgin?"
>
> "You mean you have values until temptations ride into town, then the values sneak out during the night? The town ain't big enough for both values and temptations. Values keep us steady through times of deep temptation. They are our road map through the minefields of challenge. It is easy to say you have values, and easier still to live up to them when you're by yourself in the middle of the ocean."
>
> "That's true."
>
> "Values are truly only shown to exist when they are tested. If it is meaningful for you to reserve sexual intimacy for marital vows, if you feel that doing so elevates sex and you, that is admirable."
>
> "Yeah, but how do you make the values do their thing to keep you from doing something else?"
>
> "Values only have the power you infuse into them with your respect for them and yourself, and your will. Values without temptations are merely lofty ideas. Expediting them is what makes you, and them, special. That requires grit, will, sacrifice, courage, and discomfort. But it is in the difficulty that both the values and you gain importance. The measure of you as a human being is how you honor the values.
>
> "When you begin dating him, clarify your position of intercourse only within marriage. If he tries to push you away from that position, you know he values you only as a means of sexual gratification. If he gets seductive and you're lubricating from your eyeballs to your ankles, this is the moment when you choose between momentary pleasure and long-term self-respect."
>
> "That is the real choice I'm making at that point, isn't it?"
>
> There is no fast lane to self-esteem. It's won on these battlegrounds where immediate gratification goes up against character. When character triumphs, self-esteem heightens.

One caller asked, "What if I'm too weak?" I answered that the road to unhappiness and low self-esteem is paved with the victories of immediate gratification.[1]

Copyright © 1996 by Dr. Laura C. Schlessinger. Reprinted by permission of HarperCollins Publishers, Inc.

Exercise

Purpose: To understand the difference between real and ideal values.

List five of your real values and five of your ideal values.

1. Describe what it would take for these ideal values to become real values for you. Think about why you have not made these ideal values real in your life.

2. Then explain what changes in your habits and your priorities would be involved in order for these values to be real for you.

Example:

"One of my ideal values is physical fitness. I believe it is important for everyone to keep their bodies strong through exercise and good eating habits.

"As a student, I don't take the time to exercise every day or even every other day. Since I quit the swim team, I hardly exercise at all. When I do have spare time, I sleep or go out with my girlfriend. Also, I eat a lot of fast foods or canned foods because I don't cook.

"For this ideal value to become real for me, I would have to graduate and have more time. Or, I would have to make the time to exercise. The best way would be to combine going out with my girlfriend with exercising. She likes to skate and play basketball, so we could do that together. Getting more exercise is a real possibility.

"Eating right is probably not going to happen soon. I would have to learn to cook or to marry someone who would cook for me. At this point in my life, I can't see how I could have a healthier diet, even though it is an ideal for me. But it's just not important enough for me to learn at this time."

Ethics in Argumentation

"It is terrible to speak well and be wrong."
　　　　　　　　　　　Sophocles, *Electra* (c. 418–14 B.C.)

Ethical concerns are central to any message. Those who seek to influence votes, sales, or the personal decisions of others need to:

- be honest about their conclusions and reasons
- not leave out or distort important information
- have thoroughly researched any claims they make

- listen with respect, if not agreement, to opposing viewpoints
- be willing to revise a position when better information becomes available
- give credit to secondary sources of information

Exercise

Purpose: To examine the ethical dimensions of an argument.

Listen to a political speech or a sales pitch or read an editorial essay. Then evaluate the message, stating whether the writer or speaker met the criteria given for ethical argumentation.

You might also use one of your own essays or speeches; analyze it to see whether you were as honest as you could have been and whether you credited secondary sources of information.

Ethical Decision Making

> "Every man takes care that his neighbor shall not cheat him. But a day comes when he begins to care that he does not cheat his neighbor. Then all goes well."
> Ralph Waldo Emerson, "Worship," *The Conduct of Life* (1860)

The first step in clear-headed decision making is knowing your principles and standards. In considering difficult decisions, there are several "tests" that can be useful to apply to your known principles. These tests can help you to assess how well your decision adheres to your standards.

1. **The Role Exchange Test.** This test asks you to empathize with the people who will be affected by the action you take. You try to see the situation from their point of view. You ask yourself how the others affected by your decision would feel and what consequences they would face.

    You also ask whether it would be right for the other person to take the action if you were going to be the one experiencing the consequences of the decision. Using your imagination, you change places with the person or persons who would receive the effects of your decision. In short, you decide to treat the other person as you would want to be treated in his or her place.

    For example, you see your brother's girlfriend out with other men. You hesitate to tell him because of the hurt it would cause and because you feel it's not really your business to interfere. However, when you do the role exchange test, you decide to tell him because you realize you would want to know if you were in his situation.

2. **The Universal Consequences Test.** This test focuses on the general results (consequences) of an action you might take. You imagine what would happen if everyone in a situation similar to yours took this action—would the results be acceptable?

Under the universal consequences test, if you would find it unacceptable for everyone in a similar situation to take this action, then you would reject the action.

For example, imagine that you are asked to join a community program for recycling cans, bottles, and paper. You enjoy the freedom of just throwing everything together in the trash, but you stop and assess the consequences of everyone refusing to recycle. Your assessment causes you to join the program.

3. **The New Cases Test.** This test asks you to consider whether your action is consistent with other actions that are in the same category. You choose the hardest case you can and see if you would act the same way in that case as you plan to act in this case. If you would, then your decision is consistent with your principles.

    For example, you are deciding whether to vote to continue experiments that may be successful in finding a cure for AIDS but involve injecting animals with the HIV virus. Your principle is that cruelty to animals is not justified in any circumstance. To formulate a new, harder case you might ask yourself if you would allow the research to be conducted if it would save your life or the life of your child. If you would, then you might reconsider your voting decision and reassess your principles.

    Another example involves our previous article on whether a photographer should turn over negatives to the police if it would help detectives identify and prosecute murder suspects. You may believe that freedom of the press cannot be compromised and, therefore, the photographer should be able to keep the negatives out of the investigation. Using the new cases test, imagine that someone you love dearly was the murder victim and that these photographs are the link to catching the person who killed him or her. Would that knowledge change your value priorities in this case?

4. **The Higher Principles Test.** This test asks you to determine whether the principle on which you are basing your action is consistent with a higher or more general principle you accept.

    For example, let's say your roommates are not doing their share of the housework so you are considering not doing your own share. However, because you value promise-keeping and integrity, you realize that it is important to keep your part of the bargain regardless of what they are doing with their part. You decide to keep doing your share and to talk with them about keeping their part of the agreement.

Exercise

Purpose: To be able to utilize tests for ethical decision making.

Option one: Think about an ethical dilemma you are facing or have faced in the past. If you did the exercise on being ethical for a week, you may have a recent example.

You may also use the examples listed in that exercise. In addition, you might consider a difficult ethical dilemma from your past. Then, follow the directions given below.

Option two: Think about an ethical dilemma your community or nation is facing; you might also consider an international ethical dilemma. Some examples include the use of scientific information gained by Nazi experimentation on holocaust victims, the apportionment of funds to poverty-stricken nations, the exporting of cigarettes to other nations, and the rationing of health care. Then, follow the directions.

Directions:

1. On your own or in class groups, take the dilemma through each of the four tests. Write about what each test tells you about the course your decision should take.
2. Come to a conclusion about the decision. Justify your conclusion by referring to the cumulative results of the tests.

Example:
"My friend helped me to get a job at his company and, after only a few months, I was told that he and I were both being considered for a promotion to management. He worked at the job for a year and he's getting married soon, so he really needs this job. I wouldn't even have known about the possibility of working there if he hadn't told me about it and arranged an interview for me. The dilemma is, should I take the promotion if it's offered to me or refuse it, knowing that it will then go to him?"

The role exchange test asks me to look at the situation from his point of view. It would hurt him in two ways if I took this promotion: mainly, he would lose the income and the chances for advancement that go with this position. Also, he would be hurt because he helped me to get this job and then I took a promotion he might have had. There's nothing wrong with my looking out for my own future, but in this case, it would be at his expense.

The universal consequences test asks me to look at general consequences of my decision and determine if it would be acceptable for everyone in this situation to take a similar action. A positive general consequence might be that all of the best people would be given promotions regardless of who needs the promotion most. The negative general consequence would be that people would routinely put their own desires ahead of what might be more fair and what might be best for other people, a "me-first" mentality.

The new cases test asks me to pick the hardest case I can and see if I would act the same way in that case, to determine whether I am consistent. To me, the hardest case would be if my parent would be given the promotion if I didn't take it. I don't live with my parents anymore, but I would step down if it meant that either of them could have the promotion.

The higher principles test asks me to look at my own ethical standards to see if my actions fit into these standards. This test is hard to use, because I value both my own advancement and my friend's welfare. But I can find the higher principle of fairness; I don't feel that it would be fair for me to take a job that he would have had since he is the person responsible for my being in the position to take it.

In conclusion, I won't take this job if it is offered to me. It would be hurtful to my friend, who cared enough about me to help me get a job. Also, I wouldn't want to live in a world where people always climbed over one another to achieve success. If it were my parents, I wouldn't take a job that they wanted, even if it would benefit me personally. Finally, I believe in the principle of fairness, and I don't think it would be fair to take a promotion from a friend who gave me the opportunity to work for his company.

When we make ethical decisions, it is important that the actions taken are congruent with our values. When our actions go against what we believe is right, we are prone to rationalize our behavior, rather than to admit we are not always ethical. Consider this list of common rationalizations used to justify unethical conduct.

Common Rationalizations
Ethics in Action, January–February, 1991

I. **"If It's Necessary, It's Ethical."**
Based on the false assumption that necessity breeds propriety. Necessity is an interpretation, not a fact. But even actual necessity does not justify unethical conduct. Leads to ends-justify-the-means reasoning and treating assigned tasks or desired goals as moral imperatives.

II. **"If It's Legal and Permissible, It's Proper."**
Substitutes legal requirements (which establish minimal standards of behavior) for personal moral judgment. Does not embrace full range of ethical obligations, especially for those involved in upholding the public trust. Ethical people often choose to do less than they are allowed to do and more than they are required to do.

III. **"I Was Just Doing It for You."**
Primary justification of "white lies" or withholding important information in personal or professional relationships, especially performance reviews. Dilemma: honesty and respect vs. caring. Dangers: violates principle of respect for others (implies a moral right to make decisions about one's own life based on true information), ignores underlying self-interest of liar, and underestimates uncertainty about other person's desires to be "protected" (most people would rather have unpleasant information than be deluded into believing something that isn't so). Consider perspective of persons lied to: if they discovered the lie, would they thank you for being considerate or feel betrayed, patronized, or manipulated?

IV. **"I'm Just Fighting Fire with Fire."**
Based on false assumption that deceit, lying, promise-breaking, etc. are justified if they are the same sort engaged in by those you are dealing with.

V. "It Doesn't Hurt Anyone."
Rationalization used to excuse misconduct based on the false assumption that one can violate ethical principles so long as there is no clear and immediate harm to others. It treats ethical obligations simply as factors to be considered in decision making rather than ground rules. Problem areas: asking for or giving special favors to family, friends, or politicians, disclosing nonpublic information to benefit others, using one's position for personal advantages (e.g., use of official title/letter head to get special treatment).

VI. "It Can't Be Wrong, Everyone's Doing It."
A false "safety in numbers" rationale fed by the tendency to uncritically adopt cultural, organizational, or occupational behavior systems as if they were ethical.

VII. "It's OK If I Don't Gain Personally."
Justifies improper conduct done for others or for institutional purposes on the false assumption that personal gain is the only test of impropriety. A related more narrow excuse is that only behavior resulting in improper financial gain warrants ethical criticism.

VIII. "I've Got It Coming."
Persons who feel they are overworked or underpaid rationalize that minor "perks" or acceptance of favors, discounts, or gratuities are nothing more than fair compensation for services rendered. Also used to excuse all manner of personnel policy abuses (sick days, insurance claims, overtime, personal phone calls or photocopying, theft of supplies, etc.)

IX. "I Can Still Be Objective."
Ignores the fact that a loss of objectivity always prevents perception of the loss of objectivity. Also underestimates the subtle ways in which gratitude, friendship, anticipation of future favors, and the like affect judgment. Does the person providing you with the benefit believe that it will in no way affect your judgment? Would the benefit still be provided if you were in no position to help the provider in any way?

Reprinted by permission of the Joseph and Edna Josephson Institute of Ethics.

Exercise

Purpose: To understand common rationalizations used to excuse unethical behavior and to see how these apply to specific cases.

Give examples for each of the above rationalizations. For example, under **I. "If It's Necessary, It's Ethical,"** you might cite unethical behavior on the part of campaign representatives carried out to ensure the election of their candidate. Or, consider the following case:

Ohio Reverend, Feeding Poor with Illegal Stamps, Faces Jail
by Mitch Weiss
Associated Press, Contra Costa Times, November 17, 1996

TOLEDO, OHIO. The Rev. Slim Lake sees nothing wrong with buying food stamps illegally and using them to feed the homeless, recovering alcoholics, and drug addicts—he's an urban Robin Hood to some.

Authorities, however, say the "Rev. Slim" is breaking the law and have charged him with food stamp trafficking.

The ex-con and founder of God's Church of the Streets faces 15 to 40 years in jail. He seems undaunted.

"You know, I've been buying food stamps to feed my congregation since I started my ministry," Lake said. "How can you put somebody in jail for feeding the hungry? If that's a crime, then put me in jail."

Lake has served barbecued ribs, chicken and ham sandwiches to as many as 300 people at an inner city park every Sunday for seven years.

He buys the food with the stamps and some of the $1,600 in disability pay he receives each month since he hurt his back in 1980 while working as a city street cleaner.

Not everyone loves Lake, a former drug dealer, crack addict and street hustler who has been arrested more than 30 times. Some residents of a housing project near the park say the man born Charles Lake is bad news.

"I just don't trust him," said Charles Robinson, 52. "I don't know what it is. He brings in a bad group of people. Bad group."

Lake has been in and out of jail since 1978, when he accidentally shot a friend in the head.

The friend survived, but Lake served six months in jail and once he got out, he sold drugs and stolen goods.

He says God told him to establish his church, and to some residents Lake is a godsend.

They say he helps when they are in trouble, takes them to supermarkets to buy groceries and is around just to talk.

"He's just like a brother and good friend," said Willie Valliant, a 37-year-old recovering alcoholic and drug addict.

Lake admits he buys the food stamps at discount rates on the street and exchanges them for food, but said he was set up.

His arrest came after an undercover police officer offered him $500 worth of food stamps for $300, he said.

Try to come up with a variety of situations—personal, social, and political—in which these rationalizations are used. If the class is doing this exercise in groups, the examples can be shared with the entire class.

Consider whether you rationalize any of your behavior in the ways mentioned on the list of common rationalizations.

Chapter Highlights

1. Value assumptions are beliefs about what is good and important or bad and unimportant; because these beliefs are taken for granted, they are part of the foundation of a person's argument.
2. Conflicts between value assumptions need to be addressed before fruitful discussion over value-saturated conclusions can take place.
3. Ethics are standards of conduct that reflect values.
4. There are several schools of thought about ethics, including libertarianism, utilitarianism, egalitarianism, Judeo-Christian principles, and universal ethical norms.
5. Ideal values are held by an individual in a theoretical sense; real values are held theoretically and also practiced.
6. Ethics are evident in our behavior as we advocate for ideas and make decisions.
7. Several "tests" have been developed to help people make ethical decisions: these include the role exchange test, the universal consequences test, the new cases test, and the higher principles test.
8. Ethical decision making is undermined when common rationalizations are used to support unethical practices.

Articles for Discussion and Composition

It May Not Be Plagiarism, But It's a Rip-Off
by Howard Rosenberg
Los Angeles Times, July 11, 1990

TV news fibs in so many ways.

If it's not the playacting of ratings sweeps series, it's the false promise made to hold viewers through a commercial, that titillating stories are "coming up next." If it's not on-camera reporters taking bows for the work of off-camera field producers, it's newscasts blending electronic press kits in with staff-gathered news.

These are relatively small deceptions.

As the following episode shows, the more you perpetuate the small lie, the easier it is to step up to the big one.

It was last Thursday and featured on KCAL Channel 9s "Prime 9 News" at 10 p.m. was a breezy story lamenting the decline of that great American institution, the drive-in movie. The tape package was introduced live from the studio and given a voice-over narration by KCAL's hammy entertainment reporter, John Corcoran.

Afterward, anchors Larry Carroll and Kate Sullivan seemed pleased with Corcoran's story.

One problem. A small one, really ...

It *wasn't* Corcoran's story. It was Gloria Hillard's story.

"I was angry," said Hillard, a CNN reporter covering entertainment from the network's Los Angeles bureau. "One of the most sacred tenets of journalism is that you don't take someone else's words and pass them on as your own."

Not sacred to everyone, obviously.

Hillard's story aired July 4 on CNN, a witty, charming enterprise piece that was shaped in such a personal way that it bore her signature as a reporter. "I guess Corcoran saw my piece, liked it and decided to make it his own," Hillard said.

The story is small, but the principle big, with the terrible P-word looming. "I would be highly offended to be called a plagiarist," Corcoran said later.

Like slapping your own dust jacket on someone else's book, Corcoran gave the drive-in story a brief live intro and close from the anchor desk. Otherwise, the story presented as his on KCAL was virtually a twin of Hillard's—but about a minute shorter.

Gone were a few fleeting sound bites, including Hillard's stand-up in the parking lot of a Culver City drive-in—couldn't have that if it was Corcoran's piece. Gone also was Hillard's voice. But her written words remained with only slight changes, spoken instead by Corcoran as if they were his.

How is it that Hillard's two-minute 40-second story—not only her footage and interviews but also her 226-word script—were at Corcoran's disposal?

Along with KTLA Channel 5 and KTTV Channel 11 in Los Angeles and many other independent stations throughout the nation, KCAL has a reciprocal agreement with CNN for mutual use of stories. Wire services such as the Associated Press have similar agreements with their clients.

In another way that deceit is built into the system, stations don't even have to credit CNN, who thus becomes a party to the deception.

"They are free to use our material in any way they want," said CNN's Los Angeles bureau chief, David Farmer. He said that he'd heard of nothing akin to the Hillard-Corcoran matter previously happening in Los Angeles. "But I feel it must happen quite a bit around the country," he added. "We facilitate it by sending out scripts."

There surely are newspapers, too, that attach their own reporters' by-lines to wire stories—but no newspapers with integrity.

Hillard said she knew CNN had agreements with stations for exchanging footage, but didn't know that these agreements provided for verbatim use of scripts without attribution.

Legal it may be.

Ethical it isn't.

Corcoran sounded almost shocked that anyone would think that his usurping Hillard's words without giving credit was either misleading or unethical. "I don't have any problem with it ethics-wise," Corcoran said. "Ninety-nine percent of my stuff I write. I didn't rewrite that one, and part of the reason is that I'm moving my family into a new house." Well, as long as there's a valid reason.

Corcoran noted that using words written by others without attribution "is standard procedure throughout television. When anchors read copy written for them by others," he added, "they don't say, 'written by so-and-so.'"

Because CNN allows its scripts to be used "word-for-word," Corcoran insisted, his voice-over with Hillard's words was not plagiarism. Besides, he added, "I put my own inflections on a story."

Words by Hillard, inflections by Corcoran.

"I'm not the kind of guy who's gonna go out and steal anybody's work," Corcoran said. "Trust me."

Yet the narrations on the CNN and KCAL stories track almost identically, as the following excerpts show.

Hillard: And remember that pizza? It's still here, and of course kids even work up a real good appetite at the drive-in's playground. And the drive-ins are a pretty good bargain at $4.50 for adults, and kids under 12 are free.

Corcoran: And remember that pizza? It's still here, and of course kids even work up a real good appetite at the drive-in's playground. And the drive-ins are pretty good bargains. That's $4.50 for adults. Kids under 12 are free.

Hillard: And how about a kid's point of view on drive-ins over walk-ins?

Corcoran: What about drive-ins over walk-ins?

Hillard: But they're disappearing. The Studio Drive-In is one of only a couple dozen left in Southern California. And it's scheduled for the bulldozer. The high cost of land outbid the box office, and soon the condos will be here.

Corcoran: But drive-ins are disappearing. The Studio Drive-In is one of only a couple of dozen left here. And it's scheduled for the bulldozer. The high cost of land outbid the box office, and soon the condos will be here.

And so on and so on the two stories went . . .

KCAL news director Bob Henry saw nothing improper in what Corcoran did and, incredibly, refused to discount the possibility that the same thing could happen again with his blessing.

He called this "a non-issue." Making Hillard's work sound almost too trivial to matter, he said that "a feature on drive-ins is sort of a discretionary story."

Yet it was significant enough for KCAL to use in an evening newscast and then repeat the next day in its noon newscast. KCAL, Henry snapped, can "use news from CNN any way we want."

While ethics, like drive-in movies, fade into the sunset.

© 1990, *Los Angeles Times*. Reprinted by permission.

Questions for Discussion

1. What is the ethical problem discussed by the author of this article?
2. Do you agree with the author's conclusions?
3. Are there situations you can think of in which something may be legal but is not ethical? What about situations in which something is not legal but is ethical?

Music, to Wal-Mart Ears, Should be "Clean"
by Steve Morse
Boston Globe, Dec. 9, 1996

Today's pop music stars are more and more running up against the Wal-Mart—meaning the 2,300 stores across the nation that won't carry record albums with "parental advisory" stickers and will even ask artists to change objectionable lyrics and CD covers.

These "clean versions" are then stocked on the shelves of the retail giant, which last year accounted for nearly 10 percent of the 615 million compact discs sold domestically in what has become an annual $12 billion dollar recording industry.

Wal-Mart is the country's leading pop music retailer, but there are growing fears among musicians, record executives and media watchdogs that Wal-Mart's role of "Morality Police," to quote one record executive, may change the way that music is made.

"Wal-Mart is a great place to buy shirts, but I wouldn't buy my music there," cautions Chuck D of the rap group Public Enemy, who admits to cleaning up select versions of the group's last record to appease Wal-Mart.

"It's a bible-belt mentality, but as an artist, you have to decide whether you're going to put up or shut up," Chuck D added during a recent stop in Boston.

An extensive letter-writing campaign, fueled by anti-censorship groups like the Massachusetts Music Industry Coalition, the California-based Parents for Rock and Rap and Ohio-based Rock Out Censorship, is now taking complaints to Wal-Mart directly.

More Support than Complaints

Yet Wal-Mart spokesman Dale Ingram, reached at the company's headquarters in Bentonville, Arkansas, says that letters of support for Wal-Mart's policies far outnumber the complaints. "Many of our customers understand what we're attempting to do here." he says, "We don't have a bank of censors. We're really just like all retailers. We want to know what our products are."

Wal-Mart has asked artists and their labels to clean up records for years, but the issue crystallized with a recent *New York Times* article and the banning of Sheryl Crow's new album because of the lyric: "Watch our children as they kill each other with a gun they bought at Wal-Mart discount stores." Crow refused to change the verse.

(Not all Wal-Marts sell guns and company spokesman Ingram says that stores comply with local laws regarding firearms. However, Wal-Mart has been sued twice by relatives of people killed with guns bought at its stores.)

The number of albums affected is small—about 10 to 15 out of the several hundred albums released each month—it's the principle of censorship that has rankled many musicians.

However, as singer Adam Duritz of the Counting Crows notes, "It's a legal form of censorship. It's a shame, but I don't see how you can possibly legislate against it."

Even other retailers are upset. "I'm disgusted, but not with Wal-Mart," says Russ Solomon, owner of Tower Records. "They have a right to sell anything they want, as we all do. I'm disgusted by the record companies that pander to them by changing the albums."

The profit motive is the culprit here. "We would change an album if an artist went along with it," says Andre Harrell, president and CEO of Motown Records. "We've changed records by (rapper) Da Brat. We found out that a lot of little kids buy her records, even 9-year-old kids. So we felt this was one way to reach them."

"The key informing principle is that everybody is apprised of it and everybody agrees to it," says Timothy White, editor of Billboard.

Covering the Covers

Many artists have made adjustments. Alternative pop singer Beck agreed to delete an obscenity for a cleaned-up version of his first album. "Mellow Gold," sent to Wal-Mart and K-Mart stores. Rappers Busta Rhymes and Junior M.A.F.I.A. have done clean versions of albums (which have the words "clean version") written on them.

The Butthole Surfers agreed to change their name to B.H. Surfers on CD jackets. John Mellencamp recently agreed to airbrush out images of Jesus Christ and the devil on his latest CD, "Mr. Happy Go Lucky."

Mellencamp spokeswoman Dawn Bridges says, "John didn't design the cover or conceive it, so he doesn't feel terribly personal about it. He said. 'It's OK, fine.' It's not like he was asked to change his music."

Meanwhile, Wal-Mart is adamant about doing nothing wrong. "When you serve 70 million customers a week, you're going to have some people who disagree with you sometimes," says Ingram.

Reprinted courtesy of *The Boston Globe*.

Questions for Discussion

1. What is the conflict of values between stores like Wal-Mart and musicians? What priority do you put on these values?
2. To what extent do you think the "profit motive" is involved on both sides of this controversy?
3. Have big retailers gained too much control over consumer choices or are there other ways to have convenient access to CDs?
4. How do you define broad terms like *censorship* and *obscenity*? Is it censorship for a retailer to refuse to sell music when it believes the majority of its customers would find the music offensive? What kinds of lyrics, if any, would you call obscene? Would a lyric suggesting that people of one group kill people of another group be protected as free speech? Why or why not?

Student Markets Primer on the Art of Cheating

Rutgers Senior Finds His $7 How-To Is in Demand Among College Students

by Anthony Flint

Boston Globe, February 3, 1992

One of the hottest books on college campuses isn't the latest collection of Calvin and Hobbes—it's a book about cheating.

"Cheating 101" is a how-to guide on shortcuts to a degree—effective places to hide crib sheets, systems of foot signals for sharing multiple-choice answers, places to buy term papers, and dozens of other tips.

Michael Moore, 24, a Rutgers University senior and author of the book, has sold 5,000 copies, mostly at Rutgers, Ohio State and the University of Maryland. He recently returned from a marketing road trip to Penn State. And he plans to go to Boston, home to 11 colleges and universities, to hawk the $7 book around spring break.

"We're going to hit Boston right after we hit Daytona Beach in March."

Moore, a journalism major, contracts with a printer to produce the 86-page book and sells it mostly out of his home in Hopewell, N.J. But because of the book's popularity, he takes sales operations on the road from time to time. Sometimes aided by a pre-visit article in a student newspaper, he sets up a table in a fraternity house or a room on campus and watches the money roll in.

"Students love it," said Moore, who described his weekend selling session at Penn State University and St. Francis College as "a mob scene." The trip was good for 1,150 copies.

Moore said that in addition to students snapping up the guide, several college administrators, lawyers and clinical psychologists have ordered it too—presumably as a form of counterintelligence.

Moore makes no excuses about the profits he reaps from the book, and acknowledges that he set out to make money. But he also considers "Cheating 101" to be a commentary on the shortcomings of higher education: ill-prepared professors more concerned with research, dreary required courses and the lack of training for real-world applications.

"I thought it would be a good opportunity to point out what I believe are the permanent problems in education," said Moore, who said his experience in college has been sour. "It's an indictment of the system. Maybe somebody will make some changes, to curb cheating and make college a better place."

Cheating, Moore said, is a response to the shortcomings that students see. It flourishes because often professors are not interested or look the other way, he said.

"Students just don't cheat because they're lazy or hung over," he said. "They see a professor who's not interested in what they're doing, so students aren't going to be interested in learning. That's a natural defense mechanism."

Rutgers officials, while praising Moore's entrepreneurial skills, have sharply criticized "Cheating 101" as a blatant violation of academic ethics. Some have drawn parallels to Michael Milken and Ivan Boesky, describing the book as the scholar's quick—and dishonest—route to success.

The penalties for cheating vary from school to school, but frequently include suspension or expulsion. Most colleges spell out the rules against cheating or plagiarizing in student codes provided to all freshmen.

Some educators are using the book as an opportunity to teach about ethics. Carol Oppenheim, a communications professor at Boston's Emerson College, recently led a discussion with students on whether a student newspaper should run an advertisement for the book.

"It's an interesting teaching opportunity about a real ethical dilemma," Oppenheim said.

Moore said the wrath of college administrators is to be expected. "It's a manual about their mistakes, their shortcomings and failures. It's like a bad audit."

But he denies that he is engaging in anything dishonest or unethical.

"I don't think people that are buying the book have never cheated before. They already know a lot of the methods. I'm not making a cheater out of anybody," he said.

"There's 'Final Exit,' a book on how to get out of drunk driving, a book on how to get out of speeding tickets," Moore said. "I'm making an honest living. I'm not dealing drugs. I'm just exercising my First Amendment rights."

Reprinted courtesy of *The Boston Globe*.

Questions for Discussion

1. Comment on Moore's statements: "They see a professor who's not interested in what they're doing, so students aren't going to be interested in learning. That's a natural defense mechanism."

    "It's an indictment of the system. Maybe somebody will make some changes, to curb cheating and make college a better place."

    "I don't think people that are buying the book have never cheated before. They already know a lot of the methods. I'm not making a cheater out of anybody."

    "I'm making an honest living. I'm not dealing drugs. I'm just exercising my First Amendment rights."

2. If your professor for a particular course looked the other way when students cheated, would you feel justified in cheating? Why or why not?

3. Do you find that the discussion of this book by the *Boston Globe* and advertisements for the book in student newspapers gives the book a legitimacy that it might not otherwise have? Would it make students feel more or less inclined to read it? On what do you base your answer?

4. Should Moore be allowed to advertise in student newspapers and to sell his book on campus? Why or why not?

5. What is the "real ethical dilemma" concerning this book that is mentioned by Professor Oppenheim? Do you believe there are other ethical dilemmas involved?

6. Is it OK to cheat if you feel that the system is cheating you?

Ideas for Writing or Speaking

1. Take a position on Moore's criticisms of "ill-prepared professors more concerned with research, dreary required courses, and the lack of training for real-world applications." To what extent, if any, is Moore's perception valid? If not, why not? If so, what should be done about these problems? Give reasons for your conclusion.

2. Consider Moore's comment that the book "Cheating 101" is an effective "commentary on the shortcomings of higher education." Write on either the shortcomings or benefits of higher education as if you were trying to convince someone who was considering going to college. Use your own experience as support, but include objective sources of evidence as well.

3. See if your college has a code of ethics about cheating and plagiarizing. If so, write about this code; take a position on the principles given (agree or disagree with them) and give support for your conclusions. If your college does not have a code of ethics, write one and justify (give reasons for) each of the principles you include.

4. "The Legacy I'd Like to Leave"

    Imagine that you are eighty years old. Your son, daughter, niece, nephew, husband, wife, friend, or co-worker is making a speech about you at a party held in your honor. In this speech, he or she mentions your fine qualities and the things you have accomplished in your life. He or she talks about the special traits you have that are treasured by those who know and love you. Write the speech, using this format:

    a. List personal qualities and how they have been specifically evidenced in your life.

    b. List the accomplishments you will have achieved. Again, be specific in your descriptions.

    c. Then, analyze what you would need to do (either internally or externally, or both) to merit that kind of tribute in your senior years. What ideal values would have to become real for you? What choices would you have to make about your career, your personal life, and your priorities?

5. Write an essay in which you take a position (agree or disagree) on one of the following quotes. Support your conclusion about the quote with specific reasons.

    a. "Uncle Sam has no conscience. They don't know what morals are. They don't try to eliminate an evil because it's evil, or because it's illegal, or because it's immoral; they eliminate it only when it threatens their existence."
    Malcolm X, *Malcolm X Speaks* (1965), p. 3

    b. "The difference between a moral man and a man of honor is that the latter regrets a discreditable act, even when it has worked and he has not been caught."
    H.L. Mencken, *Prejudices: Fourth Series* (1924), p. 11

    c. "The great secret of morals is love."
    Percy Bysshe Shelley, *A Defence of Poetry* (1821)

    d. "We must never delude ourselves into thinking that physical power is a substitute for moral power, which is the true sign of national greatness."
    Adlai Stevenson, speech, Hartford, Connecticut, September 18, 1952

    e. 1. Judgments are absolutely necessary. Without them, the issue of choice has no meaning because everything is equal.

       2. I believe we are the sum total of all that we do, i.e. what we "do" is who we "are." This is true because as adults we make deliberate choices in our actions. Therefore, our actions describe our inner selves, what

sacrifices we're willing to make, what evil we're willing to perpetrate. It is with awareness that we persist in negative, ugly, and destructive deeds in one or more areas. Our actions are the blueprint of our character.

3. Values give meaning to live, and all its otherwise mundane aspects.

Dr. Laura Schlessinger, *How Could You Do That?* HarperCollins (1996), p. 189

Notes

1. Dr. Laura Schlessinger, *How Could You Do That?*: (New York: HarperCollins Publishers, Inc., 1996) pp. 151–152.

CHAPTER 11

Reality Assumptions

It's Eleven O'Clock:
Do You Know Where Your Assumptions Are?

> *A critical thinker understands that people have different assumptions about the world that form the basis for their opinions; he or she also examines these assumptions.*
>
> *A critical thinker understands basic patterns of deductive and inductive reasoning.*

This chapter will cover:

- Reality assumptions
- Patterns of deductive reasoning
- Introduction to inductive reasoning

We learned in the last chapter that when an issue involves a conflict of values, we need to examine those values foundational to the argument under consideration; in other words, there is no point in bringing in evidence to support a point of view until we address the issue of clashing values.

For example, if someone believes that legalizing drugs is morally wrong, he or she will probably not be moved by a lot of statistics that show that we could save money and cut down on crime by legalizing drugs. An individual with a strong value assumption on an issue is not usually swayed by a discussion of practical benefits of a policy or an action that contradicts his or her values. When a discussion neglects to consider conflicting value assumptions on both sides of an issue, stalemates occur, and new and improved evidence does little to help these stalemates.

The critical thinker who wants to argue on a value-saturated issue needs to clearly and directly address the conflict in values and try to persuade the other side to rethink their value assumptions on that issue.

Reality Assumptions

Another foundational aspect to any argument is the underlying assumptions about reality that the various advocates for an issue hold. Reality assumptions are beliefs about what is true and factual about the world. They are based on the unique experience and education of each individual. Reality assumptions are sometimes directly stated by a writer or speaker and they are sometimes implied.

The fascinating element of assumptions is that they are often hidden to the people arguing for different conclusions. Finding hidden assumptions in arguments is like reading or watching mysteries; you accumulate clues from what people say and then make guesses about what important things they *believe* but aren't directly *stating*.

One person may assume that the only way to deal with terrorists is through a show of strength, whereas another person assumes that the only effective approach is negotiation. Notice that these two individuals probably hold the same values; both believe terrorism is wrong and is a global problem.

They also may share the value of the importance of world peace. Their conflict is about effective methodology; that is, they have different ideas (assumptions) about what terrorists are like and what works best in dealing with them. They have different views of reality.

When two people or two groups hold different assumptions, they need to stop and examine the underlying assumptions that frame their arguments rather than building arguments on those assumptions. As hidden assumptions are brought to the surface, light is shed on the different positions taken on an issue. Then "all the cards are on the table" and people have the opportunity to modify assumptions or to see more clearly why they have a strong conviction about an assumption.

Detecting Reality Assumptions

One reason that some assumptions are hidden from us is that they are so deeply ingrained; they may only surface when we come across a person or a group who holds different assumptions. We may be confronted with a set of assumptions different than our own when we are involved in a classroom debate. Or, this process of confronting the "facts" that we take for granted may occur when we are in an unfamiliar situation, like when we travel to a new place and are exposed to a different culture.

Most North Americans assume if an interview or meeting is set for 1:00, then the arrival time should be slightly before 1:00, but people from other cultures may view time more loosely. The expected arrival time could be anywhere between 1:00 and 3:00 for members of some cultures. Because of the differing assumptions across cultures, North Americans who are sent abroad by their organizations are often given training about the assumptions commonly made in the country they will be visiting.

When traveling to another country, we can be sensitive to what is expected of us as visitors. In defending our conclusions on an issue, however, we need to bring the differing assumptions to light so that the discussion is clear and rational.

Examples of Differing Reality Assumptions

- Some people assume that anyone can change and, therefore, that any prisoner can be rehabilitated. Other people assume there are individuals who are "career criminals" with no hope of being rehabilitated.
- Some people assume that the way to increase employment is to lower taxes. Other people assume that the way to increase employment is to establish more federal programs that would provide jobs for the unemployed.
- Some people assume that homosexuality is a condition established in the genetic code before birth. Other people assume that homosexuality is a result of a set of environmental circumstances.

Other assumptions involve differing definitions of words:

- One person assumes that "love" is an emotion that may or may not be permanent. Another person assumes that "love" is a commitment that is not based on emotional changes.

In an article on the dispute among obesity experts over the definition of fat, Steve Rubenstein writes:

> The United States defines a fat person as anyone with a "body mass index," or BMI, of 27.6 or higher. The World Health Organization defines a fat person as anyone with a BMI of 25 or higher." As a result of these different definitional assumptions, "Americans don't actually weigh any more, according to the latest numbers. But, in keeping with the leaner international threshold for fatness, more of them are fat."[1]

The key here is to realize that individuals make assumptions about reality, whether we realize it or not. We need to examine the assumptions we make and try to detect the assumptions that others make. When we have a foundational disagreement about reality assumptions, we should discuss those assumptions before we discuss any arguments built upon them. For example, if we believe that people can be rehabilitated, we must understand why we believe that and be able to defend our basic belief. We also need to understand why someone else would believe that people cannot be rehabilitated.

Often, individuals presenting arguments will comment: "you are assuming that . . ." or "this argument is based on the assumption that. . . ." These phrases help us identify the foundational, but unstated, elements of an argument.

For example, in a *New York Times* report on the efforts of both Democratic and Republican candidates to present themselves as champions of the fight against breast cancer, cancer researchers questioned the politicians' assumptions about the disease. One politician from New York claimed that he would shut down an incinerator plant that is throwing carcinogens into the air and water. A New Jersey politician, running for the senate, stated, "The breast cancer rates in New Jersey remain the highest in the nation. There must be a reason, an environmental cause."

The article continues with the scientists' responses to these claims:

> Scientists are disturbed by the misleading information in some campaigns. Dr. Sheila Zahm, deputy chief of the occupational epidemiology branch at the National Cancer Institute, said: "There's not a lot of information linking environmental exposures to breast cancer," even though researchers have looked. What's more, she said that the statement that New Jersey has the nation's highest cancer rate is wrong. The District of Columbia has that distinction, with Delaware second. New Jersey is tied for third with Rhode Island.
>
> ... Other scientists are repelled by what they see as the condescending assumption in these campaigns: that mentioning breast cancer is a sure way to win the female vote.
>
> Dr. Barbara Weber, a breast cancer researcher at the University of Pennsylvania calls the breast cancer strategy "pretty demeaning." The assumption, she said, is that "women don't care about the deficit or education or Medicare." It suggests, she said, that "what we care about is whether we ourselves will get breast cancer."[2]

The Need to Examine Assumptions

In our age of accelerated research in many fields, ideas that were once readily accepted have come into question. Researchers discover that what was assumed to be factual may not be true; it may have been true at one time or it may never have been true at all. When we build an argument on assumptions that are not grounded in fact, our arguments are faulty and the actions we recommend will not achieve our desired ends. We may sound logical and reasonable, but we are leading ourselves and others astray.

Consider, for example, the following excerpt from an article on suicides in the state of Washington:

> Contrary to perceptions, far more people in King County die by their own hand each year than are murdered.
>
> In 1994, 207 people in King County killed themselves, while 109 people were victims of homicide, according to a report on suicide being released by the Seattle-King County Department of Public Health.
>
> "Suicide is one of the major public-health problems in our community," the report begins.
>
> It is the second most common cause of death in the county among adults ages 20 to 24. White and Native American men have the highest suicide rates of all race and gender groups.
>
> ... The study also debunks a stubborn myth: that the area's often gloomy weather contributes to high suicide rates. The study shows no significant seasonal trend in the rate of deaths. In fact, the number of suicides in King County in 1994 was highest for the month of July.
>
> Other findings: terminal or chronic illness is the top probable cause for suicide.

> Other factors: a decline in the quality of life, unemployment, marital and financial problems, relationship problems.
>
> ... People may think suicides are rarer than they are because the media seldom report them. The media's attention to homicides might lead people to think someone is murdered on every street corner, says Bill McClure, a medical investigator in the King County medical examiner's office. "You're much more likely to pick up your own gun," he said. "The media is very skewed in what they report. Unless you're Kurt Cobain, it doesn't get covered."
>
> ... Most media don't report suicides, but make exceptions when they are committed in a public place and attract a great deal of attention, or when the person is very prominent in the community.[3]

Good researchers and investigative reporters often uncover questionable assumptions like the ones noted in this article. When we examine assumptions with the goal of discovering what is true, we can take more useful action. Some of the reality assumptions that were discovered to be false about King County include:

1. Homicide is more common than suicide.
2. Gloomy weather is a major factor in the area's high suicide rates.

Considering the new research from the county's Department of Public Health, supervisors in the Seattle–King County may want to put more funding into preventing suicides instead of concentrating their efforts mainly on homicides. In so doing, they can focus on fighting the most common causes of suicide. Rather than looking for antidotes to gloomy weather, they can support efforts to control pain for those who suffer from terminal or chronic illness; also, county officials can offer more services to people who are unemployed or struggling with financial and relationship problems.

Assumptions should be examined in the light of the best available research; then decisions can be optimally helpful and productive.

Another example of the need to examine assumptions relates to the use of prescription medicine. Because of the availability of a variety of new medications and treatments, doctors and pharmacists have to consider more factors in treating patients than they may have in the past. Since harmful, and even fatal, side effects can occur when two different drugs are prescribed to the same patient, pharmacists have to make judgment calls about whether to assume that doctors understand about the drug interactions they have prescribed. An investigation by *U.S. News and World Report* states:

> The most crucial link is the doctor. Thus, many pharmacists told *U.S. News* that when the same doctor prescribes two interacting drugs, they are less likely to question his judgment. "If the prescriptions came from two different doctors, that would warrant a call," says pharmacist Gordon Tom of San Francisco. "But if it's the same doctor, we assume he's aware of the interaction." Recent studies show that such trust is often misplaced. The Seldane-erythromycin interaction (which can cause irregular heartbeat, cardiac arrest, and sudden death) is a case in point: despite widely disseminated warnings by the drugs' manufacturers and the federal Food and Drug Administration, 3 to 10 percent of doctors last April still were prescribing the two drugs together.[4]

This investigative report also warns consumers not to assume that pharmacy computer systems that check for drug interactions are always accurate. Dr. David Kessler, past commissioner of the federal Food and Drug Administration, is quoted as saying, "It is simply untenable in 1996 to walk into a pharmacy and receive a bottle of pills and no other information. It is not good patient care."[5]

To prevent patients from making harmful assumptions, pharmacists now ask patients to wait for consultations about the medications they are receiving.

As critical thinkers, we need to actively discover and then question the assumptions underlying arguments so we are not building on a foundation of falsehood. Conversely, when we critically examine what it is we take for granted, we have the advantage of gaining a strong and solid conviction for those ideas and principles we believe to be true. Knowing *why* we believe *what* we believe helps us to be more credible and effective when we present an argument. Examining the reality assumptions of others helps us to understand and assess their arguments more fully.

Exercise

What are the assumptions?
Purpose: To detect unstated reality assumptions.

One way to detect reality assumptions is to create a brief outline of an argument you hear. Consider the following examples:

Trials and executions should be televised—the public has the right to know what's going on in our courts. Information about the judicial system needs to be more widely disseminated.

Analyzing this brief argument with the skills we've discussed far, we could outline the argument as follows:

Conclusion: Trials and executions should be televised.
Reason: The public has the right to have more information about the courts and the judicial system.
Value assumption: Freedom of information is an important value.
Reality assumption: Televising trials and executions would inform the public about our judicial system.

Let's look at another brief argument, outlining the conclusion, reasons, value assumptions, and reality assumptions.

All teenagers should have the Hepatitus B vaccination starting at twelve years old. Hepatitus B is a sexually transmitted disease that can be fatal. It can also be transmitted through I.V. drug use.

Conclusion: All teenagers should have the Hepatitus B vaccination.
Reasons: Hepatitus B is a sexually transmitted disease.
Hepatitus B can be fatal.
It can be transmitted through I.V. drug use.
Value Assumption: Health and prolonged life are important.
Reality Assumptions: Teenagers are all at risk of being sexually active or using

drugs. Children are at risk for these activities starting at age twelve. A vaccination will protect teenagers from the effects of this disease.

Taking these examples, can you create different arguments based on different assumptions about reality?

Now, look at the statements below and find possible assumptions that are being made by the speaker. Often, more than one possible assumption can be found.

After you have completed this exercise, discuss whether you agree with the assumptions you discovered.

1. This is a receptionist position, so we need a mature woman for the job. It's important that our clients feel comfortable as soon as they walk in here.
2. You can't go to the party in that outfit. Everyone will think you're completely clueless about how to dress, and no one will want to be seen with you.
3. The death penalty is proof that we value revenge more than we value people. We should save and rehabilitate people rather than giving up on them.
4. Charlene is really successful—she's only 28 and she's making $70,000 a year!
5. There is good news in that rape is on the decline in this county—there are 20 percent fewer police reports this year than last year at this time.
6. Bolger's coffee is the best—it's mountain grown. That gives it great taste.
7. The people in that town don't care about the homeless—their city council voted against contributing $2000 to a county fund to help the homeless.
8. They won't trade their lunches if you give them Twinkle cupcakes, and Twinkle will give them the energy they need to do well in school.
9. You're going to love this blind date—I've known him since fourth grade and he's a great friend of mine.
10. Let's put the county dump in Smallville—they haven't had a turn as a dump site yet.
11. Let's just live together—why do we need a piece of paper to prove our love?
12. I believe in legalizing marijuana for medicinal purposes. Marijuana should not be legalized for recreational use because it is a mind-altering and habit-forming drug; marijuana is also a gateway to harder drugs like cocaine.

Read the following article about a jury trial, keeping in mind the various assumptions that contribute to the outcome of the trial.

Acquittal Outrages Women

Jury Blames Provocative Miniskirt for Assault

by Brian Murphy
Associated Press

FORT LAUDERDALE, FLA.—Sexual assault counselors and women's groups reacted with anger and disbelief Thursday to a jury's acquittal of a rape suspect on the grounds that the woman wore a lace miniskirt without underwear.

"It's a fairly horrendous verdict," said Ellen Vargyas at the National Women's Law Center in Washington, D.C. "No one, regardless of how they are dressed, should be allowed to be raped under a knife."

The three male and three female Broward Circuit Court jurors publicly justified their verdict Wednesday to acquit a 26-year-old drifter, who then was ordered returned to Georgia to face several other rape and assault charges.

"We felt she asked for it for the way she was dressed," said jury foreman Roy Diamond. "The way she was dressed with that skirt, you could see everything she had. She was advertising for sex."

"She was obviously dressed for a good time, but we felt she may have bit off more than she could chew," said juror Mary Bradshaw.

The 22-year-old woman testified that Steven Lord abducted her at knife-point from a Fort Lauderdale restaurant parking lot in November 1988 and raped her repeatedly during a trip north on Interstate 95. She said she escaped five hours later.

Defense attorney Tim Day told jurors the woman agreed to have sex with Lord in exchange for $100 and cocaine, but later changed her mind.

Jurors said they also were swayed by the woman's calm demeanor in court, compared to the emotional testimony of a 24-year-old Georgia woman who claims Lord raped her at knife-point last year.

"When the Georgia woman testified, my heart sank," said juror Dean Medeiros. "But when the other one testified, she didn't appear to be shaken up. Basically, we didn't believe her story."

"I thought this was 1989," said Alexander Siegel, attorney for the woman, who was jailed six days in June after failing to answer subpoenas for court appearances. "I guess this means every pervert and nut out there has a license to rape any person who dresses in a manner they think is provocative."

"The whole idea that a woman is asking for it is horrendous," said Dorothea Gallagher of the National Organization for Women's Broward County chapter.

Questions for Discussion

1. What are the underlying assumptions made by the prosecution, the jurors, and the defense in this case?

2. If the plaintiff (the raped woman) had agreed to sex in exchange for $100 and cocaine, but later changed her mind, as stated by the defense, could the defendant have justified or defended his actions? What assumption guides your answer?

3. What assumption underlies the juror's comment, "She didn't appear to be shaken up . . . we didn't believe her story"?

Exercise

Purpose: To find assumptions made by professionals in various fields.

Consider your major area of study. What are some assumptions made by people in that field? For example, if you study dance therapy, then you must assume that dance can be psychologically helpful to people. If you study ecology, then you must believe that the environment is a system that needs to be balanced.

Example:
"I am studying Early Childhood Education. It's because I assume children need some structured experiences before they get to kindergarten. I also assume they learn best if they have lots of time to be creative and explore. And I assume they need lots of interaction with other kids to learn to share and relate.

"I have argued with some of my teachers who assume children should learn to read before kindergarten. We know that children can learn to read early and they can learn some math, but my assumption is they'll burn out if they have to study so young. And I also assume they'll catch up and be happier than kids who had to read so soon."

Notes

1. Steve Rubenstein, "Millions Suddenly Became Fat Without Gaining Any Weight," *San Francisco Chronicle*, October 11, 1996, page A6.
2. Gina Kolata, "Vying for the Breast Vote," *New York Times*, November 3, 1996.
3. Jennifer Bjorhus and Peyton Whitely, "New Report Debunks Myths on Suicide," *Seattle Times*, February 15, 1996.
4. Susan Headden, *U.S. News & World Report*, August 26, 1996, p. 53.
5. Ibid.

CHAPTER 12

Logic: The Practical Science of Inference

By Lou Ascione

Introduction

While the term 'thinking' may refer to any number of mental activities, such as decision making, evaluating, interpreting, explaining, predicting and calculating, there is one mental process which is a fundamental and integral part of all types of thinking, and it is called *inference*. Without inference, thinking is not possible, and effective inference is a necessary requirement for intelligent thinking of any kind. *Logic* is the 'practical science' of inference, which means that it is the study of inference for the purpose of its continuous improvement. Through logic, we learn the nature of inference, and we develop the criteria for evaluating it so that we can maintain a high level of quality regarding both our own inferences and those of others by means of criticism. In fact, the best way to conceive of logic is as an activity of 'quality control management' for the process of inference.

Understanding inference is not an easy matter because it is such a basic mental activity that it is most often carried out unconsciously. Although we all make inferences constantly in life, we rarely speak or think about them directly, and this means that the average person tends to lack both the vocabulary and concepts needed to understand the nature of inference as well as the criteria with which to evaluate it. Therefore, a great deal of logic involves the tedious but essential activity of learning somewhat technical and often abstract vocabulary and concepts. Only by learning the language of logic are we able to understand inference to such a degree that we are able to effectively evaluate inference as well as communicate our evaluations to others.

We will begin our study of logic with the concept of inference in general, and then we will work through the more specific aspects of inference by means of definition and example.

The Function of Inference

The most general way to define inference is in terms of its function: the generation of new information using only information which is given either through experience or communication. In other words, inference is the activity of taking existing information and using it to produce further information. Inference is therefore a productive process that takes the following form.

| Given Information | → INFERENCE → | New Information |

Let's look at some examples:

1. A person playing chess relies on inference to decide what move to make. He or she is given a specific situation, namely the setup of the board, and must use this information to produce further information regarding the best move to make.
2. A detective, who is given clues regarding a crime, must use this information to generate more information regarding the identity of the criminal.
3. Scientists, trying to explain a particular physical phenomenon, are given information regarding the phenomenon itself but need to produce additional information which will unify it with a particular theory of physics.
4. A doctor who is given a patient's symptoms and test results must use this information in conjunction with his or her medical knowledge to generate a diagnosis of the patient's problem.

In all four cases something is being figured out, calculated or concluded using only a given set of information; this is the defining feature of all inference.

Propositions and Arguments

Because of the fact that inference involves the manipulation of information, it can only take place within the medium of a representational system, such as a natural or an artificial language. While computer inference takes place within an artificial language, human inference (which is what we are concerned with at this time) takes place within a natural language, i.e. English. The basic unit of representation in natural language is a *proposition,* and propositions make up the basic unit of inference which is called an *argument.* Propositions constitute the content of inference, while arguments constitute its structure. In ordinary language we refer to the basic units of representation in natural language as 'beliefs,' and the basic unit of inference as an 'idea' or a 'thought.' The problem with these words, however, is that they are too vague and ambiguous to be used in logic. Therefore, the logical analysis of inference begins with a technical understanding of both propositions and arguments.

Understanding Propositions

As it was just mentioned, propositions are the basic units with which we represent the world in natural language. A proposition is a sentence that states something about the world and as such has a 'truth value,' meaning that it is either true or false. We do not have to know the truth value of a sentence for it to be a proposition; we only have to know that is has a truth value. In other words, we can identify a sentence as a proposition without actually knowing whether it is true or false; we only have to know *that* it is either true or false. For example, the following sentences are all propositions:

1. Chicago is a city in the United States.
2. No one has ever run the mile in under three minutes.
3. There are four sides to a square.
4. Some people in London own cars.
5. All animals know how to swim.
6. France is a country in Africa.
7. If we win, then I'm going to celebrate.
8. Today is Tuesday.
9. Tomorrow it will rain.
10. There is life outside our solar system.

What qualifies these sentences as propositions is the fact that they all claim something about the world and are therefore either true or false. If a sentence claims something about any aspect of the world, either past, present or future, it is a proposition. Propositions may be claims that are well known facts such as sentences 1 and 3. They may be well known falsehoods such as sentence 6, or sentences that are sometimes true and sometimes false such as 8 and 9. Propositions may be lesser known facts such as sentence 2, or conditional claims such as sentence 7. However, propositions may also be claims about the world which we have no idea if they are true or false such as sentences 5 and 10. The point is, it is not necessary to know the truth value of a sentence for it to be a proposition because it does not matter if they are true or false; it only matters that we know one of the two must be the case. Take sentence 10 for example. We may not know for sure if there is life outside of the solar system, and in fact we may never know. However, we do know that it is true that there either is or there is not life outside of the solar system at this point in time. Therefore sentence 10 is a proposition.

Non-Propositions

While it is true that all propositions are sentences, it is not the case that all sentences are propositions. There are many sentences which do not claim anything about the world because they have a different function in language. Sentences that do not claim anything about the world do not have truth values and are therefore not propositions. The following are examples of non-propositions.

1. Close the door!
2. What color is that?
3. Thank you for coming in on such short notice.
4. Don't do that, it's dangerous.

What makes these sentences non-propositions is that they do not claim anything about the world. These sentences perform other duties. For instance, sentence 1 is an order or a command and therefore does not claim anything about the world. Sentence 2 is a question, not a claim. Sentence 3 is an activity of 'thanking,' and sentence 4 is an activity of 'warning.' None of these is an activity of claiming. Even though the second part of sentence 4, 'it's dangerous,' by itself would be a proposition, as it stands, it is part of a non-proposition. In fact, the proposition 'it's dangerous' is being used as the reason to justify the activity of warning in the sentence, namely, 'don't' do it.'

Exercise

Determine which of the following sentences are propositions. Write "yes" next to any sentence that is a proposition, and "no" next to any sentence that is not a proposition.

1. Take the money and run.
2. Sometimes you win, sometimes you lose.
3. There is no evidence to back the assertion that Homer, the epic Greek poet, was blind.
4. Were the Middle Ages really like that?
5. Most people who live in South America speak French.
6. Everyone knows the meaning of the word 'wergild.'
7. Invisible people cannot see.
8. When you find out what time the party starts, let me know.
9. The speed of light is a constant.
10. People should never treat each other with disrespect.

The Nature of Arguments

An argument is a set of propositions structured in a such a way that the truth of one of the propositions is intended to be logically justified by the other propositions. Another way of saying the same thing is that arguments are sets of propositions in which some of the propositions are meant to be reasons for believing another proposition. The propositions that are used as reasons for believing another proposition are called *premises,* and the proposition that the reasons are intended to justify is called the *conclusion.* Every argument has at least one premise (although it may have any number of premises) and exactly one conclusion.

Here is an example of an argument:

If something has mass, then it is affected by gravity. Apples have mass, therefore apples are affected by gravity.

In this argument there are three propositions:

1. If something has mass, then it is affected by gravity.
2. Apples have mass.
3. Apples are affected by gravity.

The first two propositions of this argument are intended to justify the third proposition. In other words, propositions 1 and 2 are meant to be reasons for believing proposition 3. Therefore, propositions 1 and 2 make up the premises of the argument and 3. is the conclusion.

Standard Form

In order to see this argument more clearly we can put it into what is called *standard form*, which looks like this:

1. If something has mass, then it is affected by gravity.
2. Apples have mass.

Therefore, apples are affected by gravity.

When we put an argument into standard form, we list and number the premises and then we draw a line underneath the premises and we place the conclusion beneath the line so that the premises are clearly separated from the conclusion. Standard form helps us not only to see the argument more clearly but it also organizes an argument so that it is much easier to evaluate, which is our ultimate objective. The same holds true in math. It is much easier to do a math problem if we first put it into standard form. For example, it is much easier to multiply 103 x 58 by hand if we first line it up as such:

$$\begin{array}{r} 103 \\ \times 58 \\ \hline \end{array}$$

One thing we must remember is that in everyday speech or writing, arguments are not always presented in such a neat form. Premises are not always individual sentences that are easily distinguished from the conclusion. Our first task in logic is to be able to identify arguments and organize them into standard form. For instance, the above argument might have been stated as such:

It is clear that apples are affected by gravity because it is true that if something has mass then it is affected by gravity, and apples certainly do have mass.

Although this is one long sentence, it still contains the same three distinct propositions, namely,

1. If something has mass, then it is affected by gravity.
2. Apples have mass.
3. Apples are affected by gravity.

Also, proposition 3 is still the conclusion while 1 and 2 are the premises. Therefore, these propositions retain the same inference structure as above and are organized precisely the same in standard form. The only distinction to be made between this statement of the argument and the one stated above is in the wording and order of the propositions. However, the exact words used in a proposition and their order are irrelevant to the nature of the argument. Both statements of the argument contain the same propositions, therefore it is the same argument.

For example, the word 'because' replaced the word 'therefore' in the second statement of this argument, but since they both indicate a separation between the premises and the conclusion, the meaning remains the same. Phrases like 'it is clear' and 'certainly' do not change the nature of the propositions of which they are part because they mean the same thing. In this case, both phrases simply affirm that we believe these statements to be true. In logic there is no difference between 'it is clear that apples are affected by gravity,' 'apples are affected by gravity,' or 'it is true that apples are affected by gravity' because they are all logically equivalent in meaning.

Identifying Arguments

Because of the fact that arguments can be stated in many different forms, it is often not so easy to figure out if a set of sentences forms an argument. Remember, for a set of sentences to be an argument the sentences must be propositions and related in such a manner that one proposition is a conclusion and the others are premises. That is, there must be an instance of inference. To identify an argument, we must therefore determine if there are premises and a conclusion. One helpful hint for identifying arguments is by looking for specific words or phrases that indicate premises and conclusions. For instance, the word 'therefore' is a conclusion indicator. If we see the word 'therefore' in a sentence, it is guaranteed that the statement that follows it is a conclusion, and if there is a conclusion then there is an argument, so that the only goal remaining is to find the premises that support the conclusion.

The word 'because' is a classic premise indicator. If we see the word 'because' in a sentence, the statement or statements that follow it are premises. Unfortunately, while there are many words that indicate premises and conclusions, they are not always present in every argument. Therefore, it is a good idea to learn them, but it is not a good idea to depend on them. The following are lists of the most common premise and conclusion indicators.

Premise indicators	*Conclusion indicators*
because	therefore
since	then
as	thus
for	so
given that	hence
assuming that	accordingly
	consequently
	which implies
	as a result

Keep in mind that these lists are by no means exhaustive. There are many words that can indicate premises or conclusions depending on the context in which they are used, so that we must often rely on our knowledge of English to determine whether or not a set of propositions constitutes an argument. Furthermore, these words are also not always used as indicators. For example, in the sentence 'The United States has been a country since 1776,' the word 'since' does not indicate a premise but has another meaning entirely.

Exercise

Determine which of the following sets of sentences contain arguments. If a set of sentences does contain an argument, circle the conclusion and number each of the premises. If there is no argument, write" none" next to the number.

1. If there is no evidence to prove that the defendant is guilty, then the defendant must be assumed innocent of the crime. There was no evidence to prove that the defendant was guilty in this case, therefore we must assume that the defendant is innocent.

2. Because of the fact that there are more cars are on the road every year, and the fact that more cars means more accidents, we can conclude that the number of car accidents is going to increase every year.

3. Traveling in a foreign country is always more enjoyable when you are with someone who speaks the language of that country since the problem of communication is eliminated.

4. I like going to the movies. I especially enjoy adventure movies. However, sometimes there is nothing good playing in the theaters.

5 I think that I like Italian food better than Greek food because I know I like Italian food better than French food and I know that I don't like Greek food as much as French food.

6. Panicking is a form of irrationality. Therefore, if you panic, you are acting irrationally.

7. Antarctica is nothing but a block of ice, so why would anyone want to live there?

8. Anyone who eats well and exercises regularly is more likely to live a long and healthy life than anyone who does not. My uncle does not exercise at all, and as a result, he is less likely to live a long and healthy life.

9. When you gamble, you either win or lose. If you win, then you are lucky and if you lose then you are not. Last week I went to Las Vegas and won at craps, so that means I was lucky.

10. People who give up smoking and never start again tend to be the strongest proponents of anti-smoking laws. It seems that these people are the most offended by smokers, especially in public places.

Enthymemes

One of the challenges we run into when trying to identify an argument is that arguments are often presented in a compact format that is efficient for communicating to others but very difficult to express in standard form. Take, for example, the following argument:

I'm not going to buy a new car this year because I can't afford the one I want.

If we leave the wording of this argument as it is and try to put it into standard form, it would come out looking like this:

1. I can't afford the one I want

Therefore, I'm not going to buy a new car this year.

While this is literally accurate, it is not a correct expression of all the propositions that make up this argument because it is incomplete. In order to express this argument completely and correctly in standard form, we must expand on the meaning of each proposition and alter the grammar accordingly. A better version of this argument would be this:

1. There is a specific car that I want to buy.
2. I cannot afford to buy that car this year.

Therefore, I am not going to buy it.

Notice that the argument was not changed, just the wording. No propositions were added or taken away, we only expanded on that which was stated in a more compact form. Sometimes, however, an argument is presented in such a way that it is necessary to add premises that are not explicitly stated in an argument but are clearly intended by the person presenting the argument. This occurs because some reasons for believing a conclusion are so obvious that we do not bother mentioning them; we just assume the person to whom we are presenting the argument understands certain things to be the case. For example, the argument:

We will never make it to the stadium before the game starts. We are ten miles away, and the game starts in less than a minute.

The unstated premise in this argument is the fact that 'we cannot travel ten miles in less than a minute.' This is so obvious to anyone that we would never bother to state it in an argument. However, if we were to put this argument into standard form, we would still include this unstated premise to clearly present the entire argument so that we make no mistakes when we evaluate it. We do this by putting the unstated premise in parenthesis to mark the fact that it is understood and not stated explicitly. In standard form the argument would look like this:

1. We are ten miles away from the stadium.
2. The game starts in less than a minute.
3. (we cannot travel ten miles in less than a minute)

Therefore, we will never make it to the stadium before the game starts.

Another example of an argument with an unstated premise is the following:

Francine broke her back while skiing on Saturday. So, I guess she won't be going dancing with us this weekend.

The implicit premise here is the obvious claim that people with broken backs cannot go dancing. In standard form this argument would look like this:

1. (people with broken backs cannot go dancing)
2. Francine has a broken back.

Therefore, Francine cannot go dancing with us this weekend.

When adding unstated premises to an argument we have to be careful not to include anything that is not clearly implied in the context of the argument. All we are doing when we add unstated premises to an argument is making explicit that which was previously only implicit in the argument. We call arguments that have unstated premises *enthymemes*.

Exercise

State the following enthymemes in standard form.

1. I will never eat at that new restaurant on 3rd street again, because I had lunch there yesterday, and the food was terrible.
2. Given the fact that the Greeks were vastly outnumbered by the Persians, it was unlikely that they could have defeated them.
3. Of course, the defendant is guilty, we found the murder weapon in his house.
4. Frank was involved in six car accidents this month, so I imagine his insurance rates will be going up.
5. Angela had her purse stolen on the way to work and therefore had no money to buy lunch.

Evaluating Arguments

As it was mentioned in the introduction, logic is the activity of quality control management for the process of inference, and the function of logic is to evaluate the process of inference in order to maximize its effectiveness. Because of the fact that arguments are the basic units of inference, the major activity of logic is the evaluation of arguments. There are two criteria by which we evaluate arguments: content and structure. We evaluate the content of an argument in terms of *truth,* and the structure of an argument in term of *validity.* We call an argument *true,* if and only if, **all** its premises are true. We call an argument *valid,* if and only if its structure is such that true premises guarantee a true conclusion. If an argument is found to be acceptable in both content and structure, meaning that it is both true **and** valid, the argument as a whole is also acceptable, and we call it a *sound* argument. Sound arguments are the only acceptable arguments, meaning that they are the only arguments that produce reliable conclusions. In fact, if an argument is determined to be sound, we **must** accept the conclusion; to do otherwise would be irrational.

The Concept of Validity

Although the concept of truth is so familiar to us that there is no need to explain it, the concept of validity is not, and it requires special attention when studying logic. Validity is the central focus of logic, and in an important sense, logic can be thought of as the study of validity because it consists almost entirely of strategies and techniques for testing the validity of arguments. As a logical concept, validity is notorious for being rather difficult to grasp, partly because it is so unfamiliar to us to us in its technical meaning, and partly because it is so abstract. Some people grasp the notion of validity immediately, while others must struggle to comprehend it. Most people, however, fall somewhere in the middle and only come to understand the concept of validity once they have seen several examples and have practiced evaluating a number of arguments on their own. Therefore, the best way to learn the nature of validity is by examining some clear examples.

Our first example is the following argument:

> 1. The Eiffel Tower is taller than the Washington Monument.
> 2. The Washington Monument is taller than the Clock Tower.
> Therefore, the Eiffel Tower is taller than the Clock Tower.

The reason this is a valid argument is that the premises are related to the conclusion in such a way that if the premises were true, the conclusion would also have to be true. That is, if it is the case that the Eiffel Tower is taller than the Washington Monument, and the Washington Monument is taller than the Clock Tower, then it must also be the case that the Eiffel Tower is taller than the Clock Tower. In other words, it is not possible for the premises to be true and the conclusion to be false. Indeed to claim that the premises of this argument are true and that the conclusion is false would be a contradiction. Another example of a valid argument is the following:

1. If a car has no gas, it will not start.
2. This car has no gas.

Therefore, this car will not start.

Once again, this argument is valid because the truth of the premises would guarantee the truth of the conclusion.

When we test an argument for validity, we are trying to determine whether the inference structure of the argument is such that true input yields true output. If we take a step back and recall that an argument is the basic unit of inference, and inference is the activity of producing new information from given information, we can see that an argument is the production of new information (a conclusion) from given information (the premises). However, information is only valuable to us if it is true. In fact, we have a specific word for true information, namely, knowledge,' and the production of knowledge is the ultimate objective of inference. This is why an inference structure is only valuable to us if its output is as reliable as its input. If we input knowledge, we want the output to be knowledge as well. Therefore, good inference is that which takes true premises and generates a true conclusion: true input yields true output. Only certain inference structures are capable of guaranteeing this relationship between premises and conclusions, and these inference structures define the nature of validity.

Once again, good inference means 'truth in, truth out,' and a valid inference structure is one which ensures this relationship. We can illustrate the definition of a valid inference structure as such:

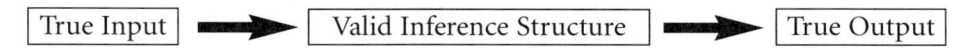

| True Input | ➡ | Valid Inference Structure | ➡ | True Output |

A common example of a valid inference structure is a calculator. Calculators are designed in such a way that if you enter the correct numbers, then you will get the correct answer. If you do not get a correct answer from a calculator it means that either the machine is not functioning properly or you did not press the correct keys. However, if a calculator is functioning properly, by pressing the correct keys you are guaranteed a correct answer.

One common misconception regarding the nature of valid inference structures is the belief that false input guarantees false output. That is, many people think that false premises necessarily lead to a false conclusion in a valid argument. However, if we use the calculator as an example, it is evident that while false input into a valid inference structure most often yields a false output, it is certainly possible to get a true output by accident. For instance, if we want to multiply 2 x 2 using a calculator, and we accidentally enter 2 + 2, we will get the correct answer to our intended calculation by 'dumb luck.' The same holds true for any valid argument in that true premises guarantee a true conclusion, but false premises only mean that we might get a false conclusion because we could be right by accident. The following is an example of a valid argument with false premises and a true conclusion:

1. All fish fly.
2. All flying animals live in water.

Therefore all fish live in water.

The conclusion in this argument happens to be true, not by virtue of this argument, but by accident. Of course, if we know that the premises of a valid argument are false, we must still reject the argument, but only because the conclusion is unreliable, meaning we do not know if the conclusion is true or false, not because it is necessarily false. We can thus make an addition to our previous illustration regarding valid inference structures to include this concept:

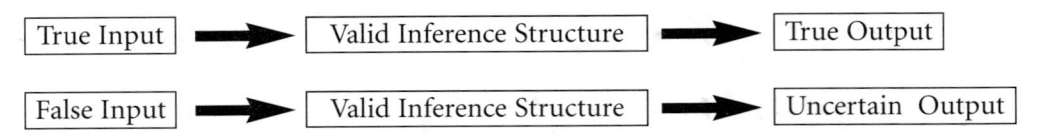

| True Input | ➡ | Valid Inference Structure | ➡ | True Output |

| False Input | ➡ | Valid Inference Structure | ➡ | Uncertain Output |

Testing Validity

One of America's first logicians, Charles S. Peirce, summarized the concept of validity in the following way:

> The object of reasoning is to find out, from the consideration of what we already know, something else which we do not know. Consequently, reasoning is good if it be such as to give a true conclusion from true premises, and not otherwise. Thus, the question of validity is purely one of fact and not of thinking. A being the premises and B being the conclusion, the question is, whether these facts are really so related that if A is B is. If so, the inference is valid, if not, not. (95)

Unfortunately, the problem with any definition of validity is that it is always ambiguous to a certain degree, and this ambiguity becomes apparent when learning to test the validity of an argument. Because the definition of a valid argument is one in which true premises guarantee a true conclusion, there is often a confusion as to whether the premises of an argument have to be true in order for an argument to be valid. In other words, it seems that the definition might imply that we have to first know if the premises of an argument are true before we can determine if the structure of the argument is valid. In order to eliminate this ambiguity regarding the definition of validity and thus preclude any confusion about how to go about testing the validity of an argument, it is necessary to elaborate on the definition of validity as well as explain the method by which we test the validity of arguments.

Because validity is determined solely by the logical structure of an argument, the actual content of the argument is irrelevant. In other words, we do not need to know the actual truth value of any of the premises in an argument to determine whether or not it is valid; the actual truth or falsity of premises has nothing to do with the logical structure of an argument. The only kind of truth we are concerned about when testing the validity of an argument is the 'hypothetical' truth of the premises. We imagine or assume the premises of an argument to be true when we are testing for validity, and by doing so we can see whether or not the conclusion necessarily follows. Only after we discover that an argument is valid do we go back to see if the premises are in fact true. If an argument is invalid, it cannot possibly be sound and thus is not an acceptable form of inference. Therefore, we do not even bother checking to see if the premises are true but simply reject the argument as a whole.

To illustrate this point, let's go back and examine how we went about determining the validity of the following argument:

1. The Eiffel Tower is taller than the Washington Monument.
2. The Washington Monument is taller than the Clock Tower.

Therefore, the Eiffel Tower is taller than the Clock Tower.

We knew that this argument was valid without ever knowing whether the premises are really true or false. That is, we were able to test the validity of this argument without worrying about questions such as; 'Is the Eiffel Tower really taller than the Washington Monument?' and 'Is the Washington Monument really taller than the Clock Tower?' The only question we had to ask regarding this argument to test its validity is 'If these premises were true, would the conclusion have to be true as well?' These premises happen to be true, but even if these premises were false, the argument would still be valid.

The following is an example of an argument which is valid in form but false in content:

1. England is one of the United States.

Therefore, any city in England is in the United States.

We can see that this argument is valid even though the premise 'England is one of the United States' is certainly false because **if** it were true that 'England is one of the United States,' then it would also have to be true that any city in England would be in the United States. Once again, the method for determining validity requires us to be able to hypothetically imagine all the premises to be true and then judge whether the conclusion given would be logically entailed by these hypothetical truths. The fact that we use hypothetical truths to evaluate the validity of arguments also implies that, technically, we can test an argument for validity even if the premises do not have any real truth value at all. A clear example of this is the following argument:

1. A is greater than B.
2. B is greater than C.

Therefore, A is greater than C.

This argument is certainly valid, and its validity is due to its logical structure alone.[1] After all, it has no content. We determine the validity of such an argument in precisely the same way as we determine the validity of any other argument, i.e. by asking whether the (hypothetical) truth of the premises would guarantee the truth of the conclusion. It makes no sense, however, to ask if the premises in this argument are really true. The only reasonable answer to such a question is 'who knows?' After all, what could such a question mean? It is not just that we are unable to answer this question, the question itself is meaningless and therefore cannot be answered. The sentences that make up the premises in this argument are not really propositions because they do not refer to anything and thus do not make any claims about the world. These sentences, therefore, can have no real truth value. They are artificial propositions that we use to examine the logical structure of an argument.

Common Terms

What makes an argument valid or not is the relationship between all the propositions that make up the argument. So much is clear. However, there still remains the question of how propositions are related at all. What relates propositions to each other? The answer is the existence of *common terms*. For example, in the argument:

1. A is greater than B
2. B is greater than C

   Therefore, A is greater than C.

There is a common term between the premises, namely 'B,' and each premise has a common term with the conclusion. Premise 1 has 'A' as a common term with the conclusion, and premise 2 has 'C' as a common term with the conclusion. Because of the fact that 'B' is a common term between premise 1 and 2, a logical relationship is established between 'A' and 'C' which is expressed as the conclusion. In other words, B is being used in this argument as a means for comparing both A and C as seen here:

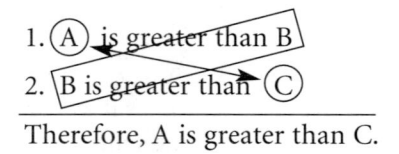

1. A is greater than B
2. B is greater than C

   Therefore, A is greater than C.

On the other hand, the existence of common terms does not by any means guarantee a valid argument structure. The common terms must be related in a valid inference structure to allow for the production of a valid conclusion. For instance, if it turned out that both A and C were greater than B, no valid inference could have been made and therefore no conclusion could have been drawn. As we will soon see, there are very specific valid inference structures for establishing logical relationships between propositions by means of common terms. Once these valid argument structures are learned, another, more straightforward, and easier method for testing the validity of an argument becomes available to us.

Invalid Arguments

An invalid argument is simply an argument that fails the test of validity, meaning that the truth of the premises would not guarantee the truth of the conclusion because of an improper inference structure. For example:

1. Any student who has a B average will graduate.
2. Judy did not get a B average.
   Therefore, Judy will not graduate

Even if Judy does not get a B average, it does not mean she will not graduate; after all, she might get an A or a C average which would still allow her to graduate. Therefore, it is possible for the premises to be true and the conclusion false. The premises only claim that people with a B average will graduate; they do not claim that *only* people with a B average will graduate.

Frequently Asked Questions About Validity

1. Can an argument be valid and have false premises?

   Yes, the actual truth value of the premises has nothing to do with validity.

2. Can a valid argument have a false conclusion?

   Yes, *but* only if the premises are also false because in a valid argument, by definition, true premises must lead to a true conclusion. A valid argument cannot have true premises and a false conclusion.

3. If both the premises and the conclusion in a argument are true, does that mean that the argument is valid?

   No. Once again the actual truth values of the propositions in an argument have nothing to do with the question of validity. Validity is a matter of the structure of an argument. All the premises may be true and the conclusion might be true as well but the argument can still have an invalid structure.

   E.g.

   1. France is in Europe.
   2. New Jersey is in the United States.
      Therefore, Phoenix is in Arizona.

   As can clearly be seen, there is no connection between the two premises and there is no connection between the premises and the conclusion. The argument lacks a valid structure due to the fact that there is no common term. However, all the premises are true and the conclusion is true.

4. Can an argument be valid and have true premises and a false conclusion?

   No. By definition a valid argument with true premises must have a true conclusion.

5. Can an argument be sound and not be valid?

   No. By definition a sound argument must be both true and valid.

Exercise

Using the assigned truth values for each proposition (T = true, and F = false), determine whether each argument is (a) true, (b) valid and (c) sound.

1. All people desire to be rational. (T)
   My brother is a person. (T)
   Therefore, my brother desires to be rational.

2. All rational people have brown hair. (F)
   My sister has brown hair. (T)
   Therefore, my sister is rational.

3. Everyone who speaks English is American. (F)
   My students all speak English. (T)
   Therefore they are all Americans.

4. All my students are American. (T)
   Sam is a student of mine. (F)
   Therefore, Sam is American.

5. If Frank goes to the concert, then Sharon will not. (T)
   Frank did go to the concert. (T)
   Therefore, Sharon did not go to the concert.

6. If Alice goes to the concert, then Sharon will not. (T)
   Sharon did not go to the concert. (T)
   Therefore, Alice did go to the concert.

7. All professional athletes are competitive. (T)
   Business is competitive. (T)
   Therefore, all competition is a business.

8. Next term I have to take either Physics or Chemistry. (T)
   I'm not going to take Chemistry because its boring. (F)
   Therefore, I'm going to take Physics next term.

Fallacies

Although everyone has an intuitive notion of validity, meaning that people naturally reject clearly invalid arguments because they simply don't make sense, many people (and perhaps most people) have no formal conception of validity and therefore lack the necessary criteria for effectively identifying the more subtle forms of invalidity.

As a result, people often accept the conclusions of certain invalid argument forms because they mistakenly believe them to be valid. We call these invalid argument forms *fallacies,* and they are extremely problematic because they so often convince people to make and accept false conclusions. In fact, some people use fallacies as a means for getting others to believe certain false propositions in an attempt to manipulate the behavior of those people. Therefore, we must always be on guard against fallacies in our own inferences as well as in the inferences of others since to believe the conclusion of any fallacious argument is, by definition, irrational.

Because of the fact that fallacies are errors of inference and are the root of a great deal of irrationality, the recognition and avoidance of fallacies is one of the major objectives of logic. One difficulty in learning to recognize and avoid fallacies, however, is that some fallacies are so common that they are accepted by many people as a matter of course. This can make the recognition of fallacies difficult to teach people. However, once they are made clear with examples, and it is understood why fallacies are invalid arguments, it becomes a lot easier to avoid committing them in one's thinking as well as to uncover them in other people's thinking. While there are a great many types of fallacies, we are only going to cover some of the most common and important fallacies listed below.

Nine Basic Fallacies

1. Appeal to Majority
2. Appeal to Emotion
3. Appeal to Ignorance
4. Ad Hominem
5. Begging the Question
6. Post Hoc Ergo Propter Hoc
7. Non-Sequitur
8. Denying the Antecedent
9. Affirming the Consequent

1. Appeal to Majority

Definition: Attempting to justify a conclusion based on the fact that large numbers of people believe it to be true.

Example: There must be life on other planets; everyone believes that.

This is certainly one of the most common fallacies because so many people base their beliefs on popular opinion. We know that it is invalid because we have clear cases in which large numbers of people believe something to be true that turns out to be false. For instance, not long ago virtually everyone believed that the Earth was flat. Today it is evident that everyone was wrong. The number of people who believe something can never be used as evidence for its truth. A more subtle example of Appeal to Majority can be found in the following argument:

Of course the Beatles were the best Rock and Roll band ever. They had more top ten hits than any other band in history.

2. Appeal to Emotion

Definition: Trying to convince people to accept a conclusion based on the emotion it evokes in them.

Example: If you take that new job out west, you will break your mother's heart because she will not be able to visit you every weekend. Don't you care about your mother?

This fallacy is often used in conjunction with appeal to majority as means for persuading people to believe something. Therefore, we must be particularly aware of these two fallacies and not let ourselves get caught in their 'appealing' traps. This fallacy is very common in courts of law in which lawyers often try to convince a jury to find a defendant innocent or guilty based on feelings of pity or outrage. For example, murder trial lawyers often bring the victim's family before the jury, such as a crying widow or the now fatherless children, in order to generate some sort of emotion that might lead the jury to lean one way or another when deliberating on the verdict.

3. Appeal to Ignorance

Definition: Accepting a specific proposition because it has not been proven false.

Example: I will believe in unicorns until someone can prove to me that they do not exist.

The fact that some propositions cannot be proven or demonstrated to be false is no justification for accepting them. Only evidence for the truth of a proposition can be used to justify its acceptance; not a lack of evidence for its falsity. For instance, while we suspect that there are no complex life forms on any other planet in our solar system, based on the information we have at this time regarding our solar system, it may be the case that we cannot *prove* this to be true. However, this inability to prove that there are no complex life forms on other planets in our solar system cannot be used as evidence to justify the proposition that there *are* complex life forms on other planets in our solar system. Just because there is no way to prove a proposition to be false does not mean that we have any evidence to support its truth.

Furthermore, to accept a proposition as true unless it can be proven false most often involves a case of intellectual dishonesty because the same level of proof is not being required to accept the proposition to be true. For example, if someone believes in unicorns and will not give up this belief unless it can be proven that they do not exist, it is almost certainly the case that this person did not require proof that unicorns exist as a condition for believing in them. People that believe in unicorns must do so in the face of a lot of evidence supporting the claim that unicorns are in fact mythical. Surely, the existence of unicorns has never been proven. Therefore, to insist that the non-existence of unicorns be proven before abandoning the belief that they do exist is being intellectually dishonest.

To commit this fallacy is thus most often a matter of being biased towards a particular belief and not genuinely considering the possibility of it being false. In fact, we can see the intellectual dishonesty inherent in appeals to ignorance because most people who claim that they will give up a belief if they are given proof that it is false are actually lying because no matter how much proof one presents to them, they will find a way to argue that the evidence is inconclusive. That is, any time evidence is presented as proof that a proposition is false, a new story will be generated that demonstrates the evidence to be insufficient. For instance, how could anyone possibly demonstrate that there are no unicorns in the world? No matter what is done to prove that unicorns do not exist, someone could always come up with a counter argument which could neutralize any evidence whatsoever. Even if a group of super-investigators undertakes a mission to search the whole world over and somehow covers every inch of the Earth and never sees a unicorn, someone might explain this lack of success by the fact that unicorns hide extremely well or even that they can make themselves invisible when people are looking for them. In any case, the fact that I can never prove with complete certainty that unicorns do not exist is no justification for believing in them. Only some sort of evidence that unicorns do exist counts as justification for believing in them.

4. Ad Hominem

Definition: An argument that attempts to justify or refute a conclusion based on a premise that attacks the person who stated the conclusion.

Example: Of course you say that skydiving is safe, you're a skydiver and skydivers are crazy.

Ad Hominem (which literally means "at the man" in Latin) is the fallacy of discarding the truth of a proposition because of some characteristic of the person who stated it. This fallacy is most commonly the result of some irrational bias such as racism, sexism, religious bias, etc. It is therefore often stated in crude and vulgar language. Racial, sexual and/or religious slurs are common accompaniments to this fallacy.

5. Begging the Question

Definition: Answering a question by repeating the question in another form, or any argument in which the conclusion is stated either explicitly or implicitly in one of the premises.

Example: First juror: "What makes you think that the defendant is guilty of murder?"

Second juror: "Because he killed that woman in cold blood."

This fallacy is perhaps the most subtle to detect. When someone commits this fallacy we often get the feeling that something is wrong with that person's reasoning, but we can't quite place our finger on the problem. The reason for this is that Begging the Question is a type of circular argument and is therefore not a fallacy in the same sense as the other fallacies. Circular arguments are actually valid, but they are valid in such a way that is unacceptable in an argument because the premises do not justify the conclusion. In other words, in an argument that 'Begs the Question' the premises are not actually reasons for accepting the conclusion because the conclusion is somehow already stated in all or part of the premises.

Take, for example, the following, obviously circular argument:

1. Michelangelo was a great artist.
   ─────────────────────────────────
   Therefore, Michelangelo was a great artist.

Technically, this argument is clearly valid since it is impossible for the premises to be true and the conclusion to be false. Indeed, if the premises are true, technically it must also be a sound argument. Unfortunately, this type of argument breaks the rules of inference at a more basic level and is therefore neither valid nor sound. If we recall, the function of inference is the production of new information using given information. This argument clearly does not accomplish this function because it simply repeats given information; there is no new information being generated. Therefore this argument is not even an example of inference so it cannot possibly have an acceptable inference structure.

Most often, however, Begging the Question is not so blatant and involves answering a question by simply restating the question in another form so that the question is not really being answered. For example:

First juror: "What makes you think that the defendant is guilty of murder?"

Second juror: "Because he killed that woman in cold blood."

We can see by the question that the defendant is accused of murdering some woman. This question actually means 'what evidence do you have to support the claim that the defendant is guilty of murdering this woman?' Therefore, the question cannot be answered by the proposition "He killed that woman in cold blood." Such an argument would look like this:

1. He murdered the woman.
   ─────────────────────────────────
   Therefore, he is guilty of murdering the woman.

What is in question here is whether or not the defendant actually murdered the woman. We are not questioning whether or not killing the woman in cold blood makes him guilty of murder. Killing the woman in cold blood is the same thing as being guilty of murder, therefore this cannot qualify as a reason for believing it to be true.

6. Post Hoc Ergo Propter Hoc (Post Hoc)

Definition: An argument which concludes that some event caused another event just because the first event preceded the second event.

Example: It started raining just before I took the test, and I got an A. Therefore, the rain must have brought me good luck or something.

Post hoc ergo propter hoc is Latin for 'after this, therefore because of this,' and we usually shorten it to simply 'Post Hoc.' Post Hoc fallacies always have to do with causes, and they are the basis for most superstitions. The mistake they make is to assume that just because an event occurred before another, that it must have caused that event. While it is certainly true that causes always precede effects; it is not true that just because one event precedes another that it must have caused it. Evidence that some event caused another involves more than just temporal order.

7. Non-Sequitur

Definition: *Non-sequitur* is Latin for "does not follow." In this fallacy it can be said that the premises do not follow from the conclusion or that the conclusion is irrelevant to the premises because there are no common terms.

Example: Exercise is good for your health, and so is eating a balanced diet, therefore you should not smoke.

Although all fallacies are non-sequitur at some level because their conclusions do not necessarily follow from their premises, the lack of a logical relationship between the premises and the conclusion of Non-Sequitur fallacies is often more pronounced. We use the term 'non-sequitur' as a default term to refer to any fallacious arguments that cannot be categorized more specifically. In the other fallacies, we have a general understanding as to the nature of the mistake being made. However, sometimes the premises and the conclusion are so unrelated that there is no way to classify the error. In common parlance we say that the conclusion 'has nothing to do with' the premises. We cannot find any connection between the premises and the conclusion and therefore we often describe a non-sequitur argument as an idea that 'makes no sense.' Indeed, if a person commits the non-sequitur fallacy too frequently, we tend to classify that person as 'crazy.'

DENYING THE ANTECEDENT AND AFFIRMING THE CONSEQUENT

These last two fallacies involve a specific type of premise known as a *conditional premise*. Conditional premises are premises that take the form 'If . . . then. . . .'

For example: '*If* it snows, *then* it's cold outside.'

Conditional premises are comprised of two parts: the 'if' part and the 'then' part. We call the 'if' part of the conditional premises the *antecedent,* and we call the 'then' part of the conditional premise the *consequent.* In the above example, 'If it snows' is the antecedent, and 'then it's cold outside' is the consequent. When we assert the truth of either the antecedent or the consequent of a conditional premises in an argument, we are 'affirming' that part of the premise. When we assert that either the antecedent or the consequent of a conditional premise is false, we are 'denying' that part of the argument.

Since there are two parts to a conditional premise (antecedent and consequent) and two possible truth values to assert for each part of the conditional premise (true and false), there are four possible argument structures that we can produce in an argument with conditional premises. Two of these structures are always valid, and two are always invalid. We will only study the two structures that are invalid at this time because they are fallacies. Later on, we will examine the two valid argument structures regarding conditional premises in detail. The two invalid argument structures that can be produced from conditional premises are 'Denying the antecedent' and 'Affirming the Consequent.'

8. Denying the Antecedent

Definition: An argument which tries to use the negation of the antecedent in a conditional premise to justify the negation of the consequent.

Example: If it snows, then it's cold outside. It did not snow today. Therefore, it is not cold outside.

In standard form it would look like this:

> 1. If it snows, then it's cold outside.
> 2. It did not snow today.
> Therefore, it is not cold outside.

Premise number 1 is the conditional premise. Premise number 2 is an assertion that the antecedent in the conditional premise is false, and therefore it is said to 'deny' the antecedent. The word 'not' is what makes the second premise a denial of the antecedent. It is the same proposition as the antecedent, but only negative, meaning it includes the word 'not.'

Once again an argument is only valid under the conditions that 'if the premises are true then the conclusion must be true as well.' However, if we reflect a little on this argument, we can see that this is not the case. If we know that premise number 1 is true, and we know that premise number 2 is also true, we cannot conclude that it is not cold outside. After all, it can be cold even when it does not snow. Therefore, this is an invalid argument. Here is another example of Denying the Antecedent:

> 1. If Aristotle wrote it, then it is ancient.
> 2. Aristotle did not write it.
> Therefore, it is not ancient.

If we assume that both these premises are true, must the conclusion also be true? Of course not. The fact that Aristotle did not write something does not mean that it is not ancient. After all, Plato (who is older than Aristotle) could have written whatever it is that is being considered. What must be understood is the fact that premise number 1 does not state that *only* Aristotle's writings are ancient. It merely states that all of Aristotle's writings are ancient. Denying the Antecedent is most often the result of misunderstanding the meaning of the conditional premise in an argument.

9. Affirming the Consequent

Definition: An argument which tries to use the truth of a consequent in a conditional premise as justification for the truth of the antecedent.

Example:

1. If it rains, then the street gets wet.
2. The street is wet.
   Therefore, it rained.

Premise number 1 is the conditional premise. Premise number 2 asserts the truth of the consequent of premise number 1. This fallacy is obviously very similar to Denying the Antecedent in that it is most often committed because people misunderstand the actual meaning of the conditional premise. The premises in this argument can be true and the conclusion false thus making it invalid. Even if it is true that 'the street gets wet when it rains'; a wet street does not necessarily mean that it rained. The street could have gotten wet by other means, such as a broken water main or an open fire hydrant.

Exercise

Name the following fallacies. Keep in mind the fact that an argument may commit more than one fallacy at a time.

1. No one doubts that Elvis is the king of rock and roll. Everyone thinks he's the greatest.
2. First person: "Why is Phillip so boring?"
   Second person: "Because he is not very interesting."
3. If the government increases income tax 200%, a lot of people will refuse to pay it. However, the government will never increase income tax that much, so no one will ever refuse to pay their income tax.
4. Exercise is good for your health, so you should not smoke.
5. How can you say that you do not believe the teachings of our religion? Our family has been devoted to this religion for over a hundred years. Are you so unconcerned about tradition to just throw it all away? What makes you any smarter than the rest of us?
6. Employee: "Why do I have to work overtime every weekend?"
   Boss: "Hey, you gotta do what you gotta do."
7. There is no reason to study Darwin's theory of natural selection. After all, it has never been proven.
8. The reason why Sylvia has such a bad temper is that she was born during a hurricane.

9. I knew that Ralph would try to argue that marijuana should be legalized; he's such a loser.
10. If you think that skydiving is not fun, then you're crazy. Dan thinks skydiving is fun, therefore he is not crazy.
11. Why ask why? All the cool people just do whatever they want to do, whenever they want to do it. What are you, some kind of nerd?
12. Of course you think that Russian history should be taught in school, you're a communist.
13. "Why do you sit out here all alone?" said Alice, not wishing to begin an argument. "Why, because there's nobody with me!" cried Humpty Dumpty. "Did you think I didn't know the answer to *that*? Ask another." (From *Through the Looking-Glass,* by Lewis Carroll.)
14. First person: "There is no evidence that ghosts exist."
    Second person: "So what? You can't *prove* that."
15. I broke a mirror last week and now all sorts of bad things are happening to me. I guess that brought me bad luck.
16. Student: "How do scientists test people's level of intelligence?"
    Teacher: "By giving them an intelligence test."
17. If they spend all their money on a new house, then they will not be able to afford a new car. They did not have enough money for a new car, therefore they must have spent all their money on a new house.
18. English must be an easy language to learn. Look how many people speak English as a second language.
19. Lying is wrong because it is immoral.
20. You should be proud of your country and be willing to fight for everything for which it stands. Sign up for military service now and become one of the brave people who made this great nation possible.
21. An attorney: "The witness claims to have seen the crime take place, but we should not believe her because she is a drug user."
22. Last week, Tom told me that I would probably get into a car accident because I drive so fast, and when I did get into an accident this week I knew it was because he jinxed me. It's all his fault.
23. There is nothing wrong with speeding. Who doesn't speed?
24. My cold went away as soon as I got to California. There must be something about the climate in California that helps the body to fight off a cold.
25. First person: "There is no reason to believe that women are less intelligent than men."
    Second person: "Yeah but no one can prove that they are not less intelligent than men."

26. Child: "Why is it wrong to steal?"
    Parent: "It just is, that's why."
27. People shouldn't be so greedy when it comes to money because they should care more about their families and friends.

Symbolic Language

One of the problems with trying to determine whether or not an argument is valid is the fact that we first receive arguments in natural language, e.g. English, which often makes our analysis of the logical structure of an argument extremely difficult. Because we are only trying to examine the logical structure of an argument, a great deal of the actual content of the argument is irrelevant and extraneous material that hinders our analysis. More specifically:

> Arguments presented in English or any other natural language are often difficult to appraise because of the vague and equivocal nature of the words used, the ambiguity of their construction, the presence of misleading idioms or confusing metaphor, or the distraction of emotional impacts.... (Copi and Cohen, 342)

Of course it is true that there are many arguments in natural language which are simple and clear enough for us to analyze their logical structure without any problems whatsoever. For example, the validity of the following argument is evident in natural language:

> All metals expand when heated. Copper is a metal. Therefore, copper expands when heated.

In standard form this argument looks like this:

1. All metals expand when heated.
2. Copper is a metal.
   Therefore, copper expands when heated

However, the logical structure of the next argument is not quite so simple to evaluate:

> The United States should slowly but surely eliminate its policy of mandatory taxation. Such a bold claim can easily be justified by making reference to the fact that coercion of any form is unacceptable given both the ethical and legal principles on which this nation is founded. If it is the case that mandatory taxation is a form of governmental coercion of United States citizens, then this policy should be eliminated, albeit, in an incremental fashion in order to avoid too drastic a change all at once. Mandatory taxation by the government necessarily implies the coercion of citizens to pay taxes by threat of punishment and thus makes such a policy equivalent to legalized extortion.

Even in standard form, the logical structure of this argument is not so easy to evaluate in natural language.

1. If it is the case that mandatory taxation is a form of governmental coercion of United States citizens, then this policy should be eliminated, albeit, in an incremental fashion in order to avoid too drastic a change all at once.

2. Mandatory taxation by the government necessarily implies the coercion of citizens to pay taxes by threat of punishment making such a policy equivalent to legalized extortion.

Therefore, the United States should slowly but surely eliminate its policy of mandatory taxation.

This argument is valid, and in fact it has the same exact logical structure as the previous argument. The difficulty that we run into when trying to evaluate such an argument is a combination of its length, organization, extraneous detail, and emotive content.

In order to avoid these problematic aspects of trying to determine the validity of arguments as they are given to us in natural language, a system has been developed for translating natural language into an entirely general, content-free and unambiguous format of symbolic language.[2] Like in algebra, the utilization of a symbolic language in logic eliminates the irrelevant and confusing content of arguments and allows us to examine the logical structure of the argument more clearly and directly. Furthermore, symbolic language simplifies the activity of evaluating the validity of arguments because it introduces a completely formal understanding of validity. This formal understanding of valid inference structures is what makes the process of evaluating the logical structure of arguments much more mechanical and procedural. Indeed, it is the fact that valid inference structures could now be formalized and mechanized that led to the emergence of a new generation of technology known as the computer age.

Evaluating the logical structure of an argument using symbolic language requires three fairly simple steps: (1) Put the argument into standard form, (2) translate all the propositions which comprise the argument, and (3) determine whether the conclusion of the argument can be deduced from the premises while using only the set of rules which define the basic forms of valid inference. Since we already know how to put an argument into standard form, learning how to translate propositions into symbolic language is our next objective.

Translation

When translating arguments into symbolic form, we begin by classifying the premises and the conclusion according to the nature of the propositions that make them up. There are two basic types of propositions: *atomic propositions* and *compound propositions*. An atomic proposition is any proposition that has a single subject and predicate and is not directly related to any other propositions. For instance, the proposition 'John is tall' is an atomic proposition since it stands by itself. 'John' is the subject and 'is tall' is the predicate. Compound propositions are propositions composed of two atomic propositions which are related in a specific way. There are only three possible relationships between atomic propositions that make up a compound proposition, and the nature of these relationships determines the truth value of the proposition as a whole. Therefore, there are three types of compound propositions: *conjunctive, disjunctive* and *conditional,* and each is defined according to the kind of logical connection it establishes between atomic propositions and is represented by a special symbol called a *connective.*

The letters of the alphabet are used to symbolize propositions. A single letter is used to symbolize an atomic proposition while two letters and a connective symbol are used to symbolize a compound proposition. Because of the fact that the ability to symbolize atomic propositions is a prerequisite for being able to symbolize compound propositions, we will begin with atomic propositions and then work our way through each type of compound proposition.

Atomic Propositions

There are two types of atomic propositions: *affirmative* and *negative.* An atomic proposition is said to be affirmative if there is no use of the word 'not' (in any form including contractions). Likewise, an atomic proposition is said to be negative if it includes any form of the word 'not.' Any affirmative atomic proposition can be transformed into a negative atomic proposition simply by adding the word 'not' and any negative atomic proposition can be transformed into an affirmative atomic proposition by eliminating the word 'not.' For example, the affirmative atomic proposition 'John is tall' can be transformed into a negative atomic proposition 'John is *not* tall,' and vice versa. An atomic proposition and its negation are logically inconsistent with each other in that we cannot assert both at the same time without contradicting ourselves.

As it was mentioned, we symbolize all atomic propositions with a single letter, and although we can use any letter we want, it is always best to use letters that help us to remember which proposition they represent.[3] Most often we use the first letter of the major subject or predicate. Given the proposition 'John is tall' we would probably choose the letter 'J' (for John) or 'T' (for tall) to symbolize the whole proposition. However, we have to make sure that we only use any given letter to represent one proposition within an argument. For example, if an argument contained two premises, the first being 'John is tall' and the second being 'Jane is tall,' you could not use 'J' to represent both propositions. If you use 'J' to represent 'John is tall,' you would probably use some other letter in the word 'Jane,' e.g. 'A', to represent the proposition 'Jane is tall.' We symbolize negative atomic propositions just as we do atomic propositions with the addition of a single negation sign in front of the letter. This negation sign is called a 'tilde' and looks like this; '~.' We would symbolize the proposition 'John is not tall' as '~J,' which is nothing more than asserting the affirmative proposition and then negating it.

Conjunctions

The second type of proposition is a compound proposition called a conjunction, and this type of proposition connects two atomic propositions using the word 'and,' 'but' or any other word that has the same function which is to assert the truth of two atomic propositions in the same premise. For example, 'It is late, and I have to study' asserts that both 'It is late' and 'I have to study' to be true propositions. In this case, we would probably use 'L' to represent the propositions 'It is late' and 'S' to represent 'I have to study.' A single dot is used to connect both of these propositions, so that the proper translation of 'It is late, and I have to study' would look like this: 'L • S.' In order for a conjunctive compound to be true, *both* its components must be true.

Disjunction

The third type of proposition is another compound proposition called a disjunction, and this type of compound connects two atomic proposition using the word 'or.' Unlike a conjunction, however, a disjunction asserts that *at least one* of the propositions it connects is true. For example, in the proposition 'Tonight I will go to the movies or I will study' the 'or' means that at least one of these things will be true. Therefore, if I go to the movies *and* study, the proposition 'Tonight I will go to the movies or I will study' is still true. This can be a little confusing because of the fact that in English we use the word 'or' in two different senses: *exclusive* and *inclusive.* The exclusive sense of the word 'or' means that only one aspect of the disjunctive proposition can be true but not both. For instance, in the exclusive sense of the word 'or' the proposition 'Tonight I will go to the movies or I will study' means that I will definitely do one of these things, but not both. Given this meaning of the word 'or' we understand the sentence to imply that there is only time for one activity tonight, so the speaker must choose between the two.

In an inclusive sense of the word 'or' the same sentence means that the speaker will do at least one of these things tonight and maybe both. It is this latter sense of 'or' that we use in logic, and this often causes students of logic some difficulty because it is not the most common usage of the word 'or' in English, but we do use it. One helpful trick is to think of the word 'or' in logic as meaning 'and/or.' For example, someone might state the proposition that 'Driving in New York City during the holidays is always unpleasant because there is either nowhere to park or there is too much traffic.' In this case, it is certainly implied that there might be nowhere to park and too much traffic during the holidays in New York City. It is not being claimed that only one of these things can be true. What is being claimed is that at least one of these things is always the case. It is best to keep examples such as this in mind when dealing with disjunctions. We use the symbol '~' called a 'wedge' or a 'vee' to represent the word 'or' in disjunctions. The proposition 'Tonight I will go to the movies or I will study' would translate as 'M ~ S' using 'M' to stand for 'I will go to the movies' and 'S' for 'I will study.'

Conditionals

The forth type of proposition is a compound proposition called a conditional proposition. As we have already mentioned, conditional premises connect two atomic propositions using the words 'if' and 'then' such that one proposition will be true if another is true. We use the symbol '⊃', called a 'horseshoe' to represent the 'If . . . then' relationship between two propositions. For example, the proposition 'If I study hard, then I'll get good grades' would translate to 'S ⊃ G,' using 'S' to stand for 'I study hard' and 'G' to stand for 'I'll get good grades.' A conditional proposition is considered true only if the truth of the antecedent leads to the truth of the consequent. For example, the conditional 'If I study hard, then I'll get good grades' is a true proposition only if studying hard does in fact yield good grades.

Remember that the proposition 'S ⊃ G' only states 'If I study hard, then I'll get good grades.' It does **not** say that I'll get good grades *only* if I study hard. After all, I could get good grades by other means such as bribing the teacher or cheating. This proposition simply says that studying is one sure way to get good grades. As we mentioned earlier, people who do not completely understand the meaning of conditional propositions are more likely commit one of the conditional fallacies, namely Denying the Antecedent or Affirming the Consequent. It is important to keep in mind the fact that conditional premises do not actually have to have the word 'then' stated explicitly. The word 'if' implies the word 'then.' For instance, the sentence 'if I win the lottery, I'll be rich' is a perfectly good conditional proposition even though it does not contain the word 'then.' However, a conditional must include the word 'if.'

To briefly review, there are four types of propositions: atomic (affirmative and negative), conjunctive, disjunctive and conditional; and there are three logical connective symbols associated with each type of compound propositions. Below is a quick reference for using these connectives as well as the negative indicator for translating premises and conclusions into symbolic form.

	Meaning	*Symbol*	*Compound form*
Negation	not	~	~p (not p)*
Conjunction	and	•	p • q (p and q)
Disjunction	or	~	p ~ q (p or q)
Conditional	If . . . then	⊃	p ⊃ q (if p then q)

*Although negation of an atomic proposition is not technically a compound form, it is nonetheless listed here because it does involve a modification of an atomic proposition and requires a specific symbol to represent this modification.

Exercise

Translate the following sentences into symbolic form:

1. It's hot outside.
2. It's not cold today.
3. Hot days are good for swimming.
4. At night I study and watch T.V.
5. During the day I study but I don't watch T.V.
6. Tomorrow will be either hot or cold.
7. If it's hot tomorrow, then I'll go swimming.

8. If it's not cold, then I won't go skiing.
9. Tomorrow I will either go skiing or swimming.
10. If it's hot tomorrow, then I'll go swimming but not jogging.
11. Regardless of the weather tomorrow, I will study.
12. Tonight I will study at the library and either stay home or go to the movies.
13. Tomorrow, I will either study again or go downtown and meet some friends.
14. If I do not go downtown tomorrow, then I will either study and watch T.V. or I'll go to the movies.
15. I like swimming and skiing, but I do not like surfing or snowboarding.

Evaluating Arguments in Symbolic Form

Once we are able to translate arguments into symbolic form, the process of testing their validity becomes a relatively easy matter. The general principle behind testing symbolic arguments for validity is the same as we use in mathematics, and since mathematics is more familiar to us, it is worthwhile examining this general principle in mathematics in order to better understand how it works in logic. If we want to add, subtract, multiply or divide any numbers over 9 by hand, we have to already know a certain amount of very basic arithmetic which we rely on to generate a correct answer. For example, if we want to add 114 and 56, the first thing we do is put these numbers into standard form as such:

$$\begin{array}{r} 114 \\ +56 \end{array}$$

Then we follow a standard procedure for generating a correct answer which involves adding up each column of numbers starting at the right and working our way to the left and 'carrying over' the left side of any sums that exceed the number 9. If we follow this procedure correctly, we will generate the correct answer, namely, 170. Therefore, we begin by adding 6 and 4, which is 10, and we carry over the 1, etc.

However, how do we know that 6 + 4 = 10? Certainly we cannot use the same procedure that we used on the previous problem to answer this simple problem. The answer is that we figured out the most basic sums in mathematics ahead of time by literally counting, and we memorized the sums of any two numbers between 0 and 9. Without this knowledge of basic sums such as 2+2 = 4, 5+3=8, 6+3=9, and so on, we would clearly not be able to add any numbers larger than 9. We depend on such basic knowledge in mathematics to help us figure out the more complex problems in math.

Logic is no different from math in this respect. In order to determine the validity of any complex arguments, we must generate a small number of basic argument forms which we know for certain to be valid, and then we use these valid argument forms as the criteria for evaluating more complex arguments. Just as we used counting as the means for determining the most basic sums in arithmetic, we use a simple method called 'truth table analysis' to generate the most basic argument forms which we know for certain to be valid. Truth table analysis begins with the construction of a truth table, which is a list of every possible truth value for a given argument form. Once we have a completed truth table, all we have to do to determine whether or not the argument form is valid is check to see that whenever all the premises are true the conclusion is also true. If it is the case that true premises always lead to a true conclusion in a particular argument form, then we know that it is valid, since the existence of true premises guarantees the existence of a true conclusion. If we discover any instances in which true premises lead to a false conclusion, then we know that the argument form is, by definition, invalid.

Once again, the reason for truth table analysis is to test the most basic argument forms to determine which ones are valid and which are not. We can then use the basic argument forms that are proven to be valid as a means for testing the validity of more complex arguments. The most important part of truth table analysis is the proper construction of the truth table. However, as long as the arguments for which we are constructing the truth tables are simple, the process is not difficult.

The most basic argument forms are those in which the premises are atomic propositions, and the conclusion is a single compound. Take for example, the following argument:

1. The movie was realistic.
2. The movie was interesting.

Therefore, the movie was both realistic and interesting.

Both premises are atomic propositions, and the conclusion is the conjunction of these two propositions. The symbolic translation of this argument yields its general argument form:

$$p$$
$$q$$
$$\therefore q \cdot p^4$$

To construct a truth table of this basic argument form we first make three columns; one for each of the premises and one for the conclusion like this:

Premises		Conclusion
p	q	p · q

Next we list out all the possible truth values for the premises. In this case, there can only be four. Both p and q can be true, both p and q can be false, p can be true and q false, or p can be false and q true. The partial truth table now looks like this:

Premises		Conclusion
p	q	p · q
T	T	
F	F	
T	F	
F	T	

284 / LOGICAL REASONING TOOLS

Once this is completed, we plug these truth values into the conclusion and determine whether or not it is true or false. In the case of a conjunction, both components must be true in order for the conjunction to be true. Only a line in which both premises are true can the conclusion be true, and any lines in which either of the premises is false will yield a false conclusion. The complete truth table is now looks like this:

Premises		Conclusion
p	q	p • q
T	T	T
F	F	F
T	F	F
F	T	F

We then examine the truth table to see if there are any instances of having true premises and a false conclusion. We start by looking for a false conclusion, and we find three instances of this. Then we go back and look at these instances to check if they come from true premises. The answer is 'no.' There is no instance of having true premises and a false conclusion. So far this argument form is not invalid. Now we look to see if there are any cases in which there are true premises, and the answer is yes, in the first line. We then check to see if this instance of true premises leads to a true conclusion. It clearly does, and therefore we know that this argument is undeniably valid and can be used as a means for evaluating more complex arguments.

Let's quickly look at an obviously invalid argument of the same form, namely:

* p
r
∴ p • q

The truth table would look like this:

p	r	p • q
T	T	F
F	F	F
T	F	F
F	T	F

Are there any instances of true premises leading to a false conclusion? Yes, in the first line. This argument form is therefore invalid and thus must be avoided. Any argument that has this same form is necessarily invalid as well.

The Rules of Inference

Although the truth table method of analyzing argument structure is the best method for evaluating basic inference structures, it is not the most efficient way to test validity. Truth tables are good for evaluating only the most simple argument structures. When it comes to larger and more complex arguments, truth tables become highly impractical. They not only require a large amount of space, but their construction can be extremely time consuming. Furthermore, truth tables must be exactly correct in order to be of any value, and given the amount of work that goes into their construction, the possibility of error is fairly high. Therefore, we only use truth tables as a means for testing the most basic inference structures, and we then utilize the most basic valid inference structures as rules with which to test the validity of more complex arguments. These valid inference structures that we use as rules for testing the validity of arguments are equivalent to the basics of mathematics, such as knowing the sums and the multiplication tables between the numbers 0 and 9. As a prerequisite for being able to use these rules to test the validity of arguments, we must not only understand these rules, but practice using them so that we become familiar with them just as we have to memorize the basic sums of the numbers between 0 and 9 in order to efficiently work out the answers to math problems.

There are only nine rules of inference that have been proven by truth table analysis to be basic valid forms of inference and can therefore be used as a means for evaluating the validity of arguments. Although we cannot use these rules to prove an argument to be invalid (only a truth table can do that), we can use these rules to prove an argument to be valid. When we use these rules of inference to demonstrate that an argument is valid, we call it a logical *proof* and this is one of the most important logical skills to know when trying to evaluate the logical structure of an argument. Proofs help us to efficiently and effectively evaluate an argument's structure regardless of the complexity of the argument. Constructing a proof is a rather mechanical process, but to do it well requires practice, skill and insight. Some people are naturally much more proficient than others at constructing proofs, but everyone can improve through practice because the key to being able to effectively evaluate the logical structure of arguments is to develop a familiarity with the rules and an understanding of how they work. We therefore begin with the rules.

The Rules of Inference

1. Modus Ponens (MP)

$$p \supset q$$
$$p$$
$$\therefore q$$

2. Modus Tollens (MT)

$$p \supset q$$
$$\sim q$$
$$\therefore \sim p$$

3. Disjunctive Syllogism (DS)

$$p \sim q \qquad p \sim q$$
$$\sim p \quad \text{or} \quad \sim q$$
$$\therefore q \qquad \therefore p$$

4. Hypothetical Syllogism (HS)

$$p \supset q$$
$$q \supset r$$
$$\therefore p \supset r$$

5. Absorption (Abs.)

$$p \supset q$$
$$\therefore p \supset (p \cdot q)$$

6. Constructive Dilemma (CD)

$$(p \supset q) \cdot (r \supset s)$$
$$p \sim r$$
$$\therefore q \sim s$$

7. Conjunction (Conj)

$$p$$
$$q$$
$$\therefore p \cdot q$$

8. Simplification (Simp.)

$$p \cdot q \qquad p \cdot q$$
$$\therefore p \quad \text{or} \quad \therefore q$$

9. Addition (Add.)

$$p$$
$$\therefore p \sim q$$

Understanding the Rules

We will now take some time to briefly explain the nature of each rule and give some simple examples.

1. *Modus Ponens*

$$p \supset q$$
$$p$$
$$\therefore q$$

If a conditional proposition is true, and its antecedent is also true, then the consequent must be true as well. If 'if p then q' is a true proposition, and 'p' is a true proposition, then 'q' must also be a true proposition. For example:

1. If it is snowing, then it is cold outside.
2. It is snowing.
∴ It is cold outside.

In symbolic form this argument would look like this:

S = It is snowing.
C = It is cold outside.

1. $S \supset C$
2. S
∴ C

Notice that the form of this argument matches the rule exactly while the content is different. The following argument forms are all variations of Modus Ponens:

$$\sim p \supset q \qquad \sim p \supset \sim q \qquad p \supset \sim q$$
$$\sim p \qquad\qquad \sim p \qquad\qquad p$$
$$\therefore q \qquad\qquad \therefore \sim q \qquad\qquad \therefore \sim q$$

What makes all these argument forms instances of Modus Ponens is that in each case the antecedent is being affirmed and therefore the consequent is being affirmed as the conclusion. It makes no difference whether the antecedent or the consequent are negative as long as the antecedent matches the second premise, and the consequent matches the conclusion. Of course, if we make a mistake and deny the antecedent, then we would be committing a fallacy. The following are all variations on the fallacy of Denying the Antecedent:

$$* \sim p \supset q \qquad * \sim p \supset \sim q \qquad * p \supset \sim q$$
$$p \qquad\qquad p \qquad\qquad \sim p$$
$$\therefore \sim q \qquad\qquad \therefore q \qquad\qquad \therefore q$$

* means that the argument form is invalid.

When we deny the antecedent, the antecedent and the second premise are negations of each other. We must be very careful not to confuse Modus Ponens with arguments in which the antecedent is denied.

2. *Modus Tollens*

$$p \supset q$$
$$\underline{\sim q}$$
$$\therefore \sim p$$

If a conditional proposition is true, and its consequent is false, then the antecedent must be false as well. If "if p then q" is a true proposition, and '~q' is a true proposition, then '~p' must also be a true proposition. For example,

    1. If it is snowing, then it is cold outside.
    2. It is not cold outside.
    It is not snowing.

Which would translate as such:

S = It is snowing.
C = It is cold outside

    1. $S \supset C$
    2. $\sim C$
    $\therefore \sim S$

Like Modus Ponens, there are several variations of Modus Tollens:

$$p \supset \sim q \qquad \sim p \supset q \qquad \sim p \supset \sim q$$
$$\underline{q} \qquad\qquad \underline{\sim q} \qquad\qquad \underline{q}$$
$$\therefore \sim p \qquad\qquad \therefore p \qquad\qquad \therefore p$$

All variations of Modus Tollens deny the consequent of the conditional and therefore deny the antecedent as well. Once again we must be careful not to confuse Modus Tollens with the fallacy of Affirming the Consequent. The following are variations of Affirming the Consequent:

$$*\ p \supset q \qquad *\ \sim p \supset \sim q \qquad *\ p \supset \sim q$$
$$\underline{q} \qquad\qquad \underline{\sim q} \qquad\qquad \underline{\sim q}$$
$$\therefore \sim p \qquad\qquad \therefore q \qquad\qquad \therefore q$$

3. *Disjunctive syllogism*

$$p \sim q \qquad\qquad p \sim q$$
$$\underline{\sim p} \quad \text{or} \quad \underline{\sim q}$$
$$\therefore q \qquad\qquad \therefore p$$

This says that if we know that 'p or q' is true, and we know that 'p' is not true, then we can conclude that 'q' is true. Likewise, if we know that 'p or q' is true and we know that 'q' is not true, then we can conclude that 'p' is true.
For example:

1. Either the blue team won or the red team won.
2. The red team did not win.

Therefore, the blue team won.

We can express this symbolically as such:

B = the blue team won.

R = the red team won.

1. B ∼ R
2. ∼R

∴ B

We normally refer to the use of this rule as the process of elimination and it is essential to the activity of troubleshooting. This is a simple but powerful inference structure.

4. *Hypothetical syllogism*

$$p \supset q$$
$$q \supset r$$
$$\therefore p \supset r$$

This says that if we know that 'if p then q' is a true proposition, and we know that 'if q then r' is a true proposition, then we also know that 'if p then r' is a true proposition. Notice that 'q' is the common term which creates the valid relationship between 'p' and 'r.'

For example:

1. If it snows then the school will be closed.
2. If the school is closed, then I get to stay home.

Therefore, if it snows, then I get to stay home.

We would translate this as follows;

S = it snows
C = school will be closed
H = I get to stay home

1. S ⊃ C
2. C ⊃ H

∴ S ⊃ H

Of course there are many variations of this rule, but every variation has a common term that is the consequent of one conditional premise and is the antecedent of the other.

5. *Constructive dilemma*

$$(p \supset q) \cdot (r \supset s)$$
$$p \sim r$$
$$\therefore q \sim s$$

This says if we know that 'if p then q' and 'if r then s' are both true propositions, and we know that 'p or r' is a true proposition, then we can conclude that 'q or s' is also a true proposition.

For example:

1. If it snows, then I will stay home and if it rains then I need to bring an umbrella to school.
2. Today it will either snow or rain.

Therefore, Today either I will stay home or bring an umbrella to school.

We can translate this:

    S = It snows
    R = It rains
    H = I will stay home
    U = I will bring an umbrella to school

$$1.\ (S \supset H) \cdot (R \supset U)$$
$$2.\ \underline{\quad S \sim R \quad}$$
$$\therefore H \sim U$$

If we split a Constructive Dilemma right down the middle we can see that it is really only two Modus Ponens put together, and is therefore subject to the same cautions and variations.

    6. *Absorption*

$$\underline{\quad p \supset q \quad}$$
$$\therefore p \supset (p \cdot q)$$

This says that if we know that 'if p then q' is a true proposition, then we know that 'if p then p and q' is a true proposition. For example:

    1. $\underline{\text{If it snows, then it's cold outside.}}$
    Therefore, if it snows, then it's snowy and cold outside.

This translates as such:

    S = it snows
    C = it's cold outside

$$1.\ \underline{\quad S \supset C \quad}$$
$$\therefore S \supset (S \cdot C)$$

    7. *Conjunction*

$$p$$
$$\underline{\quad q \quad}$$
$$\therefore p \cdot q$$

This says that if we know that 'p' is a true proposition, and we know that 'q' is a true proposition, then we can conclude that 'p and q' is a true proposition. For example:

1. I am tired.
2. I am hungry.
Therefore, I am tired and hungry

We can translate this as such:
T = I am tired
H = I am hungry

1. T
2. H
T • H

This is a very simple but extremely useful rule of inference. We use it so often and so naturally that it seems unnecessary to state.

8. *Simplification*

$$\frac{p \cdot q}{\therefore p} \quad \text{or} \quad \frac{p \cdot q}{\therefore q}$$

This says that if we know that 'p and q' is a true proposition, then we can conclude that p is a true proposition or we can conclude q is a true proposition. For example:

1. I have a car and a motorcycle
Therefore, I have a car (or motorcycle).

We can translate this;
C = I have a car
M = I have a motorcycle

$$\frac{1. \; C \cdot M}{\therefore C}$$

This is another argument form that is so basic that it seems unnecessary to state explicitly. However, it is still an important argument form that we use all the time.

9. *Addition*

$$\frac{p}{\therefore p \sim q}$$

This says that if 'p', is a true proposition, then 'p or q' is true as well. Because of the fact that a disjunction only requires one proposition to be true in order for the whole compound to be true, we can add anything we want to a true proposition by means of a disjunction and its truth value will never change. For example:

1. There are three sides to a triangle.
Therefore, there are three sides to a triangle or four sides to a square.

We can translate this as:

T = there are three sides to a triangle
F = there are four sides to a square

1. T
∴ T ~ F

Because of the fact that the proposition 'there are three sides to a triangle' is true, then this proposition *or* any other proposition whatsoever is also true, even if the second proposition is false. This is the most unusual rule of inference and it is certainly the most difficult to explain. Here is another example.

1. The sky is blue.
Therefore, the sky is blue or the Earth is flat.

We can translate this as:

B = the sky is blue
F = the Earth is flat

1. B
∴ B ~ F

Again, if a proposition is true, then that proposition or any other proposition at all is also true because only one aspect of a disjunction has to be true in order for the whole disjunction to be true. Therefore, if 'p' is true, then 'p' or any proposition (q, r, s, t . . .) is still true regardless of the truth value of the added proposition. It is important to remember that while this rule is called 'addition,' it has to do with disjunctions, i.e 'or' propositions, not 'and' propositions.

Exercise

Identify the following argument forms using the rules of inference.

1. 1. ~M
   2. ~M ⊃ S
   ∴ S

2. 1. I ⊃ H
   2. H ⊃ T
   ∴ I ⊃ T

3. 1. L
   2. C
   ∴ L • C

4. 1. X ~ Z
   2. ~Z
   ∴ X

5. 1. T ⊃ N
   2. ~N
   ∴ ~T

6. 1. (A ⊃ D) • (F ⊃ G)
   2.   A ~ F
   ∴ D ~ G

Exercise

Translate the following arguments and identify their logical structures using the rules of inference.

1. If I had enough money, then I could purchase the car I want. If I can purchase the car I want, then I'll be happy. Therefore, if I had enough money, I would be happy.
2. If I get good grades, then I'll pass the course. I got good grades this semester. Therefore, I will pass the course.
3. I always take either the subway or a cab to work. I do not have enough money to pay for a cab tomorrow. Therefore, I'll take the subway.
4. If you have a mother, then you also have a father. Therefore, if you have a mother, you must have both a mother and a father.
5. If I miss too much work, then I will get fired. I have not gotten fired yet. Therefore, I must not have missed too much work.

Proving Validity

Now we will learn how to use these rules to evaluate the validity of arguments. First of all, we know that any argument that takes the exact form of one of these rules is automatically valid. When this happens we use the rule and the justification for the validity of the argument. For example, if we have an argument that translates into the form;

1. $T \supset S$
2. T
$\overline{}$
S

We can just say that it is valid by Modus Ponens and put an "1,2 MP" next to the conclusion. This means that S can be generated from the premises 1 and 2 by means of Modus ponens. It is understood that Modus Ponens is a valid rule of inference.

1. $T \supset S$
2. T
$\overline{}$
∴ S   1,2 MP

As we can see, the construction of truth tables is a long and tedious process, but it is the only way to prove that an argument is invalid. On the other hand, there are much better ways to prove that an argument is valid. For example, imagine the argument: "If I get an A or a B on the test, then I will pass the course. I did get an A, therefore I will pass the course.

In symbolic form, the argument looks like this;

A = I get an A.
B = I get a B.
P = I pass the course.

$$1.\ (A \sim B) \supset P$$
$$2.\ A$$
$$\therefore P$$

At first glance this argument may look like Modus Ponens. However, if we look carefully at the rule for Modus Ponens it is clear that the antecedent is not a disjunction as it is with this argument. Therefore, this argument does not conform to the rules of inference exactly making it necessary to construct a proof of its validity. The fact that an argument does not conform exactly to one rule of inference does not mean that it is invalid. It may be that the conclusion was produced by the use of more than one rule of inference. This is perfectly acceptable and is indeed true of most arguments. The rules of inference must be thought of as different types of bridges that are used to connect premises in such a way that they justify a conclusion. Most arguments utilize several types of bridges to connect the premises to the conclusion. The objective of a proof is to figure out which bridges were used to make these connections. Of course there are only eight acceptable bridges (the rules of inference), and we must make sure that only these bridges are used in the construction of an argument. A proof is essentially a 'reconstruction' of an argument and we do this by applying the rules of inference to the premises to see if we can generate the conclusion. In other words, we begin with the premises and see if we can get to the conclusion only using our logical bridges, namely the nine rules of inference.

The procedure for constructing a proof is therefore to begin adding new premises to the argument until the conclusion is produced. In a valid argument, the conclusion must be contained somewhere inside the premises. In a proof we try to isolate the conclusion. So we first look at the conclusion and try to find it in the premises. Then we ask ourselves "what rules can we use to get the premise by itself. In the case of the example just used, the conclusion is P. We see that P is in the first premise, so that all we have to do is isolate it from the rest of the premise. There is *no* specific procedure for doing this. Constructing proofs requires a little creativity, and there is very often more than one way to prove an argument.

Let's look at how we can prove the argument:

$$1.\ (A \sim B) \supset P$$
$$2.\ A$$
$$\therefore P$$

First we assume all the premises to be true since if they were true the conclusion would also have to be true. Therefore, if we assume the premises to be true and we can use the rules of inference to prove the conclusion to be true also, then we know the argument is valid. We then look for the conclusion and see that it is in premise 1, then we determine how to isolate it from that premise. We isolate a premise so that we know that it alone is true. We remember that in order for a consequent to be true, the antecedent must be true. Therefore, if we can produce a true antecedent of premise 1 we know that the consequent must also be true. Now we need to be a little creative and look at our resources to see what rules we can apply to our premises to get the antecedent (A ~ B). We know already that A is true because we have it isolated in premise 2 and (using a little insight) we can see that if we apply the rule of addition to premise 2 and add B then we will have (A ~ B).

The proof so far looks like this;

    1. (A ~ B) ⊃ P
    2. A
    ──────────────
    ∴ P

    3. A ~ B   2, Add

We add new premises to the argument underneath the conclusion. State the premise or premises which we used to create the new premise and name the rule used to do so. In this case, we added B to A to get A ~ B, and we got A from premise 2. Now we do have a true Modus Ponens. Between premise 1 and 3 we can conclude 'P' by Modus Ponens. This is the conclusion, so we have completed the proof of this argument. It is officially valid. The finished proof looks like this:

    1. (A ~ B) ⊃ P
    2. A
    ──────────────
    ∴ P

    3. A ~ B   2   Add
    4. P   1,3   MP

In order to better understand the activity of generating a logical proof we can first practice the general activity of using the rules of inference to deduce any possible conclusions from the premises. After we become proficient at this, we can then aim our deductions at specific conclusions. In fact, a proof is nothing but the demonstration that a specific conclusion can be deduced from given premises using only the rules of inference. For instance, given the following premises;

    1. C • D
    2. C ⊃ R

we can conclude several things using the rules of inference. To begin with, if we know that 'C • D' is true, then we also know that 'C' is true and that 'D' is true. Therefore, we can list these premises as valid conclusions as such:

1. C · D
2. C ⊃ R
3. C   1 Simp.
4. D   1 Simp.

What we did here was to use the rule of simplification to deduce 3 and 4 from premise 1. Once we demonstrate that 3 and 4 are valid conclusions from the premises, we can use all four propositions as premises for deducing further valid conclusions using the rules of inference. For example, now that we know 'C' to be true and that 'C ⊃ D' is true, we can combine them to deduce 'R' by means of Modus Ponens, so that our argument looks like this;

1. C · D
2. C ⊃ R
3. C   1 Simp.
4. D   1 Simp.
5. R   2, 3 MP

In this manner we have shown that 3, 4, and 5 are all valid deductive inferences from premises 1 and 2. For any given argument we can determine what all the possible valid conclusions are that can be generated from the premises. In other words, using only the rules of inference we can create a hypothetical list of all valid conclusions from any set of premises. Of course, this task would often be tedious and time consuming, but it could be done. When we want to find out whether or not a particular conclusion is valid from specific premises, we are really only asking if it is included in this hypothetical list of valid conclusions.

The objective of a proof is to eliminate the need to generate the entire list of valid conclusions from a set of premises just to see if one particular conclusion is on it. When generating a proof, we therefore look at the conclusion and try to deduce it using only the rules of inference. Creating a proof is thus similar to a maze on a piece of paper in which we see the starting point as well as the end and we must try to get to the conclusion by following specific paths. Some paths may be dead ends and some will lead to the conclusion. Therefore, creating a proof is more of an art than a science. There is no scientific method for solving mazes and there is no scientific method for creating logical proofs; however, there are general rules of thumb that make it a lot easier. Furthermore, like any other craft, practice yields improvement when it comes to generating proofs. Although some people are naturally more talented than others in this skill and develop more efficient habits for demonstrating validity, everyone improves their skill in proving validity by practicing. People who are more skilled at proofs are merely able to complete a proof in less steps than other people. Their proofs are thus more 'elegant' than others, but are no more correct. Efficiency is nice when it comes to proofs, but the end result is all that really matters.

Exercise

Here are some valid arguments to practice generating proofs:

1. 1. R ~ T
   2. L • ~T
   ∴ R

2. 1. S ⊃ W
   2. M ⊃ S
   ∴ M ⊃ W

3. 1. D
   2. D ⊃ N
   3. ~N ~ Z
   ∴ Z

4. 1. S ⊃ C
   2. S ~ A
   3. A ⊃ G
   ∴ C ~ G

5. 1. (F ~ J) ⊃ H
   2. D • F
   ∴ H

6. 1. ~(K • B)
   2. ~X
   3. ~(N ~ X) ⊃ (K • B)
   ∴ N

7. 1. E • L
   2. L ⊃ T
   3. T ⊃ R
   ∴ L ⊃ (L • R)

8. 1. T ⊃ D
   2. C • P
   3. ~F ~ ~C
   4. (~F ~ A) ⊃ (A • T)
   ∴ D ~ W

9. 1. (H ~ J) ⊃ ~(R ~ S) • M
   2. J ⊃ ~(D • L)
   3. D
   4. ~J ⊃ H
   5. L
   ∴ ~(R ~ S)

10. 1. W • (~A ⊃ N)
    2. (D ~ T) ⊃ R
    3. ~A ~ (D ~ T)
    4. ~N
    ∴ R

11. 1. L
    2. G • P
    3. [(P • L) ~ C] ⊃ Z
    4. E ~ ~Z
    ∴ (E • G) ~ X

Works Cited

Copi, Irving M. and Cohen, Carl. *Introduction to Logic.* Upper Saddle River, New Jersey: Prentice Hall, 1998.

Peirce, Charles S. *Charles S. Pierce: Selected Writings (Values in a Universe of Chance.)* Ed. Philip P. Wiener. New York: Dover Publications, Inc., 1958.

Footnotes

1. Notice that this argument has the exact same logical form as the argument:

   1. The Eiffel Tower is taller than the Washington Monument.
   2. The Washington Monument is taller than the Clock Tower.
   Therefore, the Eiffel Tower is taller than the Clock Tower.

2. The specific type of symbolic language that is used in modern logic is called 'Boolean Logic,' named after George Booles, an English mathematician who began developing this system of symbolic language in the nineteenth century.

3. Although we can use any letters in the alphabet to represent propositions, it is standard practice to use the letters "p" and "q" as examples. Notice that it is also standard practice to use lower case letters in examples that are not actually symbolic translations of anything, and to use upper case letters in actual translations in which the letters are symbolizing something particular.

4. The symbol '∴' is used as a conclusion indicator in symbolic language. In English it reads 'therefore.'

APPENDICES

APPENDIX A

Quality

(revised by Rebecca Dozier and Jennifer McNeill)

Quality is ubiquitous; it pervades all aspects of today's engineering work environment. Employers seek to employ graduates who can work effectively in a quality dominated work environment[1]; engineers are expected to use quality processes to create quality products; and, universities are expected to teach students about quality principles. Basic quality principles and tools are presented in this section of the workbook. Some of the material is presented in an *active learning* format; this format requires that you think about a question, and perhaps write down your thoughts, before you read the subsequent paragraph. You will maximize your understanding of the material if you take the time to perform these suggested exercises.

Quality: What Is It?

Take a few minutes and write down your definition of a *quality product*.

_____

_____

_____

_____

_____

Did you find this hard to do? We certainly did; quality is not easy to define. Does your definition include *'better'* as a descriptor (e.g., the better the product the higher its quality)? Did you define quality in terms of the attributes of the product (e.g., a quality product costs less or goes faster)? How does your definition compare to any of the following definitions:

1. a) Superiority of kind, e.g., an intellect of unquestioned quality.
   b) Degree or grade of excellence, e.g., yard goods of low quality.[2]
2. Quality is the totality of features and characteristics of a product or service that bear on its ability to satisfy implied or stated needs.[3]
3. The least expensive method of achieving quality is to deliver a design that cannot fail to satisfy the customer.[4]
4. Quality is a measure of customer satisfaction with a product or process.[5]

These are perfectly adequate definitions, but how useful are they? Take a few minutes to consider how you could use any of these definitions (including yours) to establish which of two similar products had the higher quality.

_____

_____

_____

_____

_____

_____

How did you do? We did not feel our definitions were very operational. The definitions that equate quality to 'better' are meaningless unless you know what 'better' means. Our last three definitions use the concept of 'customer satisfaction'; what exactly is customer satisfaction and how is it measured? The most useful definitions appear to be those that equate quality to a product **attribute**; e.g., low cost. Such definitions apply to particular products; however, there seems to be no attribute, or set of unique attributes, that applies to all products. Consequently, these definitions of quality are not universal. Robert Pirsig notes:[6]

> Quality is a characteristic of thought and statement that is recognized by a non-thinking process. Because definitions are a product of rigid, formal thinking, quality cannot be defined. But even though Quality cannot be defined, *you know, what Quality is!*

So which definition is correct? None? All? All the definitions, including yours, are correct for some situations. We like the general nature of the second, third and fourth definitions; however, they all require an understanding of customer needs.

Customer Needs

Assume that you are going to purchase a new video game for the Super Nintendo Entertainment System® you received for Christmas. Since you are purchasing the game with all the pennies you've saved from working at Burger King®, you are considered a customer. Make a list of your needs, features that will lead to your satisfaction with the game. For instance, you might need a game that two people can play simultaneously. What other needs do you have?

_____
_____
_____
_____
_____
_____

How long was your list? Did it include the game's graphics, cost, level of difficulty? Categorize the needs you have listed. What categories do you have?

In the mid 1980s Noriaki Kano addressed categorizing customer desires. According to Kano[7], customer desires (requirements) can be categorized as either an Expected Requirement, a Revealed Requirement, or an Exciting Requirement.

Expected Requirements

Expected requirements are those basic characteristics that customers **assume** are present in generically similar products or services. These characteristics are so basic that the customer seldom mentions them, and all similar products do in fact include these characteristics. For example, one of the **expected** requirements for a video game is that it will have a hard casing around the delicate computer chips. It is **assumed** by the customer that all video games have this characteristic and it is unlikely that a customer would mention it to a design engineer. Can you list any other expected requirements?

_____
_____
_____
_____
_____

Did your list include that the game will fit in your Nintendo, have color, have sound, and that you'll be able to control what's happening on the screen?

Revealed Requirements

Revealed requirements are those characteristics that customers discuss when describing the characteristics that would improve a product or service. These characteristics are generally related to the **performance** of the product or service. For example, some **revealed** requirements for the video game would be the game's difficulty level and cost. These are the requirements that are normally discussed with design engineers. Can you list any other revealed requirements?

_____

_____

_____

_____

_____

_____

Did your list include the number of levels, the number of lives you start with, the number of hidden items, and whether or not there's a published hint book?

Compare your list of revealed and expected requirements. Are there any items that appear on both lists? If so, on which list do you now think they belong?

Exciting Requirements

Exciting requirements are those characteristics that cause a customer to say WOW! Generically similar products (e.g., video games) from competing companies will include different exciting requirements. For example, an exciting requirement for a video game would be that it was able to wake you up in the morning. Exciting requirements are only recognized when they are present; thus, they are seldom mentioned to design engineers. Can you list any other exciting requirements?

_____

_____

_____

_____

_____

_____

Did you list include three dimensional graphics, a video game that has a screen saver, or a video game that sounds like you're cleaning your room so that your parents don't get mad at you for not doing your chores.

Review your initial list of requirements and your three new lists. Were there any needs on your first list that didn't show up on any of the new lists? If so, put them on the appropriate list.

Customer Satisfaction

What is the relationship between customer needs and customer satisfaction? Does increasing the number of requirements in each category lead to higher customer satisfaction? Review your categorized lists; would more characteristics in any of the categories increase your satisfaction?

_____

_____

_____

_____

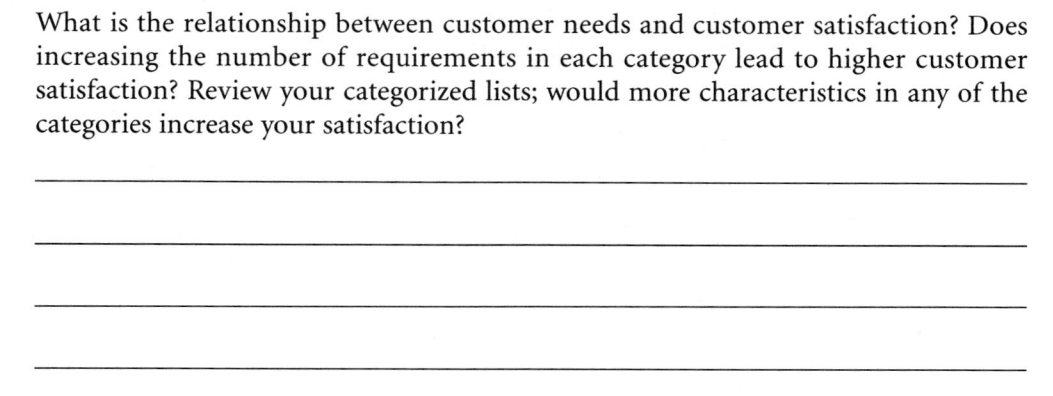

What did you conclude? Does your satisfaction increase because your game works with your system (expected requirement), or because it takes longer to win (revealed requirement) or has cool 3D graphics (exciting requirement)? How do your results compare with those proposed by Kano (see Table A–1)?

Table A–1. Relationship Between Customer Needs and Satisfaction

Requirement Type	Not Present	Present	More
Expected	dissatisfaction	unaware	no effect
Revealed	dissatisfaction	satisfaction	increased satisfaction
Exciting	unaware	satisfaction	increased satisfaction

Table A–1 illustrates that 'more' is 'better' only for the **revealed** and **exciting** requirements; more of an **expected** requirement has no impact on satisfaction (is this true for the expected requirements in your list?). Table 1 also illustrates that there are two ways to produce dissatisfied customers: **omitting expected** requirements and/or including a minimum number of a **revealed** requirements. Absence of exciting requirements does not lead to dissatisfaction. Look at your list of requirements to confirm these observations.

Identifying Customer Needs

If quality products are those that satisfy customers, how are these customer needs identified? Did asking you to write down your needs as a video game customer work well? Do you feel your list is complete? Probably not, but why? Only the **revealed** requirements are characteristics that customers think of prior to obtaining or using a product or service. Generally, customers are unaware of expected and exciting requirements; therefore, asking the customer what she wants seldom produces a satisfied customer. Furthermore, it is difficult for customers to evaluate an exciting requirement until they actually see or experience the product. For example, market surveys in the early 1970s suggested that there was no market for engineering hand held calculators.

Establishing a good set of customer needs is one of the important tasks that must be performed during the Problem Definition Stage of the Problem Solving Heuristic[8]. What are some alternative ways of identifying expected and/or exciting requirements?

The assessment process and the checklists used to evaluate your work products in ECE 100 are discussed in Sections B and J (Part III) of this workbook. Are these checklists *expected, revealed, or exciting* customer requirements?

A Quality Culture

Do you recognize the name Dr. W. Edwards Deming? What word or phrase would you associate with Deming? If you do not recognize, or have only a passing familiarity with, the name Deming, you should spend some time on, the WEB and seek out more information.

Deming defined a way of thinking about quality and summarized his philosophy in a set of fourteen points (Figure A–1). Deming's fourteen points work together to

---

1. Create constancy of purpose
2. Adopt the new philosophy
3. Cease dependence on inspection to achieve quality
4. End the practice of awarding business on the basis of price tag
5. Constantly improve the system of production and service
6. Institute training on the job
7. Institute leadership
8. Drive out fear
9. Break down barriers between departments
10. Eliminate slogans and exhortations
11. Eliminate quotas and management by objective
12. Remove barriers that rob people of their pride of workmanship
13. Institute a vigorous program of education and self-improvement
14. Put everybody to work to accomplish the transformation

Figure A–1. Deming's Fourteen Points.[9]

create a quality 'culture'. The items on the list are not intended to be used selectively; all fourteen points must be implemented as a total 'package'. The ECE 100 course was designed to implement Deming's fourteen points in the classroom.

Read the points. Which of the points do you instantly agree with, which do you not understand, which do you think would be the hardest for you to implement?

Improving Quality

There are two methods that can be used to bring about a change in the quality of a product: Re-engineering (*Ishinsuru*) and Continuous Improvement (*Kaizen*). Figure A–2 highlights the differences in these two methods; what do you think is the major difference in the two methods? **Re-engineering** involves **major changes** (quantum leaps, radical new designs); a shift in paradigm is often involved. **Continuous improvement,** on the other hand, involves a **steady, continuous change** in quality (small steps, restructuring); paradigm shifts are not involved.

• Continuous Improvement (Kaizen)	• Re-Engineering (Ishinsuru)
• Continuous incremental improvement	• Quantum leaps
• Small steps	• Revolutionary thinking
• Restructuring	• Radical new designs
• Team work	• Team work
• Customer focused	• Customer focused
• Sequential processing	• Whole process responsibility
• Push down decision making	• Push down decision making

Figure A–2. Comparison of Quality Improvement Methods

Figure A–3 shows how these two process can work together: the bottom line shows that a product's quality steadily declines without a concerted effort to improve it's quality. The *Kaizen* method reverses this trend by **continually** improving the quality (shown by the slightly upward sloping lines). Using *Kaizen* can reverse the natural quality decay; however, it will seldom lead to radical new ideas (changes in quality). When *Ishinsuru* is used there is a **step increase** in quality. Note that if *Kaizen* is not used after the *Ishinsuru* change then the quality will begin its natural decaying process. Can you think of how quality was improved by Kaizen and by Ishinsuru for the video game?

For Kaizen, did you consider the gradual increase in the quality of graphics and sound used in video games or the increase in the sensitivity of player control? For Ishinsuru, did you consider the development of systems intended exclusively to play video games from the systems (i.e., personal computers) where video games made up only a portion of the functions?

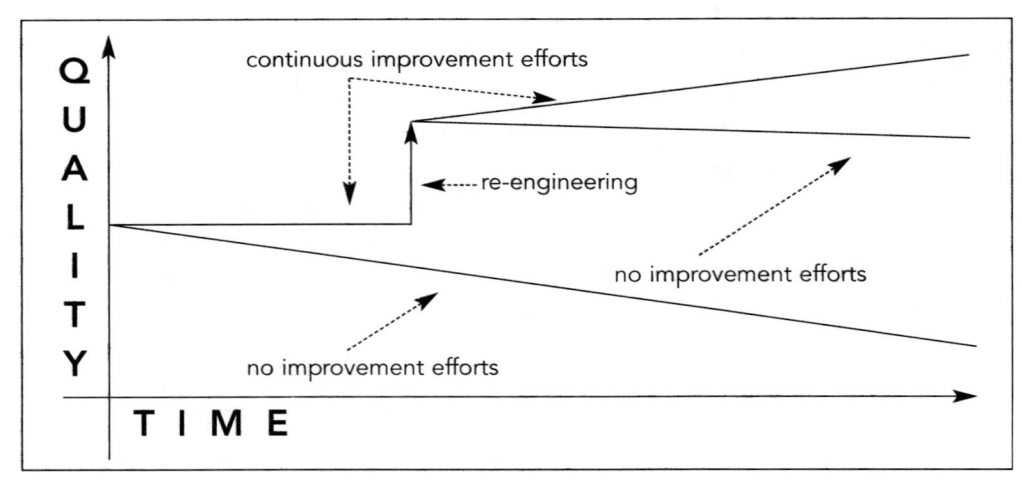

Figure A-3. Quality versus Time: With and Without Continuous Improvement.[10]

Re-engineering (Ishinsuru)

Re-engineering is sometimes defined by its three R's: Rethink, Redesign, Retool. Rethinking is the 'paradigm busting' aspect of the process, creating new visions and defining critical success factors. After a new vision is created new products, processes, and/or services are designed, which are followed by the creation of new jobs and manufacturing processes.

Continuous Improvement (Kaizen)

Figure A–4 illustrates a typical continuous improvement cycle. The process is initiated by identifying and selecting a problem. If solutions to the problem are known, they are implemented and evaluated; if solutions are unknown solutions must be created (a multistep process). The process cycle ends with an evaluation of the solution, i.e., did the solution work. If the solution did not work, what would you do next?

Continuous improvement cycles are often called Plan Do Check Act (PDCA) cycles. Continuous improvement comes from repeated execution of the PDCA cycle. Figure A–5 briefly summarizes the steps in the PDCA cycle. 1) **Plan**: this step involves the collection of data to support the selection of the problem and is generally the most time consuming step. 2) **Do**: this step involves the generation and implementation of

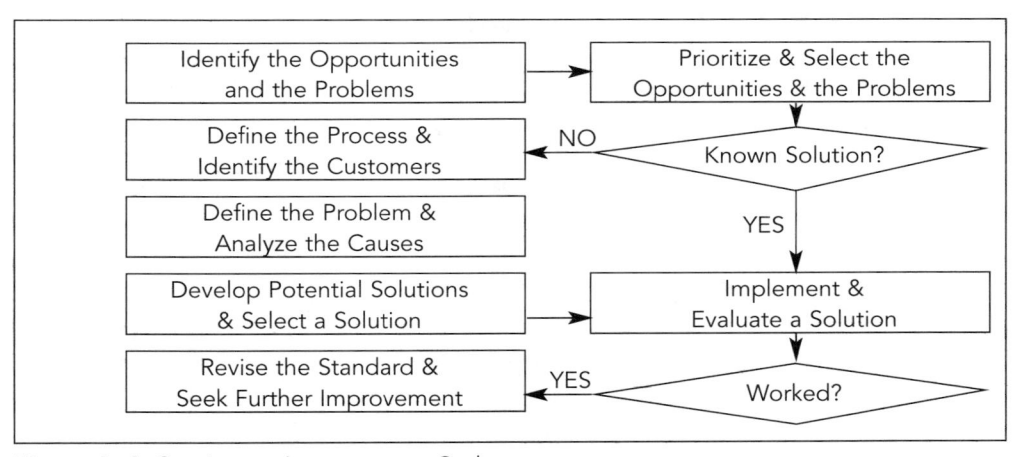

Figure A–4. Continuous Improvement Cycle.

Plan
• define the process
• identify the real problem (collect data to confirm) typically 50% of the time is spent on this part of the cycle

Do
• generate and select a solution
• implement the proposed improvement
• typically 10% of the time is spent on this part of the cycle

Check
• measure the effect of the change
• typically 15% of the time is spent on this part of the cycle

Act
• standardize the change
• document the project
• typically 25% of the time is spent on this part of the cycle

Figure A–5. Plan Do Check Act Cycle.

a solution, and is generally less time consuming. 3) **Check**: this is a critical step. PDCA cycles require that the solution be evaluated, using collected data, to determine if the process, product or service was actually improved, i.e., it can not be **assumed** that the solution improved the process. 4) **Act**: this step involves institutionalizing (standardizing) and documenting the change. Note that one quarter of the effort goes into this step.

Process

Process is a very important aspect of quality. Take a few minutes and write down your definition of process.

_____

_____

_____

_____

Does your definition address the making of something (e.g., a process is the way something is done)? Did you use an analogy (e.g., a process is like a recipe for making apple pie)? Does your definition include the fact that there are multiple steps or tasks in a process (e.g., a process is a collection of steps used to make something)? Was there any sense of order or organization in your definition (e.g., a process is a sequential set of tasks used to make something). All of these items are important aspects of a process. Our definition, which includes all of the above, is:

> A process is an organized collection of interrelated tasks that converts 'inputs' into desired 'outputs'

Figure A–6 is a 'blackbox' description of a process. Inputs are converted (changed) into desired (not unexpected or unwanted) outputs. This transformation takes place through the completion of a number of interrelated tasks.

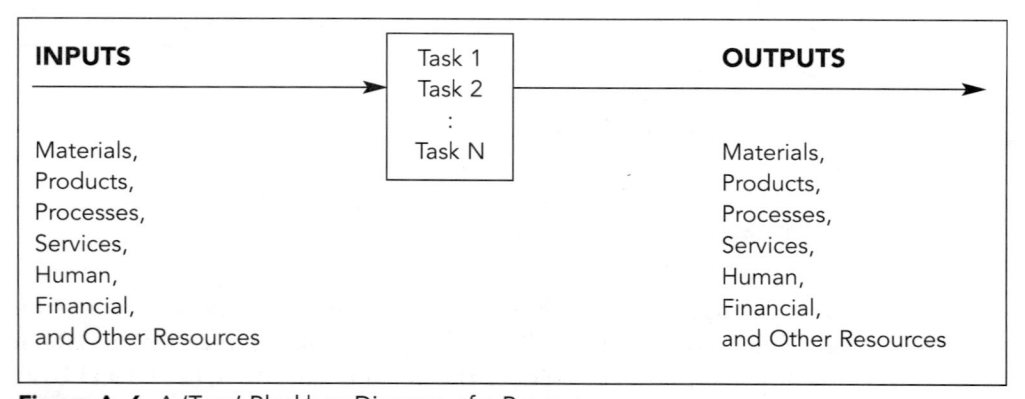

INPUTS	Task 1	**OUTPUTS**
	Task 2	
	:	
Materials,	Task N	Materials,
Products,		Products,
Processes,		Processes,
Services,		Services,
Human,		Human,
Financial,		Financial,
and Other Resources		and Other Resources

Figure A–6. A 'True' Blackbox Diagram of a Process.

Flowcharts

Processes are complex and often hard to describe with words. Thus, processes are generally described using a visual representation called a flowchart. Flowcharts show the various tasks and the relationships among the tasks. There are two general types of flowcharts, process flowcharts and deployment flowcharts:

> A **process flowchart** is a chart (picture) that uses symbols to describe the tasks and decisions and lines to describe the interrelationships among the tasks and decisions required to convert available inputs into desired outputs for a specific process

and

> A **deployment flowchart** is a process flowchart that also-includes: 1) the *people* responsible for completing the tasks and making the decisions, 2) the *time* required to complete each task, and 3) the *quality issues* associated with each task.

Several example flowcharts are included in this Workbook. What type of flowchart is Figure **3** in Section **B**? If you said "deployment flowchart" that is correct. Why? If you said "because the figure is a process flowchart (symbols for tasks and decisions, lines for interrelationships) and it shows 1) the responsibilities of three groups of people involved in the process", and 2) the time involved, and 3) the quality issues, then you answered completely. Figure A–7 is another example of a deployment flow chart. Who are the people involved in planning a meeting; what are their responsibilities?

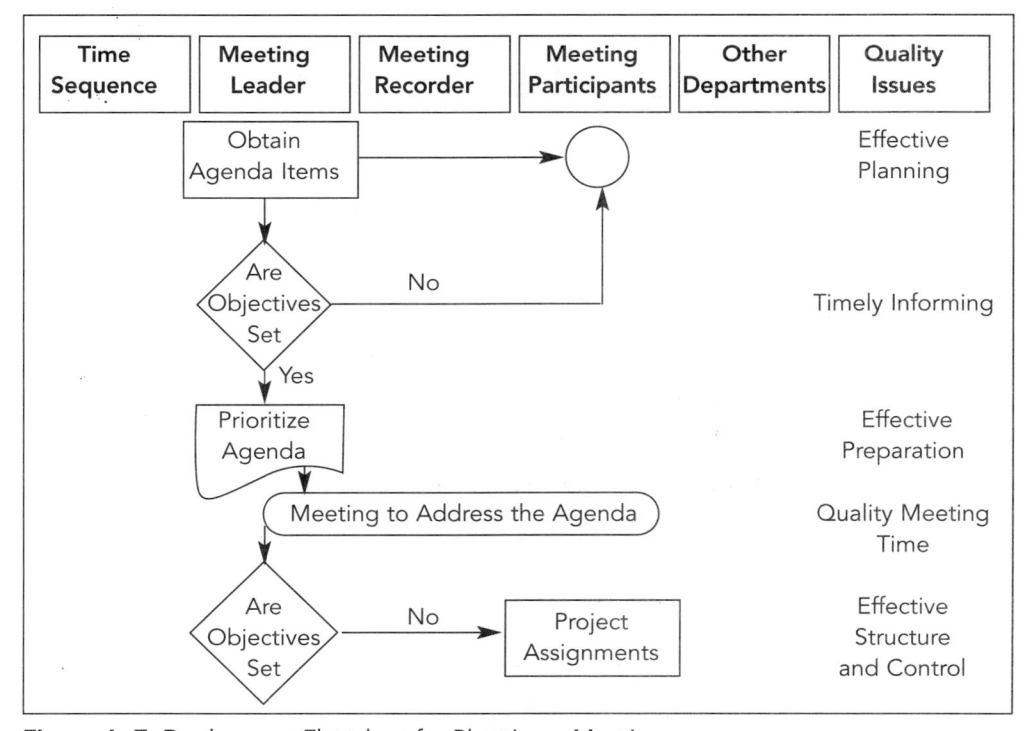

Figure A–7. Deployment Flowchart for Planning a Meeting.

Creating Deployment Flowcharts

The process used to create deployment flowcharts is summarized below.

1. Identify and name the process.
2. Determine the start and finish points of the current process.
3. List the steps involved between the start and the finish using verbs and nouns.
   a) Brainstorm macro (large) steps (write on post-its, one step per post-it).
   b) Sequence the steps (move post-its around).
   c) Brainstorm smaller steps (write on post-its, one step per post-it).
   d) Sequence and integrate the smaller steps into macro steps.
4. Assign symbols (see Figure A–8) to the appropriate tasks and decisions.
5. Divide a blank chart into columns; one column for each key person or group responsible for completion of a task in the process. Draw the chart using the symbols.

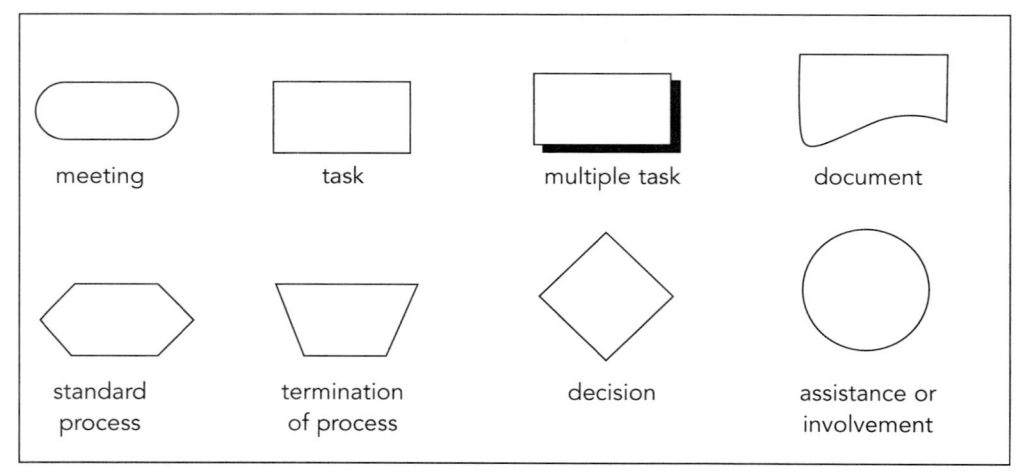

Figure A–8. Standard Flowchart Symbols.

6. Identify the control points (i.e., locations in the flowchart where something can be counted or evaluated.

Can you create a flow chart for playing a Nintendo game?

_____

_____

_____

_____

_____

Figure A–9 illustrates our suggestion as to what a flowchart for setting up a Nintendo game might look like. Did you come up with something similar?

Can you think of other examples of flowcharts that you have seen. What type of flowchart is the cynically humorous example in Figure A–10. Can you analyze this flowchart?

_____
_____
_____
_____
_____
_____

Did you notice that the flowchart in Figure A–10 does not use the correct symbols? Which boxes should be replaced with diamonds? What about the symbol terminating the process? Is there anything else wrong with this flowchart? What about the process itself? Do you think that the flowchart presents an ethical approach to problem solving? We think not. In a **quality** environment employers and employees focus on **identifying** and **fixing** problems, rather than focusing on blame. Continuous Improvement, which is the essence of **quality**, requires that problems be identified, brought out in the open (i.e., problems are not hidden), and analyzed to see how the problem can be eliminated. While this flowchart may represent the way some businesses are run, we can predict that in the long run these businesses will not succeed.

The following article from a local newspaper illustrates the importance of quali-

314 / APPENDIX A

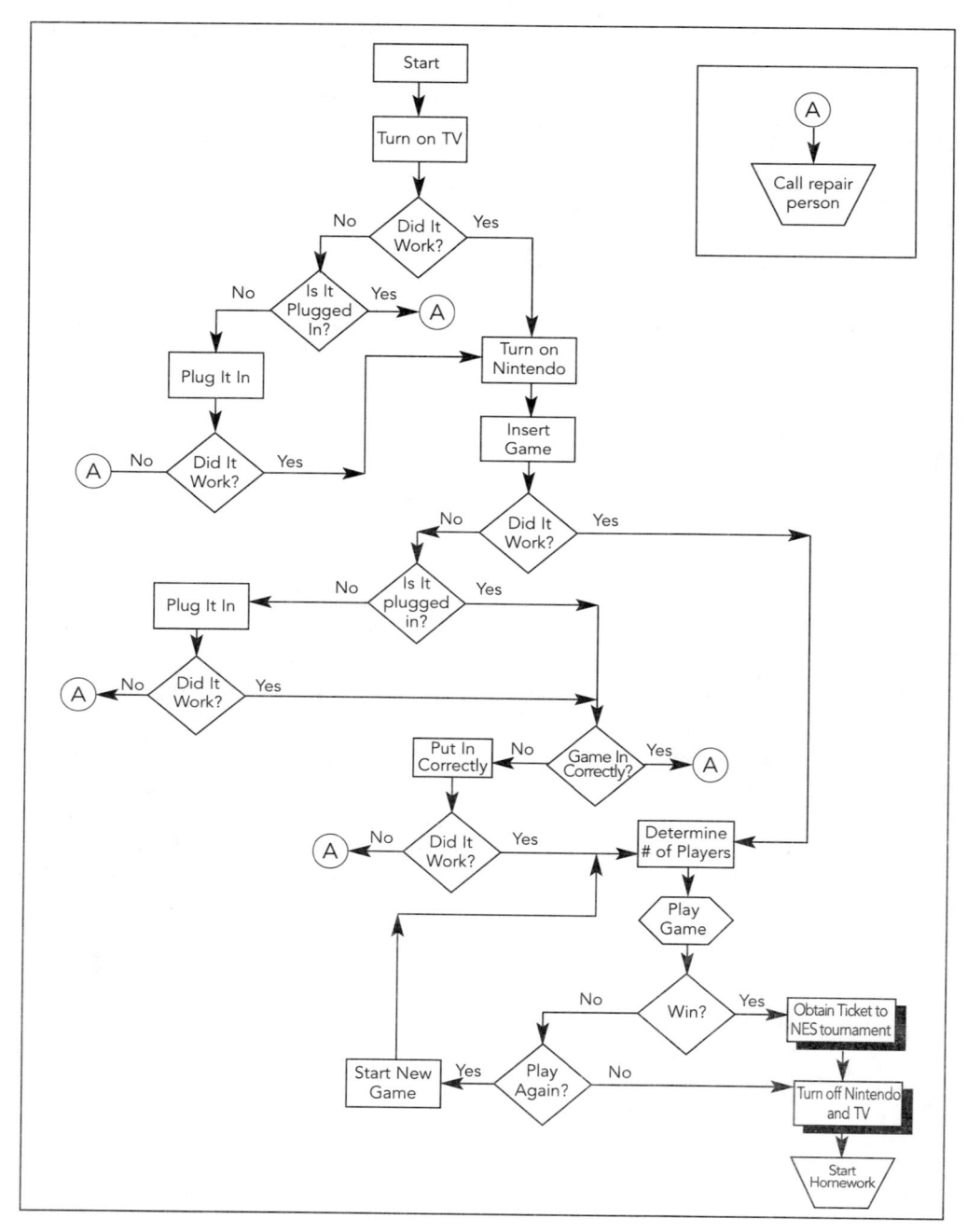

Figure A–9. Flowchart for Setting Up a Nintendo Game.

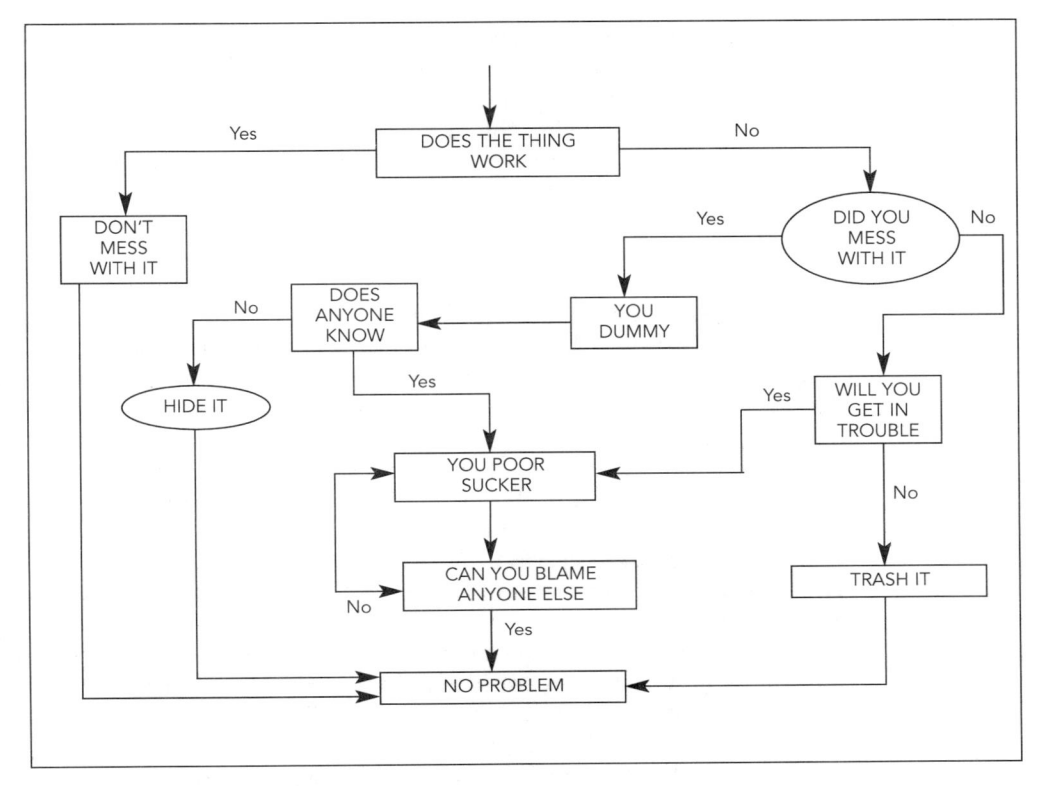

Figure A-10. An Often Used Problem Solving "Flowchart."

ty in the engineering workplace.

Concept creates team players: For AlliedSignal, proof is in figures
By Ed Foster Staff writer
Arizona Republic, June 28, 1996

In recent months, Dino Clark has seen the time and manpower that goes into producing jet-engine fan hubs drop drastically at AlliedSignal's aircraft engine-parts plant here. Clark doesn't like the word *kaizen*, or continuous improvement, the theory the company is using. Neither does he care for Japanese consultants. For the past 1-1/2 years, two consulting firms associated with Toyota have worked with AlliedSignal factory teams, implementing kaizen. But Clark is enthusiastic about the manufacturing improvements in his machining cell. "I've been here 24 years," Clark said. "We tried different concepts. We could never put the people together, the machinery together. "Now we've got everybody, from the president all the way down, working together. They really work with you. Everybody's got a chance to make it work."

Since late 1994, the company has paired teams of workers in various factory areas with outside consultants. The consultants, whose firms have relationships with Toyota, considered a model manufacturer, push the team members toward high goals, and the workers find ways to cut waste to get there. Clark's area, which machines the center hub of the front fan on jet engines, formerly produced fewer than two hubs per day. After being studied and improved, production rose to eight hubs per day. Meanwhile, the number of machine operators dropped from 14 to six. The time required to set up the machines was 10–15 hours. Through *kaizen* the machinists got that down to six hours, then three and now 1-1/2h in most cases. Some machines now are being set up in 30 minutes, and the consultants are pushing for 10 minutes.

Clark is enthusiastic about the improvements, but he complains that the Japanese want too much. They have "a lot to learn about reality and life itself," Clark said. Not all the factory workers are as positive as Clark. Some, such as Sherry Brightwell, are far more skeptical. But even Brightwell says *kaizen* has worked, if not as well as management believes. "They have taken out a lot of wasted steps," she said.

Kaizen is being driven by Marc Hoffman, vice president of operations, who came to AlliedSignal in 1994 from one of the consulting companies. Before that, he was a plant manager for General Electric. The effort has been implemented in aircraft-engine factories here and in Connecticut, South Carolina and Ireland. According to Hoffman and his director of operations, Rich Barlow, improvements have been substantial.

Production at the parts plant, which is on the edge of Phoenix Sky Harbor International Airport, **has improved 20 percent** in the past 18 months, Barlow said. "The way we measure is output per human being," he said. "We are getting more widgets from the same people."

Typically, the consultants come in for a week to focus on a particular area. Workers from that area form a team to help find waste and root it out. Barlow said the kind of production gains made in Clark's cell have enabled the engines division to exceed a corporate demand for 6 percent annual production growth easily. Hoffman, 40, said an important key in the improvements has been just-in-time production. Historically, AlliedSignal has produced parts in batches, which sit until they are needed at the next step. Just-in-time production requires that parts be produced as they are needed for the next step.

Hoffman compared it to a bucket brigade. "Problems rise to the surface, and you are forced to address them immediately," he said. The result is reduced inventory and costs, and improved delivery, Hoffman added. He said the factory workers were skeptical when he arrived in 1994. He came from TBM, a North Caroline consulting firm and one of the companies he uses today.

One of his problems has been the word *kaizen*. "If I had to do it over, I might not have used it," Hoffman said. But he made no apology for using outside consultants. Because they don't have friends or an emotional investment in the plant, they are perfectly willing to push wholesale changes. "There is value to not being concerned about hurt feelings," Hoffman said, adding that the consultants bring in a wealth of experience. "They know it is achievable," he said. "They fundamentally believe it can happen."

One technique is videotaping operations, so workers can see waste. "it is almost embarrassing," Hoffman said. AlliedSignal is also passing along its lessons to its suppliers. AlliedSignal teams recently visited Stolper-Fabralloy Co. in Phoenix to help it streamline its operations. Mark Russell, quality assurance manager for Stolper-Fabralloy said the company expects a $54,000 saving from the two-day session. "We consider it (the training) a great privilege," he added. "They don't do this for all of their vendors." Stolper-Fabralloy makes sheet-metal parts for AlliedSignal engines.

Most of the theories for improvement have been lifted from Toyota and some American companies, including Motorola and Texas Instruments, but Hoffman said they are really just extensions of Henry Ford's ideas. But American industry lost its way and discounted Ford's ideas, he said, especially after World War II, when U.S. industry had little competition and huge markets. "In my opinion, it was arrogance. I remember when I was in college, all the excuses while we were getting the hell beaten out of us," said Hoffman, a 1978 graduate of Cornell University. "Things didn't change because they didn't need to change."

Today, he said, AlliedSignal's customers, aircraft manufacturers and the airlines, demand higher quality and lower prices. The challenge AlliedSignal and other manufacturers face is simple, Hoffman said: Get better or die. "It is not just Boeing. It is every market we are in. Those who fail to improve cannot survive." He added that the increased **efficiency** has not led to layoffs. Instead, the company has been able to use its quality gains and lower costs to snare more business. "The whole idea of improving by laying off people doesn't make good sense," said Hoffman, who said the company must instead leverage its people and factory space to grow.

AlliedSignal has had huge layoffs in the past. The company shed thousands of workers earlier in the decade, after both the civilian and military aircraft markets collapsed. The scars remain. Workers interviewed on the factory floor invariably brought up the possibility of layoffs. Where, they asked, will the people displaced in *kaizen* go? So far, they have been absorbed in new production, as the business has grown. But people such as machinist Charlie Gilchrist, who is cautiously enthusiastic about the changes, believe that could change. "Everybody is scared they could lose their jobs," Gilchrist said. "That has been around since the beginning of *kaizen.* "I don't believe anybody can guarantee me a job these days."

Barlow said employees have been promised that no layoffs will result from kaizen. But he said the company can't make promises about recessions. However, he added that as costs continue to decline, work that is now outsourced can be done in company factories. "We only make a quarter of our parts," he said. "As we become more competitive with small parts, we can bring business in from the mom-and-pop shops." Ultimately, the workers on the floor appeared to agree that lower costs could translate to job security in the next recession. "Nobody likes change," Gilchrist said: "But it's coming, and you can't stop it. There's no sense fighting it." At least, he said, management now is willing to listen to the workers, and to tap their expertise. "It opens up communication tremendously," Gilchrist said. "They listen 200 percent better than they used to."

Notes

1. ASEE, "Educating Tomorrow's Engineers", Prism, May/June 1995, pp 11–15.
2. *The American Heritage Dictionary of the English Language,* Third Edition, licensed from Houghton Mifflin Company. Copyright © 1992 by Houghton Mifflin Company.

3. ANSI/ASQC Standard A3 - 1987, http://www.cae.wisc.edu/~ming/qlty.html (visited June 10, 1997).

4. Genichi Taguchi.

5. A compilation of definitions.

6. Pirsig, Robert M., *Zen And The Art Of Motorcycle Maintenance,* ISBN 0-688-00230-7, William Morrow & Company, Inc., New York, 1974.

7. Kano, Noriaki, Nobuhiko Seraku, Fumio Takahashi, and Shinichi Tsuji, *Attractive Quality and Must-Be Quality,* Translated by Glenn Mazur, Hinshitsu 14, no. 2, (February, 1984), pp 39–48, Tokyo: Japan Society for Quality Control (see http://www-personal.engin.umich.edu/~gmazur/tqm/tqm8.htm for a brief overview by Glenn Mazur [visited June 16, 1997]).

8. Fogler, H. Scott, LeBlanc, Steven E. *Strategies for Creative Problem Solving,* ISBN 0-13-179318-7, Prentice Hall PTR, 1994.

9. Deming, W. Edwards, *Out Of The Crisis,* Published by the Massachusetts Institute of Technology, Center for Advanced Engineering Study, Cambridge, MA 02139, 1986. (For a summary of the 14 Points see http://deming.eng.clemson.edu/pub/den/files/auth14.txt [visited June 10, 1997]).

10. Imai, Masaaki, *Kaizen,* McGraw Hill Publishing Co., 1986, p 27

APPENDIX B

Reading and Studying:
Your Keys to Knowledge

The society you live in revolves around the written word. Although the growth of computer technology may seem to have made technical knowledge more important than reading, the focus on word processing and computer handling of documents has actually *increased* the need for employees who function at a high level of literacy. As the *Condition of Education* 1996 report states, "In recent years, literacy has been viewed as one of the fundamental tools necessary for successful economic performance in industrialized societies. Literacy is no longer defined merely as a basic threshold of reading ability, but rather as the ability to understand and use printed information in daily activities, at home, at work, and in the community."

Two crucial keys to your college success are reading and studying. If you read thoroughly and understand what you read, and if you achieve your study goals, you can improve your capacity to learn and understand. In this chapter you will learn how you can overcome barriers to successful reading and benefit from defining a purpose each time you read. You will explore the PQ3R study technique, see how critical reading can help you maximize your understanding of any text, and learn to understand visual aids.

What Are Some Challenges of Reading?

Whatever your skill level, you will encounter challenges that make reading more difficult, such as an excess of reading assignments, difficult texts, distractions, a lack of speed and comprehension, and insufficient vocabulary. Following are some ideas about how to meet these challenges. Note that if you have a reading disability, if English is not your primary language, or if you have limited reading skills, you may need additional support and guidance. Most colleges provide services for students through a reading center or tutoring program. Take the initiative to seek help if you need it. Many accomplished learners have benefited from help in specific areas.

Dealing With Reading Overload

Reading overload is part of almost every college experience. On a typical day, you may be faced with reading assignments that look like this:

- An entire textbook chapter on the causes of the Civil War (American history)
- An original research study on the stages of sleep (psychology)
- Pages 1–50 in Arthur Miller's play *Death of a Salesman* (American literature)

Reading all this and more leaves little time for anything else unless you read selectively and skillfully. You can't control your reading load. You can, however, improve your reading skills. The material in this chapter will present techniques that can help you read and study as efficiently as you possibly can, while still having time left over for other things.

Working Through Difficult Texts

While many textbooks are useful teaching tools, some can be poorly written and organized. Students using texts that aren't well written may blame themselves for the difficulty they're experiencing. Because texts are often written with the purpose of challenging the intellect, even well-written, well-organized texts may be difficult and dense to read. Generally, the further you advance in your education, the more complex your required reading is likely to be. For example, your sociology professor may assign a chapter on the dynamics of social groups, including those of dyads and triads. When is the last time you heard the terms *dyads* and *triads* in normal conversation? You may feel at times as though you are reading a foreign language as you encounter new concepts, words, and terms.

Assignments can also be difficult when the required reading is from primary sources rather than from texts. *Primary sources* are original documents rather than another writer's interpretation of these documents. They include:

- historical documents
- works of literature (novels, poems, and plays)
- scientific studies, including lab reports and accounts of experiments
- journal articles

The academic writing found in journal articles and scientific studies is different from other kinds of writing. Some academic writers assume that readers understand sophisticated concepts. They may not define basic terms, provide background information, or supply a wealth of examples to support their ideas. As a result, concepts may be difficult to understand.

Making your way through poorly written or difficult reading material is hard work that can be accomplished through focus, motivation, commitment, and skill. The following strategies may help.

Approach your reading assignments head-on. Be careful not to prejudge them as impossible or boring before you even start to read.

Accept the fact that some texts may require some extra work and concentration. Set a goal to make your way through the material and learn, whatever it takes.

When a primary source discusses difficult concepts that it does not explain, put in some extra work to define such concepts on your own. Ask your instructor or other students for help. Consult reference materials in that particular subject area, other class materials, dictionaries, and encyclopedias. For convenience, try creating your own mini-library at home. Collect reference materials that you use often, such as a dictionary, a thesaurus, a writer's style handbook, and maybe an atlas or computer manual. You may also benefit from owning reference materials in your particular areas of study. "If you find yourself going to the library to look up the same reference again and again, consider purchasing that book for your personal or office library," advises library expert Sherwood Harris.

Look for order and meaning in seemingly chaotic reading materials. The information you will find in this chapter on the PQ3R reading technique and on critical reading will help you discover patterns and achieve a greater depth of understanding. Finding order within chaos is an important skill, not just in the mastery of reading, but also in life. This skill can give you power by helping you "read" (think through) work dilemmas, personal problems, and educational situations.

Managing Distractions

With so much happening around you, it's often hard to keep your mind on what you are reading. Distractions take many forms. Some are external: the sound of a telephone, a friend who sits next to you at lunch and wants to talk, a young child who asks for help with homework. Other distractions come from within. As you try to study, you may be thinking about your parent's health, an argument you had with a friend or partner, a paper due in art history, or a site on the Internet that you want to visit.

IDENTIFY THE DISTRACTION AND CHOOSE A SUITABLE ACTION

Pinpoint what's distracting you before you decide what kind of action to take. If the distraction is *external* and *out of your control*, such as construction outside your building or a noisy group in the library, try to move away from it. If the distraction is *external* but *within your control*, such as the television, telephone, or children, take action. For example, if the television or telephone is a problem, turn off the TV or unplug the phone for an hour. Figure B-1 explores some ways that parents or other people caring for children may be able to maximize their study efforts.

If the distraction is *internal*, there are a few strategies to try that may help you clear your mind. You may want to take a break from your studying and tend to one of the issues that you are worrying about. Physical exercise may relax you and bring back your ability to focus. For some people, studying while listening to music helps to

Managing Children While Studying

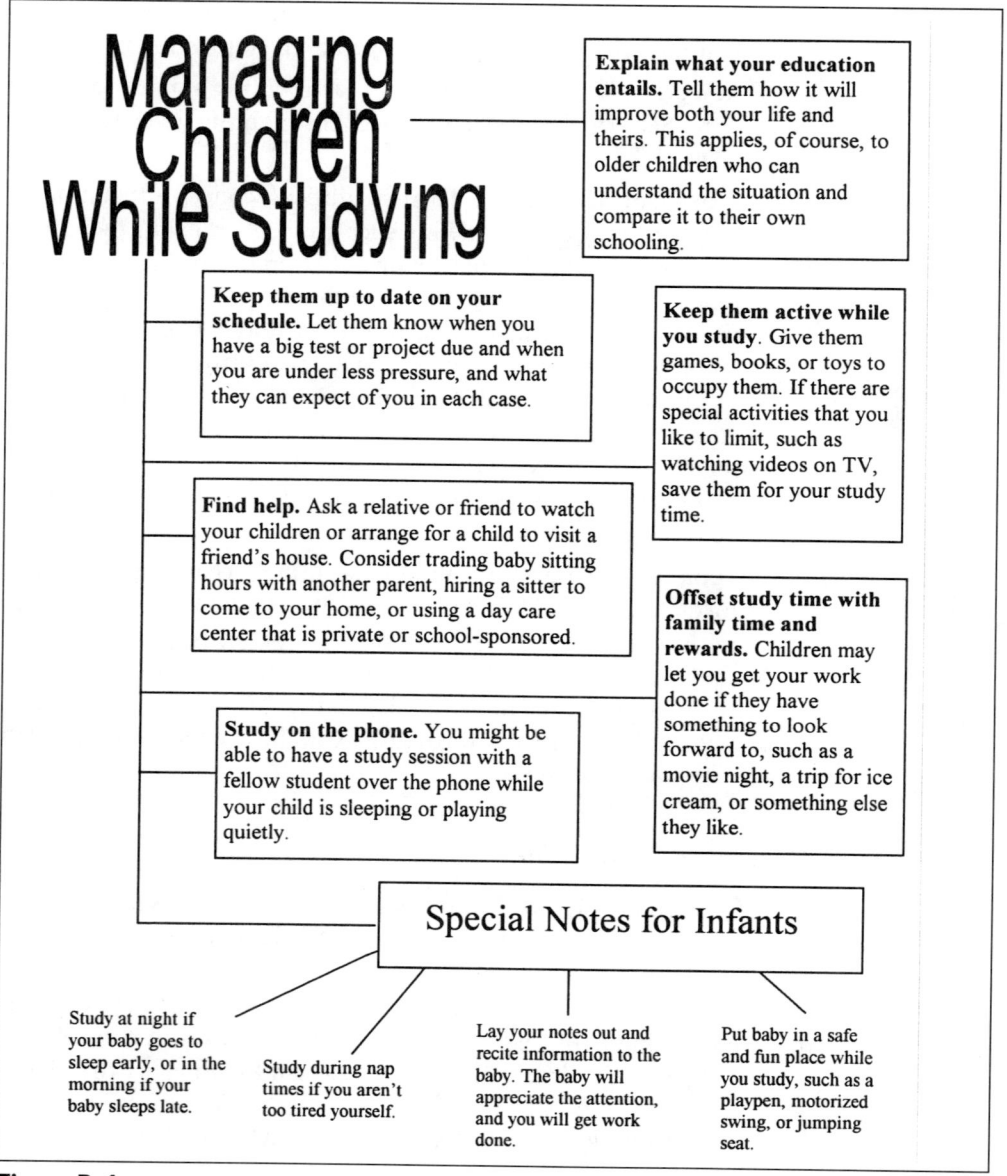

Explain what your education entails. Tell them how it will improve both your life and theirs. This applies, of course, to older children who can understand the situation and compare it to their own schooling.

Keep them up to date on your schedule. Let them know when you have a big test or project due and when you are under less pressure, and what they can expect of you in each case.

Keep them active while you study. Give them games, books, or toys to occupy them. If there are special activities that you like to limit, such as watching videos on TV, save them for your study time.

Find help. Ask a relative or friend to watch your children or arrange for a child to visit a friend's house. Consider trading baby sitting hours with another parent, hiring a sitter to come to your home, or using a day care center that is private or school-sponsored.

Offset study time with family time and rewards. Children may let you get your work done if they have something to look forward to, such as a movie night, a trip for ice cream, or something else they like.

Study on the phone. You might be able to have a study session with a fellow student over the phone while your child is sleeping or playing quietly.

Special Notes for Infants

Study at night if your baby goes to sleep early, or in the morning if your baby sleeps late.

Study during nap times if you aren't too tired yourself.

Lay your notes out and recite information to the baby. The baby will appreciate the attention, and you will get work done.

Put baby in a safe and fun place while you study, such as a playpen, motorized swing, or jumping seat.

Figure B–1.

quiet a busy mind. For others, silence may do the trick. If you need silence to read or study and cannot find a truly quiet environment, consider purchasing sound-muffling headphones or even earplugs.

FIND THE BEST PLACE AND TIME TO READ

Any reader needs focus and discipline in order to concentrate on the material. Finding a place and time that minimize outside distractions will help you achieve that focus. Here are some suggestions:

Read alone unless you are working with other readers. Family members, friends, or others who are not in study mode may interrupt your concentration. If you prefer to read alone, establish a relatively interruption-proof place and time, such as an out-of-the-way spot at the library or an after-class hour in an empty classroom. If you study at home and live with other people, you may want to place a "Quiet" sign on the door. Some students benefit from reading together with one or more other students. If this helps you, plan to schedule a group meeting where you read sections of the assigned material and then break to discuss them.

Find a comfortable location. Many students study in the library on a hard-backed chair. Others prefer a library easy chair, a chair in their room, or even the floor. The spot you choose should be comfortable enough for hours of reading, but not so comfortable that you fall asleep. Also, make sure that you have adequate lighting and aren't too hot or too cold.

Choose a regular reading place and time. Choose a spot or two you like and return to them often. Also, choose a time when your mind is alert and focused. Some students prefer to read just before or after the class for which the reading is assigned. Eventually, you will associate preferred places and times with focused reading.

If it helps you concentrate, listen to soothing background music. The right music can drown out background noises and relax you. However, the wrong music can make it impossible to concentrate; for some people, silence is better. Experiment to learn what you prefer; if music helps, stick with the type that works better. A personal headset makes listening possible no matter where you are.

Turn off the television. For most people, reading and television don't mix.

Building Comprehension and Speed

Most students lead busy lives, carrying heavy academic loads while perhaps working a job or even caring for a family. It's difficult to make time to study at all, let alone handle the enormous reading assignments for your different classes. Increasing your reading comprehension and speed will save you valuable time and effort.

Rapid reading won't do you any good if you can't remember the material or answer questions about it. However, reading too slowly can be equally inefficient because it often eats up valuable study time and gives your mind space to wander. Your goal is to read for maximum speed and comprehension. Because greater comprehension is the primary goal and actually promotes faster reading, make comprehension your priority over speed.

> Although today's college campuses are filled with 18- to 22-year-olds, they are also filled with older, nontraditional students who are returning to school. Nearly 1.5 million women and more than 700,000 men over the age of 35 are attending college—as 4-year students, in 2-year degree programs, and as graduate students. While there has been a dramatic increase in this segment of the college population, the percentage of typical college students—men and women between the ages of 18 and 22—has actually declined since 1980.
>
> This dramatic demographic shift coincides with the recognition that humans are lifelong learners with cognitive abilities that adapt to life demands. Despite societal stereotypes that the primary period for learning is over after adolescence, we now know that it is during middle age that adults acquire the information and skills they need to meet the changing demands of their jobs. This is as true for bankers as it is for computer scientists, both of whom work in fields that have changed radically in recent years as a result of an explosion in technology.
>
> In large part, middle-aged students are returning to school because they have to. Many are unemployed—the victims of corporate downsizing. Others are moving into the job market after spending time at home as full-time parents. A financial planner who stopped working for 5 years to raise her daughter may need recertification before any firm will hire her. Even adults who worked part-time during their child-rearing years may have to return to school to acquire the knowledge they need to qualify for a full-time job. This is especially true in fields with a high degree of professional obsolescence.
>
> Whatever the reason for their return, studies show that the majority of middle-aged students are conscientious about their work. They attend classes regularly and get better grades, on average, than other segments of the student population.
>
> The decision to return to school involves personal introspection and assessment of one's skills and abilities. The student role is generally different from the other roles middle-aged adults assume, and it requires considerable adaptation. A student is in a subordinate position as a learner. Also, mature adults may find themselves among a large number of students who are considerably younger than they are, and the faculty may also be younger. Initially, the age difference may be a source of discomfort.
>
> Family members must often take on new responsibilities when a middle-aged member assumes the role of college student. A husband may have to do more household chores, while a wife may have to return to work to supplement the family income. In addition, the student may need emotional support. Sometimes this involves awkward role reversals and the disruption of familiar interaction patterns.
>
> With the realization that middle-aged students are here to stay, community colleges and universities are making substantial adjustments to meet their needs. In addition many students receive the training they need at work. Many large corporations run training departments designed to maintain a competent work force.
>
> *Source:* HUMAN DEVELOPMENT, 7/E by Craig, © 1974. Adapted by permission of Prentice-Hall, Inc., Upper Saddle River, NJ.

TEST YOUR SPEED AND COMPREHENSION

To make your own personal reading-speed assessment, time how rapidly you read the following 500-word selection from start to finish without stopping. This excerpt, entitled "Back to School at Middle Age," is adapted from the seventh edition of Grace J. Craig's college text on Human Development:

Reading and Studying: Your Keys to Knowledge / 325

Use the following formula to calculate how quickly you read this material:

- Note the time it took you in minutes to read the passage. Use decimals for fractions of a minute. That is, if it took you 1 minute and 45 seconds, then write 1.75 minutes.
- Divide the number of words in the passage by your reading time.

  The number you come up with is your reading speed in words per minute. If you spent 1.75 minutes reading this 500-word selection, you would divide 500 by 1.75 to come up with a reading speed of approximately 286 words per minute.

Q Now answer the following questions without looking back at the text:

1. How many men and women over the age of 35 are now enrolled in various college programs?

   A. approximately 1.5 million women and 700,000 men

   B. 5 million men and women

   C. approximately 1.5 million men and 700,000 women

2. How has the enrollment of 18- to 22-year-old college students changed since 1980 in relationship to the total college population?

   A. The percentage of students in this age group has increased.

   B. The percentage of students in this age group has remained the same.

   C. The percentage of students in this age group has decreased.

3. According to the passage, which one of the following reasons does not describe why older adults return to school?

   A. Unemployed adults return to school to acquire new work-related skills.

   B. After spending time at home raising children, many adults are moving onto another stage of life, which involves returning to work.

   C. Adults with discretionary income are choosing to invest money in themselves.

4. According to the text, why is the student role different from the other roles middle-aged adults assume?

   A. As learners, students are in a subordinate position, which can be uncomfortable for mature adults.

   B. Adults are not used to studying.

   C. Middle-aged adults often find it difficult to talk with young adults.

A Here are the correct answers: 1A, 2C, 3C, 4A. You should have gotten at least three of the four questions correct. In general, your comprehension percentage, as judged by the number of questions like this that you answer correctly, should be above 70 percent. Lower scores mean that you are missing, or forgetting, important information.

Methods for Increasing Reading Comprehension

Following are some specific strategies for increasing your understanding of what you read:

> Continually build your knowledge through reading and studying. More than any other factor, what you already know before you read a passage will determine your ability to understand and remember important ideas. Previous knowledge, including vocabulary, facts, and ideas, gives you a **context** for what you read.
>
> Establish your purpose for reading. When you establish what you want to get out of your reading, you will be able to determine what level of understanding you need to reach and, therefore, on what you need to focus.
>
> Remove the barriers of negative self-talk. Instead of telling yourself that you cannot understand, think positively. Tell yourself: *I can learn this material. I am a good reader.*
>
> Think critically. Ask yourself questions. Do you understand the sentence, paragraph, or chapter you just read? Are ideas and supporting examples clear to you? Could you clearly explain what you just read to someone else?

> **Context,** Written or spoken knowledge that can help illuminate the meaning of a work or passage.

Methods for Increasing Reading Speed

The average American adult reads between 150 and 350 words per minute. Slower readers fall below this range, while faster readers are capable of speeds of 500 to 1000 words per minute and sometimes faster. The following suggestions will help increase your reading speed.

- Try to read groups of words rather than single words.
- Avoid pointing your finger to guide your reading, since this will slow your pace.
- Try swinging your eyes from side to side as you read a passage, instead of stopping at various points to read individual words.
- When reading narrow columns, focus your eyes in the middle of the column and read down the page. With practice, you'll be able to read the entire column width.

- Avoid **vocalization** when reading.
- Avoid thinking each word to yourself as you read it, a practice known as subvocalization. *Subvocalization* is one of the primary causes of slow reading speed.

> **Vocalization,** The practice of speaking words and/or moving your lips while reading.

Expanding Your Vocabulary

Lifelong learners consider their vocabulary a work in progress, because they never finish learning new words. A strong vocabulary increases reading speed and comprehension—when you understand the words in your reading material, you don't have to stop as often to think about what they mean. No matter how strong or weak your vocabulary is, you can improve it by using a dictionary, reading and writing words in context, and learning common prefixes and suffixes.

USE A DICTIONARY

When reading a textbook, the first "dictionary" to search is the text glossary. Textbooks often include an end-of-book glossary that explains technical words and concepts. The definitions there are usually limited to the meaning of the term as it is used in the text.

Standard dictionaries provide a broader treatment. They give you all kinds of information about each word, including its origin, pronunciation, part of speech, synonyms (words that are similar), antonyms (words with opposite meanings), and multiple meanings. By using a dictionary whenever you read, you will increase your general comprehension. Buy a standard dictionary and keep it nearby. Don't hesitate to make notations in it when you need to. Consult your dictionary when you need help understanding a passage that contains unfamiliar key words.

You may not always have time for the following suggestions, but when you can use them, they will make your dictionary use as productive as possible.

> **Read every meaning of a word, not just the first.** Think critically about which meaning suits the context of the word in question, and choose the one that makes the most sense to you.
>
> **Substitute a word or phrase from the definition for the word.** Use the definition you have chosen. Imagine, for example, that you encounter the following sentence and do not know what the word *indoctrinated* means:

The cult indoctrinated its members to reject society's values.

When you search the dictionary, you find several alternate definitions including *brainwashed, instructed,* and *trained exhaustively.* You decide that the definition closest to the correct meaning is *brainwashed.* Substituting this term, the sentence reads:

The cult brainwashed its members to reject society's values.

Keep a journal of every new word you learn, including definitions. Review the journal on a regular basis and watch your vocabulary grow.

Reading and Writing Words in Context

Most people learn words best when they read and use them in written or spoken language. Although reading a definition tells you what a word means, you may have difficulty remembering that definition because you have no former knowledge, or context, to which to connect or compare it. Using a word in context after defining it will help to anchor the information so that you can continue to build upon it.

Here are some strategies for using context to solidify your learning of new vocabulary words.

> Use new words in a sentence or two right away. Do this immediately after reading their definitions, while everything is still fresh in your mind.
>
> Reread the sentence where you originally saw the word. Go over it a few times to make sure you understand how the word is used.
>
> Use the word over the next few days whenever it may apply. Try it while talking with friends, writing letters or notes, or in your own thoughts.
>
> Consider where you may have seen or heard the word before. When you learn a word, going back to sentences you previously didn't understand may help you to broaden your understanding of its meaning. For example, when most children learn the Pledge of Allegiance, they memorize the words by rote without understanding exactly what "allegiance" means. Later, when they learn the definition of "allegiance," the pledge provides a context for the word that helps them understand it more fully.
>
> Seek knowledgeable advice. If after looking up a word you still have trouble with its meaning, ask your instructor or a friend if they can help you figure it out.

If you keep a vocabulary journal, include sentences that place the word in context. Write sentences near the word's definition.

Learn Prefixes and Suffixes

Often, if you understand part of a word, you will be able to figure out what the entire word means. Particularly helpful is a working knowledge of common prefixes and suffixes. *Prefixes* are word parts that are added to the beginning of a **root** while *suffixes* are added to the end of the root. Table B–1 contains prefixes and suffixes you may encounter.

Facing the challenges of reading is only the first step. The next important step is to examine why you are reading any given piece of material.

Root, the central part or basis of a word, around which prefixes and/or suffixes can be added to produce different words.

Table B–1. Common Prefixes and Suffixes

Prefix	Primary Meaning	Example
a, ab	from, away	abstain, avert
ad, af, at	to	adhere, affix, attain
con, cor, com	with, together	convene, correlate, compare
di	apart	divert, divorce
il	not	illegal, illegible
ir	not	irresponsible
post	after	postpone, post-partum
sub, sup	under	subordinate, suppose

Suffix	Primary Meaning	Example
-able	able	recyclable
-arium	place for	aquarium, solarium
-cule	very small	molecule
-ist	one who	pianist
-meter	measure	thermometer
-ness	state of	carelessness
-sis	condition of	hypnosis
-y	inclined to	sleepy

Why Define Your Purpose for Reading?

As with all other aspects of your education, asking important questions will enable you to make the most of your efforts. When you define your purpose, you ask yourself *why* you are reading a particular piece of material. One way to do this is by completing this sentence: "In reading this material, I intend to define/learn/answer/achieve...." With a clear purpose in mind, you can decide how much time and effort to expend on various reading assignments. Nearly 375 years ago, Francis Bacon, the great English philosopher, recognized that

> Some books are to be tasted, others to be swallowed, and some few to be chewed and digested; that is, some books are to be read only in parts, others to be read but not curiously; and some few to be read wholly, and with diligence and attention.

Table B–2. Linking Purpose to Pace

Type of Material	Reading Purpose	Pace
Academic readings • textbooks • original sources • articles from scholarly journals • on-line publications for academic readers • lab reports • required fiction	• Critical analysis • Overall mastery • Preparation for tests	• Slow, especially if the material is new and unfamiliar
Manuals • instructions • recipes	• Practical application • Slow to medium	
Journalism and nonfiction for the general reader • nonfiction books • newspapers • magazines • on-line publications for the general public	• Understanding of • Understanding of general ideas, key concepts, and specific facts for personal understanding and/or practical application	• Medium to fast
Nonrequired fiction	• Understanding of general ideas, key concepts, and specific facts for enjoyment	• Variable, but tending toward the faster speeds

Source: Adapted from Nicholas Reid Schaffzin, *The Princeton Review Reading Smart.* New York: Random House, 1996, p. 15.

Achieving your reading purpose requires adapting to different types of reading materials. Being a flexible reader—adjusting your reading strategies and pace—will help you to adapt successfully.

Purpose Determines Reading Strategy

With purpose comes direction; with direction comes a strategy for reading. Following are five reading purposes, examined briefly. You may have one or more for each piece of reading material you approach.

Purpose 1: Read to Evaluate Critically. Critical evaluation involves approaching the material with an open mind, examining causes and effects, evaluating ideas, and asking questions that test the strength of the writer's argument and that try to identify assumptions. Critical reading is essential for you to demonstrate an understanding of material that goes beyond basic recall of information. You will learn more about critical reading later in the appendix.

Purpose 2: Read for Comprehension. Much of the studying you do involves reading for the purpose of comprehending the material. The two main components of comprehension are *general ideas* and *specific facts/examples*. These components depend on one another. Facts and examples help to explain or support ideas, and ideas provide a framework that helps the reader to remember facts and examples.

> *General Ideas.* General-idea reading is rapid reading that seeks an overview of the material. You may skip entire sections as you focus on headings, subheadings, and summary statements in search of general ideas.
>
> *Specific Facts/Examples.* At times, readers may focus on locating specific pieces of information—for example, the stages of intellectual development in young children. Often, a reader may search for examples that support or explain more general ideas—for example, the causes of economic recession. Because you know exactly what you are looking for, you can skim the material at a rapid rate. Reading your texts for specific information may help before taking a test.

Purpose 3: Read for Practical Application. A third purpose for reading is to gather usable information which you can apply toward a specific goal. When you read a computer software manual, an instruction sheet for assembling a gas grill, or a cookbook recipe, your goal is to learn how to do something. Reading and action usually go hand in hand.

Purpose 4: Read for Pleasure. Some materials you read for entertainment, such as *Sports Illustrated* magazine or the latest John Grisham courtroom thriller. Entertaining reading may also go beyond materials that seem obviously designed to entertain. Whereas some people may read a Jane Austen novel for comprehension, as in a class assignment, others may read Austen books for pleasure.

Purpose Determines Pace

George M. Usova, senior education specialist and graduate professor at The Johns Hopkins University, explains: "Good readers are flexible readers. They read at a variety of rates and adapt them to the reading *purpose* at hand, the *difficulty* of the material, and their *familiarity* with the subject area." As Table B–2 shows, good readers link the pace of reading to their reading purpose.

So far, this chapter has focused on reading. Recognizing obstacles to effective reading and defining the various purposes for reading lay the groundwork for effective *studying*—the process of mastering the concepts and skills contained in your texts.

Thinking Back

1. List four purposes for reading.

    a. _____

    b. _____

    c. _____

    d. _____

2. Identify at least five methods for increasing reading speed.

    a. _____

    b. _____

    c. _____

    d. _____

    e. _____

3. Identify three methods for increasing reading comprehension.

    a. _____

    b. _____

    c. _____

4. Explain how using a dictionary and analyzing words can help improve reading comprehension.

    _____

    _____

    _____

Thinking Ahead

1. Do you think there is a relationship between effective reading and effective studying? Why or why not?

    _____

    _____

    _____

2. If you were to design a study method that works for you, what would that method involve?

_____

_____

_____

_____

3. When tables and charts appear in your textbooks, do they help you? What do you think their value is when studying?

_____

_____

_____

_____

How Can PQ3R Help You Study Reading Materials?

When you study, you take *ownership* of the material you read. You learn it well enough to apply it to what you do. For example, by the time students studying to be computer-hardware technicians complete their coursework, they should be able to assemble various machines and analyze hardware problems that lead to malfunctions.

Studying also gives you mastery over *concepts*. For example, a dental hygiene student learns the causes of gum disease, a biology student learns what happens during photosynthesis, and a business student learns about marketing research.

This section will focus on a technique that will help you learn and study more effectively as you read your college textbooks.

> **Skimming,** rapid superficial reading of materials that involves glancing through to determine central ideas and main elements.
>
> **Scanning,** reading material in an investigative way, searching for specific information.

Preview-Question-Read-Recite-Review (PQ3R)

PQ3R is a technique that will help you grasp ideas quickly, remember more, and review effectively and efficiently for tests. The symbols P-Q-3-R stand for *preview, question, read, recite,* and *review—all* steps in the studying process. Developed more than 55 years ago by Francis Robinson, the technique is still being used today because it works. It is particularly helpful for studying texts. When reading literature, read the work once from beginning to end to appreciate the story and language. Then, reread it using PQ3R to master the material.

Moving through the stages of PQ3R requires that you know how to skim and scan. *Skimming* involves rapid reading of various chapter elements, including introductions, conclusions, and summaries; the first and last lines of paragraphs; boldface or italicized terms; pictures, charts, and diagrams. In contrast, *scanning* involves the careful search for specific facts and examples. You will probably use scanning during the *review* phase of PQ3R when you need to locate and remind yourself of particular information. In a chemistry text, for example, you may scan for examples of how to apply a particular formula.

Preview

The best way to ruin a "whodunit" novel is to flip through the pages to find out how everything turned out. However, when reading textbooks, previewing can help you learn and is encouraged. *Previewing* refers to the process of surveying, or pre-reading, a book before you actually study it. Most textbooks include devices that give students an overview of the text as a whole as well as of the contents of individual chapters. As you look at Figure B-2, think about how many of these devices you already use.

Question

Your next step is to examine the chapter headings and, on your own paper, write questions linked to those headings. If your reading material has no headings, develop questions as you read. These questions will focus your attention and increase your interest, helping you relate new ideas to what you already know and building your comprehension. You can take questions from the textbook or from your lecture notes, or come

PREVIEWING DEVICES

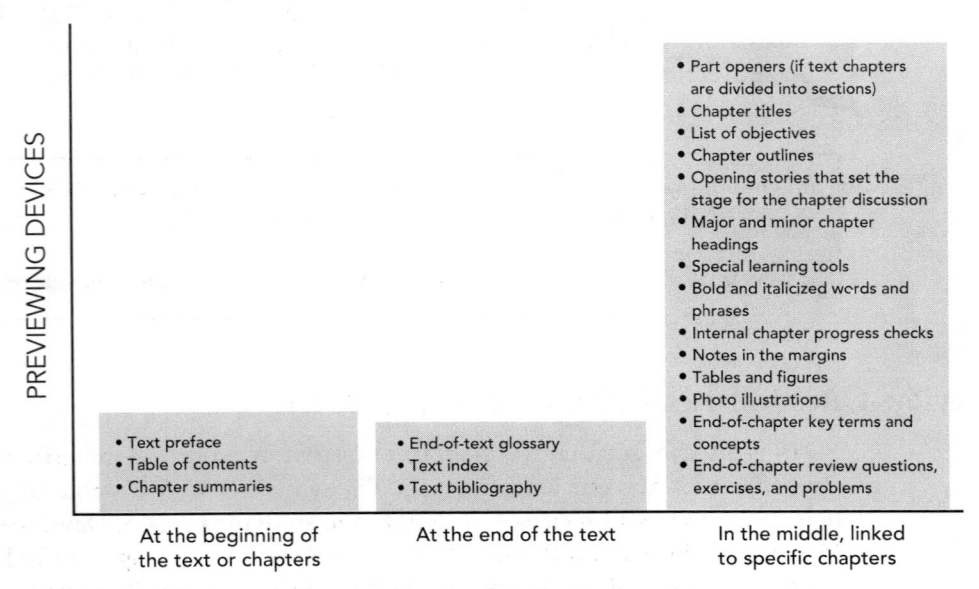

At the beginning of the text or chapters	At the end of the text	In the middle, linked to specific chapters
• Text preface • Table of contents • Chapter summaries	• End-of-text glossary • Text index • Text bibliography	• Part openers (if text chapters are divided into sections) • Chapter titles • List of objectives • Chapter outlines • Opening stories that set the stage for the chapter discussion • Major and minor chapter headings • Special learning tools • Bold and italicized words and phrases • Internal chapter progress checks • Notes in the margins • Tables and figures • Photo illustrations • End-of-chapter key terms and concepts • End-of-chapter review questions, exercises, and problems

Figure B-2. Text and Chapter Previewing Devices

up with them on your own when you preview, based on what ideas you think are most important.

Here is how this technique works. The column on the left contains primary- and secondary-level headings from a section of *Business*, an introductory text by Ricky W. Griffin and Ronald J. Ebert. The column on the right rephrases these headings in question form.

1. THE CONSUMER BUYING PROCESS	1. WHAT IS THE CONSUMER BUYING PROCESS?
A. Problem/Need Recognition	A. Why must consumers first recognize a problem or need before they buy a product?
B. Information Seeking	B. What is information seeking and who answers consumer's questions?
C. Evaluation of Alternatives	C. How do consumers evaluate different products to narrow their choices?
D. Purchase Decision	D. Are purchasing decisions simple or complex?
E. Postpurchase Evaluation	E. What happens after the sale?

There is no "correct" set of questions. Given the same headings, you would create your own particular set of questions. The more useful kinds of questions are ones that engage the critical-thinking mind actions and processes.

Read

Your questions give you a starting point for *reading*, the first R in PQ3R. Read the material with the purpose of answering each question you raised. Pay special attention to the first and last lines of every paragraph, which should tell you what the paragraph is about. As you read, record key words, phrases, and concepts in your notebook. Some students divide the notebook into two columns, writing questions on the left and answers on the right. This method is known as the Cornell note-taking system.

If you own the textbook, marking it up—in whatever ways you prefer—is a must. The notations you make will help you to interact with the material and make sense of it. You may want to write notes in the margins, circle key ideas, or highlight key sections. Some people prefer to underline, although underlining adds more ink to the lines of text and may overwhelm your eye. Although writing in a textbook makes it difficult to sell it back to the bookstore, the increased depth of understanding you can gain is worth the investment.

Highlighting may help you pinpoint material to review before an exam. Here are some additional tips on highlighting:

Get in the habit of marking the text *after* you read the material. If you do it while you are reading, you may wind up marking less important passages.

Highlight key terms and concepts. Mark the examples that explain and support important ideas. You might try highlighting ideas in one color and examples in another.

Highlight figures and tables. They are especially important if they summarize text concepts.

Avoid overmarking. A phrase or two is enough in most paragraphs. Set off long passages with brackets rather than marking every line.

Write notes in the margins with a pen or pencil. Comments like "main point" and "important definition" will help you find key sections later on.

Be careful not to mistake highlighting for learning. You will not necessarily learn what you highlight unless you review it carefully. You may benefit from writing the important information you have highlighted into your lecture notes.

One final step in the reading phase is to divide your reading into digestible segments. Many students read from one topic heading to the next, then stop. Pace your reading so that you understand as you go. If you find you are losing the thread of the ideas you are reading, you may want to try smaller segments, or you may need to take a break and come back to it later.

Recite

Once you finish reading a topic, stop and answer the questions you raised about it in the Q stage of PQ3R. You may decide to *recite* each answer aloud, silently speak the answers to yourself, tell the answers to another person as though you were teaching him or her, or write your ideas and answers in brief notes. Writing is often the most effective way to solidify what you have read. Use whatever techniques best suit your learning-style profile.

After you finish one section, move on to the next. Then repeat the question-read-recite cycle until you complete the entire chapter. If during this process you find yourself fumbling for thoughts, it means that you do not yet "own" the ideas. Reread the section that's giving you trouble until you master its contents. Understanding each section as you go is crucial because the material in one section often forms a foundation for the next.

Review

Review soon after you finish a chapter. Here are some techniques for reviewing.

- Skim and reread your notes. Then try summarizing them from memory.
- Answer the text's end-of-chapter review, discussion, and application questions.
- Quiz yourself, using the questions you raised in the Q stage. If you can't answer one of your own or one of the text's questions, go back and scan the material for answers.
- Review and summarize in writing the sections and phrases you have highlighted.
- Create a chapter outline in standard outline form or think-link form.
- Reread the preface, headings, tables, and summary.
- Recite important concepts to yourself, or record important information on a cassette tape and play it on your car's tape deck or your Walkman.
- Make flashcards that have an idea or word on one side and examples, a definition, or other related information on the other. Test yourself.
- Think critically: Break ideas down into examples, consider similar or different concepts, recall important terms, evaluate ideas, and explore causes and effects.
- Make think links that show how important concepts relate to one another.

Remember that you can ask your instructor if you need help clarifying your reading material. Your instructor is an important resource. Pinpoint the material you want to discuss, schedule a meeting with him or her during office hours, and come prepared with a list of questions. You may also want to ask what materials to focus on when you study for tests.

If possible, you should review both alone and with study groups. Reviewing in as many different ways as possible increases the likelihood of retention. Figure B-3 shows some techniques that will help a study group maximize its time and efforts.

Repeating the review process renews and solidifies your knowledge. That is why it is important to set up regular review sessions—for example, once a week. As you review, remember that refreshing your knowledge is easier and faster than learning it the first time.

As you can see in Table B-3, using PQ3R is part of being an active reader. Active reading involves the specific activities that help you retain what you learn.

Study Groups

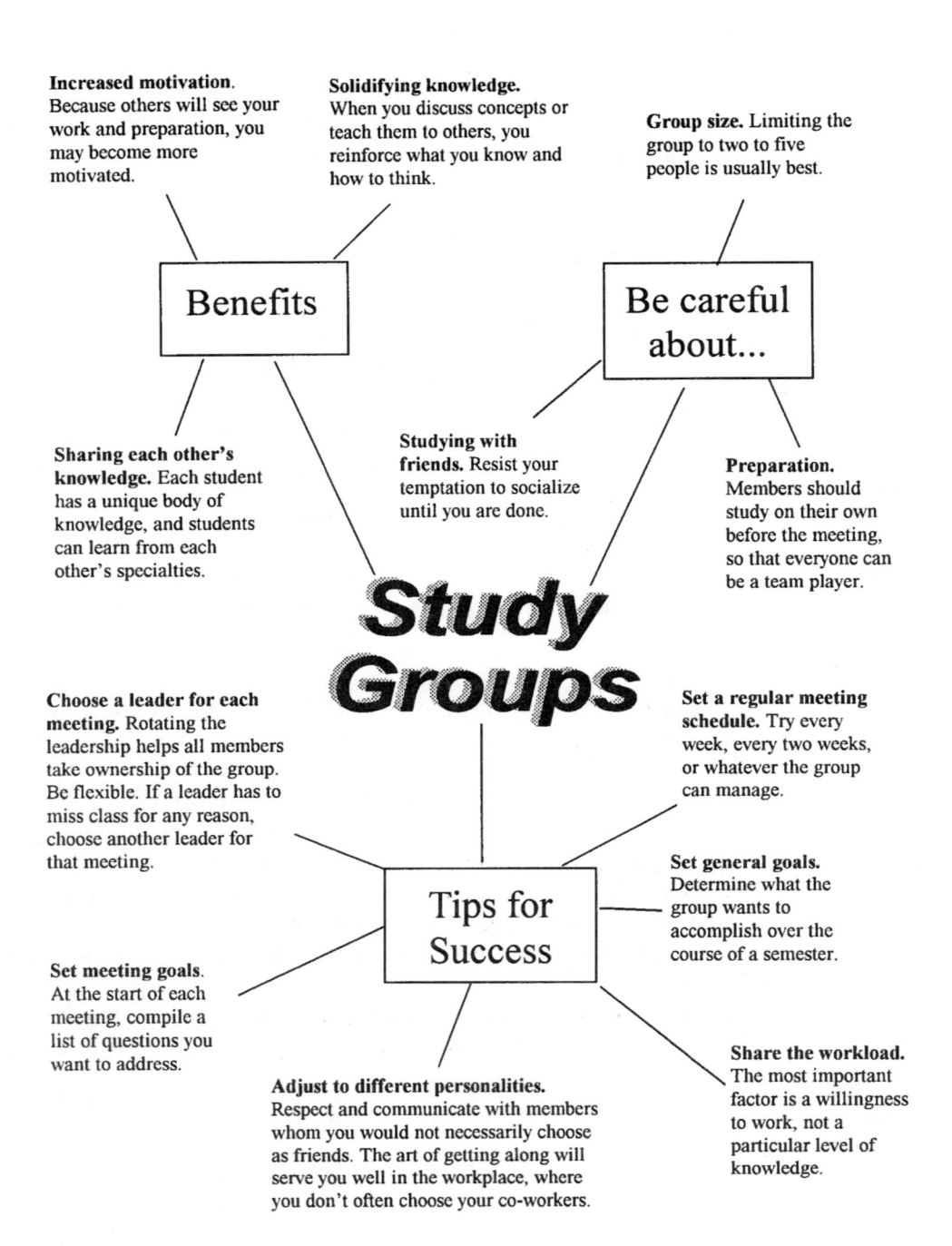

Benefits

Increased motivation. Because others will see your work and preparation, you may become more motivated.

Solidifying knowledge. When you discuss concepts or teach them to others, you reinforce what you know and how to think.

Sharing each other's knowledge. Each student has a unique body of knowledge, and students can learn from each other's specialties.

Be careful about...

Group size. Limiting the group to two to five people is usually best.

Studying with friends. Resist your temptation to socialize until you are done.

Preparation. Members should study on their own before the meeting, so that everyone can be a team player.

Tips for Success

Choose a leader for each meeting. Rotating the leadership helps all members take ownership of the group. Be flexible. If a leader has to miss class for any reason, choose another leader for that meeting.

Set meeting goals. At the start of each meeting, compile a list of questions you want to address.

Adjust to different personalities. Respect and communicate with members whom you would not necessarily choose as friends. The art of getting along will serve you well in the workplace, where you don't often choose your co-workers.

Set a regular meeting schedule. Try every week, every two weeks, or whatever the group can manage.

Set general goals. Determine what the group wants to accomplish over the course of a semester.

Share the workload. The most important factor is a willingness to work, not a particular level of knowledge.

Figure B–3. Study Group Techniques

Table B–3. Use PQ3R to Become an Active Reader

Active Readers Tend to . . .

Divide material into manageable sections.	Answer end-of-chapter questions and applications.
Write questions.	Create chapter outlines.
Answer questions through focused note-taking.	Create think links that map concepts in a logical way.
Recite, verbally and in writing, the answers to questions.	Make flashcards and study them.
Highlight key concepts.	Recite what they learned into a tape recorder, and play the tape back.
Focus on main ideas found in paragraphs, sections, and chapters.	Rewrite and summarize notes and highlighted materials from memory.
Recognize summary and support devices.	Explain what they read to a family member or friend.
Analyse tables, figures, and photos.	Form a study group.

Putting PQ3R to Work

The following is an excerpt from Principles of Microeconomics by Karl E. Case and Ray C. Fair. Apply the PQ3R technique as you read it. Think through the major points of the passage and use the margins and/or the space provided below to make any notes, comments, or questions.

_____

_____

_____

_____

Firms and Households: The Basic Decision-Making Units

Throughout this book, we discuss and analyze the behavior of two fundamental decision-making units: *firms*—the primary producing units in an economy—and *households*—the consuming units in an economy. Both are made up of people performing different functions and playing different roles. In essence, then, what we are developing is a theory of human behavior.

firm
An organization that transforms resources (inputs) into products (outputs). Firms are the primary producing units in a market economy.

A **firm** exists when a person or a group of people decides to reproduce a product or products by transforming *inputs* (that is, resources in the broadest sense) into *outputs* (the products that are sold in the market). Some firms produce goods; others produce services. Some are large, some are small, and some are in between. But all firms exist to transform resources into things that people want. The Colorado Symphony Orchestra takes labor, land, a building, musically talented people, electricity, and other inputs and combines them to produce concerts. The production process can be extremely complicated. The first flutist in the orchestra, for example, uses training, talent, previous performing experience, a score, an instrument, the conductor's interpretation, and her own feelings about the music to produce just one contribution to an overall performance.

Most firms exist to make a profit for their owners, but some do not. Columbia University, for example, fits the description of a firm: It takes inputs in the form of labor, land, skills, books, and buildings and produces a service that we call education. Although it sells that service for a price, it does not exist to make a profit, but rather to provide education of the highest quality possible.

Still, most firms exist to make a profit. They engage in production because they can sell their product for more than it costs to produce it. The analysis of firm behavior that follows rests on the assumption that *firms make decisions in order to maximize profits*.

entrepreneur
A person who organizes, manages, and assumes the risks of a firm, taking a new idea or a new product and turning it into a successful business.

An **entrepreneur** is one who organizes, manages, and assumes the risks of a firm. It is the entrepreneur who takes a new idea or a new product and turns it into a successful business. All firms have implicit in them some element of entrepreneurship. When a new firm is created—whether a proprietorship, a partnership, or a corporation—someone must organize the new firm, arrange financing, hire employees, and take risks. That person is an entrepreneur. Sometimes existing companies introduce new products, and sometimes new firms develop or improve an old idea, but at the root of it all is entrepreneurship, which some see as the core of the free enterprise system.

At the root of the debate about the potential of free enterprise in formerly socialist Eastern Europe is the question of entrepreneurship. Does an entrepreneurial spirit exist in that part of the world? If not, can it be developed? Without it the free enterprise system breaks down.

households
The consuming units in an economy.

The consuming units in an economy are **households**. A household may consist of any number of people: a single person living alone, a married couple living with four children, or 15 unrelated people sharing a house. Household decisions are presumably based on the individual tastes and preferences of the consuming unit. The household buys what it wants and can afford. In a large, heterogeneous, and open society such as the United States, wildly different tastes find expression in the marketplace. A six-block walk in any direction on any street in Manhattan or a drive from the Chicago loop south into rural Illinois should be enough to convince anyone that it is difficult to generalize about what people like and do not like.

Even though *households* have wide-ranging preferences, they also have some things in common. All—even the very rich—have ultimately limited incomes, and all must pay in some way for the things they consume. While households may have some control over their incomes—they can work more or less—they are also constrained by the availability of jobs, current wages, their own abilities, and their accumulated and inherited wealth (or lack thereof).

Source: Principles of Economics, 4/E by Case/Fair, © 1994. Reprinted by permission of Prentice-Hall, Inc., Upper Saddle River, NJ.

After reading the excerpt using PQ3R, answer the following questions. Try not to look back at the material. Instead, examine whether the PQ3R system helped you remember the key points of the passage.

1. What are the two decision-making units called?

_____

_____

_____

2. Most firms exist to make a profit. True or false? _____

3. Someone who organizes, manages, and assumes risks is called a(n):

_____

4. A household:
   a. is the consuming unit in an economy.
   b. may consist of any number of people.
   c. has ultimately limited incomes.
   d. is constrained by the availability of jobs.
   e. all of the above.

How Can You Read Critically?

Your textbooks will often contain features that highlight important ideas and help you determine questions to ask while reading. As you advance in your education, however, many reading assignments will not be so clearly marked, especially if they are primary sources. You will need critical-reading skills in order to select the important ideas, identify examples that support them, and ask questions about the text without the aid of any special features or tools.

Critical reading enables you to consider reading material carefully, developing a thorough understanding of it through evaluation and analysis. A critical reader is able to discern what in a piece of reading material is true or useful, such as when using material as a source for an essay. A critical reader can also compare one piece of material to another and evaluate which makes more sense, which proves its thesis more successfully, or which is more useful for the reader's purpose.

Critical reading is reading that transcends taking in and regurgitating material. You can read critically by using PQ3R to get a basic idea of the material, asking questions based on the critical-thinking mind actions, and engaging your critical-thinking processes.

Use PQ3R to "Taste" Reading Material

Sylvan Barnet and Hugo Bedau, authors of *Critical Thinking, Reading, and Writing—A Brief Guide to Argument*, suggest that the active reading of PQ3R will help you form an initial idea of what a piece of reading material is all about. Through previewing, skimming for ideas and examples, highlighting and writing comments and questions in the margins, and reviewing, you can develop a basic understanding of its central ideas and contents.

Summarizing, part of the review process in PQ3R, is one of the best ways to develop an understanding of a piece of reading material. To construct a *summary*, focus on the central ideas of the piece and the main examples that support those ideas. A summary does *not* contain any of your own ideas or your evaluation of the material. It simply condenses the material, making it easier for you to focus on the structure of the piece and its central ideas when you go back to read more critically. At that point, you can begin to evaluate the piece and introduce your own ideas. Using the mind actions will help you.

> **Summary**, a concise restatement of the material, in your own words, that covers the main points.

Ask Questions Based on the Mind Actions

The essence of critical reading, as with critical thinking, is asking questions. Instead of simply accepting what you read, seek a more thorough understanding by questioning the material as you go along. Using the mind actions of the Thinktrix to formulate your questions will help you understand the material.

What parts of the material you focus on will depend on your purpose for reading. For example, if you are writing a paper on the causes of World War II, you might spend your time focusing on how certain causes fit your thesis. If you are comparing two pieces of writing that contain opposing arguments, you may focus on picking out their central ideas and evaluating how well the writers use examples to support these ideas.

You can question any of the following components of reading material:

- the central idea of the entire piece
- a particular idea or statement
- the examples that support an idea or statement
- the proof of a fact
- the definition of a concept

Following are some ways to critically question your reading material, based on the mind actions. Apply them to any component you want to question by substituting the component for the words "it" and "this."

Similarity: What does this remind me of, or how is it similar to something else I know?

Difference:	What different conclusions are possible?
	How is this different from my experience?
Cause and Effect:	Why did this happen, or what caused this?
	What are the effects or consequences of this?
	What effect does the author want to have, or what is the purpose of this material?
	What effects support a stated cause?
Example to Idea:	How would I classify this, or what is the best idea to fit this example(s)?
	How would I summarize this, or what are the key ideas?
	What is the thesis or central idea?
Idea to Example:	What evidence supports this, or what examples fit this idea?
Evaluation:	How would I evaluate this? Is it valid or pertinent?
	Does this example support my thesis or central idea?

Engage Critical-Thinking Processes

Certain thinking processes can help to deepen your analysis and evaluation of what you read. These processes are establishing truth, constructing an argument, and shifting perspective. Within these processes you will ask questions that use the mind actions.

ESTABLISHING TRUTH

With what you know about how to seek truth, you can evaluate any statement in your reading material, identifying it as fact, opinion, or assumption and challenging how it is supported. Evaluate statements, central ideas, or entire pieces of reading material using questions such as the following:

- Is this true? How does the writer know?
- How could I test the validity of this?
- What assumptions underlie this?
- What else do I know that is similar to or different from this?
- What information that I already know supports or disproves this?
- What examples disprove this as fact or do not fit this assumption?

For example, imagine that a piece of writing states, "The dissolving of the family unit is the main cause of society's ills." You may question the truth of this statement by looking at what facts and examples support it. You may question the writer's sources of information. You may investigate its truth by reading other materials. You could discern that some hidden assumptions underlie this statement, such as an assumed definition of what a family is or of what constitutes "society's ills." You could also find examples that do not fit this assumption, such as successful families that don't fit the definition of "family" used by the writer.

REAL WORLD PERSPECTIVE
How can I cope with a learning disability?

Clacy Albert, Washington State University—Pullman, Washington, Communications Major

All my life I've felt different. I just couldn't seem to learn the way other kids did. I felt stupid and afraid that other people would think I couldn't do anything right. I wouldn't raise my hand in class because I was afraid of being laughed at. I wouldn't volunteer for games because I was afraid I'd let my team down. Study groups were impossible for me. I didn't want anyone to know that I was different. Because of this, my self-esteem really suffered. I became very quiet.

It wasn't until I was a sophomore in high school that a teacher recognized something was wrong with the way I learned. It was my math teacher who saw that I couldn't recognize certain patterns. I would see things in reverse or not be able to recognize a pattern at all. He sat down with my parents and helped them understand something was wrong. Unfortunately, the school I attended didn't have any testing for learning disabilities, so I let it go until I was in college. When I enrolled at WSU they told us about the learning disability resource center. My mom suggested I finally get the testing I needed. I'm glad I did because now I know that I have dyslexia and need special assistance to handle my studies. I wish there was mandatory testing for this disability in grade school. If there had been I wouldn't have suffered so deeply all these years. What suggestions do you have for helping me cope with this disability?

Edith Hall, Senior Sales Representative—Prentice Hall

I have a different disability but one that causes similar problems. I have Attention Deficit Hyperactivity Disorder and the fact that it was undiagnosed and untreated for many years has caused lots of problems in my life. It wasn't until I was six years out of college that I was diagnosed ADHD. And the great thing about it is I don't feel crazy anymore. Now I know why I can't sit still for long periods and why I can't complete large and/or long projects like other non-ADHD people can.

I think acknowledging that I had a disorder and then accepting it were the biggest steps to coping and living with this disorder. The other thing I have done is to get educated. I have read almost anything I can get my hands on. I am also involved in a support group. Having other people I can talk with about how my brain affects my behavior and my life truly is one of the best coping strategies I know.

Having a disability or disorder is not a bad thing. Ennis Cosby, slain son of comedian Bill Cosby, said of his dyslexia, "The day I found out I had dyslexia was the best day of my life." Finding out he had dyslexia relieved him of the belief that he was dumb or stupid or slow. For me, like Ennis Cosby, finding out I had ADHD was a great day in my life because I now had tools and help to be different and I no longer felt alone.

Constructing an Argument

When your reading material contains one or more arguments, you can use what you know about arguments to evaluate whether the writer has constructed his or her argument effectively. Ask questions like the following:

- What is the purpose of the writer's argument?
- Do I believe this? How is the writer trying to persuade me?
- If the author uses cause-and-effect reasoning, does it seem logical?
- Do the examples adequately support the central idea of the argument?
- What different and perhaps opposing arguments seem just as valid?
- If I'm not sure whether I believe this, how could I construct an opposing argument?

Don't rule out the possibility that you may agree wholeheartedly with an argument. However, use critical thinking to make an informed decision, rather than accepting it outright.

Shifting Perspective

Your understanding of perspective will help you understand that many reading materials are written from a particular perspective. Perspective often has a strong effect on how the material is presented. For example, if a recording artist and a music censorship advocate were to each write a piece about a controversial song created by that artist, their different perspectives would result in two very different pieces of writing.

To analyze perspective, ask questions like the following:

What perspective is guiding this? What are the underlying ideas that influence this material?

Who wrote this, and what may be the author's perspective? For example, a piece on a new drug written by an employee of the drug manufacturer may differ from a doctor's evaluation of the drug.

What does the title of the material tell me about its perspective? For example, a piece entitled "New Therapies for Diabetes" may be more informational, and "What's Wrong with Insulin Injections" may intend to be persuasive.

How does the material's source affect its perspective? For example, an article on health management organizations (HMOs) published in an HMO newsletter may be more favorable and one-sided than one published in *The New York Times*.

Seek Understanding

Reading critically allows you to investigate what you read so that you can reach the highest possible level of understanding. Think of your reading process as an archaeological dig. The first step is to excavate a site and uncover the artifacts. In reading, that corresponds to your initial preview and reading of the material. As important as the excavation is, the process would be incomplete if you stopped there and just took home a bunch of items covered in dirt. The second half of the process is to investigate each item, evaluate what all of those items mean, and to derive new knowledge and ideas from what you discover. Critical reading allows you to complete that crucial second half of the process.

As you work through all the different requirements of critical reading, remember that critical reading takes *time* and *focus*. Finding a time, place, and purpose for reading, covered earlier in the appendix, is crucial to successful critical reading. Give yourself a chance to gain as much as possible from what you read.

Visual aids can provide valuable information as you study. Explore how to "read" them and make the most of their value as study tools.

How Can You "Read" Visual Aids?

Visual aids, including tables and charts, are commonly used in texts and other college materials. They highlight statistical comparisons that show:

- *trends over time* (for example, the number of televisions per household in 1997 as compared to the number in 1957)
- *relative rankings* (for example, the size of the advertising budgets of four major consumer-products companies)
- *distributions* (for example, student performance on standardized tests by geographic area)
- *cycles* (for example, the regular upward and downward movement of the nation's economy as defined by periods of prosperity and recession)

Tables and charts also summarize concepts that are presented in paragraph form.

Knowing what to look for in visual aids will help you learn to "read" the information they present. The visuals in the following section are from actual textbooks published by Prentice Hall.

Understanding Tables

The two basic types of tables are data tables and word tables. Data tables present numerical information—for example, the numbers of students taking a standardized test in fifty states. *Word tables* summarize and consolidate complex information, making it easier to study and evaluate. Table B–4 is a model of a typical table, including the individual parts and their arrangement on the page.

Table B-4. The Parts and Arrangements of a Table

TABLE NO.
TITLE OF TABLE

Stub Head	Caption		Caption	
	Subcaption	Subcaption	Subcaption	Subcaption
Stub	XXXX	XXXX	XXXX	XXXX
Stub	XXXX	XXXX[a]	XXXX	XXXX
Stub	XXXX	XXXX	XXXX	XXXX
Stub	XXXX	XXXX	XXXX	XXXX
Stub	XXXX	XXXX	XXXX	XXXX
Total	XXXX	XXXX	XXXX[b]	XXXX

[a]Footnote

[b]Footnote

Source:

Source: "THE PARTS AND ARRANGEMENTS OF A TABLE" from BUSINESS WRITING, 2E by J. HAROLD JANIS and HOWARD R. DRESNER. Copyright © 1956, 1972 by J. Harold Janis. Reprinted by permission of HarperCollins Publishers, Inc.

The table is arranged in columns and rows and has the following elements:

- The *table number* identifies the table and is usually referred to in the text.
- The *table title* helps readers focus on the table's message.
- *Captions*, also known as column titles, identify the material that fall below.
- *Subcaptions* divide the columns into smaller sections.
- The *stubs* refer to the captions running along the horizontal rows. The nature of the stubs is identified by the *stub head*.
- *Footnotes* are used to explain specific details found in the table.
- The *source* acknowledges where the information comes from.

Understanding Charts

Charts, also known as graphs, present numerical data in visual form in order to show relationships among the data. Types of charts include pie charts, bar charts, and line charts.

The *pie chart* is the most common and easy-to-understand visual aid. It presents data as wedge-shaped sections of a circle in order to show the relative size of each item as a percentage of the whole. The pie chart in Figure B–4 compares the amount of money each of the top five television network advertisers spends each year to the total spent by all five advertisers.

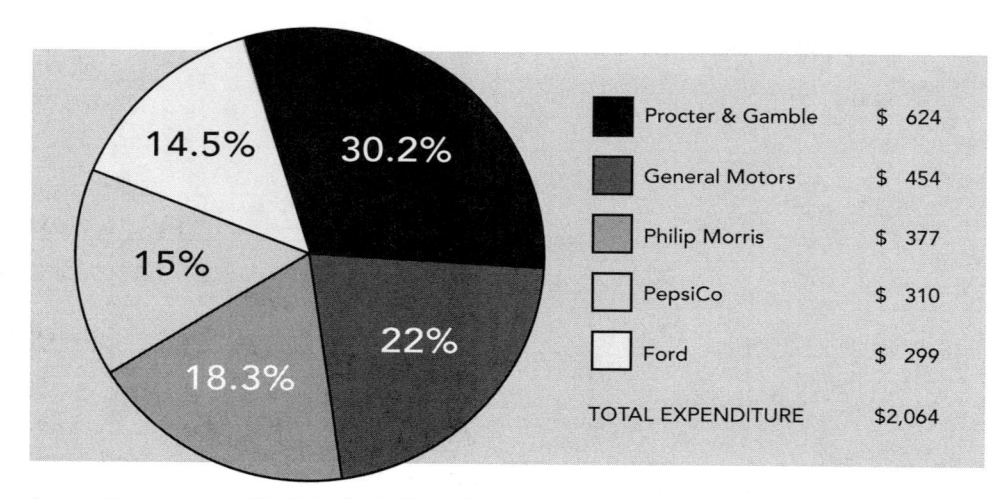

[Pie chart showing TV Ad Expenditures percentages: 30.2%, 22%, 18.3%, 15%, 14.5%]

■	Procter & Gamble	$ 624
■	General Motors	$ 454
■	Philip Morris	$ 377
□	PepsiCo	$ 310
□	Ford	$ 299
	TOTAL EXPENDITURE	$2,064

Source: Data presented in Ricky W. Griffin and Ronald J. Ebert. Business, 4th ed. Upper Saddle River, NJ: Prentice Hall, 1996, p. 526.

Figure B–4. TV Ad Expenditures in Millions of Dollars

AGENCY	NUMBER of MULTINATIONAL CLIENTS
Grey Advertising	83
McCann-Erickson Worldwide	74
Ogilvy & Mather Worldwide	56
Saatchi & Saatchi Advertising	41
DDB Needham Worldwide	40

Source: Information courtesy of DDB Needham Worldwide.

Figure B–5. Number of Multinational Clients of Major Advertising Agencies

Bar charts consist of horizontal bars of varying lengths and show the relative rankings of each bar. While pie charts focus on the size of individual components in relationship to the whole, bar charts demonstrate how items compare with one another.

The bar chart in Figure B–5 shows the number of multinational clients of five major advertising agencies. The information presented from left to right is on the *horizontal axis*. The information presented from the top to the bottom of the chart is on the *vertical axis*. Here the horizontal axis shows the number of clients, while the vertical shows agency names. Since the values of the horizontal bars are clear, no scale is needed (scales are used to clarify values).

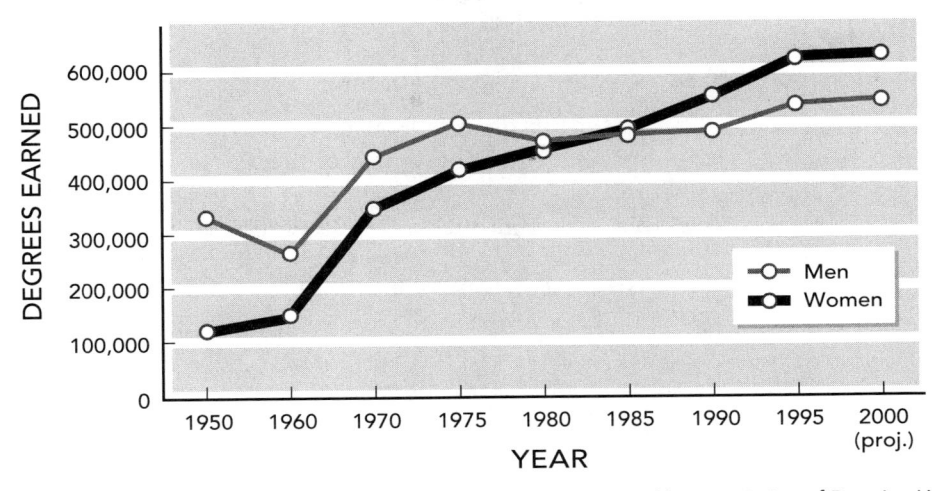

Reading and Studying: Your Keys to Knowledge / 349

Source: PSYCHOLOGY, 2/E by Davis and Palladino, © 1997. Reprinted by permission of Prentice-Hall, Inc., Upper Saddle River, NJ.

Figure B–6. Number of Men and Woman Earning Bachelor's Degrees

Finally, the lines in *line charts* show continuous trends over time. The horizontal axis shows a span of time, while the vertical axis represents a specific measurement such as dollars or units of various kinds. The line chart in Figure B-6 shows how the number of men and women earning bachelor's degrees has increased in the past fifty years.

Tables and charts help to make information appealing to the reader. They are a valuable study aid that can add to your understanding of what you read.

читать

This word may look completely unfamiliar to you, but anyone who can read the Russian language and alphabet will know that it means "read." People who read languages that use different kinds of characters, such as Russian, Japanese, or Greek, learn to process those characters as easily as you process the letters of your native alphabet. Your mind learns to process individually each letter or character you see. This ability enables you to move to the next level of understanding—making sense of those letters or characters when they are grouped to form words, phrases, and sentences.

Think of this concept when you read. Remember that your mind is an incredible tool, processing immeasurable amounts of information so that you can understand the concepts on the page. Give it the best opportunity to succeed by reading as often as you can and by focusing on all of the elements that help you read to the best of your ability.

Important Points to Remember

Q. 1. What are some challenges of reading?

A. College students often experience an overload of assignments and too little time to complete them. Conceptually difficult or poorly written texts can present another roadblock. Distractions, the need to build comprehension and speed, and the need to expand vocabulary are three other challenges.

Q. 2. Why define your purpose for reading?

A. Defining your purpose means asking yourself why you are reading a particular piece of material. Having a purpose helps you structure your approach toward reading assignments, since different purposes require different levels of time and effort. The four main purposes are critical evaluation, comprehension (both general ideas and specific examples), practical application, and pleasure.

Q. 3. How can PQ3R help you study?

A. PQ3R, the process of *previewing, questioning, reading, reciting,* and *reviewing,* encourages active studying. *Previewing* refers to surveying a book before studying it. During the *questioning* phase, you write questions linked to chapter headings. During the *reading* stage, you read the material in order to answer these questions and take notes. During the *reciting* stage, you answer the questions you raised by reciting aloud or silently to yourself, telling answers to another person, or writing them in a notebook. The *review* stage involves skimming and rereading your notes. Forming a study group may also help to maximize your review efforts.

Q. 4. How can you read critically?

A. Critical-reading skills help you select important ideas, identify supporting examples, and ask questions about any text, developing an understanding of the material through evaluation and analysis. Critical reading involves using PQ3R to "taste" the material, asking questions based on the seven mind actions, and engaging your critical-thinking processes (establishing the truth of what you read, evaluating its arguments, and analyzing its perspective).

Q. 5. How can you "read" visual aids?

A. Visual aids, including tables and charts, highlight statistical comparisons and summarize information. Learning to read visual aids depends on understanding their value as learning tools and on learning how tables and charts are constructed and the messages they convey.

Appendix B: Applications

Name _____ Date _____

Taking Stock: Refining Your Thoughts

Look back at the statements you explored at the start of the appendix. Observe whether your attitudes have changed and what you have learned by studying this chapter.

1. Explain four reasons why many students have trouble handling their reading assignments.

   _____
   _____
   _____
   _____

2. Identify at least two strategies that will help you get through difficult texts.

   _____
   _____

3. Name two ideas for increasing your reading speed and two ideas for increasing your comprehension that you would be likely to use.

   _____
   _____
   _____

4. Explain three ways you can remember the vocabulary words you learn.

   _____
   _____
   _____

5. Describe your reaction to PQ3R as a study tool. What parts of the strategy do you think will help you most?

_____

_____

_____

6. How might studying with others help you learn?

_____

_____

7. Explain how text tables and charts might help you learn assigned material.

_____

_____

_____

8. Choose one reading or studying strategy you learned in this chapter and explain how you will apply it to your schoolwork during the next week.

_____

_____

_____

Key Into Your Life: Opportunities to Apply What You Learn

EXERCISE 1: PREVIEWING YOUR TEXTBOOK

Previewing is an important step in PQ3R (preview, question, read, recite, review). Use the following form to conduct this preview on one text you are using this year:

Textbook Preview Form

1. Textbook name and authors: _____
2. Describe the mission of the book as defined in the Preface. ("Mission" is defined by the scope of the book's contents, what it is trying to accomplish, and the readers for whom it is intended):

_____

_____

Reading and Studying: Your Keys to Knowledge / 353

3. List three important features that will help you study the material covered in the text. (You will find a list of these features in the Preface.):

   a. _____

   b. _____

   c. _____

4. What does the Table of Contents tell you about the contents and focus of the book? Does the book intend a comprehensive overview of the field or does it focus on a narrow part of the field?

   _____
   _____
   _____
   _____

5. Based on your preview, write a short statement about what you expect studying this text will be like.

   _____
   _____
   _____

EXERCISE 2: PREVIEWING INDIVIDUAL CHAPTERS[10]

Conduct the same type of analysis on an individual chapter of the text you just previewed.

Chapter Review Form

1. Chapter title: _____

   What does the title tell you about the chapter's focus? _____

   _____
   _____

2. From the list below, check the study aids contained in the chapter:

- ☐ list of objectives
- ☐ chapter outline
- ☐ opening vignette
- ☐ major and minor chapter headings
- ☐ bold and italicized words and phrases
- ☐ internal chapter reviews
- ☐ marginal notes
- ☐ tables, charts, and figures
- ☐ photo illustrations, including captions
- ☐ end-of-chapter summaries
- ☐ end-of chapter key terms and concepts
- ☐ end of chapter review questions, exercises, and problems
- ☐ other _____

3. Based on your analysis of these elements, which seem likely to provide you with the most studying assistance? Why?

_____

_____

_____

4. Identify at least three break points in the chapter that will help you divide it into manageable segments (page # and location on page).

   a. _____

   b. _____

   c. _____

EXERCISE 3: STUDYING A TEXT PAGE

The following page is from the Groups and Organizations chapter in the sixth edition of John J. Macionis's *Sociology*, a Prentice Hall text.
Using what you learned in this chapter about study techniques, complete the following items:

1. Identify the headings on the page and the relationship among them. Which headings are primary level headings; which are secondary; which are tertiary (third-level heads)? Which heading serves as an umbrella for the rest?

_____

_____

_____

SOCIAL GROUPS

Virtually everyone moves through life with a sense of belonging; this is the experience of group life. A **social group** refers to *two or more people who identify and interact with one another.* Human beings continually come together to form couples, families, circles of friends, neighborhoods, churches, businesses, clubs, and numerous large organizations. Whatever the form, groups encompass people with shared experiences, loyalties, and interests. In short, while maintaining their individuality, the members of social groups also think of themselves as a special "we."

Groups, Categories, and Crowds

People often use the term "group" imprecisely. We now distinguish the group from the similar concepts of category and crowd.

Category

A *category* refers to people who have some status in common. Women, single fathers, military recruits, homeowners, and Roman Catholics are all examples of categories.

Why are categories not considered groups? Simply because, while the individuals involved are aware that they are not the only ones to hold that particular status, the vast majority are strangers to one another.

Crowd

A *crowd* refers to a temporary cluster of individuals who may or may not interact at all. Students sitting together in a lecture hall do engage one another and share some common identity as college classmates; thus, such a crowd might be called a loosely formed group. By contrast, riders hurtling along on a subway train or bathers enjoying a summer day at the beach pay little attention to one another and amount to an anonymous aggregate of people. In general, then, crowds are too transitory and too impersonal to qualify as social groups.

The right circumstances, however, could turn a crowd into a group. People riding in a subway train that crashes under the city streets generally become keenly aware of their common plight and begin to help each other. Sometimes such extraordinary experiences become the basis for lasting relationships.

Primary and Secondary Groups

Acquaintances commonly greet one another with a smile and the simple phrase "Hi! How are you?" The response is usually a well-scripted "Just fine, thanks. How about you?" This answer, of course, is often more formal than truthful. In most cases, providing a detailed account of how you are *really* doing would prompt the other person to beat a hasty and awkward exit.

Sociologists classify social groups by measuring them against two ideal types based on members' level of genuine personal concern. This variation is the key to distinguishing *primary* from *secondary* groups.

According to Charles Horton Cooley (1864–1929), who is introduced in the box, a **primary group** is *a small social group whose members share personal and enduring relationships.* Bound together by *primary relationships*, individuals in primary groups typically spend a great deal of time together, engage in a wide range of common activities, and feel that they know one another well. Although not without periodic conflict, members of primary groups display sincere concern for each other's welfare. The family is every society's most important primary group.

Cooley characterized these personal and tightly integrated groups as *primary* because they are among the first groups we experience in life. In addition, the family and early play groups also hold primary importance in the socialization process, shaping attitudes, behavior, and social identity.

Source: Sociology, 6/E by John J. Macionis, ©1997. Reprinted by permission of Prentice-Hall, Inc., Upper Saddle River, NJ.

2. What do the headings tell you about the content of the page?

3. After reading the chapter headings, write three study questions. List the questions below:

   a. _____

   b. _____

   c. _____

4. Using a marker pen, highlight key phrases and sentences. Write short marginal notes to help you review the material at a later point.

5. After reading this page, list three key concepts that you would need to study:

   a. _____

   b. _____

   c. _____

EXERCISE 4: FOCUSING ON YOUR PURPOSE FOR READING

Read the paragraphs on the next page on kinetic and potential energy and the first law of thermodynamics. When you have finished, answer the questions that follow.

   a. *Reading for critical evaluation.* Evaluate the material by answering these questions:

   Were the ideas clearly supported by examples? If you feel one or more were not supported, give an example.

   _____
   _____
   _____
   _____

   Did the author make any assumptions that weren't examined? If so, name one or more.

   _____
   _____

   Do you disagree with any part of the material? If so, which part, and why?

   _____
   _____
   _____

Among the fundamental characteristics of all living organisms is the ability to guide chemical reactions within their bodies along certain pathways. The chemical reactions serve many functions, depending on the nature of the organism: to synthesize the molecules that make up the organism's body, to reproduce, to move, even to think. Chemical reactions either require or release **energy**, which can be defined simply as *the capacity to do work*, including synthesizing molecules, moving things around, and generating heat and light. In this chapter we discuss the physical laws that govern energy flow in the universe, how energy flow in turn governs chemical reactions, and how the chemical reactions within living cells are controlled by the molecules of the cell itself. Chapters 7 and 8 focus on photosynthesis, the chief "port of entry" for energy into the biosphere, and glycolysis and cellular respiration, the most important sequences of chemical reactions that release energy.

Energy and the Ability to Do Work

As you learned in Chapter 2, there are two types of energy: **kinetic energy** and **potential energy**. Both types of energy may exist in many different forms. Kinetic energy, or *energy of movement*, includes light (movement of photons), heat (movement of molecules), electricity (movement of electrically charged particles), and movement of large objects. Potential energy, or *stored energy*, includes chemical energy stored in the bonds that hold atoms together in molecules, electrical energy stored in a battery, and positional energy stored in a diver poised to spring (Fig. 4-1). Under the right conditions, kinetic energy can be transformed into potential energy, and vice versa. For example, the diver converted kinetic energy of movement into potential energy of position when she climbed the ladder up to the platform; when she jumps off, the potential energy will be converted back into kinetic energy.

To understand how energy flow governs interactions among pieces of matter, we need to know two things: (1) the quantity of available energy and (2) the usefulness of the energy. These are the subjects of the laws of thermodynamics, which we will now examine.

The Laws of Thermodynamics Describe the Basic Properties of Energy

All interactions among pieces of matter are governed by the two **laws of thermodynamics**, physical principles that define the basic properties and behavior of energy. The laws of thermodynamics deal with "isolated systems," which are any parts of the universe that cannot exchange either matter or energy with any other parts. Probably no part of the universe is completely isolated from all possible exchange with every other part, but the concept of an isolated system is useful in thinking about energy flow.

The First Law of Thermodynamics States That Energy Can Neither Be Created nor Destroyed

The **first law of thermodynamics** states that within any isolated system, energy can neither be created nor destroyed, although it can be changed in form (for example, from chemical energy to heat energy). In other words, within an isolated system *the total quantity of energy remains constant*. The first law is therefore often called the law of conservation of energy. To use a familiar example, let's see how the first law applies to driving your car (Fig. 4-2). We can consider that your car (with a full tank of gas), the road, and the surrounding air roughly constitute an isolated system. When you drive your car, you convert the potential chemical energy of gasoline into kinetic energy of movement and heat energy. The total amount of energy that was in the gasoline before it was burned is the same as the total amount of this kinetic energy and heat.

An important rule of energy conversions is this: Energy always flows "downhill," from places with a high concentration of energy to places with a low concentration of energy. This is the principle behind engines. As we described in Chapter 2, temperature is a measure of how fast molecules move. The burning gasoline in your car's engine consists of molecules moving at extremely high speeds: a high concentration of energy. The cooler air outside the engine consists of molecules moving at much lower speeds: a low concentration of energy. The molecules in the engine hit the piston harder than the air molecules outside the engine do, so the piston moves upward, driving the gears that move the car. Work is done. When the engine is turned off, it cools down as heat is transferred from the warm engine to its cooler surroundings. The molecules on both sides of the piston move at the same speed, so the piston stays still. No work is done.

Source: Life on Earth by Audesirk/Audesirk, © 1997. Reprinted by permisson of Prentice-Hall, Inc., Upper Saddle River, NJ.

b. *Reading for practical application.* Imagine you have to give a presentation on this material the next time the class meets. On a separate sheet of paper, create an outline or think link that maps out the key elements you would discuss.

c. *Reading for comprehension.* Answer the following questions to determine the level of your comprehension.

Name the two types of energy.

_____

_____

Which one "stores" energy? _____

Can kinetic energy be turned into potential energy? _____

What term describes the basic properties and behaviors of energy?_____

_____

Mark the following statements as true (T) or false (F).

_____Within any isolated system, energy can be neither created nor destroyed.

_____Energy always flows downhill, from high concentration levels to low.

_____All interactions among pieces of matter are governed by two laws of thermodynamics.

_____Some parts of the universe are isolated from other parts.

EXERCISE 5: STUDYING CHARTS AND TABLES

Following is a series of four pie charts that appear in the Family chapter of the Macionis *Sociology* text. Look at the charts and answer the following questions:

1. Based on these charts, what specific points is this chapter section likely to cover?

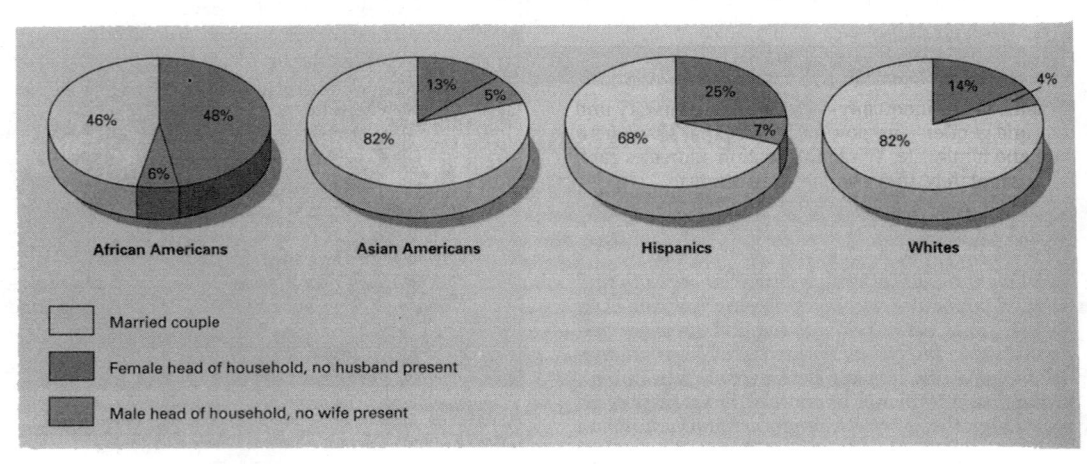

African Americans: 46%, 48%, 6%
Asian Americans: 82%, 13%, 5%
Hispanics: 68%, 25%, 7%
Whites: 82%, 14%, 4%

☐ Married couple
■ Female head of household, no husband present
■ Male head of household, no wife present

Family Form in the United States, 1993
Source: U.S. Bureau of the Census (1995).

Source: Sociology, 6/E by John J. Macionis, © 1997. Adapted by permission of Prentice-Hall, Inc., Upper Saddle River, NJ.

READING AND STUDYING: YOUR KEYS TO KNOWLEDGE / 359

2. What do these charts tell you about the different composition of African American, Asian American, Hispanic, and White families?

3. What does the title tell you about the content of the charts?

4. How might this chart will help you to understand key concepts?

Later in the Macionis *Sociology* text the following line chart appears in the Population and Urbanization chapter. Analyze the chart and answer the following questions:

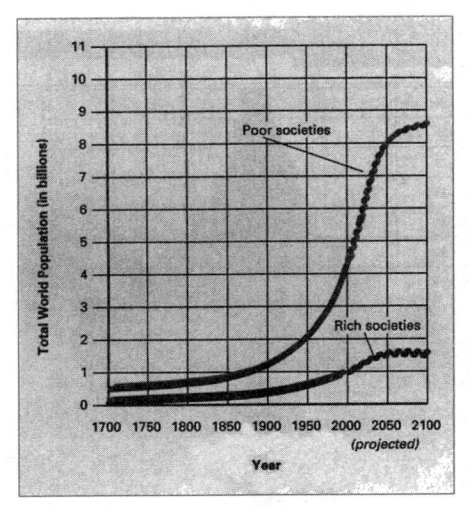

The Increase in World Population, 1700–2100

Source: Sociology, 6/E by John J. Macionis, © 1997. Adapted by permission of Prentice-Hall, Inc., Upper Saddle River, NJ.

1. Based on this chart, what specific points is this chapter section likely to cover?

   _____

   _____

2. What does the chart tell you about population trends in poor and rich societies?

   _____

   _____

   _____

3. What information is presented on the chart's vertical axis? What information is presented on the horizontal axis?

   _____

   _____

4. How will this chart help you to understand key concepts?

   _____

   _____

   _____

Key to Cooperative Learning: Building Teamwork Skills

Reading and Group Discussion. Divide into small groups, ideally groups of four. Take five minutes to read independently the excerpt from *Tools For Life* magazine. Each person should select one of the following questions to focus on while reading. If your group is smaller than four, eliminate unselected questions. If your group is larger than four, some questions may have to be shared between two group members.

1. What role do internships play in today's corporate hiring process?
2. If you were a manager for a company, why would you want to hire someone who had had one or two internships during college?
3. What did Dan Kosta gain from taking a semester off from school for his internship?
4. How would an intern learn about business from the bottom up?

Use your critical-reading skills to achieve your purpose of exploring your selected question. Focus on finding ideas that help to answer the question and examples that support those ideas. Consider other information you know, relevant to your question, that may be similar to or different from the material in the passage. If your questions looks for causes or effects, scan for them in the passage. Be sure to make notes as you write.

From "The New Rung on the Corporate Ladder,"
by Emma J. Taylor.

Gone are the days of the entry-level jobs; the internship has replaced it as the low rung on the corporate ladder. Summer internships have long been the de facto third semester of school, adding ballast and diversity to otherwise short résumés, but these days even three summer stints aren't always enough to secure you the right position. Recent grads are now turning to year-long postcollege internships, and undergrads are taking time off from school to fill low-paying or unpaid positions, all in the effort to prove they're ready to face the responsibility of full-time jobs. And employers are taking note.

"Work experience has a higher value than most educational experiences," says Patrick Scheetz, author of a nationwide hiring survey and director of the Collegiate Employment Research Institute at Michigan State University. "It is the employer's expectation," he explains. "If you went into heart surgery, you would ask if the surgeon had ever operated on a heart before. Why wouldn't an employer ask the same question of you?" Of last year's new hires, according to the survey, nearly 50 percent had completed career-related internships. "Work plays a big part in your development as a prospective employee," Scheetz says.

In other words, employers like to see you pay your dues.

Dan Kosta paid his when he took a semester off to intern with Paul Shaffer on *The Late Show with David Letterman*. He dealt with a lot of downtime and pulled some gofer details, but in the entertainment industry, as in many others, the mudsucking internship is virtually a prerequisite.

"It's backroom to backstage," Kosta says of his experience at *The Late Show*. "It's really about being there. I learned more about the entertainment industry in the first two weeks I was there than I could have taking any kind of class or reading any kind of book. It's just hands-on knowledge. You see how everything works, from the top to the bottom. And you're the bottom."

Source: An excerpt from "The New Rung on the Corporate Ladder."

When you have finished reading critically, gather together as a group. Each person (or pair) should take a turn presenting the question, the response and/or answer to the question that was derived through critical reading, and any other ideas that came up while reading. The group then has an opportunity to present any other ideas that they want to add to the discussion of that question. Continue until each person has had a chance to present what they worked on.

Key to Self-Expression: Discovery Through Journal Writing

To record your thoughts, use a separate journal.

Reading Challenges. What is your most difficult challenge when reading assigned materials? A challenge might be a particular kind of reading material, a reading situation, or the achievement of a certain goal when reading. Considering the tools this chapter presents, make a plan that addresses this challenge. What techniques might be able to help you most? How and when will you try them out? What positive effects do you anticipate they may have on you?

Key to Your Personal Portfolio: Your Paper Trail to Success

Evaluate Your Reading and Study Skills. On a separate sheet of paper, evaluate your current reading and studying skills. Analyze the current status of each of the following skill areas, what you are doing to improve your performance in each area, and your long-term and short-term goals for skill improvement. Define your short-term goal in terms of what you hope to accomplish after one month and your long-term goal in terms of what you hope to accomplish in one year.

Skill Areas

- Ability to define your reading purpose
- Progress in increasing your reading speed
- Progress in increasing your reading comprehension
- Vocabulary building
- Use of PQ3R
- Identification and use of text-previewing devices
- Participation in a study group
- Ability to understand and use visual aids

Use your item-by-item analysis as an action plan that will help you improve your skills. For example, if you currently spend no time building your vocabulary, your short-term goal may be to add five new words a week to your vocabulary, with your end-of-year goal the "ownership" of more than 200 new words. To accomplish this, you could do more reading and upgrade the quality of your reading material. One way to do this is to start reading a national paper like *The New York Times, Washington Post,* or *Wall Street Journal,* all of which are available on line and at your library. You may also want to keep a list of the unfamiliar words you encounter as you read, look them up in a dictionary, and use them in a sentence.

As part of your plan, prioritize the items on the list. For example, you may decide that your number-one priority is perfecting the use of PQ3R, while the item of least importance is forming a study group, since you study best alone.

As the year progresses, monitor your accomplishments in each area. You may decide to modify your action plan based on how the elements of the plan affect your school performance. If you work as well as attend class, consider the reading you have to do on the job—newspapers, journals, or any other information—along with your school reading when you activate your plan and monitor your progress.

APPENDIX C

Note Taking And Research:
Learning from Others

Both in school and out, you spend much of your time like a detective in search of knowledge. When you listen to your instructors during class lectures, do independent research, or learn on the job, you are uncovering and gathering information that you may put to use, now or in the future. Note-taking and research can empower you to create new ideas from what you learn. The more knowledge you gather in your "detective work," the more resources you have at your disposal when you soar ahead into new realms of thinking.

The search for knowledge requires varied skills. First, you need to use an effective note-taking system to record what you hear or read. Second, you need to know how to harness the vast resources of your college library. This chapter will show you note-taking and research skills that can help you make your searches for information successful.

How Does Taking Notes Help You?

Note-taking isn't always easy to do. You might feel that it prevents you from watching your instructor, or that you can't write fast enough, or that you seem to remember enough material even when you don't take notes. The act of note-taking, however, involves you in the learning process in many beneficial ways. Whatever you feel are the negative effects of note-taking, try weighing them against the potential positive effects. You may see why good note-taking can be a useful habit (see Table C-1).

Notes help you learn when you are in class, doing research, or studying. Since it is virtually impossible to take notes on everything you hear or read, the act of note-taking encourages you to think critically and evaluate what is worth remembering. Asking yourself questions like the following will help you judge what is important enough to write down.

- Do I need this information? •
- Is the information important to the lecture or reading or is it just an interesting comment?
- Is the information fact or opinion? If it is opinion, is it worth remembering?

Your responses will guide your note-taking in class and help you decide what to study before an exam. Similarly, the notes you take while doing research will influence your research efforts.

You have a number of different note-taking styles to choose from, including outlines, think links (mind maps), and the Cornell note-taking system. After you read about each one, base your choice on what feels right to you and what works best for the situation. For example, a student who generally prefers to take notes in think-link style might feel more comfortable using outline form for research.

Before you decide on a system, explore what class notes and research notes are and how to use each to your advantage.

How Can You Make the Most of Class Notes?

Class notes—the notes you take while listening to an instructor—may contain key terms and definitions (for example, Marketing research is . . .), explanations of complex concepts and processes (how a computer works; what happens during photosynthesis), or narratives of who did what to whom and when (The events that led to the Persian Gulf War include . . .). If lectures include material that is not in your text or if your instructor talks about specific test questions, your class notes become even more important as a study tool.

Table C–1. The Value of Notes

- Your notes provide written material that helps you study information and prepare for tests.
- When you take notes, you become an active, involved listener and learner.
- Notes help you think critically and organize ideas.
- The information you learn in class may not appear in any text; you will have no way to study it with outwriting it down.
- If it is difficult for you to process information while in class, having notes to read and make sense of later can help you learn.
- Note-taking allows you to compile information from different research sources and use the information in your writing.
- Note-taking is a skill that you will use on the job and in your personal life.

Preparing to Take Class Notes

Your class notes have two purposes: First, they should reflect what you heard in class, and second, they should be a resource for studying, writing, or comparing with your text material. Taking good class notes depends on good preparation, including the following:

- Use separate pieces of 8 1/2 -by-11-inch paper for each class. If you use a three-ring binder, punch holes in papers your instructor hands out and insert them immediately following your notes for that day.
- Take a comfortable seat where you can easily see and hear, and be ready to write as soon as the instructor begins speaking.
- Choose a note-taking system that helps you handle the instructor's speaking style (you'll be more able to determine this style after a few classes). While one instructor may deliver organized lectures at a normal speaking rate, another may jump from topic to topic or talk very quickly.
- If your instructor assigns reading on a lecture topic, you may choose to complete the reading before class so that the lecture becomes more of a review than an introduction.
- Set up a support system with a student in each class. That way, when you are absent, you can get the notes you missed.

What to Do During Class

Because no one has the time to write down everything he or she hears, the following strategies will help you choose and record what you feel is important, in a format that you can read and understand later.

- Date each page. When you take several pages of notes during a lecture, add an identifying letter or number to the date on each page: 11/27A, 11/27B, 11/27C, or 11/27—1 of 3, 11/27—2 of 3, 11/27—3 of 3. This will help you keep track of the order of your pages.
- Add the specific topic of the lecture at the top of the page. For example: 11/27A—*U. S. Immigration Policy After World War II*

    Since an instructor may revisit a topic days or even weeks after introducing it, this suggestion will help you gather all your notes on the same topic when it is time to study.

- If your instructor jumps from topic to topic during a single class, it may help to start a new page for each new topic.
- Some students prefer to use only one side of the note paper, because this can make notes easier to read and avoid the problem of flipping back and forth when studying. Others prefer to use both sides, which can be a more economical paper-saving option. Choose what works best for you.

- Record whatever your instructor emphasizes. See Figure C–1 for more details about how an instructor might call attention to particular information.
- Write down all key terms and definitions. If, for example, your instructor is discussing the stages of mental development in children, as defined by psychologist Jean Piaget, your notes should certainly mention the following terms: *sensorimotor, preoperational, concrete operations, formal operations.*
- Continue to take notes during class discussions and question-and-answer periods. When your fellow students ask for help, the explanations may help you as well.
- Write down all questions raised by the instructor, since the same questions may appear on a test.
- Leave one or more blank spaces between points. This white space will help you review your notes, because information will be in self-contained segments. (This suggestion does not apply if you are using a think link.)
- Draw pictures and diagrams that help illustrate ideas.
- Write quickly but legibly. This may involve using a form of shorthand (see the section on shorthand on p. 375 of this appendix).
- Indicate material that is especially important with a star, underlining, a highlighter pen, a different color pen, or capital letters.
- If you cannot understand what the instructor is saying, leave a space where the explanation belongs and place a question mark in the margin. Then ask the instructor to explain it again after class or discuss it with a classmate. Fill in the blank when the idea is clear.

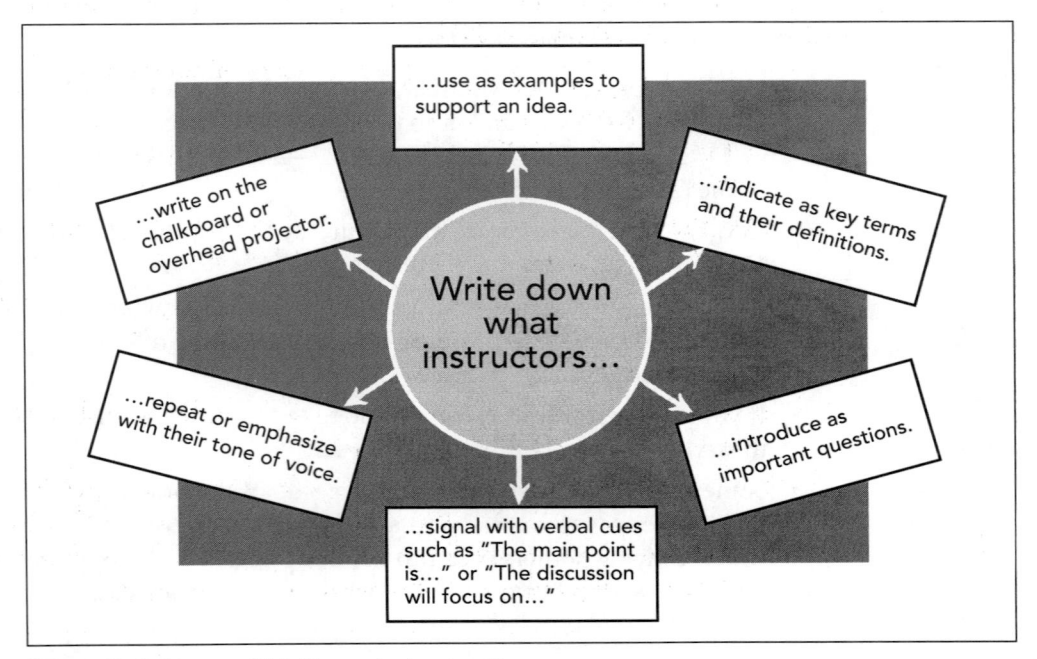

Figure C–1. How to Pick Up on Instructor Cues.

- Take notes until the instructor stops speaking. Students who stop writing a few minutes before the class is over may miss critical information.
- Make your notes as legible, organized, and complete as possible. Your notes are only useful if you can read and understand them.

Make Notes a Valuable After-Class Reference

Class notes are a valuable study tool when you review them regularly. The act of reviewing helps you remember important concepts and links new information to information you already know.

If you can, try to begin your review within a day of the lecture. Read over your notes to learn the information, clarify difficult concepts and shorthand abbreviations, fill in missing information, and underline or highlight key points. You may also want to add headings and subheadings, and insert clarifying phrases or sentences. Try to review each week's notes at the end of that week. Think critically about the material, in writing, study-group discussions, or quiet reflective thought, using the following questions.

Can I easily recall the facts I have written?

What do these ideas mean? What examples support or negate them?

How do I evaluate these ideas? Why are they important? How fully do I understand them?

What similar facts or ideas does this information call to mind?

How does this information differ from what I already know?

What new ideas can I form from learning this information?

How do these ideas, facts, and statements relate to one another? Do any of them have cause and effect relationships?

Writing a **summary** of your notes is another important review technique. Summarizing involves critically evaluating which ideas and examples are most important and then rewriting the material in a shortened form, focusing on those important ideas and examples. You may prefer to summarize as you review your notes, although you might also try summarizing your notes from memory after you review them.

> **Summary,** The substance of a body of material, presented in a condensed form by reducing it to its main points.

Study groups can be a useful way to review notes, because group members can benefit from each other's different perspectives and abilities. For example, if you happened to focus well on one particular part of the lecture and lost concentration during another, a fellow student may have been taking good notes on the part you missed. If you are a part of a study group, compare your notes with the notes of other group members to make sure they are complete and accurate. If there are gaps, fill them in. If another explanation seems to make more sense than the one you have, copy it down.

Your class notes will help you study for tests. Use them along with your textbook, text study notes, and other sources. Your notes may help you predict what will be covered on a test and may even point to specific test questions.

Class notes are only one form of note-taking. Research notes are another key to school success.

What Are Research Notes and How Can You Use Them?

Research notes are the notes you take while gathering information to answer a research question. Research notes take two forms: source notes and content notes.

Source notes are the preliminary notes you take as you review available research. They include vital bibliographic information as well as a short summary and critical evaluation of the work. Write these notes when you consider a book or article interesting enough to look at again. They do not signal that you have actually read something all the way through, only that you plan to review it later on.

The bibliographic information that every source note should include is the author's full name; the title of the work; the edition (if any); the publisher, year, and city of publication; and the page numbers you consulted. (Depending on the source, other information may also be needed, such as an issue and volume number for a magazine.) Many students find that index cards work best for source notes. See Figure C–2 for an example of how you can write source notes on index cards.

The second type of research notes are *content notes*. Unlike brief informational source notes, content notes provide an in-depth look at the source, taken during a thorough reading. Use them to record the information you need to write your draft. Here are some suggestions for taking effective content notes:

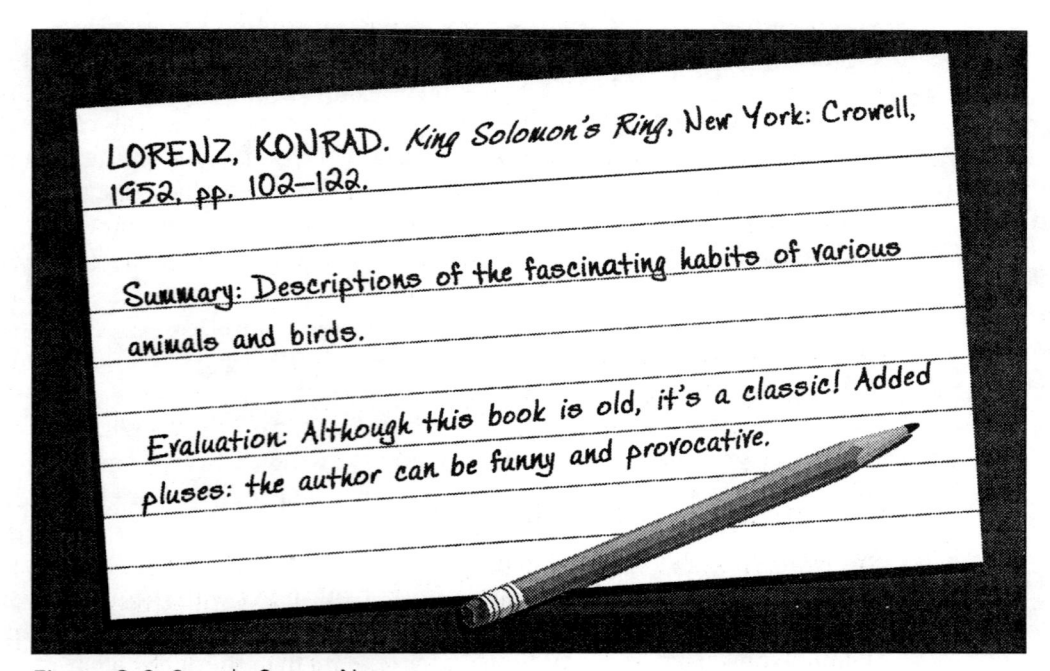

LORENZ, KONRAD. *King Solomon's Ring.* New York: Crowell, 1952. pp. 102–122.

Summary: Descriptions of the fascinating habits of various animals and birds.

Evaluation: Although this book is old, it's a classic! Added pluses: the author can be funny and provocative.

Figure C–2. Sample Source Note.

- When a source looks promising, begin reading it and summarizing what you read. Use standard notebook paper that fits into a three-ring binder. This gives you space to write as well as the flexibility to rearrange the pages into any order that makes sense. (If you prefer using large index cards for content notes, choose four-by-six or five-by-eight-inch sizes.)
- Include bibliographic information and page numbers for every source.
- Limit each page to a single source.
- If you take notes on more than one subject from a single source, create a separate page for each subject.
- If the notes on a source require more than one page, label the pages and number them sequentially. Reference the title of the source in how you label the pages. For example, if the particular source is a magazine entitled *Business Week*, your pages might be labeled BW1, BW2, BW3, and so on.
- Identify the type of note that appears on each page. Evaluate whether it is a summary in your own words, a quotation, or a **paraphrase**.
- Write your summary notes in any of the note-taking systems described later in this appendix.

> **Paraphrase.** A restatement of a written text or passage in another form or other words; often to clarify meaning.

Different kinds of notations that you make directly on photocopies of sources—marginal notes, highlighting, and underlining—can supplement your content notes. Say, for example, that you are writing a paper on the psychological development of adolescent girls. During your research, you photocopy an article written by Dr. Carol Gilligan, who is an expert in the field. On the photocopy, you highlight important information and make marginal notes that detail your immediate reactions to some of the author's key points. Then you take content notes on the article. When it is time to write your paper, you have two different and helpful resources to consult.

Try to divide your time as equally as possible between photocopy notes and content notes. If you use photocopies as your primary reference without making any of your own content notes, you may have more work to do when you begin writing, because you will need to spend time putting the source material in your own words. Writing paraphrases and summaries in content notes ahead of time will save you some work later in the process.

Whether you are taking notes in class or while doing research, there are different note-taking systems from which you can choose.

What Note-Taking System Should You Use?

The choice is yours. You will benefit most from the system that feels most comfortable to you. Everyone has a different learning and working style, so don't wedge yourself into a system that doesn't work for you. The most common note-taking systems include outlines, the Cornell system, and think links.

Taking Notes in Outline Form

When a reading assignment or lecture seems well organized, you may choose to take notes in outline form. *Outlining* shows the relationships among ideas and their supporting examples through the use of line-by-line phrases set off by varying indentations. When you use an outline, you construct a line-by-line representation of how ideas relate to one another and are supported by facts and examples.

FORMAL VS. INFORMAL OUTLINES

Formal outlines indicate ideas and examples using Roman numerals, capital and lowercase letters, and numbers. The rules of formal outlines require at least two headings on the same level. That is, if you have a II A you must also have a II B. Similarly, if you have a III A 1 you must also have a III A 2. In contrast, *informal outlines* show the same relationships but replace the formality with a system of consistent indenting and dashes. Figure C–3 shows the difference between the two outline forms. Because making a formal outline can take time and focus, many students find that the time pres-

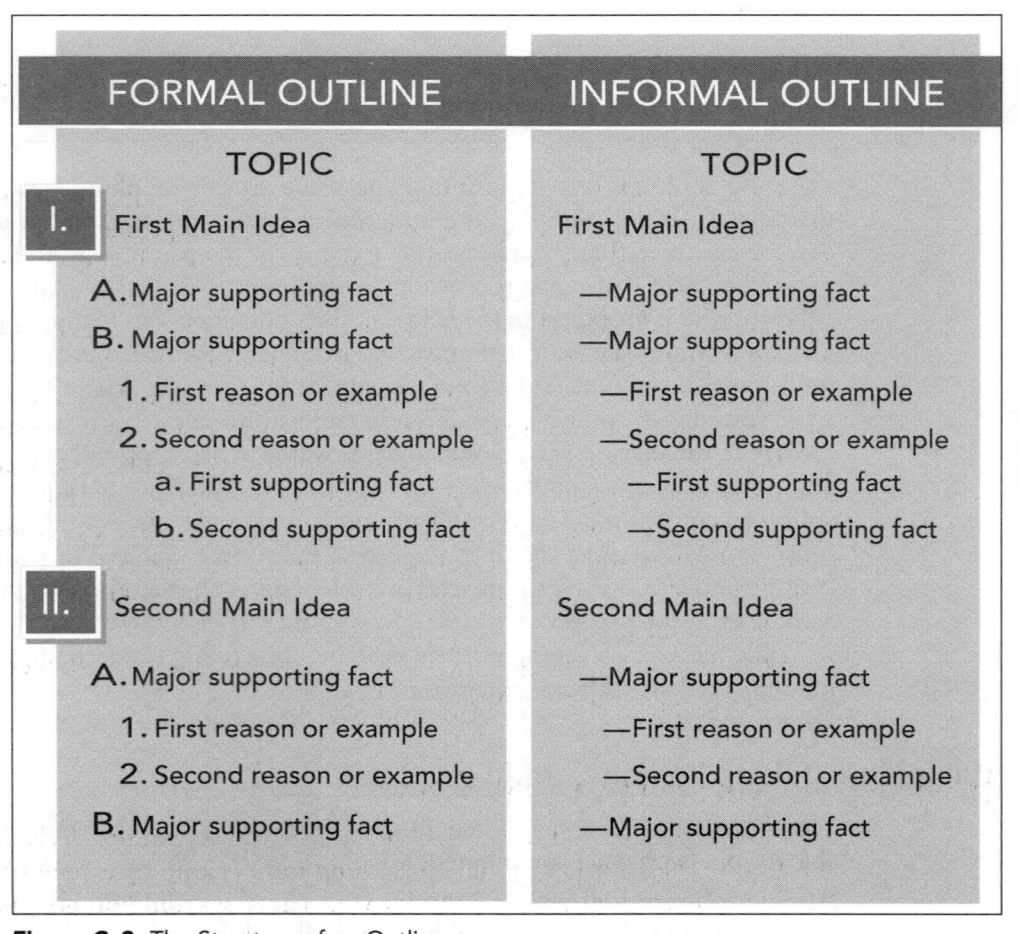

FORMAL OUTLINE	INFORMAL OUTLINE
TOPIC	TOPIC
I. First Main Idea	First Main Idea
A. Major supporting fact	—Major supporting fact
B. Major supporting fact	—Major supporting fact
1. First reason or example	—First reason or example
2. Second reason or example	—Second reason or example
a. First supporting fact	—First supporting fact
b. Second supporting fact	—Second supporting fact
II. Second Main Idea	Second Main Idea
A. Major supporting fact	—Major supporting fact
1. First reason or example	—First reason or example
2. Second reason or example	—Second reason or example
B. Major supporting fact	—Major supporting fact

Figure C–3. The Structure of an Outline.

sures of in-class note-taking make using formal outlines difficult. You might be more able to keep up if you use an informal one instead.

Figure C–4 shows how a student has used the structure of a formal outline to write notes on the topic of civil-rights legislation.

When you use an outline to write class notes, you may have trouble when an instructor rambles or jumps from point to point. The best advice in this case is to abandon the outline structure for the time being. Focus instead on taking down whatever information you can and on drawing connections among key topics. After class, try to restructure your notes and, if possible, rewrite them in outline form.

GUIDED NOTES

From time to time an instructor may give you a guide to help you take notes in the class, usually in the form of an outline. This outline may be on a page that you receive at the beginning of the class, on the board, or on an overhead projector.

Civil Rights Legislation: 1860–1968

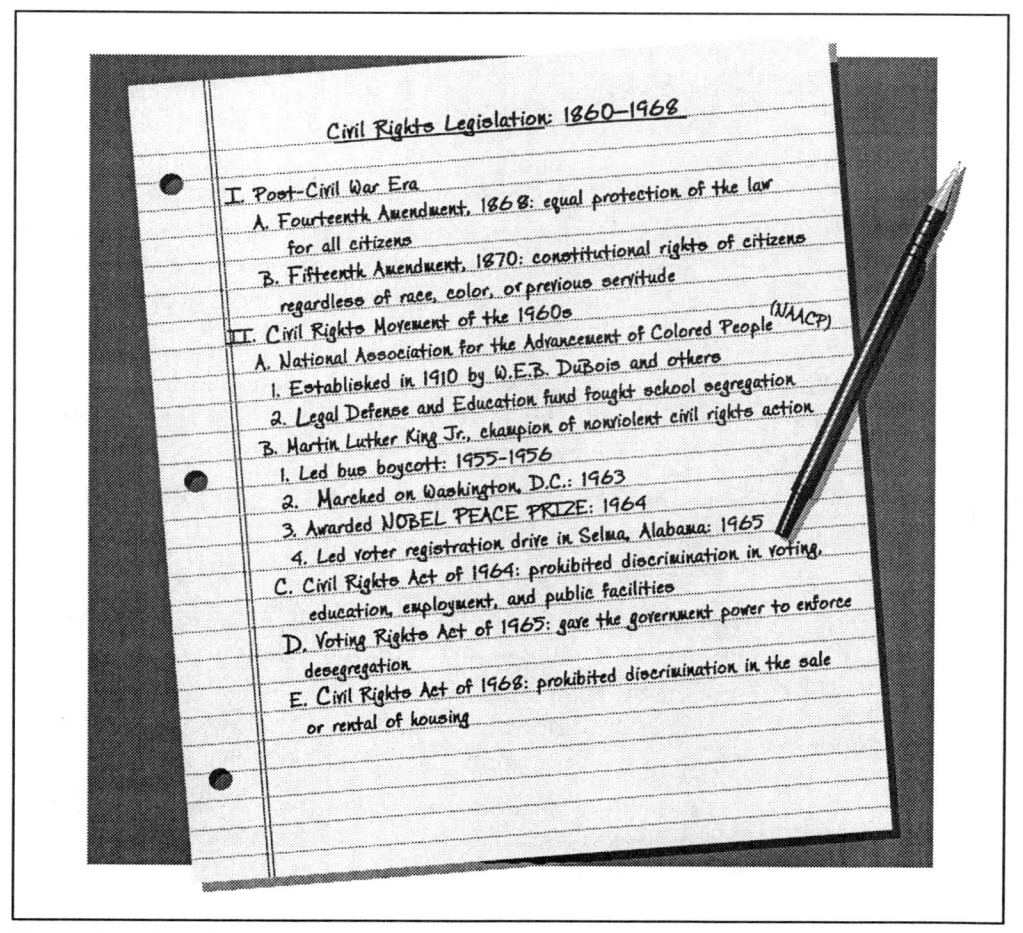

I. Post-Civil War Era
   A. Fourteenth Amendment, 1868: equal protection of the law for all citizens
   B. Fifteenth Amendment, 1870: constitutional rights of citizens regardless of race, color, or previous servitude
II. Civil Rights Movement of the 1960s
   A. National Association for the Advancement of Colored People (NAACP)
     1. Established in 1910 by W.E.B. DuBois and others
     2. Legal Defense and Education fund fought school segregation
   B. Martin Luther King Jr., champion of nonviolent civil rights action
     1. Led bus boycott: 1955–1956
     2. Marched on Washington, D.C.: 1963
     3. Awarded NOBEL PEACE PRIZE: 1964
     4. Led voter registration drive in Selma, Alabama: 1965
   C. Civil Rights Act of 1964: prohibited discrimination in voting, education, employment, and public facilities
   D. Voting Rights Act of 1965: gave the government power to enforce desegregation
   E. Civil Rights Act of 1968: prohibited discrimination in the sale or rental of housing

Figure C–4. Sample Formal Outline.

Although *guided notes* help you follow the lecture and organize your thoughts during class, they do not replace your own notes. Because they are more of a basic outline of topics than a comprehensive coverage of information, they require that you fill in what they do not cover in detail. If you tune out because you think that the guided notes are all you need, you will most likely miss out on important information.

When you receive guided notes on paper, write directly on the paper if there is room. If not, use a separate sheet and write on it the outline categories that the guided notes suggest. If the guided notes are on the board or overhead, copy them down, leaving plenty of space in between for your own notes.

Using the Cornell Note-taking System

The *Cornell note-taking system*, also known as the T-note system, was developed more than forty-five years ago by Walter Pauk at Cornell University. Since then, the system has become widely accepted and is now used by students throughout the world.

The system is successful because it is simple—and because it works. It consists of three sections on ordinary note paper:

- *Section 1*, the largest section, is on the right. Here you record your notes in informal outline form.
- *Section 2*, to the left of your notes, is known as the *cue column.* Leave it blank while you read or listen, then fill it in later as you review. You might fill it with comments that highlight main ideas, clarify meaning, suggest examples, or link ideas and examples. You can even draw diagrams.
- *Section 3*, at the bottom of the page, is known as the *summary area.* Here you use a sentence or two to summarize the notes on the page. Use this section during the review process to reinforce concepts and provide an overview of what the notes say.

When you use the Cornell system, create the note-taking structure before class begins. Picture an upside-down letter T as you follow these directions, and use Figure C–5 on the next page as your guide.

- Start with a sheet of standard loose-leaf paper. Label it with the date and title of the lecture.
- To create the *cue column*:
  Draw a vertical line about two and a half inches from the left side of the paper. End the line about two inches from the bottom of the sheet.
- To create the *summary area*:
  Starting at the point where the vertical line ends (about two inches from the bottom of the page), draw a horizontal line that spans the entire paper.

Figure C–5 shows how a student used the Cornell system to take notes in an introduction-to-business course.

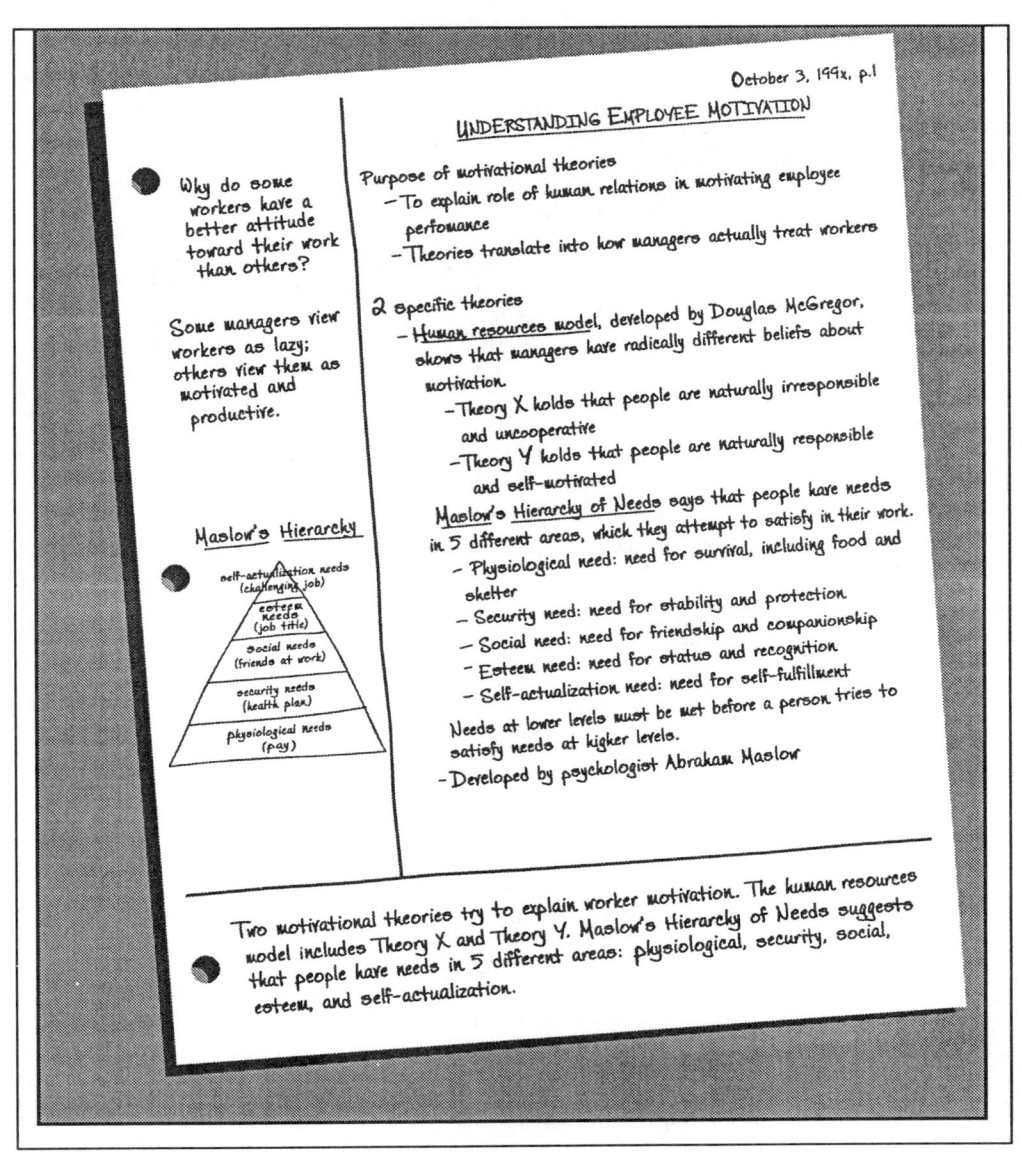

Figure C–5. Notes Taken Using the Cornell System.

Creating a Think Link

A *think link*, also known as a mind map, is a visual form of note-taking. When you draw a think link, you diagram ideas using shapes and lines that link ideas and supporting details and examples. The visual design makes the connections easy to see, and the use of shapes and pictures extends the material beyond just words. Many learners respond well to the power of **visualization**. You can use think links to brainstorm ideas for paper topics as well.

> **Visualization,** The interpretaton of verbal ideas through the use of mental visual images.

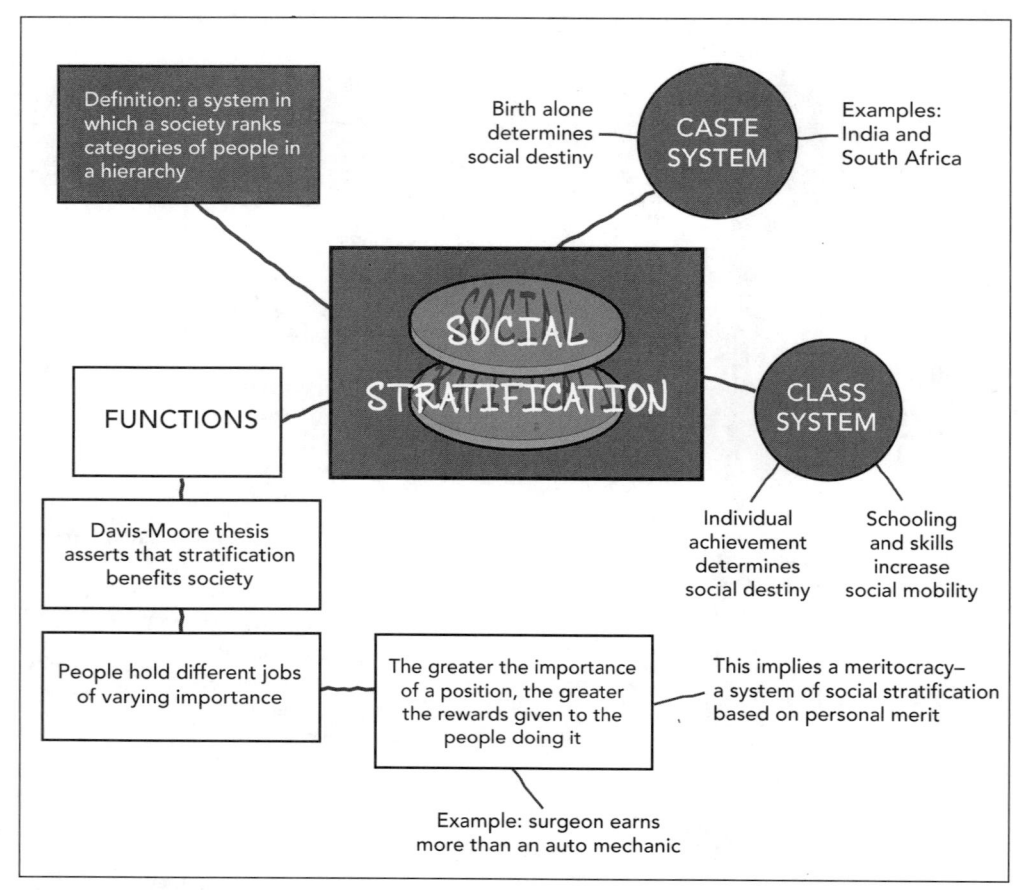

```
                        CASTE
Definition: a system in    Birth alone    SYSTEM    Examples:
which a society ranks    determines                India and
categories of people in   social destiny            South Africa
a hierarchy
                    
                    SOCIAL
                    STRATIFICATION
                                            CLASS
         FUNCTIONS                          SYSTEM

                                    Individual      Schooling
                                    achievement     and skills
                                    determines      increase
                                    social destiny  social mobility
Davis-Moore thesis
asserts that stratification
benefits society

People hold different jobs   The greater the importance   This implies a meritocracy—
of varying importance        of a position, the greater    a system of social stratification
                             the rewards given to the     based on personal merit
                             people doing it

                        Example: surgeon earns
                        more than an auto mechanic
```

Figure C–6. Sample Think Link

One way to create a think link is to start by circling your topic in the middle of a sheet of unlined paper. Next, draw a line from the circled topic and write the name of the first major idea at the end of that line. Circle the idea also. Then draw lines from that circle, noting at the ends of those lines specific facts related to the circled idea. Continue the process, connecting thoughts to one another using circles, lines, and words. Figure C–6 shows a think link on social stratification—a concept presented during a sociology class—that follows this particular structure.

You can design any kind of think link that feels comfortable to you. Different examples include stair steps showing connected ideas that build toward a conclusion, a tree shape with roots as causes and branches as effects, or a sun shape with a central idea and facts radiating out from the center. Figure C–7 shows a type of think link sometimes referred to as a "jellyfish."

A think link may be difficult to construct in class, especially if your instructor talks quickly. In this case, use another note-taking system during class. Then make a think link as part of the process of reviewing your notes.

Once you choose a note-taking system, your success will depend on how well you use it to record vital information. Learning some form of personal shorthand will help you make the most of whatever system you choose.

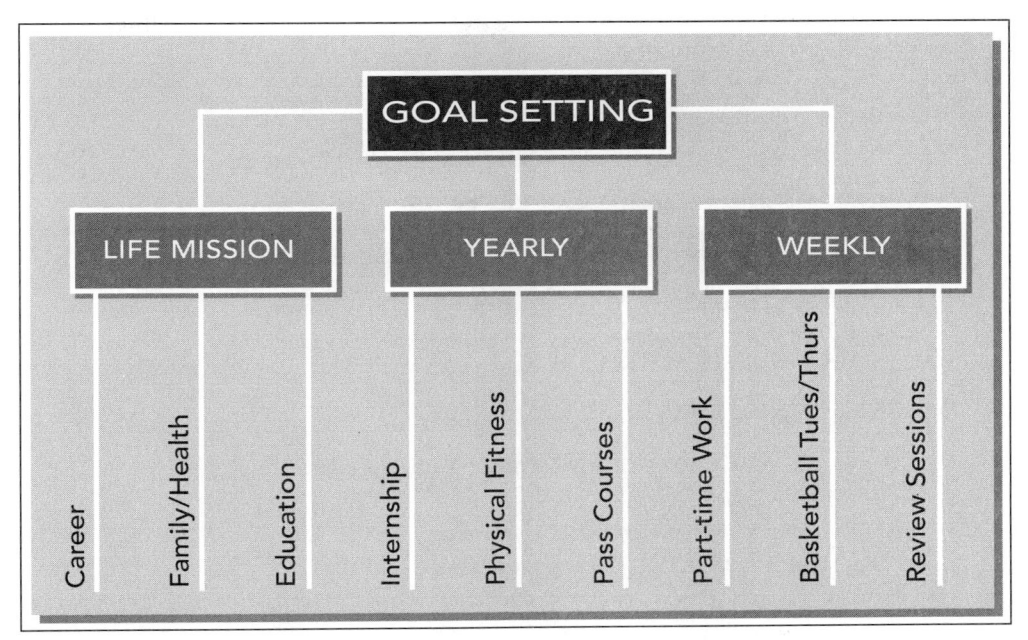

Figure C-7. The "Jellyfish" Think Link

How Can You Write Faster When Taking Notes?

When taking notes in class, many students feel they have trouble keeping up with the instructor. You may have had this feeling, hurrying along in a game of catch-up, sensing that you are always a few sentences behind. Using some personal shorthand (not standard secretarial shorthand) can help to push the pen faster.

Personal shorthand uses abbreviations and shortened words in addition to replacing words or parts of words with symbols. Because you are the only intended reader, you can misspell and abbreviate words in ways that only you understand. The only danger with shorthand is that you might forget what your writing means. To avoid this problem, review your shorthand notes while your abbreviations and symbols are fresh in your mind. If there is any confusion, spell out words as you review.

How do you write shorthand? Here are some suggestions that will help you master this important skill:

1. Use the following standard abbreviations in place of complete words:

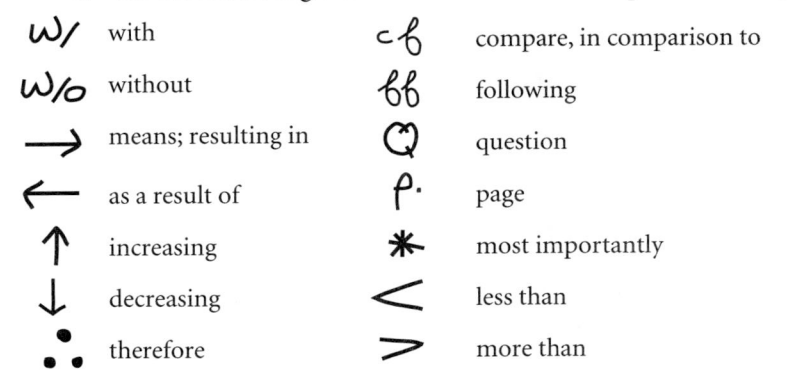

w/	with	cf	compare, in comparison to
w/o	without	ff	following
→	means; resulting in	Q	question
←	as a result of	p.	page
↑	increasing	*	most importantly
↓	decreasing	<	less than
∴	therefore	>	more than

☺	because	=	equals
≈	approximately	%	percent
+ or &	and	Δ	change
—	minus; negative	2	to; two; too
NO. or #	number	vs	versus; against
i.e.	that is,	eg	for example
etc.	and so forth	c/o	care of
ng	no good	lb	pound

2. Shorten words by removing vowels from the middle of words:
   - prps = purpose
   - knlge = knowledge
   - lwyr = lawyer
   - Crvtte = Corvette (as on a vanity license plate for a car)
   - hstry = history
   - cmptr = computer

3. Substitute word beginnings for entire words:
   - assoc = associate; association
   - info = information
   - subj = subject
   - mixt = mixture
   - chem = chemical; chemistry
   - rep = representative
   - min = minimum
   - max = maximum

4. Form plurals by adding s to shortened words:
   - prblms = problems
   - mchns = machines
   - drctrys = directories
   - prntrs = printers

5. Make up your own symbols and use them consistently:
   - b/4 = before
   - 4tn = fortune
   - 2thake = toothache

6. Learn to rely on key phrases instead of complete sentences.
   For example, write "German—nouns capitalized" instead of "In the German language, all nouns are capitalized."

7. Use standard or informal abbreviations for proper nouns such as places, people, companies, scientific substances, events, and so on.
   LA—Louisiana
   D.C. —Washington, D.C.
   It. —Italy
   FMC—Ford Motor Company
   H_2O—water
   Moz. —Wolfgang Amadeus Mozart
   WWII—World War II
8. If you know you are going to repeat a particular word or phrase often throughout the course of a class period, write it out once at the beginning of the class and then establish an abbreviation that you will use through the rest of your notes, writing that abbreviation in parentheses following the full name. For example, if you are taking notes on the rise and fall of Argentina's former first lady Eva Peron, you might start out writing "Eva Peron (EP)" and then use "EP" throughout the rest of the class period.

One important reason for taking notes is to record information you gather during research. Research involves a systematic search for information.

Thinking Back

1. List three reasons why note-taking is important in college.

   a. _____

   b. _____

   c. _____

2. Identify two steps for each stage of class note-taking (before, during, and after class).

Before class: _____

_____

_____

During class: _____

_____

_____

After class: _____

_____

_____

_____

3. Explain the differences between source notes and content notes.

_____

_____

4. Look back at the different note-taking systems discussed in this chapter. Consider one particular course you are currently taking. Which system are you likely to use in that class, and why? Which system are you likely to use while doing research for a paper for that class, and why?

_____

_____

_____

5. Rewrite, and shorten, the following paragraph using shorthand symbols.

When you start a new writing project, you face many decisions even before you sit at a keyboard or pick up a pen. What is the most efficient way to sort out all you need to think about? Start by focusing separately on groups of decisions about topic, purpose, audience, and the specific writing situation. Then try to fit the groups together, adjusting them to create a whole.

_____

_____

_____

Thinking Ahead

1. How do you think you will use research in the career you plan to enter? If you currently work, how do you use research on the job right now?

_____

_____

2. What specific search tools do you expect to find in your school library?

_____

_____

3. How have you used computers to explore the resources of your library? Why do you think library computers have changed the research process?

_____

_____

What Is the Research Process?

When you use sources available at your library and through your computer to systematically search for information, you are engaged in the *research process.* It is through this process that you attempt to find information that will answer your research question. The most useful research sources are usually those that are well known, well supported, balanced, and current.

How do you begin the research process? One of your first steps should be to learn about your library, its resources, and its layout. While some schools have only one library, other schools have a library network that includes one or more central libraries and smaller, specialized libraries that focus on specific academic areas such as math, science, or business. Answer these questions and you will be well on your way to understanding how your library operates:

1. Where is the general reference collection?
2. Where is the specialized reference collection?
3. Is the book catalog computerized or on cards or are both systems available?
4. What periodical (journal, magazine, and newspaper) indexes does the library have, and are they in book form or on computer?
5. Does the library use an open-stack system for books (you are allowed to find materials on your own) or does it have a closed system (library holdings are off limits to everyone but official personnel who get you what you need)?
6. Do you have access to magazines and journals and in what form will you find them? (Many libraries display periodicals that are a year or two old and convert older copies to microfilm or microfiche.)
7. Does the library have any special collections, including files of corporate annual reports and local, state, and federal government documents?

The answers to these questions can be found in the library itself. Take advantage of library tours, training sessions, and descriptive pamphlets for students. Also, spend time walking around the library on your own to discover what it has to offer. If you still have questions, ask a librarian. A simple question can save hours of searching.

How Do You Use a Search Strategy To Conduct Research?

When you have a general idea of where everything is, you can begin your search for information. This involves following a specific *search strategy*—a step-by-step method for finding information that takes you from general to specific sources as you investigate your research question. Starting with general sources usually works best, because they give you an overview of your research topic and lead you to more specific information. For example, an encyclopedia article on your topic may include the name of an important book or expert in the area that you can then track down.

A library search strategy involves checking general and specific reference works, the catalog of books, periodical indexes, and electronic sources, including the Internet (see Figure C–8).

Use General Reference Works

Begin your research with *general reference works*. These works cover hundreds—and sometimes thousands—of different topics in a broad, nondetailed way. General reference guides are found in the front of most libraries and are often available on

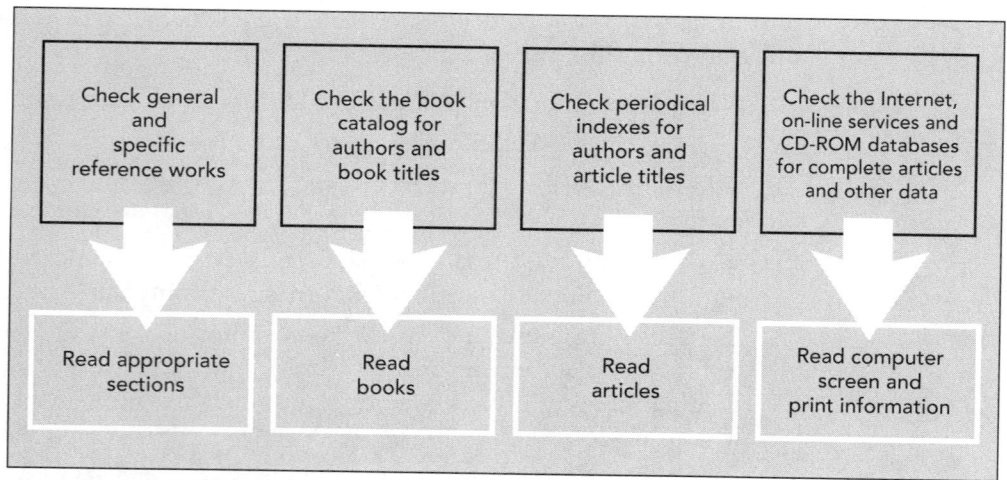

Check general and specific reference works	Check the book catalog for authors and book titles	Check periodical indexes for authors and article titles	Check the Internet, on-line services and CD-ROM databases for complete articles and other data
↓	↓	↓	↓
Read appropriate sections	Read books	Read articles	Read computer screen and print information

Figure C–8. Library Search Strategy.

CD-ROM. You access this information by inserting the disk into a specially designed computer. Among the works that fall into this category are:

- encyclopedias—for example, the multivolume *Encyclopaedia Britannica* and the single-volume *New Columbia Encyclopedia*
- almanacs—*The Word Almanac* and *Book of Facts*
- yearbooks—*The Statistical Abstract of the United States*
- dictionaries—*Webster's New World College Dictionary*
- biographical reference works—*Who's Who in America* and *Webster's Biographical Dictionary*
- bibliographies—*Books in Print*

> **CD-ROM** A computer disk, containing millions of words and images, that can be read by a computer. (CD-ROM stands for "compact disk read-only memory.")

Search Specialized Reference Works

After you have a general overview of your topic, look at *specialized reference works* to find more specific facts. Specialized reference works include encyclopedias and dictionaries that focus on a narrow field. Although the entries you find in these volumes are short summaries, they focus on critical ideas and on the key words you will need to conduct additional research. Bibliographies that accompany the articles point you to the names and works of recognized experts. Here are some titles of specialized reference works organized by subject area:

Fine Arts (including music, art, film, television and theater)
- *International Cyclopedia of Music and Musicians*
- *Oxford Companion to Art*
- *International Encyclopedia of Film*
- *International Television Almanac*

History
- *Dictionary of American Biography*
- *Encyclopedia of American History*
- *New Cambridge Modern History*

Science and Technology
- *Encyclopedia of Computer Science and Technology*
- *The Encyclopedia of Biological Sciences*
- *The McGraw-Hill Encyclopedia of Science and Technology*

Social Sciences
- *Dictionary of Education*
- *Encyclopedia of Psychology*
- *International Encyclopedia of the Social Sciences*

Use the Library Book Catalog

Usually found near the front of the library, the *book catalog* lists every book the library owns. The listings usually appear in three separate categories: authors' names, book titles, and subjects. Not too long ago, most libraries stored their book catalog on index-sized cards in hundreds of small drawers. Today, many libraries have replaced these cards with computer systems. Using a terminal that has access to the library's computer records, you can conduct an electronic search by specific author, title, and subject.

The computerized catalog in your college library is probably connected to the holdings of other college and university libraries. This gives you an on-line search capacity, which means that if you don't find the book you want in your local library, you can track it down in another library and request it through an interlibrary loan. *Interlibrary loan* is a system used by many colleges to allow students to borrow materials from a library other than the one at their school. Students request materials through their own library, where the materials are eventually delivered by the outside library. When you are in a rush, keep in mind that an outside library may take a substantial amount of time to deliver the materials you request.

Use Periodical Indexes to Search for Periodicals

Periodicals are magazines, journals, and newspapers that are published on a regular basis throughout the year. Examples include *Time*, *Newsweek*, *Business Week*, *Journal of the American Medical Association*, and *Science*. Many libraries display periodicals up to a year or two old and convert older copies to **microfilm** or **microfiche**. Reading microfilm or microfiche requires special viewing machines, available in most libraries.

> **Microfilm,** A reel of film on which printed materials are photographed at greatly reduced size for ease of storage.
>
> **Microfiche,** A card or sheet of microfilm that contains a considerable number of pages of printed text and/or photographs in reduced form.

Finding articles in publications involves a search of periodical indexes. The most widely used general index is the *Reader's Guide to Periodical Literature*, available on CD-ROM and in book form. *The Reader's Guide* indexes articles in more than 100 general-interest magazines and journals. Two general indexes that appear only in computerized form are *Info-trac* and *Academic Abstracts*.

REAL WORLD PERSPECTIVE
How can I conduct a successful research project?

Kathleen Cole, Gonzaga University
I returned to school when I was 41 years old. My marriage had broken up, so I wanted to develop new skills that would help me better provide for myself and my daughter. I had already gone to school for three years when I was just out of high school but it was a conservatory of music and I didn't have to use any research or study skills, other than to memorize songs. Now that I'm at a university, I'm realizing just how limited I am at some of these skills. I'd eventually like to go on to get a master's degree, so it is crucial I learn how to function in the library and research information.

Whenever I'm given a research project, I go right to the help desk and whoever is there finds everything I need for me. I'd like to be able to do it myself. After that, I check out the books, take them home, and read the chapters I think are relevant to my paper. But here's the dilemma: I don't know how to reference the materials I use. If I summarize, do I still need to refer to the author? Also, how much of my research paper should be about what others believe? Am I supposed to just quote the current and past beliefs or do I add my own opinions and conclusions? Finally, when I reference, do I put the small numbers at the bottom of the page or do I write a full bibliography in the back?

Giuseppe Morella, Public Relations Major, Gonzaga University
Most libraries provide orientation sessions to show students how to use the library. A library worker can help you learn to find what you need. Even if you know a lot about libraries in general, getting to know your school's library is essential, since each library has special resources that you might never find out about if you don't ask.

Before you take books home from the library, you can skim them to see which ones will be most useful. Then, at home, you can take notes on index cards so that it will be easier to organize and reference your paper. Label a top corner of each card with the general topic of the fact or quotation. In another corner, write the name of the book you're citing from, and in a third corner, mark the page number. As for referencing, you need to cite everything that is not either your own idea or general knowledge. If you summarize another's material, you do not need to use quotation marks, but you still need to cite the author. You can use either footnotes, parentheticals, or endnotes, depending on what your professor wants. You also need a bibliography or "works cited" page at the end. There are many good style books that give detailed instructions for citing all kinds of material.

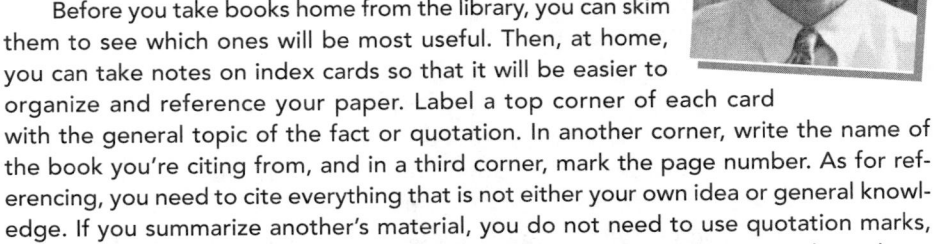

Deciding how much of your own opinion to use can be tricky. If you are unsure about a particular assignment, you can check with the professor. In general, a "research paper" indicates that you are supposed to find out what others believe. But you should also think critically. After assessing the information, what conclusions do you reach, and why? A research paper is an exercise in learning from others and deciding for yourself.

Specialized periodical indexes focus on magazines and journals in narrow subject areas, such as history, art, and nursing. Many of the following indexes can be found in electronic or book form:

Business and Economics	*ABI-Inform*	*Art Index*
Education Index	*Humanities Index*	*Music Index*
Medicine and Nursing	*Medline*	*Psychological Abstracts*
Religion and History	*Science and Technology*	*Social Science Index*

Almost no library owns all the publications listed in these and other specialized indexes. However, journals that are not part of your library's collection may be available via interlibrary loan.

Conduct Electronic Research

You will also find complete source material through a variety of electronic sources, including the Internet, on-line services, and CD-ROM. Here is a sampling of the kind of information you will find:

- complete articles from thousands of journals and magazines
- complete articles from newspapers around the world
- government data on topics as varied as agriculture, transportation, and labor
- business documents, including corporate annual reports

Your library is probably connected to the Internet, a worldwide computer network that links government, university, research, and business computers along an electronic network often referred to as the Information Superhighway. Tapping into the World-Wide Web—a tool for searching the huge libraries of information stored on the Internet—gives you access to billions of written words and graphic images.

As a researcher, your main challenge is to navigate the Internet without wasting hours trying to find what you need. Because the Internet is so vast, this book contains an Internet Research Appendix to help you explore it. After reading this Appendix, you will have many tools to aid you on your journeys along the Information Superhighway. A good place to begin is with your own school: If your college has its own Internet home page, spend some time browsing through it.

Although most libraries do not charge a fee to access the Internet, they do charge when you connect to commercial on-line services, including Nexis, CompuServe, and Prodigy. When you use these services, you may have to pay for time used and/or for the number of requests you make. To minimize your expense, see your librarian before you begin and ask about all fees and restrictions. If there is a fee, using an efficient keyword search will slash your on-line time (the final section of this chapter will look at keyword searches).

Libraries also have electronic databases on CD-ROM. A database is a collection of data—in most library cases, a list of related resources that all focus on one specific subject area—arranged so you can search through it and retrieve specific items easily. For example, the DIALOG Information System includes hundreds of small databases in specialized areas, such as business, psychology, and science. CD-ROM databases are generally smaller than on-line databases and are updated less frequently. However, there is never a user's fee.

Conduct a Keyword Search

Knowing how to conduct a *keyword* search will help you find what you are looking for on the Internet and in the book catalog and other print and electronic library indexes. Keywords are codes that give you access to information. Without these codes, it may be difficult to tap into the library's vast resources to find the exact spot that contains the information you need.

How do you find keywords? The best way is to search a multivolume catalog, known as the *Library of Congress Subject Headings* (*LCSH*), which is available in book and electronic form. Although you won't find any authors or titles in this volume, you will find a list of subject headings used consistently in all library indexes. Keeping a list of these words and using them in your research can head off hours of frustration. For example, although the library card catalog doesn't list any volumes that deal with the topic of "ghost towns," it covers the topic under the Library of Congress Subject Heading: "Cities and Towns: Ruined and Extinct." Figure C–9 shows how the LCSH system works.

Gestalt

The German word *gestalt* refers to a whole that is greater than the sum of its parts. When you can think in terms of *gestalt*, you are able to see both the whole picture and how each individual part contributes to that whole. To refer to a common phrase, gestalt is seeing the whole forest as well as individual trees.

Think of this concept as you consider how note-taking and research can help you build your knowledge and store of information. When you're reading your notes, ask yourself: Do I truly understand the material, or am I just trying to cram facts into my head? When you're writing a paper from your research, ask yourself: Am I stepping back to see the central idea clearly, so that I can express my thoughts in the best way possible? As important as the individual facts and examples may be, the *gestalt* is what helps the individual parts of your notes and your research gain a new and important meaning as a whole.

Important Points to Remember

Q 1. How does taking notes help you?

A Notes help you learn when you are in class, doing research, or studying. The positive effects of taking notes include having written study material, becoming an active and involved listener, and improving a skill that you will use on the job and in your personal life. Note-taking also encourages you to think critically and evaluate what is worth remembering. The notes you take during library research record what you learn from the sources you consult.

386 / Appendix C

Agriculture—Equipment and supplies
  see
Agricultural machinery

Crops—Machinery
  see
Agricultural machinery

Farm machinery
  see
Agricultural machinery

Machinery
  see also
Agricultural machinery

Farm equipment
  see also
Agricultural machinery

Farm mechanization
  see also
Agricultural machinery

Machine-tractor stations
  see also
Agricultural machinery

Agricultural machinery
  see also subdivision Machinery
  under names of crops, e.g.
  Corn—Machinery

Agricultural machinery
  see also
Agricultural implements

Agricultural machinery
  see also
Agricultural instruments

Agricultural machinery (May Subd Geog)
  UF Agriculture—Equipment and supplies
      Crops—Machinery
      Farm machinery
  BT Machinery
  RT Farm equipment
      Farm mechanization
      Machine-tractor stations
  SA subdivision Machinery under names
      of crops, e.g. Corn—Machinery
  NT Agricultural implements
      Agricultural instruments
      ...

Abbreviations

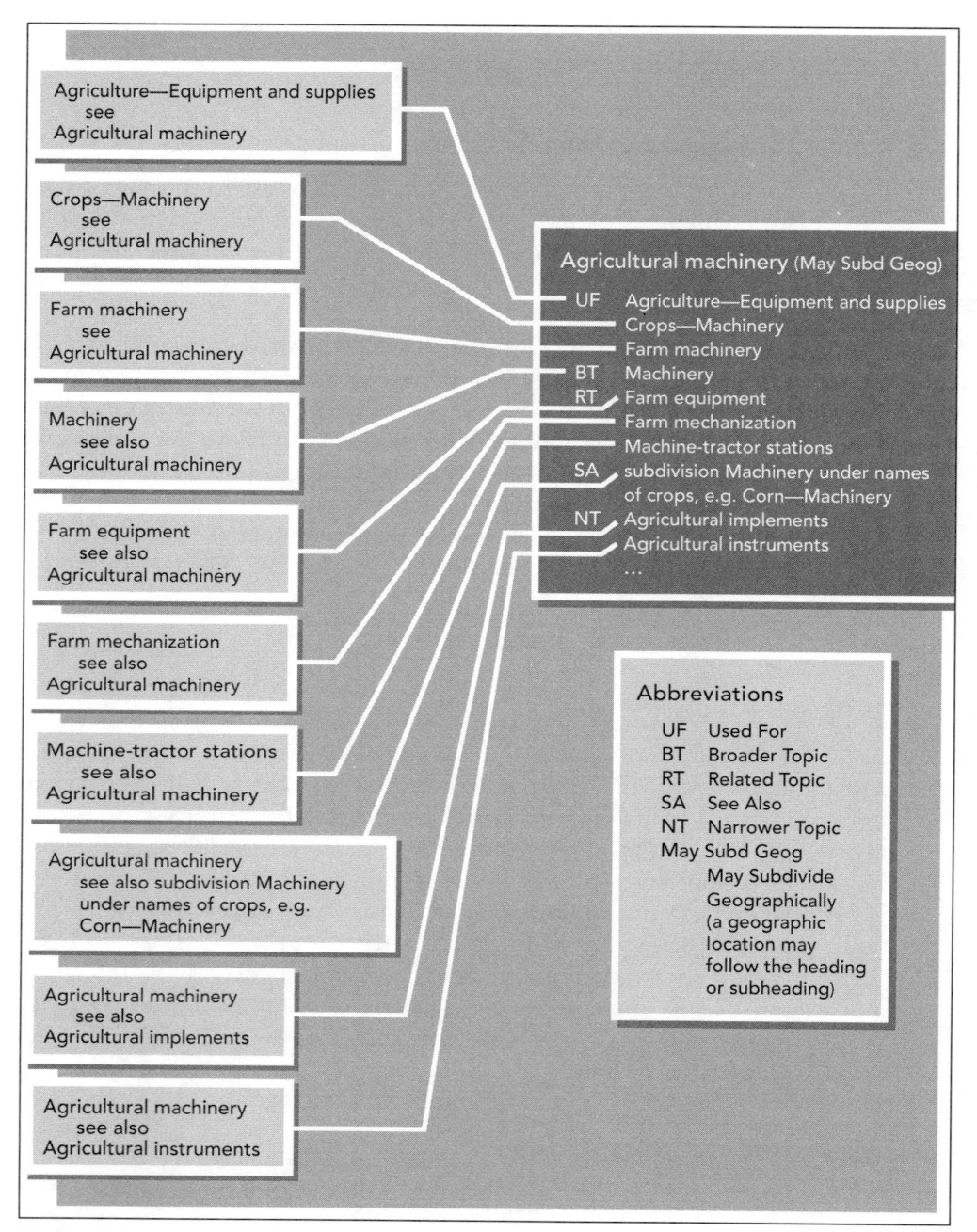

  UF Used For
  BT Broader Topic
  RT Related Topic
  SA See Also
  NT Narrower Topic
  May Subd Geog
      May Subdivide
      Geographically
      (a geographic
      location may
      follow the heading
      or subheading)

Figure C–9. How to Read Library of Congress Subject Headings.

Q 2. How can you make the most of class notes?

A Class notes may contain critical definitions, explanations of difficult concepts, and narratives of events. Taking comprehensive class notes requires pre-class preparation, the skill to report accurately what you hear during class, and a commitment to review the notes after class.

Q 3. How do you use research notes?

A Research notes, the notes you take while gathering information to answer a research question, consist of source notes and content notes. Source notes are preliminary notes that you take as you briefly review available research. Content notes are an in-depth, critical look at each source. Index cards work well for either source notes or content notes. Marginal notes and highlighting on photocopied research materials are also helpful.

Q 4. What note-taking system should you use?

A You can choose among several note-taking systems for class and research. These include formal or informal outlining, the Cornell system, and think links. Your goal is to find a system you are comfortable using, one that fits the special needs of the situation. For example, the Cornell system or informal outlining may work best during class, while think links and formal outlining may be most useful for rewriting your notes during review sessions.

Q 5. How can you write faster when taking notes?

A Note-taking often requires rapid writing, especially in class. Using a version of personal shorthand, which replaces words with shorter words or symbols, will help you accurately record what the instructor says. To avoid the problem of forgetting what your shorthand means, review your notes while the abbreviations and symbols are fresh in your mind, and spell out words as you review.

Q 6. What is the research process?

A Library research is the systematic search for information that involves finding and evaluating sources. Knowing your library's resources and layout will enable you to search skillfully. Work to locate particular reference collections, the card catalog, periodical indexes and periodicals, and special collections. Take advantage of library tours and training sessions to solidify your knowledge.

Q 7. How do you use a search strategy to conduct research?

A A library search strategy is a step-by-step method for finding information that moves you from general to specific sources. The strategy starts with general reference works and then moves to specialized reference works, the library book catalog, periodical indexes, and electronic sources, including the Internet and CD-ROMs. Conducting a successful search involves learning how to conduct a keyword search.

Appendix C: Applications

Name _____ Date _____

Taking Stock: Refining Your Thoughts

Look back at the statements you explored at the start of the chapter. Observe whether your attitudes have changed and what you have learned by studying this chapter.

1. Name two specific ways in which taking good notes will help you succeed at school.

   _____

   _____

   _____

   _____

2. Identify three ways to take better class notes.

   _____

   _____

   _____

3. Explain the kinds of information you plan to include in source notes and content notes.

   _____

   _____

   _____

4. Briefly describe your reactions to the note-taking systems described in this chapter, including outlines, the Cornell system, and think links. What system will help you the most? Why?

   _____

   _____

   _____

5. Name three ways to create your own shorthand. For each, show how you would shorten a word in your own notes.

_____
_____
_____
_____

6. List the stages in the library search strategy.

_____
_____
_____
_____

7. Identify three specific ways in which computers will help you find information at the library.

_____
_____
_____
_____

8. Choose one note-taking or research strategy you learned in this chapter, and explain how you will apply it in your schoolwork during the next week.

_____
_____
_____
_____

Key Into Your Life: Opportunities to Apply What You Learn

EXERCISE 1: HOW GOOD ARE YOUR NOTES?

Look back at two sets of notes that you recently took in two different courses. For each set, evaluate your level of success, using the questions given.

First set of notes

Do these notes make sense to you? Why or why not? If they aren't as clear as you'd like them to be, evaluate why that happened (fatigue, distraction, dislike of class material, etc.).

_____

_____

_____

_____

Are these notes complete and accurate? Why or why not?

_____

_____

Did you feel that you kept up with the lecture? If not, how does that show in the notes?

_____

_____

How do you evaluate your handwriting?

_____

What note-taking system did you use? Did it work for this class or not, and why?

_____

_____

_____

Did you give supporting facts and examples to back up important ideas?

_____

_____

Do you feel comfortable studying from these notes? Why or why not? If not, what do you need to do to make them more complete?

_____

_____

Second Set of Notes

Do these notes make sense to you? Why or why not? If they aren't as clear as you'd like them to be, evaluate why that happened (fatigue, distraction, dislike of class material, etc.)

_____

_____

Are these notes complete and accurate? Why or why not?

_____

Did you feel that you kept up with the lecture? If not, how does that show in the notes?

_____

_____

How do you evaluate your handwriting?

_____

_____

What note-taking system did you use? Did it work for this class or not, and why?

_____

_____

Did you give supporting facts and examples to back up important ideas?

_____

Do you feel comfortable studying from these notes? Why or why not? If not, what do you need to do to make them more complete?

_____

_____

_____

EXERCISE 2: IMPROVE YOUR NOTES

To improve your note-taking skill, use the following questions to think about your current skills and your goals for improvement.

What are your strengths and weaknesses as a note-taker in class?

_____

_____

_____

_____

What are your strengths and weaknesses as a research note-taker?

_____

_____

_____

_____

Identify three goals for improving your note-taking ability.

Goals for improving class notes
First goal:

_____

_____

Second goal:

_____

_____

Third goal:

_____

_____

Goals for improving research notes
First goal:

_____

_____

Second goal:

_____

_____

Third goal:

_____

_____

The next time you take notes in the two courses from Exercise 1, take the opportunity to work toward your class-notes goals. Evaluate your two sets of notes in terms of how you wanted to improve. Did you achieve any or all of your goals?

_____

_____

_____

_____

EXERCISE 3: MAKE SHORTHAND WORK FOR YOU

Look again at the shorthand techniques and symbols discussed in this chapter. Which abbreviations do you already use all the time?

_____

_____

Which symbols and abbreviations do you plan to use that are new to you?

_____

_____

Identify what you can do after class to make sure you understand your shorthand.

_____

_____

Plan one specific class period to make use of as many shorthand abbreviations as you can. Then evaluate your notes after class.

Do you understand your notes clearly? _____

Which shorthand abbreviations were you most likely to use? _____

_____

_____

Which shorthand abbreviations do you think were most successful for you?

_____

_____

Did any shorthand abbreviations seem to require extra concentration instead of saving you time? If so, which ones? _____

Exercise 4: Follow a Search Strategy

Choose a research topic that interests you—anything from how the Super Bowl has changed sports in America to the communication differences between men and women. Take a trip to the library and use the search strategy described in this chapter to identify the different sources you could use to research your topic. At the library, list three sources in each of the following categories:

TOPIC:

_____

_____

General reference works:

_____

_____

Specialized reference works:

_____

_____

Books found by searching the book catalog:

_____

_____

Periodicals found by searching periodical indexes:

_____

_____

Sources found on the Internet and/or through on-line services:

_____

_____

Exercise 5: Notes on Student Financial Aid

Imagine for a moment that you are doing a research project on student financial aid. After reading an article on financial aid, use a separate piece of paper to take content notes on what you read. Your notes may be in whatever form you choose: a formal or informal outline, the Cornell system, or a think link. Supplement your notes with marginal notes and underlining in the book itself.

Key To Cooperative Learning: Building Teamwork Skills

This teamwork exercise will show you how your note-taking techniques compare with those of other students. It will also help you analyze what makes one set of notes more useful than another set:

- Start by choosing a two-to three-page excerpt from your text. The excerpt should contain a lot of "meaty" information, but should have no tables or figures. Don't read the excerpt before you start the exercise.
- Form groups of four students. Within each group, one student will play the role of instructor and the other three will be students. Assign different note-taking strategies to each student—one will use outlining, one the Cornell system, and one think links. The "instructor" will read the excerpt as if he or she were delivering a classroom lecture. The "students" will take notes on the material. You will then have three different sets of notes on the same material.
- Now come together with all four group participants to review and compare all three versions. Read each version carefully and answer the following questions:

1. Did all three note-takers record all the important information? If there are differences in the versions, why do you think these differences occurred? (You can ask the note-takers to explain why they chose to include some information and omit others.)

   _____

   _____

   _____

2. How did each student feel about his or her note-taking strategy? Who felt comfortable and who didn't, and why?

   _____

   _____

   _____

3. Evaluate the different sets of notes. For this material and situation, which set of notes is likely to be the most helpful study tool for you?

___

Key To Self-Expression: Discovery Through Journal Writing

To record your thoughts, use a separate journal.

Read the following statements:

- When I use a library search strategy, I feel like an investigative reporter in search of the facts I need to write story. The more useful sources I find, the better."
- When I use a library search strategy, I feel like I'm overdoing it. I can usually find everything I need in one source, and looking for more information seems like a waste of time."

Which of these statements reflects your attitude toward library research? Describe in more detail how you feel about research. How do you think you might use research skills both in school and on the job? How did reading this chapter affect your attitude toward the usefulness of library research skills?

Key To Your Personal Portfolio: Your Paper Trail to Success

Suppose that you have to write a paper for your introduction-to-business course, and you decide to explore the following topic:

Privacy in an Age of Voice Mail and Electronic Mail:
Do Managers Have the Right to "Spy" on Their Employees?

Use the search strategy introduced in this chapter to develop a plan for researching this topic. List the types of sources you would look at and the order in which you would look at them. Be specific in the sources you mention. (This exercise will involve a visit to the library, where you will probably have to spend an hour or two doing research.)

Write up your research plan, indicating information specific to your particular library (available sources, their locations in the building, when and how they are available, what you can locate through interlibrary loan and at which libraries, what you can find at smaller libraries on campus, and so on). Include helpful basic information such as the hours of the library, special hours for particular rooms or collections in the library, and the names and phone numbers of librarians and other helpful personnel. If you have time, compare your plan with the plans developed by two or three classmates. Discuss how the plans differ and the strengths and weaknesses of each. Using what you learn, finalize your research plan for your portfolio. Use this plan as a guide whenever you need to research a topic.

APPENDIX D

Test Taking:
Showing What You Know

Testing is a fact of student life, even though many students don't look forward to taking tests. Part of the remedy for dreading tests lies in how you perceive them. If you think of them as a measure of your self-worth, having an off day that results in a low grade might give you an inaccurate opinion of yourself. Instead, think of exams as preparation for life. When you get a job, act as a volunteer, or even work through your family budget, you'll have to apply what you know and put your skills into action—exactly what you do when you take a test.

As you will see in this chapter, test taking involves more than showing up on time with a pencil in hand. It's about preparation, endurance, and strategy. It's also about conquering fears, paying attention to details, and learning from mistakes.

How Can Preparation Help Improve Test Scores?

Like a runner who prepares for a marathon by exercising, eating right, taking practice runs, and getting enough sleep, you can take steps to master your exams. The primary step, occupying much of your preparation time, is to study until you know the material that will be on the test. Other important steps are the preparation strategies that follow.

Identify Test Type and Material Covered

Before you begin studying, try to determine what will be covered on the test and the type of test it will be:

- Will it be a short-answer test with true/false and multiple-choice questions, an essay test, or a combination?

- Will the test cover everything you studied since the semester began or will it be limited to a more narrow topic?
- Will the test cover only what you learned in class and in the text or will it also cover outside readings?

Your instructors can answer these questions for you. Even though they may not tell you the specific questions that will be on the test, they will let you know what blocks of information will be covered and the question format. Some instructors may even give you a study guide or drop hints throughout the semester about possible test questions. While some comments are direct ("I might ask a question on the subject of _____ on your next exam"), other clues are subtle. For example, when instructors repeat an idea or when they express personal interest in a topic ("One of my favorite theories is . . . "), they are often letting you know that the material may be on the test.

Here are a few other strategies for predicting what may be on a test:

Use PQ3R to identify important ideas and facts. Often, the questions you write and ask yourself when you read assigned materials may be part of the test. In addition, any textbook study questions are good candidates for test material.

If you know people who took the instructor's course before, ask them about class tests. Try to find out how difficult the tests are, whether they focus more on assigned readings or class notes, what materials are usually covered, and what types of questions occur on the tests. This information can help you decide which materials to focus on during study time. Ask also about instructor preferences. For example, if you learn that the instructor pays close attention to factual and grammatical accuracy, you will be wise to focus on details and grammar as you study. If he or she has a special appreciation for neatness, you will make an impression by writing carefully and cleanly on your test.

Examine old tests. Instructors often make them available in class or on reserve in the library. Studying these exams can help you learn what type and level of questions to expect. Old tests help to answer the following questions:

- Does the instructor focus on examples and details, general ideas and themes, or a combination of both?
- Can you do well on the test through straight memorization or does the material require critical thinking?
- Are the questions straightforward or are they confusing and sometimes tricky?
- Do the tests require the integration of facts from different areas to draw conclusions?

If you can't get copies of old tests and your instructor doesn't give too many details about what the test will cover, use clues from the class to predict test questions. Ask yourself, for example, whether the instructor is interested in memorized facts or critical thinking, in obscure details or overriding themes. After taking the first exam in the course, you will have more information about what to expect in the future.

Choose Study Materials

Once you have identified as much as you can about the subject matter of the test, choose the materials that contain the information you need to study. You can save yourself time by making sure that you aren't studying anything you don't need to. Go through your notes, your texts, any primary source materials that were assigned, and any handouts from your instructor. Set aside any materials you don't need so they don't take up your valuable time.

Set a Study Schedule

Use your time-management skills to set a schedule that will help you feel as prepared as you can be. Consider all the relevant factors—the materials you need to study, how many days or weeks until the test date, and how much time you can study each day. If you establish your schedule ahead of time and write it in your date book, you will be much more likely to follow it.

Schedules will vary widely according to situation. For example, if you have only three days before the test and no other obligations during that time, you might set two 2-hour study sessions for yourself during each day. On the other hand, if you have two weeks before a test date, classes during the day, and work three nights a week, you might spread out your study sessions over the nights you have off work during those two weeks.

Prepare Through Critical Thinking

Using the techniques from Chapter 4, approach your test preparation as an active, critical thinker, working to understand the material rather than to just pass the test by repeating facts. As you study, try to connect ideas to examples, analyze causes and effects, establish truth, and look at issues from different perspectives.

In many courses, instructors want to see evidence that you can link seemingly unrelated ideas into patterns that make sense. As you study, try to explore concepts from different perspectives and connect ideas and examples that, on the surface, appear unrelated. Although you'll probably find answers to these questions in your text or class notes, you may have to work at putting different ideas together. Critical thinking takes work but may promote a greater understanding of the subject and probably a higher grade on the exam.

Using critical thinking is especially important in your preparation for essay tests that ask you to develop and support a thesis. The best way to prepare for these questions is to identify three or four essay questions your instructor is likely to ask and write out your responses as part of your test preparation.

Take a Pretest

Use questions from your textbook to create your own pretest. Most textbooks, although not all, will include such questions at the ends of chapters. If your course doesn't have an assigned text, develop questions from your notes and from assigned outside readings. Choose questions that are likely to be covered on the test, then answer them under testlike conditions—in quiet, with no books or notes to help you (unless your exam is open-book), and with a clock telling you when to quit. Try to come as close as you can to duplicating the actual test situation.

Create an Organized Study Plan

A checklist, like the one in Figure D-1, will help you get organized and stay on track as you prepare for each test.

Prepare Physically

When taking a test, you often need to work efficiently under time pressure. If your body is tired or under stress, you will probably not think as clearly or perform as well. If you can, avoid pulling an all-nighter. Get some sleep so that you can wake up rested and alert. Remember that adequate sleep can help cement your memories by reducing interference from new memories. If you are one of the many who press the snooze button in their sleep, you may want to set two alarm clocks and place them across the room from your bed. That way you'll be more likely to get to your test on time.

Eating right is also important. Sugar-laden snacks will bring your energy up only to send you crashing back down much too soon. Similarly, too much caffeine can add to your tension and make it difficult to focus. Eating nothing will leave you drained, but too much food can make you want to take a nap. The best advice is to eat a light, well-balanced meal before a test. When time is short, grab a quick-energy snack such as a banana, orange juice, or a granola bar.

Conquer Test Anxiety

A certain amount of stress can be a good thing. Your body is on alert, and your energy motivates you to do your best. For many students, however, the time before and during an exam brings a feeling of near-panic known as *test anxiety*. Described as a bad case of nerves that makes it hard to think or remember, test anxiety can make your life as a student miserable and can affect how well you do on tests. When anxiety blocks performance, you need to take steps to control it. Here are some suggestions:

> **Prepare so you'll feel in control.** The more you know about what to expect on the exam, the better you'll feel. Find out what material will be covered, the format of the questions, the length of the exam, and the percentage of points assigned to each question. You may even want to study in the room where you'll take the test, if you can.
>
> **Put the test in perspective.** No matter how important it may seem, a test is only a small part of your educational experience and an even smaller part of your life. Your test grade, whether high or low, does not reflect on the kind of person you are or on your ability to succeed in many different areas.

Pretest Checklist

Course: _____ Teacher: _____

Date, time, and place of test: _____

Type of test (e.g., Is it a midterm or a minor quiz?): _____

What the instructor has told you about the test, including the types of test questions, the length of the test, and how much the test counts in your final grade: _____

_____
_____
_____

Topics to be covered on the test in order of importance:

1. _____
2. _____
3. _____
4. _____
5. _____

Study schedule, including materials you plan to study (e.g., texts and class notes) and date you plan to complete each source:

Source	Date of Completion
1. _____	_____
2. _____	_____
3. _____	_____
4. _____	_____
5. _____	_____

Materials you are expected to bring to the test (e.g., your textbook, a sourcebook, a calculator): _____

_____

Special study arrangements (e.g., plan study-group meetings, ask the instructor for special help, get outside tutoring): _____

_____
_____

Life management issues (e.g., make child-care arrangements, rearrange work hours):

_____
_____
_____

Figure D–1.

Make a study plan. Divide the plan into a series of small tasks. As you finish each one, you'll be able to boost your sense of accomplishment and control.

Don't assume that anything less than perfection equals failure. Trying for a perfect score might overwhelm you, and the resulting anxiety could lower your score rather than raise it. Successful people aren't perfect people, they are people who constantly aim to do their best.

Practice relaxation. When you feel test anxiety coming on, take some deep breaths, close your eyes, and visualize a positive mental image related to the test. Images like the following can help propel you to success:

> *Your teacher hands your test back with a grade of A.*
>
> *Your grades in all your courses are so good that you make the dean's list.*
>
> *When you apply for a job, the employer reviews your college transcript and hires you on the spot.*

TEST ANXIETY AND THE RETURNING ADULT STUDENT

If you're returning to school after several years away, you may wonder if you can compete with younger students or if your mind is still able to learn new material. These feelings of inadequacy can block success if you let them. Telling yourself that you can't pass an exam because your test-taking skills are rusty is a formula for failure.

To counteract any negative feelings you may have, focus on how your life experiences have given you skills you can use. For example, managing work and a family requires strong time management, planning, and communication skills that can help you plan your study time, juggle school responsibilities, and interact with students and instructors. If you let these positive feelings in, they may translate into increased ability to achieve your goals.

COPING WITH MATH ANXIETY

Many students feel particular anxiety about math tests. As Sheila Tobias, author of *Overcoming Math Anxiety*[2], explains in the boxed quote on the following page, *math anxiety* is linked to the feeling that math is impossible.

Students who feel they are no good at math probably won't do well on math tests, even if they study. Their attitudes block their efforts. If you are one of these students, here are some steps you can take to begin thinking about math—and math tests—in a different way.

See the value—and benefits—in learning to use your mind in a mathematical way. Mathematical thinking is another type of critical thinking. It can help you solve the little and big problems that are part of your world, such as how to measure the amount of wallpaper you need in a room, compare the cost of different student loan programs, determine how long the 500 gallons of oil in your tank will last if the average winter temperature is 28 degrees, or analyze stock prices.

Think of math as a tool that will help you land a good job. In fields such as engineering, accounting, banking, the stock market, and computers, the abili-

> *The first thing people remember about failing at math is that it felt like sudden death. Whether it happened while learning word problems in sixth grade, coping with equations in high school, or first confronting calculus and statistics in college, failure was instant and frightening. An idea or a new operation was not just difficult, it was impossible! And instead of asking questions or taking the lesson slowly, assuming that in a month or so they would be able to digest it, people remember the feeling, as certain as it was sudden, that they would never go any further in mathematics. If we assume, as we must, that the curriculum was reasonable and that the new idea was merely the next in a series of learnable concepts, that feeling of utter defeat was simply not rational: In fact, the autobiographies of math-anxious college students and adults reveal that, no matter how much the teacher reassured them, they sensed that from that moment on, as far as math was concerned, they were through.*

ty to solve numerical problems is at the heart of the work. In real estate, retail sales, medicine, and publishing—fields that don't seem math-oriented—you may use math for **quantitative** tasks such as writing budgets and business plans and figuring mortgage rates. The more you know about math, the more you're likely to be paid. According to one expert, starting salaries increase by $2000 a year for every mathematics course you've taken since ninth grade.[3]

Quantitative, Of or relating to measurement, number, or quantity.

Turn negative self-talk into positive self-talk. Instead of telling yourself that a problem is too hard, tell yourself that if you take small, logical steps, you will succeed. Says Tobias, "If we can talk ourselves into feeling comfortable and secure, we may let in a good idea."[4] You might want to record your self-talk in a math learning journal. Write down how you feel about your math course, the progress you've made in mastering concepts, and how your feelings of math anxiety change as the year progresses.

Don't believe that women can't do math. Sheila Tobias says that when male students fail a math quiz, they don't think they worked hard enough; but when female students fail, they are three times more likely to feel that they just don't have what it takes.[5] Whether you are a man or a woman, work to overcome this stereotype.

Use the people and resources around you. Get to know your math instructor so you're comfortable asking for help. Join a math study group and make building confidence a group goal. Have a pep meeting right before a big test. Look for math-anxiety workshops. Seek out a tutor who can help you with your skills and build your confidence.

Become comfortable in the world of math. Find a computer program with math games or buy a paperback book with math puzzles. Have fun with problems and let yourself feel good as you solve them. Then transfer these feelings to your class work and tests.

Think mathematically in your everyday life. Do percentages, estimations, and other problems in your head. Have fun with them. For example, if you're driving somewhere, calculate the distance and your average speed and estimate how long it will take you to arrive. At the grocery store, as you shop, notice prices and calculate what you think the final total will be.

Understand math's relationship to your life success. Being at ease with numbers can serve you in day-to-day functions. Percentages can help you compare the financial benefits of different loan programs, adding and subtracting will allow you to balance a checkbook, and fractions will help you compare costs at work. Furthermore, even though you won't always see a connection between what you do in class and what you use in life, working with numbers helps to develop critical-thinking skills. The precise calculation and problem solving involved in math help you develop precision, cause-and-effect analysis, strategic planning, an understanding for idea-and-example relationships, a focus on detail, and a sense of order.

Studying for a Test When There Are Children Around

Parents who have to juggle child care with study time can find the challenge especially difficult right before a test. Here are some suggestions that might help:

Tell your children why this test is important. You might explain that doing well on this exam is a step toward a successful education and a better job, which will improve their lives as well as yours. Discuss the situation in concrete terms that they can understand. For example, a better job for you might mean for them a better home, nicer places to play, more money to plan fun outings and vacations, more time to spend as a family, and a happier parent (you)!

Explain the time frame. Tell them when and for how long you will study, and when the test will take place. Although children age nine and older will probably cooperate, younger children may have a harder time accepting that you can't be with them. Plan a reward outing so they can celebrate with you after you finish your test—going for ice cream, seeing a movie, having a picnic.

Keep children active while you study. Stock up on games, books, and videos. If a child is old enough, have him or her invite a friend over.

Find help. Ask a relative or friend to watch the children during the day for a couple of days before your exam, or arrange for your child to visit a friend's house. Consider trading baby-sitting hours with another parent, hiring a baby sitter who will come to your home, or enrolling your child in a day-care center.

When you have prepared using the strategies that work for you, you are ready to take your exam. Now you can focus on methods to help you succeed when the test begins.

What General Strategies Can Help You Succeed on Tests?

Even though every test is different, there are general strategies that will help you handle almost all tests, including short-answer and essay exams.

Write Down Key Facts

Before you even look at the test, write down any key information—including formulas, rules, and definitions—that you studied recently or even right before you entered the test room. Use the back of the question sheet or a piece of scrap paper for your notes (make sure it is clear to your instructor that this scrap paper didn't come into the test room already filled in!) Recording this information right at the start will make forgetting less likely.

Begin With an Overview of the Exam

Even though exam time is precious, spend a few minutes at the start of the test to get a sense of the kinds of questions you'll be answering, what type of thinking processes or mind actions they require, the number of questions in each section, and the point value of each section. Use this information to schedule the time you spend on each section. For example, if a two-hour test is divided into two sections of equal point value—an essay section with four questions and a short-answer section with sixty questions—you can divide your time in the following way:

- An hour on the essay section; no more than fifteen minutes for each question
- An hour on the short-answer section; one minute for each question

As you make your calculations, think about the level of difficulty of each section. If you think you can handle the short-answer questions in less than an hour and that you'll need more time with the essays, budget your time in a way that works for you.

Read Test Directions

Although it seems obvious, reading test directions carefully can save you a lot of trouble. For example, while a history test made up of 100 true/false questions and one essay may look straightforward, the directions may tell you that you have to answer 80 of the 100 questions, that you won't be penalized for incorrect answers, and that the essay is a nonrequired bonus question. If the directions indicate that you *are* penalized for incorrect answers—meaning that you will lose points instead of simply not gaining points—you may want to avoid guessing unless you're fairly certain of the answer. For example, incorrect questions may do some damage if you earn two points for every correct answer and lose one point for every incorrect answer.

When you read the directions, you may learn that some questions or sections are weighted more heavily than others. For example, the short-answer questions on a two-part test may be worth only thirty points, while the essays are worth seventy points. In this case, it's smart to spend a lot more time on the essays than the short answers. To keep yourself aware of the specifics of the directions, you may want to circle or underline key words and numbers.

Work From Easy to Hard

Begin with the parts or questions that seem easiest to you. One advantage of this strategy is that you will tend to take less time to answer the questions you know well, leaving more time to spend on the more difficult questions that may require increased effort and thinking. If you like to work through questions in order, mark difficult questions as you reach them and return to them after you answer the questions you know.

Another advantage of answering the easier questions first is that comfortably knowing answers to questions can boost your confidence early on in the test, helping you to continue to believe in yourself when you launch into the more difficult sections.

Watch the Clock

As you work through the test, keep track of how much time is left and whether your progress is keeping up with your schedule. You may want to plan out your time on a scrap piece of paper, especially if you have one or more essays to write. Wear a watch or bring a small clock with you to the test room. A wall clock may be broken, or there may be no clock at all!

Some students are so concerned about time that they rush through the test and actually have time left over. In situations like this, it's easy to leave early, happy that the test is over. The best move, however, is to take your time. Rushing is almost always a mistake, even if you feel you've done well. Stay till the end so you can refine and check your work—it couldn't hurt, and it might help.

Master the Art of Intelligent Guessing

When you are unsure of an answer on a short-answer test, you can leave it blank or you can guess. In most cases, provided that you are not penalized for incorrect answers, guessing will benefit you. "Intelligent guessing," writes Steven Frank, an authority on student studying and test taking, "means taking advantage of what you do know in order to try to figure out what you don't. If you guess intelligently, you have a decent shot at getting the answer right."[6]

Intelligent guessing begins by eliminating all the answers you know—or believe—are wrong. Try to narrow your choices to two possible answers, then choose the one you think is more likely to be correct. Strategies for guessing the correct answer in a multiple-choice test will be discussed later in the chapter.

When you check your work at the end of the test, ask yourself whether you would make the same guesses again. Chances are that you will leave your answers alone, but you may notice something that will make you change your mind. For example, you may have misread or failed to notice a **qualifier** that affects meaning, recalled a fact that will enable you to answer the question without guessing, miscalculated a step in a math problem, or determined that your guess didn't make sense.

> **Qualifier,** a descriptive word, such as *always, never,* or *often,* that changes the meaning of another word or word group.

Follow Directions on Machine-Scored Tests

Machine-scored tests require that you use a special pencil to fill in a small box on a computerized answer sheet. When the computer scans the sheet, it can tell whether you answered the questions correctly.

Taking these tests requires special care. Use the right pencil (a number-two pencil is usually required) and mark your answer in the correct space. Periodically, check the answer number against the question number to make sure they match. If you mark the answer to question 4 in the space for question 5, not only will you get question 4 wrong, but your responses for every question that follows will be off by a line. One helpful way to avoid getting off track is to put a small dot next to any number that you skip and plan to return to later on.

Neatness counts on these tests, because the computer can misread stray pencil marks or partially erased answers. If you mark two answers to a question and only partially erase one, the computer will read both responses and charge you with a wrong answer. Completely fill each answer space and avoid any other pencil marks that could be misinterpreted by the computer.

Use Critical Thinking to Avoid Errors

When the pressure of a test makes you nervous, critical thinking can help you work through each question thoroughly and avoid errors. Following are some critical-thinking strategies to use during a test.

Recall facts, procedures, rules, and formulas. You base your answers on the information you recall. Think carefully to make sure you recall it accurately.

Think about similarities. If you don't know how to attack a question or problem, consider any similar questions or problems that you have worked on in class or while studying.

Notice differences. Especially with objective questions, items that seem different from what you have studied may indicate answers you can eliminate.

Think through causes and effects. For a numerical problem, think through how you plan to solve it and see if the answer—the effect of your plan—makes sense. For an essay question that asks you to analyze a condition or situation, consider both what caused it and what effects it has.

Find the best idea to match the example or examples given. For a numerical problem, decide what formula (idea) best applies to the example or examples (the data of the problem). For an essay question, decide what idea applies to, or links, the examples given.

Support ideas with examples. When you put forth an idea in an answer to an essay question, be sure to back up your idea with an adequate number of examples that fit.

Evaluate each test question. In your initial approach to any question, evaluate what kinds of thinking will best help you solve it. For example, essay questions often require cause and effect and idea-to-example thinking, while objective questions often benefit from thinking through similarities and differences.

The general strategies you have just explained also can help you to address specific types of test questions.

Thinking Back

1. List three questions you can ask that will help predict test content.

2. Describe two strategies that can help you identify the material covered on a test.

3. Explain three ways you might choose to combat any text anxiety you feel.

4. List the steps to take to get an overview of an exam before you begin answering questions.

5. List three ways critical thinking can help avoid common test errors.

   a. _____

   b. _____

   c. _____

Thinking Ahead

1. Consider how you do on short-answer tests that include multiple-choice and true/false questions. What are your favorite kinds of short-answer questions? Which do you tend to make mistakes on, and why do you think this happens?

   _____
   _____
   _____
   _____

2. Describe how you generally handle essay questions. Do you plan your answers using an outline or think link, or do you write the first thing that comes to your mind?

   _____
   _____
   _____
   _____
   _____

3. Would you ever consider retaking a test if an improved grade would not count? Why or why not?

   _____
   _____
   _____
   _____

How Can You Master Different Types of Test Questions?

Although the goal of all test questions is to discover how much you know about a subject, every type of question has a different way of asking you what you know. Answering different types of questions is part science and part art. First of all, the strategy changes dramatically according to whether the question is objective or subjective.

For **objective questions**, you choose or write a short answer you believe is correct, often making a selection from a limited number of choices. Multiple-choice, fill-in-the-blank, and true/false questions fall into this category. **Subjective questions** demand the same information recall as objective questions, but they also require that you plan, organize, draft, and refine a written response. They may also require more extensive critical thinking and evaluation of the thinking processes required. All essay questions are subjective. While there are some guidelines that will help you choose the right answers to both types of questions, you must also learn to "feel" your way to an answer that works.

> **Objective questions,** Short-answer questions that test your ability to recall, compare and contrast information, and link ideas to examples.
>
> **Subjective questions,** Essay questions that require you to express your answer in terms of your own personal knowledge and perspective.

Multiple-Choice Questions

Multiple-choice questions are the most popular type of question found on standardized tests. The following strategies can help you answer these questions:

Carefully read the directions. In the rush to get to work on a question it is easy to read directions too quickly or to skip them, assuming that the questions will be self-explanatory. Directions, however, can be tricky. For example, while most test items ask for a single correct answer, some give you the option of marking several choices that are correct. For some tests, you might be required to answer only a certain number of the test questions.

Read each question thoroughly before looking at the choices. Then try to answer the question. This strategy will reduce the possibility that the choices will confuse you.

Underline key words and phrases in the question. If the question is complicated, try to break it down into small sections that are easy to understand.

Pay special attention to words that could throw you off. For example, it is easy to overlook negatives in a question ("Which of the following is *not* . . .").

If you don't know the answer, eliminate those answers that you know or suspect are wrong. Your goal is to leave yourself with two possible answers, which would give you a fifty-fifty chance of making the right choice. The following are questions you can ask as you work to eliminate choices:

- Is the choice accurate in its own terms? If there's an error in the choice—for example, a term that is incorrectly defined—the answer is wrong.
- Is the choice relevant? An answer may be accurate, but it may not relate to the essence of the question.
- Are there any qualifiers? *Absolute* qualifiers like *always, never, all, none,* or *every often* signal an exception that makes a choice incorrect. For example, the statement that "normal children always begin talking before the age of two" is an untrue statement; while most normal children begin talking before age two, some have a later start. Analysis has shown that choices containing conservative qualifiers (*often, most, rarely, may sometimes be, can occasionally result in*) are often correct.
- Do the choices give you any clues? Does a puzzling word remind you of a word you know? If you don't know a word, does any part of the word—its prefix, suffix, or root—seem familiar to you?

Look for patterns that may lead to the right answer, then use intelligent guessing. The idea is to know the material so well that you don't have to guess, but that level of knowledge is not always possible. When you really aren't sure, use these hints to help you make an educated guess. Test-taking experts have found patterns in multiple-choice questions that may help you get a better grade. Here is their advice:

- Consider the possibility that a choice that is *more general* than the others is the right answer.
- Consider the possibility that a choice that is *longer* than the others is the right answer.
- Look for a choice that has a *middle value in a range* (the range can be from small to large, from old to recent). It is likely to be the right answer.
- Look for two choices that have *similar meanings*. One of these answers is probably correct.
- Look for *answers that agree grammatically with the question.* For example, a fill-in-the-blank question that has an *a* or *an* before the blank gives you a clue as to which answer is correct.

Make sure you read every word of every answer. Instructors have been known to include answers that are almost right, except for a single word.

When questions are keyed to a long reading passage, read the questions first. This will help you, when you read the passage, to focus on the information you need to answer the questions.

On the following page are some examples of the kinds of multiple-choice questions you might encounter in an Introduction to Psychology course.[7]

1. Arnold is at the company party and has had too much to drink. He releases all of his pent-up aggression by yelling at his boss, who promptly fires him. Arnold normally would not have yelled at his boss, but after drinking heavily he yelled because_____.

    a. parties are places where employees are supposed to be able to "loosen up"
    b. alcohol is a stimulant
    c. alcohol makes people less concerned with the negative consequences of their behavior
    d. alcohol inhibits brain centers that control the perception of loudness

    (The correct answer is C)

2. Which of the following has not been shown to be a probable cause of or influence in the development of alcoholism in our society?

    a. intelligence
    b. culture
    c. personality
    d. genetic vulnerability

    (The correct answer is A)

3. Geraldine is a heavy coffee drinker who has become addicted to caffeine. If she completely ceases her intake of caffeine over the next few days, she is likely to experience each of the following EXCEPT_____.

    a. depression
    b. lethargy
    c. insomnia
    d. headaches

    (The correct answer is C)

True/False Questions

True/false questions test your recognition of facts and often concepts as well, including minor details. Read them carefully to look for qualifiers that can turn a statement that would otherwise be true into one that is false. Similarly, a statement you think is false may also be turned around with a qualifier. Qualifiers to watch out for include: *all, only,* and *always* (the absolutes that often make a statement false), and *generally, often, usually,* and *sometimes* (the conservatives that often make a statement true).

If you're truly stumped on a true/false question, guess (unless you're penalized for wrong answers). You will always have a fifty-fifty chance of being right. Here are some examples of the kinds of true/false questions you might encounter in an Introduction to Psychology course. The correct answer follows each question:

> Are the following questions true or false?
> 1. Alcohol use is clearly related to increases in hostility, aggression, violence, and abusive behavior. (True)
> 2. Marijuana is harmless. (False)
> 3. Simply expecting a drug to produce an effect is often enough to produce the effect. (True)
> 4. Alcohol is a stimulant. (False)

Essay Questions

An essay question allows you to express your knowledge and views on a topic in a much more extensive manner than any short-answer question can provide. With the freedom to express your views, though, comes the challenge to both exhibit knowledge and show you have command of how to organize and express that knowledge clearly.

Start by reading the essay questions. If you have a choice among a group of questions—such as answering two out of three given possibilities—first decide which you are going to try. Then focus on what each question is asking, the mind actions you will need to use, and the writing directions. Read the questions carefully and do everything that you are asked to do. Some essay questions may contain more than one part.

Certain action verbs can help you figure out how to think, so watch for them and know exactly what they mean. Table D-1 on the next page explains some words commonly used in essays. Underline these words as you read the essay question, and use them to guide your writing.

Next, budget your time and begin to plan. Outline or diagram the main points you want to make and indicate the examples you plan to cite to support these ideas. Let this outline be your guide as you begin to write.

You're under time pressure, so don't spend too much time on introductions or flowery prose. Start with a thesis statement or idea that states your position and tells in a basic way what your essay will say. In the first paragraph, introduce the essay's key points. These may be sub-ideas, causes, effects, or even examples. Use clear, concise language in the body of the essay. Carefully establish your ideas and support them with examples, and look back at your outline to make sure you are covering everything. Wrap it up with a conclusion that is short and to the point.

Try to write legibly—if your instructor can't read your ideas, it doesn't matter how good they are. Instructors who have to read twenty or more essays for a single class may not have the energy to decipher messy handwriting. Try printing and skipping every other line if you know your handwriting is problematic. Avoid writing on both sides of the paper since it will make your handwriting even harder to read. You may even want to discuss the problem with the instructor.

Do your best to save time to reread and revise your essay after you finish getting your ideas down on paper. Look for ideas you left out, ideas you didn't support with enough examples, and poorly phrased sentences that might confuse the reader. Also, check for mistakes in grammar, spelling, punctuation, and usage. No matter what

> **Table D-1.** Common Action Verbs on Essay Tests
>
> **Analyze**—Break into parts and discuss each part separately.
> **Compare**—Explain similarities and differences.
> **Contrast**—Distinguish between items being compared by focusing on differences.
> **Criticize**—Evaluate the positive and negative effects of what is being discussed.
> **Define**—State the essential quality or meaning. Give the common idea.
> **Describe**—Visualize and give information that paints a complete picture.
> **Discuss**—Examine in a complete and detailed way, usually by connecting ideas to examples.
> **Enumerate/List/Identify**—Recall and specify items in the form of a list.
> **Explain**—Make the meaning of something clear, often by making analogies or giving examples.
> **Evaluate**—Give your opinion about the value or worth of something, usually by weighing positive and negative effects, and justify your conclusion.
> **Illustrate**—Supply examples.
> **Interpret**—Explain your personal view of facts and ideas and how they relate to one another.
> **Outline**—Organize and present the sub-ideas or main examples of an idea.
> **Prove**—Use evidence and argument to show that something is true, usually by showing cause and effect or giving examples that fit the idea to be proven.
> **Review**—Provide an overview of ideas and establish their merits and features.
> **State**—Explain clearly, simply, and concisely, being sure that each word gives the image you want.
> **Summarize**—Give the important ideas in brief.
> **Trace**—Present a history of the way something developed, often by showing cause and effect.

subject you are writing about, having a command of these factors will make your work all the more complete and impressive.

Here are some examples of essay questions you might encounter in an Introduction to Psychology course. In each case, notice the action verbs from Table D-1.

> 1. Summarize the theories and research on the causes and effects of daydreaming. Discuss the possible uses for daydreaming in a healthy individual.
> 2. Describe the physical and psychological effects of alcohol and the problems associated with its use.
> 3. Explain what sleep terrors are, what appears to cause them, and who is most likely to suffer from them.

REAL WORLD PERSPECTIVE

How can I prepare for exams?

Jeff Felardeau, Selkirk College—Nelson, British Columbia, Adult Basic Education
I've been out of school for quite a long time, so when I returned and had to memorize material for exams, I just wasn't prepared. The labor work I was doing didn't require me to use my memorization skills. I had the most difficulty memorizing for classes like biology and any of the sciences where you have to memorize a lot of facts. I'd work hard by repeating the information over and over in my mind, but I'd only be able to recall it for a short time afterwards—long-term learning wasn't there. Whenever I'd prepare for an exam, I'd find myself in a "cram" mode because I didn't remember any of the material from class. It was like learning the material all over again.

I took a class called College Success which gave me some good study tips. They taught me things like mind-mapping, listening skills, and note-taking styles. They also taught me to use word associations and visualization to help remember the material. It's helped me improve a lot but still, I get stuck in old habits and patterns and forget to apply the methods that that will really help me improve. I know that if I don't change these old study patterns and habits, I'll hit the wall sooner or later. I can't keep using methods that served me in the past but are no longer effective for where I am today. What do you suggest?

Miriam Kapner, New England Conservatory—Boston, MA, Junior in oboe performance
Even though you have a good understanding of what it takes to prepare for an exam, the key is to remain disciplined. If your mind is wandering in class and you find you're staring out the window looking at those clouds, remember that you have control of your mind. By staying focused in class you will not have to study so much when exam time rolls around. Although we all fall victim to daydreaming, try and gain control of your mind by thinking of your goals or by using simple mind tricks. Even if the class has a very dry teacher, there are ways to keep focused. One day a friend and I sat down and figured out exactly how much each class was costing us. When we realized the amount of money we were spending for that hour, it was a real eye-opener. If I'm really having a hard time, then I make sure I ask at least two questions per class. This forces me to pay attention.

In order to memorize, you need to be able to find some order. It helps if you have a reference point to begin with and then look for certain patterns or categories. I also use mnemonic devices to help me remember. In fact, I can still remember the ones I learned in elementary school: **G**eneral **E**lectric **L**ights **N**ever **D**im for the first five books of the Bible and of course, **E**very **G**ood **B**oy **D**oes **F**ine for the lines in the treble clef. But mainly, whatever steps you take to improve your preparation for exams, remember that you are in control of your mind—not the other way around.

What Techniques Will Help Improve Performance on Math Tests?

Mathematical test problems present a special challenge to some students, especially those who suffer from math anxiety. These strategies may help you overcome any difficulties you might have:

Analyze problems carefully. Make sure that you take all the "givens" into account as you begin your calculations. Focus also on what you want to find or prove.

Write down any formulas, theorems, or definitions that apply to the problem. Do this before you begin your calculations.

Estimate a *ballpark* solution before you tackle the problem. Then work the problem and check your actual solution against your original estimate. The two answers should be close. If they're not, recheck your work. You may have made a simple calculation error.

> **Ballpark,** Being approximately proper in numerical range.

Break the calculation into the smallest possible pieces. Go step by step and don't move on to the next step until you are clear about what you've done so far.

Recall how you solved similar problems. Past experience can give you valuable clues as to how a particular problem should be handled.

Draw a picture to help you see the problem. This can be a diagram, a chart, or some other type of visual presentation.

Take your time. Precision and accuracy demand concentration and focus. For example, if you're using a calculator, it's easy to press a wrong key without realizing it, and one wrong keystroke can mean the difference between a right and wrong answer.

Be neat. When it comes to numbers, a case of mistaken identity can mean the difference between a right and a wrong answer. A 4 that looks like a 9 or a 1 that looks like a 7 can make trouble. Similarly, if you are writing numbers in columns, be sure that all decimal points are lined up under one another.

Use the opposite operation to check your work. When you come up with an answer, work backwards to see if you end up where the problem started. Arriving back at the starting point usually indicates that your calculations have been correct. Use subtraction to check your addition; use division to check multiplication; and so on.

Look back at the questions to be sure you did everything that was asked. Did you answer every part of the question? Did you show all the required work? Be as complete as you possibly can.

How Can You Learn From Test Mistakes?

The purpose of a test is to see how much you know, not merely what grade you can achieve. The knowledge that comes from attending class and studying should allow you to correctly answer test questions. Knowledge also comes, however, when you take the time to learn from your mistakes. If you don't examine what you get wrong on a test, you might repeat the same mistake again on another test and perhaps in life. Learn from test mistakes just as you learn from mistakes in your personal and business life. The following strategies will help:

Try to identify patterns in your mistakes. Look for:

- *Careless errors*—In your rush to complete the exam, did you misread the question or directions, blacken the wrong box on the answer sheet, inadvertently skip a question, or use illegible handwriting?

- *Conceptual or factual errors*—Did you misunderstand a concept or never learn it in the first place? Did you fail to master certain facts? Did you skip part of the assigned text or miss important classes in which ideas were covered?

If you have time, try to rework the questions you got wrong. Based on the feedback from your instructor, try to rewrite an essay, recalculate a math problem starting from the original question, or redo the questions that follow a reading selection. Although revisiting avoidable mistakes can be frustrating, the process can help you know what to do differently next time. If you see patterns of careless errors, promise yourself that you'll be more careful in the future and that you'll save time to double-check your work. If you pick up conceptual and factual errors, rededicate yourself to better preparation.

After reviewing your mistakes, fill in your knowledge gaps. If you made mistakes on questions because you didn't know or understand them, develop a plan to comprehensively learn the material. Solidifying your knowledge can help you in exams further down the road, as well as in life situations that involve the subject matter you're studying. You might even consider asking your instructor if you can retake the exam, if you have the time to do so. The score might not count, but you may find that focusing on learning rather than on grades can improve your knowledge and build self-respect.

If you fail a test completely, don't throw it away. First, take comfort in the fact that many students have been in your shoes and that you are likely to improve your performance. Then recommit to the process by reviewing and analyzing your errors. Finally, be sure you understand *why* you failed. This is especially important for an essay test, because while most objective questions are fact-based and clearly right or wrong, subjective questions are in large part subject to the opinion of the grader. Respectfully ask the instructor who graded the test for an explanation. You may also want to ask what you could have done to have earned a better grade.

Sine qua non

Although the Latin language is no longer commonly used, it is one of the most dominant ancestors of modern English, and many Latin words and phrases have a place in the English language. The Latin phrase *sine qua non* (pronounced "sihn-ay kwa nahn") means, literally, "without which not." Translated into everyday language, a *sine qua non* is "an absolutely indispensable or essential thing."

Think of true learning as the *sine qua non* of test taking. When you have worked hard to learn ideas and information, taking it in and using different techniques to review and retain it, you will be more able to take tests successfully, confident that you have the knowledge necessary to answer the required questions. Focus on knowledge so that test taking becomes not an intimidating challenge but an opportunity to show what you know.

Important Points to Remember

Q 1. How can preparation help improve test scores?

A Preparation is one key to test success. Strategies that can help improve your approach include identifying test type and coverage; choosing appropriate study materials; setting a study schedule; using critical thinking to prepare for possible questions; taking a pre-test; creating an organized study plan; preparing your body by getting enough sleep and eating well; recognizing and conquering test anxiety; and learning to study when you're also taking care of children.

Q 2. What general strategies can help you succeed on tests?

A Although all tests are different, there are methods that will help improve your performance on almost every test. These methods include writing down key information as soon as the test begins; taking time to skim the exam and get an overview; reading the directions; working from the easiest questions to the hardest; keeping track of time as you work; learning to guess intelligently; knowing how to fill out machine-scored tests; and using critical thinking to avoid errors.

Q 3. How can you master different types of test questions?

A Learning how to approach different types of test questions is important to your success. There are different skills for objective questions, which include multiple-choice and true/false questions, and for subjective questions, which include essay questions.

Q 4. What special techniques will help improve your performance on math tests?

A Actions you can take to improve your performance on math tests include careful problem analysis; writing down formulas or theorems that apply to problems; breaking calculations into small, easy-to-handle pieces; drawing pictures of problems; recalling how you solved similar problems; and learning to estimate.

Q 5. How can you learn from test mistakes?

A The purpose of a test is to see how much you know. Test mistakes can show you where you might need to strengthen your knowledge. When you get your test back, look for careless errors as well as those that involve concepts and facts. Instead of taking your mistakes as a defeat, treat them as a challenge to understand what you did wrong and avoid making the same mistake in the future.

Appendix D: Applications

Name _____ **Date** _____

Taking Stock: Refining Your Thoughts

Look back at the statements you explored at the start of the chapter. Observe whether your attitudes have changed and what you have learned by studying this chapter.

1. List the four exam preparation actions that seem most important to you.
   _____
   _____
   _____

2. If you were to experience test or math anxiety, what three strategies would you use to fight it?
   _____
   _____
   _____

3. Describe four general test-taking strategies that may help improve your test performance.
   _____
   _____
   _____

4. Explain how answering multiple-choice questions differs from answering true/false questions. Give one strategy for each type of question.
   _____
   _____
   _____

5. Describe a plan of action for answering essay questions.

6. Describe how you can benefit from reviewing mistakes you make on tests.

7. Identify one test-taking strategy you learned in this chapter and explain how you will apply it to your next exam.

Key Into Your Life: Opportunities to Apply What You Learn

EXERCISE 1: CREATE YOUR OWN POSITIVE SELF-TALK FOR TESTS

Because the attitude you bring to a test can influence your performance, you will benefit from believing that you can do well. In the space below, create five phrases of positive self-talk that will help you develop confidence before a test. Then list five ideas you can repeat to yourself that will increase your confidence during a test.

Positive self-talk that you can use **before** *a test:*

1. _____
2. _____
3. _____
4. _____
5. _____

Positive self-talk to use **during** *a test:*

1. _____
2. _____
3. _____
4. _____
5. _____

EXERCISE 2: ANALYZE STUDY QUESTIONS

Use a textbook, a review book, or study guide for a course you're now taking. Look at the sample study/test questions in the book and complete these exercises:

- In the space below, copy down two questions from your materials—if possible, one multiple-choice question and one true/false question. For each question, name a strategy or strategies from this chapter that will help you solve it and why.

Question 1:
_____
_____
_____
_____

Question 2:
_____
_____
_____
_____

List two essay questions from your materials. For each, describe how a particular strategy or strategies from this chapter will help you answer the question.

Question 1:
_____
_____
_____
_____

Question 2:

_____
_____
_____
_____

Look back at Table D-1, "Common Action Verbs on Essay Tests." List the verbs from this table that are found in sample essay questions in your book. Define any verbs from your book that do not appear in the table.

_____
_____
_____
_____

EXERCISE 3: RECOGNIZING AND OVERCOMING MATH ANXIETY

The following questions will help you learn whether or not you suffer from math anxiety. Answer each question in the space below. If you need more room, use additional paper.

- Do you think of yourself as a good or a poor math student? How did you arrive at this opinion of your mathematical ability?

_____
_____
_____
_____

- If you are a woman, do you feel that society's opinion about women and math has affected your confidence and performance? If so, how? If not, why not?

_____
_____
_____
_____

TEST TAKING: SHOWING WHAT YOU KNOW / 425

- Are you more likely to freeze on a math test than on any other type of test? Why? Does your performance vary according to how much you study?

- What happens when you try to do math in real-life situations?

- When you were younger, do you remember doing well in math, or did you always have problems with the subject? If you can, recall and describe a specific experience that left a lasting impression.

- After answering these questions, take a moment to think about the steps you will take to reduce your math anxiety in the future and to improve your test scores. Write down your thoughts:

EXERCISE 4: POST-TEST ANALYSIS

When you get back your next test, take a detailed look at your performance.

- Write what you think of your test performance and grade. Were you pleased or disappointed? If you made mistakes, were they careless errors or did you lack the facts and concepts?

- Next, list the test preparation activities that helped you do well on the exam and the activities you wish you had done—and intend to do—for the next exam.

Positive things I did:
_____
_____
_____
_____
_____

Positive actions I intend to take next time:
_____
_____
_____
_____
_____

- Finally, list the activities you are not likely to repeat when studying for the next test.
_____
_____
_____
_____

Exercise 5: Learning From Your Mistakes

For this exercise, use an exam on which you made one or more mistakes. Why do you think you answered the question(s) incorrectly?
_____
_____

- Did any qualifiers such as *always, sometimes, never, often, occasionally,* or *only* make the question(s) more difficult or confusing? What steps could you have taken to clarify the meaning?
_____
_____
_____

- Did you try to guess the correct answer? If so, why do you think you made the wrong choice?

_____
_____
_____

- Did you feel rushed? If you had had more time, do you think you would have gotten the right answer(s)? What could you have done to budget your time more effectively?

_____
_____
_____
_____

- If an essay question was a problem, what do you think went wrong? What will you do differently the next time you face an essay question on a test?

_____
_____
_____
_____

Key to Cooperative Learning: Building Teamwork Skills

Study Partners Choose a study partner in one of your classes other than this one. Work together to learn the required material for a particular test. Use the checklist on the following page to quiz each other and measure how well you prepare.

Go through the entire checklist before the exam. Help each other overcome areas of weakness, and try to build each other's confidence and test-taking skills. After the exam, meet with your partner to evaluate the checklist. Improve it according to your needs, adding new questions that you think should be included or crossing out questions that didn't seem to be necessary. Your improved checklist will help you do even better on the next exam.

> _____ I asked the instructor what will be covered on the exam and the format of the test questions.
>
> _____ I tried to learn as much as I could about the kinds of tests the instructor gives by talking to former students and getting copies of old exams.
>
> _____ I used critical thinking to explore difficult concepts that might be on the test.
>
> _____ I took a pretest.
>
> _____ I tried to prepare my body and mind to perform at their best.
>
> _____ I used positive self-talk and other techniques to overcome negative thoughts that might affect my performance.
>
> _____ I have gotten my personal life under control so I can focus on the exam.
>
> _____ I have a plan of action that I will follow when I see the test for the first time. I'll try to get an overview of the test, learn test ground rules, schedule my time, and evaluate questions and choices in case I have to guess.
>
> _____ I reviewed strategies for handling multiple-choice, true/false, and essay questions and feel comfortable with these strategies.

Key to Self-Expression: Discovery Through Journal Writing

To record your thoughts, use a separate journal or a lined pad.

Do you experience test anxiety? How do you feel as you walk into a testing room? Do you think your performance on tests accurately reflects what you know, or do your test scores fall short of your knowledge and capability? If there is a gap between your knowledge and your scores, why do you think this gap exists? Describe the steps you can take that will give you the confidence to do well on tests.

Key to Your Personal Portfolio: Your Paper Trail to Success

Apply Your New Study Skills As you prepare for tests, you have the opportunity to put into action many of the skills you learned, including critical thinking, reading, studying, listening, memory, note-taking, and writing, as well as specific test-taking skills. By now, you have probably read all the chapters associated with these skills. Think back on what you learned (you can also refer to the chapters), and develop a plan that shows how you will apply your new knowledge about study skills as you prepare for your next exam. Here are some of the topics you can consider:

- the specific critical-thinking techniques that will help you master the material
- the memory techniques that work best for you
- the note-taking system that allows you to take comprehensive class notes
- how you like to use PQ3R when you study

- what techniques help you write your best
- the test-taking strategies that will help you prepare for and take your exams

Using separate sheets of paper, construct your plan, using an outline or a think link.

This exercise asks you to apply what you learned in several different chapters. To successfully complete the exercise, you have to know yourself and the techniques that will work for you as you prepare for your exams. Not every suggestion in this book is right for every person. Choose the skills that will work in your life and then use them to become a better student.